Contesting Nordicness

Helsinki Yearbook of Intellectual History

Edited by Heikki Haara and Koen Stapelbroek

Volume 2

Contesting Nordicness

From Scandinavianism to the Nordic Brand

Edited by
Jani Marjanen, Johan Strang and Mary Hilson

DE GRUYTER
OLDENBOURG

ISBN 978-3-11-073501-7
e-ISBN (PDF) 978-3-11-073010-4
e-ISBN (EPUB) 978-3-11-073015-9
ISSN 2698-6205

Library of Congress Control Number: 2021948486

Bibliographic information published by the Deutsche Nationalbibliothek
The Deutsche Nationalbibliothek lists this publication in the Deutsche Nationalbibliografie;
detailed bibliographic data are available on the Internet at http://dnb.dnb.de.

© 2021 Jani Marjanen, Johan Strang, Mary Hilson and the chapters' contributors. Published by
Walter de Gruyter GmbH, Berlin/Boston
This book is published with open access at www.degruyter.com.

Cover illustration: The Brooklyn Museum's 1954 „Design in Scandinavia" exhibition launched
„Scandinavian Modern" furniture on the American market, Installation view from Design in
Scandinavia, April 20, 1954 through May 16, 1954. [https://commons.wikimedia.org/wiki/
File:Design_in_Scandinavia_exhibition.jpg]
Printing and binding: CPI books GmbH, Leck

www.degruyter.com

Table of Contents

Acknowledgements

This book draws from discussions that began at the University of Helsinki's Centre for Nordic Studies and its networks. Largely inspired by Henrik Stenius, we wanted to develop a way to analyse *Norden* as culturally constructed, while at the same time acknowledging that the region is constantly redefined in political debate. Instead of looking for the essential features of Nordic political culture, we shifted our perspective towards an examination of the many different things that were rhetorically coupled with the Nordic countries, as well as the reasons and motives for this in various historical situations.

These debates developed into the idea for this book, which was first discussed at a seminar organised by Jani Marjanen and Johan Strang in 2015. We would like to thank Letterstedtska föreningen and the Finnish Institute in Berlin for supporting this initial meeting, and the Centre for Nordic Studies and the Faculty of Arts at the University of Helsinki for sponsoring a follow up seminar in Helsinki in December 2016. After these meetings, the book matured as a dialogue between the editors and the individual authors of the chapters in this book. We also want to direct our warm thanks to those colleagues who attended these earlier meetings and made valuable contributions to the discussion, especially Matti La Mela, Jussi Kurunmäki, Malcolm Langford, Haldor Byrkjeflot and Kazimierz Musiał. We are also grateful to Ragnheiður Kristjánsdóttir, Nils Edling and two anonymous referees for suggestions and comments that helped improve the individual chapters. The foundation of the Helsinki Centre for Intellectual History and the launch of its Yearbook series provided a final impetus to complete the book. We thank the series editors and the publisher for including this volume in the series.

Andreas Hansen, Ilana Brown and Mark Shackleton provided us with valuable assistance with preparing the final manuscript.

Acknowledgements are also due to the Academy of Finland (grant number 323489), Bank of Sweden Tercentenary Foundation (grant M19-0231:1), the Independent Research Fund Denmark (grant number 8018–00023B), UiO:Nordic, and the University of Helsinki three-year project "Vernacularization and nation building" for their support of our research. Publication of the open-access edition of this volume was made possible by a grant from the NordForsk university hub ReNEW (Reimaging Norden in an Evolving World).

Helsinki and Aarhus, May 2021
Mary Hilson, Jani Marjanen and Johan Strang

Johan Strang, Jani Marjanen and Mary Hilson

A Rhetorical Perspective on Nordicness: From Creating Unity to Exporting Models

In 2020 the dairy company Arla launched a new range of plant-based drinks. Marketed under the brand name "JÖRÐ" with allusions to Old Norse mythology, the products were described as an "oat drink from Nordic nature... made by Nordic wind, rain and sun." The term "Nordic" featured prominently in the company's own descriptions of its product, with references to "Nordic flavours such as barley and hemp," and to oats "grown in the Nordics for hundreds of years."[1] This apparently trivial example picks up on real and mythical sediments of meaning at the same time as it tries to convey an image of something modern and humorous. The brand itself may be full of contradictions, especially as the Nordic countries are known for their high levels of consumption and production of dairy products, but the notion of Nordicness clearly carries a lot of rhetorical appeal in this type of marketing.

There are many other examples of the use of "the Nordic" to evoke interest in the politics, society, and culture of Denmark, Finland, Iceland, Norway and Sweden – the five countries, which together with the three autonomous regions of the Faroe Islands, Greenland, and Åland make up the Nordic region.[2] In this book, we explore the appeal and flexibility of the rhetoric of Nordicness. What, if anything, do the different uses of "Nordic" have in common, and are there any particular circumstances or historical periods in which the rhetoric has been particularly popular? The starting point for our book is our perception that there has been an upsurge in a new rhetoric of Nordicness since about 2010, which so far has not been discussed in scholarly literature in any great detail.[3] What accounts

---

1 Arla Foods, "JÖRÐ Oat Drink | Fresh & Organic," accessed December 13, 2020, https://jord-plantbased.com/en-gb/oat-drink/.
2 Examples include *The Economist*'s 2013 special issue on "The Nordic Countries: The Next Supermodel"; and the wave of literature on the Nordic way of life and political culture – see Anu Partanen, *The Nordic Theory of Everything: In Search of a Better Life* (New York: Harper Collins, 2016) or Brontë Aurell, Anna Jacobsen, and Lucy Panes, *Nørth: How to Live Scandinavian* (London: Aurum Press, 2017). There are also examples of attempts to brand design as Nordic (e.g. https://www.warmnordic.com/) and there is even a local brewery in Tampere that makes "Nordic beers" (see: https://www.gastropub.net/brewery/).
3 We are, however, aware of the fact that the rising appeal of "the Nordic" is also a feature of academic policy that has generated funding opportunities for scholarly research on Norden. This publication and its authors are therefore, at least to some extent, part of the phenomenon we

for the recent rise of "the Nordic" in politics, culture and marketing, and how does this new Nordicness relate to the history of the adjective?

If one were to describe what makes the Nordic countries Nordic a wide range of characteristics could be listed. These include notions of sparsely populated societies living in close relationship to nature, comparatively peaceful and consensual political cultures, or the strong, even dominant role of the state and the weak position of the family in societal affairs. One could also highlight some of the many paradoxes of Nordicness: the strong but secularised position of religion in society, the political traditions of equality against the competitiveness of the Nordic economies, or the peripherality of relatively poor peasant societies surviving in harsh conditions against rich and modern societies blessed with an abundance of natural resources. The list of distinguishing features might draw on geography, language, culture or politics, but cannot really be complete. Indeed, definitions of "the Nordic" seldom aim at being exhaustive but are more likely to provide different sets of characteristics that produce tailored descriptions of the region. They represent competing visions of what the Nordic region is or should be.

It is also legitimate to question whether any of the defining features associated with "the Nordic" can be said to be *exclusively* Nordic. The Nordics share historical legacies with the Baltic States, and many political features with other small and medium-sized states, such as the Netherlands, Switzerland, New Zealand or Scotland. Many cultural, religious and political traditions in the Nordic region have a German origin, while since the Second World War, the Nordics have oriented themselves heavily towards the Anglo-American world. In their peculiar outside/inside perspective on "Europe," Nordic societies are very similar to other semi-peripheries of Europe, such as the Balkans.[4] When it comes to climate and nature, the Nordics might look like parts of Canada or Russia.

Moreover, it is seldom the case that all Nordic countries share the same characteristics, a realisation that has led welfare state scholars to refer to a Nordic welfare model with five exceptions.[5] This perspective highlights tensions present

---

study. We wish to thank the Academy of Finland (grant 323489), the NordForsk-funded university hub ReNEW, the Independent Research Fund Denmark (grant number 8018–00023B), and UiO: Nordic for their support of our research.

4 Stefan Nygård, Johan Strang, and Marja Jalava, eds., *Decentering European Intellectual Space* (Leiden: Brill, 2018).

5 Niels Finn Christiansen and Klaus Petersen, "Preface," *Scandinavian Journal of History* 26, no. 3 (September 2001): 153–156, doi:10.1080/034687501750303828; see also Jóhann Páll Árnason and Björn Wittrock, eds., *Nordic Paths to Modernity* (New York: Berghahn Books, 2012).

in any notion of the Nordic.[6] The old kingdoms (Sweden and Denmark) can be contrasted with the younger nation states (Norway, Finland and Iceland). The historical legacies of the early modern monarchies can be found in differences between East *Norden* (Sweden and Finland) and West *Norden* (Denmark, Norway, and Iceland), while the core Scandinavian countries (Sweden, Denmark, and Norway) may be contrasted with Iceland and Finland, or the large countries (Finland, Sweden, Denmark, and Norway) with the much smaller Iceland. There is also the notion of the more continental European Denmark versus the more peripheral parts of *Norden*. International political affiliations are also complex, with divisions between the NATO members (Denmark, Norway, and Iceland) and the non-aligned (Sweden and Finland); and between EU members (Denmark, Sweden, and Finland) and non-EU members (Norway and Iceland). As well as the five nation states the Nordic region also includes the autonomous territories of Greenland, the Faroe Islands and Åland, the transnational Sápmi region, which spans the northern parts of the Nordic countries and the Kola Peninsula of Russia, and border regions such as the Torne valley, the Øresund region and Southern Jutland/Schleswig.

Linguistic divisions can be made between the three Scandinavian languages, Danish, Norwegian, and Swedish – which have various degrees of mutual intelligibility – and Icelandic and Faroese, which are insular versions of Scandinavian languages no longer comprehensible to speakers of Danish, Norwegian, and Swedish. Finnish is of completely different origin, though it has been claimed that there are semantic similarities between Finnish and Swedish as political languages.[7] Other non-Scandinavian languages in the region include Greenlandic and the Sámi languages.[8] But there are also many languages – such as Arabic, English, and Russian, to name only a few of the most important ones – that may be widely spoken in the region, even though they are not always associated with it. Indeed, intra-Nordic communication is to an increasing extent taking place in English, which further complicates the idea of language being the core and essence of Nordicity.

---

6 Jani Marjanen, "Nordic Modernities: From Historical Region to Five Exceptions," *International Journal for History, Culture and Modernity* 3, no. 1 (March 2015): 91–106, doi:10.18352/22130624–00301005; Pauli Kettunen, "Review Essay: A Return to the Figure of the Free Nordic Peasant," *Acta Sociologica* 42, no. 3 (July 1999): 259–269, doi:10.1177/000169939904200306.
7 Henrik Stenius, "The Finnish Citizen: How a Translation Emasculated the Concept," *Redescriptions: Yearbook of Political Thought, Conceptual History and Feminist Theory* 8 (2004): 172–188.
8 Michael P. Barnes, "Linguistic Variety in the Nordics," 2019, https://nordics.info/show/artikel/linguistic-variety-in-the-nordic-region/.

Regardless of the complicated answers to what makes *Norden* Nordic, there is one point that remains: throughout at least the past two hundred years or so, many actors have invested heavily in the notion of *Norden*. Because of this, there is a long and complicated history of defining the Nordic region and talking about things as Nordic. The aim of this book is to analyse the broad variety of ways in which "Nordic" has been used as an adjective both within and outside the region. We explore the use of the term "Nordic" – and the related term "Scandinavian" – in conjunction with concepts such as race, openness, gender equality, food, crime fiction, Nordic cooperation, and the Nordic model, from historical and contemporary perspectives. The leading idea is that all of these uses of the term Nordic have been crucial in negotiating what the region stands for, its identity or brand. By analysing the background, context, and rhetorical struggles for the claims for specific "Nordic" characteristics in different discourses, this book sheds new light on the debates on the cultural construction of the Nordic region,[9] as well as the broader international discussion on regionalism and transnational history.[10]

This book is part of a recent wave of volumes on Nordic societies and cultures, covering topics such as the Nordic model, Nordic egalitarianism, Nordic human rights, Nordic democracy, Nordic gender equality, Nordic literature, and Nordic design.[11] Some volumes even explicitly focus on the discourse and

---

9 Øystein Sørensen and Bo Stråth, eds., *The Cultural Construction of Norden* (Oslo: Scandinavian University Press, 1997); Árnason and Wittrock, *Nordic Paths to Modernity*; Johan Strang, ed., *Nordic Cooperation: A European Region in Transition* (London: Routledge, 2016), doi:10.4324/9781315755366.

10 See e. g. James Casteel, "Historicizing the Nation: Transnational Approaches to the Recent European Past," in *Transnational Europe: Promise, Paradox, Limits*, ed. Joan DeBardeleben and Achim Hurrelmann (London: Palgrave Macmillan, 2011), 153–169, doi:10.1057/9780230306370_9; M. Middell, L. Roura Aulinas, and Lluís Roura i Aulinas, eds., *Transnational Challenges to National History Writing* (Basingstoke: Palgrave Macmillan, 2013); Diana Mishkova and Balázs Trencsényi, eds., *European Regions and Boundaries: A Conceptual History* (New York: Berghahn Books, 2017); Diana Mishkova, Balázs Trencsényi, and Marja Jalava, eds., *"Regimes of Historicity" in Southeastern and Northern Europe, 1890–1945: Discourses of Identity and Temporality* (Basingstoke: Palgrave Macmillan, 2014), doi:10.1057/9781137362476; Stefan Troebst, "Introduction: What's in a Historical Region? A Teutonic Perspective," *European Review of History: Revue Europeenne d'histoire* 10, no. 2 (2003): 173–188, doi:10.1080/1350748032000140741; Maria Todorova, *Imagining the Balkans* (New York: Oxford University Press, 1997); Maria Todorova, "Spacing Europe: What Is a Historical Region?" *East Central Europe* 32, no. 1–2 (2005): 59–78, doi:10.1163/18763308–90001032.

11 Anu Koivunen, Jari Ojala, and Janne Holmén, ed., *The Nordic Economic, Social and Political Model: Challenges in the 21st Century* (London: Routledge, 2021); Synnove Bendixsen, Mary Bente Bringslid, and Halvard Vike, eds., *Egalitarianism in Scandinavia: Historical and Contempo-*

conceptualisation of these phenomena, like the recent *The Changing Meanings of the Welfare State: Histories of a Key Concept in the Nordic Countries.*[12] However, the scholarly emphasis in all of these volumes is on the Nordic version, and the appropriation or conceptualisation of particular phenomena, rather than on the explicit historical discourses in which these phenomena have been labelled Scandinavian or Nordic. As such, our volume is most closely related to the 2010 book *Rhetorics of Nordic Democracy,* which tried to describe not only the elements that are so often seen as key features of Nordic politics and culture, but also the tensions that are present in the historical and discursive construction of them as Nordic.[13] In comparing the rhetoric of Nordicness in a wide variety of discourses, our book is the first scholarly volume to put the focus on the adjective "Nordic" rather than the nouns that are used following it.

The starting point for the volume is the simple observation that "Nordic" and "Scandinavian" are flexible and contested concepts that have been, and continue to be, used in many and often contradictory ways. They have been associated with political projects and institutions (Scandinavianism, the Nordic Council) while also functioning as categories of analysis in academic research (the Nordic model, Nordic welfare states). Moreover, they have been used to pinpoint a regional identity, based on shared historical and cultural legacies, which is often said to complement, rather than compete with, the national identities in the region. "Nordic" and "Scandinavian" have often – though not always – had positive connotations. As such, they have to an increasing extent become resources for commercial and cultural branding, as in the examples of Nordic noir, New Nordic Food or Scandinavian design. The chapters of the book discuss in-

---

rary Perspectives (London: Palgrave Macmillan, 2018), doi:10.1007/978-3-319-59791-1; Hanne Hagtvedt Vik et al., eds., *Nordic Histories of Human Rights* (London: Routledge, 2021); Nicholas Aylott, *Models of Democracy in Nordic and Baltic Europe: Political Institutions and Discourse* (Farnham: Ashgate Publishing, 2014); Eirinn Larsen, Sigrun Marie Moss, and Inger Skjelsbæk, eds., *Gender Equality and Nation Branding in the Nordic Region* (London: Routledge, 2021); Steven P. Sondrup et al., eds., *Nordic Literature: A Comparative History,* Vol. 1, *Spatial Nodes* (Amsterdam: John Benjamins Publishing Company, 2017), doi:10.1075/chlel.xxxi; Tobias Hoffmann and Bröhan-Museum Berlin, eds., *Nordic Design: Die Antwort aufs Bauhaus = Nordic Design: The Response to the Bauhaus* (Stuttgart: Arnoldsche, 2019); Byrkjeflot, Haldor, Lars Mjøset, Mads Mordhorst and Klaus Petersen, eds. The Making and Circulation of Nordic Models, Ideals and Images (London: Routledge, 2021) doi:10.4324/9781003156925.

12 Nils Edling, ed., *The Changing Meanings of the Welfare State: Histories of a Key Concept in the Nordic Countries* (New York: Berghahn Books, 2019).

13 Jussi Kurunmäki and Johan Strang, "Introduction: 'Nordic Democracy' in a World of Tensions," in *Rhetorics of Nordic Democracy,* ed. Jussi Kurunmäki and Johan Strang (Helsinki: Finnish Literature Society, 2010), doi:10.21435/sfh.17.

dividual cases, but this introduction will present our methodological starting point, discuss a number of key tensions in the rhetoric of Nordicness, and, finally, highlight a number of key turning points and historical layers in this rhetoric.

"Nordic" as a contested concept

The overwhelming appeal of the term "Nordic" during the twenty-first century has made it an object of political struggle between various groups who seek to claim the term for their own purposes. During the 2010s, for example, the Nordic model was at the centre of such disputes between Social Democrats and Conservatives across the region (see Hilson and Hoctor in this volume). At the same time another rhetoric of Nordicness with nationalist, anti-immigration and even racist overtones also flourished: at the time of writing in 2021 the populist party group in the Nordic Council calls itself "Nordic Freedom" (*Nordisk frihed*), while extreme right-wing movements such as the "Nordic Resistance Movement" (*Nordiska motståndsrörelsen*) make frequent use of Old Norse mythology. Yet, Nordicness also continues to be evoked in the name of international solidarity, humanitarianism and solidarity, as for example with the *New Nordic Peace* report published by the Nordic Council of Ministers in 2019.[14] Indeed, in May 2015 the Finnish Social Democrat Erkki Tuomioja criticised a government decision to make record-breaking cuts in foreign aid by claiming that "Finland is no longer a Nordic country."[15]

If notions of Nordicness are contested in the present, they were certainly never fixed in the past. As shown in Merle Weßel's chapter, the concept of a Nordic race was widespread among scientists and politicians in the United States, Europe and Scandinavia during the late nineteenth and early twentieth centuries. The adjective "Nordic" was used politically in the 1930s by the German National Socialists as well as by the far right within the Nordic region. The Swedish National Socialists of the 1930s, for example, called their youth organisation "Nordic Youth" (*Nordisk Ungdom*). At the same time, the 1930s saw the dawn of a rhetoric of "Nordic democracy" by which Social Democrats and others sought to portray the region as a democratic haven in a Europe threatened by totalitarianism.[16]

---

14 Anine Hagemann and Isabel Bramsen, *New Nordic Peace* 524, TemaNord (Copenhagen: Nordic Council of Ministers, 2019), doi:10.6027/TN2019–524.
15 Cecilia Heikel, "Vi använder vår yttrandefrihet för att säga ifrån," *Svenska Yle*, July 28, 2015, https://svenska.yle.fi/artikel/2015/07/28/vi-anvander-var-yttrandefrihet-att-saga-ifran.
16 Kurunmäki and Strang, "Introduction: 'Nordic Democracy' in a World of Tensions."

Rhetorical struggles are most apparent in the field of politics. This book suggests, however, that it is important to take stock of the plurality of usages of the term "Nordic" and analyse the complex interplay between political, academic, cultural and commercial rhetoric. The fact that similar notions of efficiency, simplicity, and age-old traditions of liberty can be evoked in discourses claiming to defend Nordic ethnic homogeneity, promoting Nordic democratic values, creating a Nordic cuisine or selling Nordic crime fiction points towards a certain transferability of the rhetoric of Nordicness from one discourse to another. For example, in his chapter on Nordic noir, Jakob Stougaard-Nielsen argues that the appeal of Nordic crime fiction in the UK from the late 2000s lay precisely in its complex relationship with utopian and dystopian images of the Nordic welfare state.

In emphasising the contested nature of the adjectives "Scandinavian" and "Nordic" the book distances itself from the struggles to define the essence or true nature of the Nordic region and its political and cultural characteristics. Instead, we embrace a constructivist approach akin to the theoretical premises of the discussion on "historical regions."[17] As such, we build on previous studies of the Nordic region such as the seminal *The Cultural Construction of Norden*, the studies of the "images" of *Norden*, as well as the more recent discussion on "Nordic branding."[18] Our ambition, however, is to advance beyond a quest for structures or elements that made the Nordic region (the free Nordic peasant, egalitarian education, Lutheranism or Social Democracy), or the ways in which these elements or others were promoted as part of a Nordic brand, and to focus instead on the "speech acts" through which these elements were appealed to (or reject-

---

17 Troebst, "Introduction;" Todorova, *Imagining the Balkans*; Todorova, "Spacing Europe"; Diana Mishkova, *Beyond Balkanism, the Scholarly Politics of Region Making* (London: Routledge, 2018); Mishkova and Trencsényi, *European Regions and Boundaries*.
18 Sørensen and Stråth, *The Cultural Construction of Norden*; see also Árnason and Wittrock, *Nordic Paths to Modernity*; Peter Stadius, *Resan till norr: Spanska Nordenbilder kring sekelskiftet 1900* (Helsingfors: Finska Vetenskaps-societeten, 2005); Jonas Harvard and Peter Stadius, "Conclusion: Mediating the Nordic Brand – History Recycled," in *Communicating the North: Media Structures and Images in the Making of the Nordic Region*, ed. Jonas Harvard and Peter Stadius, The Nordic Experience (Aldershot: Ashgate, 2013), 319–332; Christopher S. Browning, "Branding Nordicity: Models, Identity and the Decline of Exceptionalism," *Cooperation and Conflict* 42, no. 1 (2007): 27–51, doi:10.1177/0010836707073475; Louis Clerc, Nikolas Glover, and Paul Jordan, eds., *Histories of Public Diplomacy and Nation Branding in the Nordic and Baltic Countries: Representing the Periphery* (Leiden: Brill, 2015); Svein Ivar Angell and Mads Mordhorst, "National Reputation Management and the Competition State: The Cases of Denmark and Norway," *Journal of Cultural Economy* 8, no. 2 (2015): 184–201, doi:10.1080/17530350.2014.885459.

ed) through the use of the adjective "Nordic."[19] As such, it is not the making of *Norden*, but the political and cultural struggles over "the Nordic" that lie at the heart of the book.

We suggest that the rhetoric of Nordicness needs to be analysed by unpacking the historical layers of experiences and connotations present in language. We do this by bringing together scholars working in various disciplinary backgrounds under a common framework inspired by the tradition of conceptual history (*Begriffsgeschichte*).[20] Our starting point is that referring to something as "Nordic" or "Scandinavian" is both a reflection of how something Nordic is seen at a given time and a way of forging a specific view on something as Nordic. Paraphrasing Reinhart Koselleck, we see concepts as both mirrors of and vehicles for historical change.[21] Together, the historical struggles for defining Nordicness form different layers of meaning that are available for actors who can choose to claim, reject or redefine them in order to make new assertions and form future visions for "the Nordic." Our focus is on phrases where "the Nordic" is used in order to make an explicit claim about Nordic exceptionalism or difference from other regions ("the Nordic model" and "Nordic Noir"). It is, however, important also to acknowledge that even when "the Nordic" is used as a neutral marker indicating merely the geographical extension of its noun (as in "Nordic cooperation" or "The Nordic Society for Phenomenology"), the adjective adds something evaluative or substantial to the noun. It might allude to a wide range of positive features associated with the adjective "Nordic," such as democracy, welfare, pragmatism, openness, but it might also potentially evoke different forms of negative associations: arrogance, self-righteousness, or xenophobia. The rhetorical perspective allows for a more detailed analysis of how particular

---

19 Quentin Skinner, *Visions of Politics: Regarding Method*, vol. 1 (Cambridge: Cambridge University Press, 2002), doi:10.1017/CBO9780511790812.

20 Reinhart Koselleck, "Einleitung," in *Geschichtliche Grundbegriffe: Historisches Lexikon zur politisch-sozialen Sprache in Deutschland*, ed. Otto Brunner, Werner Conze, and Reinhart Koselleck (Stuttgart: Klett-Cotta, 1972); Reinhart Koselleck, "A Response to Comments on Geschichtliche Grundbegriffe," in *The Meaning of Historical Terms and Concepts: New Studies on Begriffsgeschichte*, ed. Hartmut Lehmann and Melvin Richter (Washington, DC: German Historical Institute, 1996); Skinner, *Visions of Politics*; Jan Ifversen, "About Key Concepts and How to Study Them," *Contributions to the History of Concepts* 6, no. 1 (2011), doi:10.3167/choc.2011.060104; Willibald Steinmetz and Michael Freeden, "Conceptual History: Challenges, Conundrums, Complexities," in *Conceptual History in the European Space*, ed. Willibald Steinmetz, Michael Freeden, and Javier Fernández Sebastián (New York: Berghahn Books, 2017), doi:10.2307/j.ctvw04kcs.9.

21 Koselleck, "Einleitung."

agents have seen the Nordic region, thus acknowledging that agency belongs to particular persons and institutions and not discourses as such.

Tensions of Nordicness

In analysing the motives of individual speech acts that have framed different cultural, social and political items as "Nordic", this book takes stock of many different instances of more or less inventive rhetoric. As noted above, standard accounts of what makes *Norden* Nordic usually present a number of incongruities and contradictions. In shifting the perspective to a study of the rhetoric of Nordicness, these can be identified and analysed more clearly as tensions arising from the various purposes for which the historical actors use the concept.

Contested Nordic geographies

The geographical extension of the terms "Scandinavian" and the "Nordic" is, of course, a contested issue in itself. Within the region, the adjective "Scandinavian" (*skandinavisk, skandinaavinen, skandínaviskur*) is usually, but not always, used to denote something Danish, Norwegian and/or Swedish, whereas "Nordic" (*nordisk, pohjoismainen, norræn*) tends to include Finland and Iceland as well. In other languages and contexts, including in English, "Scandinavian" might be used of all five Nordic nations, or sometimes of just some of them. Historically, the geographical extension of *Norden* ("the North") has been disputed. In nineteenth-century travel literature, Russia was often included in "the North,"[22] while Iceland had an ambivalent position as an example of what Guðmundur Hálfdanarson has labelled "boreal alterity" – on the edge of European civilisation but at the same time associated with the European and Nordic past preserved in its Old Norse literary traditions.[23]

For much of the twentieth century, Sweden was indisputably at the core of the region, the most Nordic of all the Nordic countries.[24] For Denmark and Nor-

---

22 Stadius, *Resan till norr.*
23 Guðmundur Hálfdanarson, "Iceland Perceived: Nordic European or a Colonial Other?" in *The Postcolonial North Atlantic Iceland, Greenland and the Faroe Islands*, ed. Lill-Ann Körber and Ebbe Volquardsen (Berlin: Nordeuropa-Institut der Humboldt-Universität, 2014), 39–66.
24 Jenny Andersson and Mary Hilson, "Images of Sweden and the Nordic Countries," *Scandinavian Journal of History* 34, no. 3 (2009): 219–28, doi:10.1080/03468750903134681.

way, being Nordic has largely been equally self-evident, despite these countries' slightly more continental European and transatlantic orientations. By contrast, for Iceland, the turn to *Norden* was more controversial and demanded a conscious effort in the interwar period.[25] For Finland, the country's position as a Nordic country was far from evident in the first half of the twentieth century, until the rhetoric of Nordicness gradually became an essential tool to assert its status as part of the West from the 1930s onwards.[26] Claims to a Nordic identity have at times formed part of the political rhetoric in Estonia and the Baltic region as a whole, and more recently also in Scotland.[27] The recent wave of (New) Nordicness, in turn, seems to point in different directions. On the one hand, geopolitical developments and the increased usage of "the Nordic" for branding purposes have furthered the idea of a fixed region consisting of only five Nordic countries and three autonomous regions.[28] On the other hand, as "the Nordic" has become a brand it refers increasingly to qualities and values rather than geopolitical location or cultural community, and as such questions of the geographical extension of "the Nordic" have become increasingly irrelevant (see Kelting and Stougaard-Nielsen, both in this volume).

The relationship to the outside is, of course, a central aspect of defining the Nordic region, though this demarcation has always been fluid. In the nineteenth century, "Scandinavia" functioned as a means of distinguishing the Danish and Swedish monarchies from other northern powers such as Prussia/Germany and Russia. In early twentieth-century racial discourses, we find the idea of a common Nordic-Germanic people, as opposed to Alpine or Southern races (see Weßel in this volume). From the 1930s, and especially after 1945, *Norden* was

---

25 Ragnheiður Kristjánsdóttir, "For Equality or Against Foreign Oppression? The Politics of the Left in Iceland Leading up to the Cold War," *Moving the Social* 48 (2012): 11–28, doi:10.13154/mts.48.2012.11–28; Ragnheiður Kristjánsdóttir, "Facing the Nation – Nordic Communists and Their National Contexts, from the 1920s and into the Cold War," in *Labour, Unions and Politics under the North Star: The Nordic Countries, 1700–2000*, ed. Mary Hilson, Silke Neunsinger, and Iben Vyff (New York: Berghahn Books, 2017).
26 Max Engman, "Är Finland ett nordiskt land?" *Den Jyske Historiker* 69–70 (1994).
27 Mikko Lagerspetz, "How Many Nordic Countries?: Possibilities and Limits of Geopolitical Identity Construction," *Cooperation and Conflict* 38, no. 1 (2003): 49–61, doi:10.1177/0010836703038001003; Mart Kuldkepp, "The Scandinavian Connection in Early Estonian Nationalism," *Journal of Baltic Studies* 44, no. 3 (2013): 313–338, doi:10.1080/01629778.2012.744911; Andrew G. Newby, "'In Building a Nation Few Better Examples Can Be Found': *Norden* and the Scottish Parliament," *Scandinavian Journal of History* 34, no. 3 (2009): 307–329, doi:10.1080/03468750903134749.
28 Browning, "Branding Nordicity"; Johan Strang, "Introduction: The Nordic Model of Transnational Cooperation?" in *Nordic Cooperation: A European Region in Transition*, ed. Johan Strang (New York: Routledge, 2016), 1–26, doi:10.4324/9781315755366–1.

often construed against a German or a European conservative other, or as an exceptional region representing a third way between Western capitalism and Eastern communism.[29] These uses of "the Nordic" bear a strong similarity to what Reinhart Koselleck called "asymmetrical counter-concepts," that is, conceptual pairs that are defined solely by one part. In Koselleck's heavily laden examples "Hellenes and barbarians," "Christians and heretics," and "humans and non-humans" the second term of the pair receives its meaning from lacking a quality present in the former. "Barbarian" was simply a generic classification put against the specific name of a Hellene.[30] When it comes to "the Nordic," this use of asymmetrical counter-concepts was most extreme in the racist discourse analysed by Weßel in this volume. But, as shown by Strang, it was also strikingly apparent in the asymmetrical usage of "Europe" to define Nordic cooperation, Nordic democracy or the Nordic welfare state. In the field of culture, the asymmetrical other is usually not articulated (e. g., in the example of Nordic design), but appears in a similar way as something that *lacks* perceived distinctive Nordic qualities.

Nordicness as simultaneously age old and progressive

Closely related to these spatial connotations are the temporal dimensions of Nordicness. Recent work on the history of geo-spatial concepts has highlighted how the formation of geographical entities is deeply entrenched in ideas about progress, lagging behind and catching up.[31] As a whole, the Nordic region has at various points in history been conceived of either as a laggard at the outskirts of European modernity, or as a progressive region at the vanguards of human de-

---

29 Bo Stråth, "The Swedish Image of Europe as the Other," in *Europe and the Other, Europe as the Other*, ed. Bo Stråth (Wien: Peter Lang, 2010); Lars Trägårdh, "Sweden and the EU: Welfare State Nationalism and the Spectre of 'Europe,'" in *European Integration and National Identity: The Challenge of Nordic States*, ed. Lene Hansen and Ole Wæver (London: Routledge, 2002); see also Strang in this volume.

30 Reinhart Koselleck, *Vergangene Zukunft: zur Semantik geschichtlicher Zeiten* (Frankfurt am Main: Suhrkamp, 1979).

31 Diana Mishkova and Balázs Trencsényi, "Introduction," in *European Regions and Boundaries: A Conceptual History*, ed. Diana Mishkova and Balázs Trencsényi (New York: Berghahn Books, 2017); Diana Mishkova and Balázs Trencsényi, "Conceptualizing Spaces within Europe: The Case of Meso-Regions," in *European Regions and Boundaries: A Conceptual History*, ed. Diana Mishkova and Balázs Trencsényi (New York: Berghahn Books, 2017); Marja Jalava and Bo Stråth, "Scandinavia/Norden," in *European Regions and Boundaries: A Conceptual History*, ed. Diana Mishkova and Balázs Trencsényi (New York: Berghahn Books, 2017).

velopment.[32] As such, the rhetoric of Nordicness has involved a wide range of seemingly contradictory temporal speech-acts. On the one hand, as emphatically shown in Lily Kelting's chapter on New Nordic Food, Nordicness is often used in order to refer to historical, even primordial, features of the Nordic region, relating to nature and landscape. The Viking legacy is often evoked as an "original" pre-nation-state Nordicness. On the other hand, at least since the late nineteenth century the rhetoric of Nordicness has – as indicated above – also often been used to allude to progress, modernity, or even the avant-garde, as opposed to a more traditionalist Europe.[33] This progressive turn can be dated to "the modern breakthrough" associated with authors like Georg Brandes, Henrik Ibsen and August Strindberg in the late nineteenth century,[34] to the rise of Social Democracy in the 1930s, or to the designation of the functionalist architecture and modernist design of the mid-twentieth century as "characteristically Scandinavian."

Perhaps it is precisely this combination of tradition and progress that provides the rhetoric of Nordicness with its suggestive appeal.[35] The 1930s rhetoric of Nordic democracy is a case in point. The Social Democrats furnished their own progressive political vision of the future with allusions to its long historical roots.[36] In this sense, Nordic rhetoric touches upon another Koselleckian theme, the gap between "the space of experience" and "the horizon of expectation."[37] Today, we see a similar combination of historical tradition and modern solutions in the discourse of gender equality, in which a notion of the strong Nordic woman in early peasant societies is presented as the background to the contemporary position of women in working life, at home and as being in charge of their own bodies (see Pirjo Markkola's chapter in this volume). Building on the French historian François Hartog, it can be suggested that "the Nordic" has be-

---

32 Stefan Nygård and Johan Strang, "Conceptual Universalization and the Role of the Peripheries," *Contributions to the History of Concepts* 12, no. 1 (2017): 55–75, doi:10.3167/choc.2017.120105.

33 Tania Ørem, *A Cultural History of the Avant-Garde in the Nordic Countries 1925–1950*, vol. 1–3 (Leiden: Brill, 2012); Jenny Andersson, "Nordic Nostalgia and Nordic Light: The Swedish Model as Utopia 1930–2007," *Scandinavian Journal of History* 34, no. 3 (2009): 229–245, doi:.1080/03468750903134699.

34 Julie K Allen, *Icons of Danish Modernity: Georg Brandes and Asta Nielsen* (Seattle: University of Washington, 2012).

35 Carl Marklund and Peter Stadius, "Acceptance and Conformity: Merging Modernity with Nationalism in the Stockholm Exhibition in 1930," *Culture Unbound* 2, no. 5 (2010): 609–634, doi:10.3384/cu.2000.1525.10235609.

36 Kurunmäki and Strang, "Introduction: 'Nordic Democracy' in a World of Tensions."

37 Koselleck, *Vergangene Zukunft*.

come increasingly presentist.[38] Notions like Nordic Noir, Nordic food or even the Nordic model allude to a past that legitimates the present, but do not carry within themselves a promise of a radically better future in the same way as Scandinavianism in the nineteenth century, Nordic democracy in the 1930s, or Nordic cooperation in the Cold War period.

The rhetoric of Nordicness has also been a way of *synchronizing* the Nordic countries with each other, bringing them together at the same level of development.[39] It is well known that Nordic comparisons in domestic political debates are often used in order to show that one's own country lags behind the others in some aspect or another, with the purpose of urging political action. Pauli Kettunen, for example, has argued that the notion of the Nordic welfare state in Finland was a matter of immanent critique of Finnish society, where the temporalised rhetoric of "Nordic" represented a horizon of expectation modelled around the Swedish example. If Finland purported to be a Nordic country, it had to follow and catch up with developments in the rest of the region, particularly in Sweden.[40]

In this way, Nordic rhetoric has seldom been a matter of negotiating an average Nordic state of development, but instead it usually refers to the most progressive and advanced solutions in the region. For many decades during the post-war period, Sweden was conceived of as being ahead and by virtue of this defined "the Nordic," giving direction to developments in the other Nordic countries. More recently, this position has been challenged in at least two different ways. On the one hand, it seems as if the other Nordic countries have caught up with and even overtaken Sweden in various fields. As such, "the Nordic model" often appears in international debate as no longer synonymous with the Swedish welfare state, but as the aggregate of cherry-picked features from the different Nordic countries.[41] On the other hand, there has also been a shift in the political landscape which has meant that an increasing number of people in the region (and abroad) have begun to frame the Swedish example less as a

---

38 François Hartog, *Regimes of Historicity: Presentism and Experiences of Time*, trans. Saskia Brown (New York: Columbia University Press, 2015).

39 Helge Jordheim, "Europe at Different Speeds: Asynchronicities and Multiple Times in European Conceptual History," in *Conceptual History in the European Space*, ed. Willibald Steinmetz, Michael Freeden, and Javier Fernández Sebastián (New York: Berghahn Books, 2017), 139–174, doi:10.2307/j.ctvw04kcs.9.

40 Pauli Kettunen, "The Nordic Welfare State in Finland," *Scandinavian Journal of History* 26, no. 3 (2001): 225–247, doi:10.1080/034687501750303864.

41 Carl Marklund, "The Nordic Model on the Global Market of Ideas: The Welfare State as Scandinavia's Best Brand," *Geopolitics* 22, no. 3 (2017): 623–639, doi:10.1080/14650045.2016.1251906.

utopian and more as a dystopian vision of the future. This view has been expressed especially in connection with immigration policy, but in 2020 also with the handling of the Covid-19 pandemic, which has raised concerns that the Swedish welfare state has been wrecked by neoliberal reform.[42]

The interchangeability of "the Nordic" and the national

It is often argued that the Nordic identity is special because it is complementary, not opposed, to the five different national identities. In other words, Nordicness does not challenge, but is an integral part of Finnishness or Danishness, for example.[43] This means that there is a certain interchangeability of national adjectives (Danish, Finnish, Icelandic, Norwegian and Swedish) with the word Nordic. Using "Nordic" instead of national adjectives can be an attempt to present something as more primordial than the modern nation-state (see Lily Kelting's chapter in this volume). In Finland, the rhetoric of Nordicness can be a way of incorporating into national history traditions, events, and individuals from the country's long shared history with Sweden. In his chapter on Nordic openness, Tero Erkkilä shows how in 1990s Finland the clergyman and economic thinker Anders Chydenius (1729–1803) was branded as the father of Nordic openness, at least in part because it would have sounded awkwardly anachronistic to label him Finnish.

The substitution of Nordic for the national adjectives may also be a way of associating with the favourable image of the neighbouring countries, or even

---

42 Mikael Jalving, *Absolut Sverige: En rejse i tavshedens rige* (København: Jyllands-Postens Forlag, 2011); Bjarne Riiser Gundersen, *Svenske tilstander: En reise til et fremmed land* (Bergen: Vigmostad & Bjørke, 2019); Jeanette Björkqvist, "Både Finland och Norge öppnar för att hjälpa," *Svenska Dagbladet*, December 12, 2020, https://www.svd.se/finland-redo-att-hjalpa-sverige-med-coronavard; Anton Ösgård, "How Privatization Hobbled Sweden's Response To Coronavirus," *Jacobin Magazine*, 2020, https://jacobinmag.com/2020/11/sweden-coronavirus-covid-nordic-scandinavia; Peter S. Goodman and Erik Augustin Palm, "Pandemic Exposes Holes in Sweden's Generous Social Welfare State," *The New York Times*, October 8, 2020, https://www.nytimes.com/2020/10/08/business/coronavirus-sweden-social-welfare.html; Johan Strang, "Kommentar: Vår älskade dystopi," in *Sverigebilden i Norden: En studie i Danmark, Finland, Island och Norge* (Stockholm: Svenska institutet, 2021), https://si.se/app/uploads/2021/03/bilden-av-sverige-i-norden.pdf.

43 See e.g., Norbert Götz, "*Norden*: Structures That Do Not Make a Region," *European Review of History: Revue Europeenne d'histoire* 10, no. 2 (2003): 323–341, doi:10.1080/1350748032000140822; Lene Hansen, "Conclusion," in *European Integration and National Identity: The Challenge of the Nordic States*, ed. Lene Hansen and Ole Wæver (London: Routledge, 2001), 212–225.

hiding more troublesome aspects of the image or reputation of a particular Nordic nation.[44] For example, at various points in Finnish history the rhetoric of "Nordic democracy" was not only a way of connecting Finland with "the West", but also of smoothing over domestic political tensions and disarming threats from extremist political factions on the right and the left.[45] Moreover, the rhetoric of Nordicness has also been a way of avoiding explicitly nationalistic rhetoric. In the 1930s, Social Democrats used the same rhetoric of Nordic democracy in order to associate with contemporary trends towards cultural nationalism, without aligning too closely with extreme nationalist voices.[46] From the 1980s, Swedish Social Democrats mobilised the concept of a Nordic model in response to rising neo liberalism, while references to a Nordic model in the 2010s allowed centre-right politicians to distance themselves from the (Social Democratic) ideological connotations of the Swedish model.[47]

Despite the interchangeability of "Nordic" with national adjectives, the rhetoric of Nordicness has usually included some kind of reference to the other Nordic countries. Especially during the Cold War period, "Nordic" was customarily used either with representation from, or as an appeal to, the other Nordic countries. In an era of nation branding in the new millennium, such references have become less important and the "Nordic" is increasingly used as synonymous with Danishness or Finnishness for example, rather than as a transnational Nordic space.

There are clearly also limits to the interchangeability of the Nordic and the national. It is, for example, unusual to see athletes presented as Nordic, because they are primarily thought of as representing the nation and often in explicit opposition to Nordic "arch-enemies." In general, *Norden* seems to have become an

---

44 Marklund, "The Nordic Model on the Global Market of Ideas."

45 Petri Koikkalainen, "From Agrarian Republicanism to the Politics of Neutrality: Urho Kekkonen and 'Nordic Democracy' in Finnish Cold War Politics," in *Rhetorics of Nordic Democracy*, ed. Jussi Kurunmäki and Johan Strang (Helsinki: Finnish Literature Society, 2010), doi:10.21435/sfh.17.

46 Niels Kayser Nielsen, *Bonde, stat og hjem: Nordisk demokrati og nationalisme fra pietismen til 2. verdenskrig* (Aarhus: Aarhus universitetsforlag, 2009); Kurunmäki and Strang, "Introduction: 'Nordic Democracy' in a World of Tensions"; Nikolas Glover and Andreas Mørkved Hellenes, "A 'Swedish Offensive' at the World's Fairs: Advertising, Social Reformism and the Roots of Swedish Cultural Diplomacy, 1935–1939," *Contemporary European History* 30, no. 2 (May 2021): 202, doi:10.1017/S0960777320000533.

47 Andreas Mørkved Hellenes, "Tracing the Nordic Model. French Creations, Swedish Appropriations and Nordic Articulations," in *The Making and Circulation of Nordic Models, Ideals and Images*, ed. Haldor Byrkjeflot et al. (London: Routledge, 2021); Marklund, "The Nordic Model on the Global Market of Ideas;" see also Hilson and Hoctor in this volume.

increasingly irrelevant framework for sports. Nordic championships are rarely arranged, and Nordic records in various sports are no longer registered or simply deemed irrelevant. Even the Miss Scandinavia beauty pageants were discontinued in 2008. Internal rivalries remain, however, and important clashes between athletes or teams from different Nordic countries can still be framed in the media as "battles of Scandinavia/*Norden*." That said, even in sports the rhetoric of Nordicness can sometimes be a way of expressing sympathies with (or claiming the success of) an athlete from another Nordic country, as in the case of the Icelandic football success in the 2016 European Championship.

"The Nordic" in different parts of the region

The rhetoric of Nordicness is used differently and for different purposes in different parts of the region. Sometimes this can cause misunderstandings and frictions between people who all claim to represent "true" Nordicness. In Denmark for example, "the Nordic" has been invoked to stress the distinctiveness of Denmark from the European mainstream, whereas in Finland Nordicness has been a way of cementing Finland's status as a (West) European country. It is beyond the scope of this volume to explore the different uses of Nordicness within the subnational regions of the Nordic countries, but one might expect "the Nordic" to have a different significance in West Jutland, Northern Karelia, Skåne or the Haparanda/Tornio border regions, say, compared to Copenhagen or Helsinki.

Historians of the Nordic welfare state have documented how Nordic cooperation often functioned as an arena where particularly Danish and Swedish politicians quarrelled with each other on various social political issues, thus effectively engaging themselves in a struggle to define "the *Nordic* welfare state."[48] The rhetoric of Nordicness is thus connected to power hierarchies in the region, where the tendency of monopolising "the Nordic" as a designation for something Danish or Swedish has often generated some irritation in Finland, Iceland and Norway. Examples range from the establishment of the "Nordic Museum" (*Nordiska museet*) in Stockholm in 1873 to the advertising campaign "Stockholm – the capital of Scandinavia" in the first decade of the 2000s. Similarly, in 1874

---

48 Pauli Kettunen, Urban Lundberg, and Mirja Österberg, "The Nordic Model and the Rise and Fall of Nordic Cooperation," in *Nordic Cooperation: A European Region in Transition*, ed. Johan Strang, (London: Routledge, 2016), doi:10.4324/9781315755366; Klaus Petersen, "National, Nordic and Trans-Nordic. Transnational Perspectives on the History of the Nordic Welfare State," in *Beyond Welfare State Models*, ed. Klaus Petersen and Pauli Kettunen (Cheltenham: Edward Elgar Publishing, 2011), 41–64, doi:10.4337/9781849809603.00009.

Henrik Ibsen complained that Georg Brandes was using "Scandinavian literature" as a name for a small circle of intellectuals in Copenhagen, ignoring writers from other parts of the Nordic region.[49] Indeed, as shown by Ruth Hemstad in
her chapter, in nineteenth-century Norway there was a strong suspicion that the
cosy rhetoric of Scandinavia or *Norden* served only to conceal Swedish and Danish imperialist ambitions, a suspicion that lived on as a Norwegian scepticism of
Nordic cooperation throughout much of the latter half of the twentieth century
(see also Strang in this volume). More recently, however, Norway has become
an enthusiastic promoter of both "the Nordic" and of Nordic cooperation.[50]
This might be related to a fear of being left out when Finland and Sweden joined
the EU in 1995 and when the discourse on Baltic Sea cooperation was most intense.[51] Simultaneously, a case can undoubtedly be made that the oil-generated
economic prosperity of recent years has enabled Norwegian actors to indulge in
the rhetoric of Nordicness with the self-confidence that was previously confined
to Danes and Swedes.[52]

The ambivalent relationship to "the Nordic" is perhaps a more enduring feature of Icelandic political rhetoric, the latest Nordic country to reach full independence (1944). Ragnheiður Kristjánsdóttir has convincingly argued that the
Icelandic Social Democratic movement was severely hampered by its "Nordicness" and closeness to its Danish sister party. This meant it remained largely
in the shadow of political movements such as the conservatives, agrarians
and socialists, who could more easily flourish in a political landscape thoroughly
permeated by nationalist discourse.[53] To be sure, there was also (and continues
to be) a similar nationalist hesitation towards the Nordic in Finland, but more

---

49 Stefan Nygård, "The Southern Prism of the Northern Breakthrough: Georg Brandes and Italy"
in *Georg Brandes. Pioneer of Comparative Literature and Global Public Intellectual*, ed. Jens Bjerring-Hansen, Anders Engberg-Pedersen, and Lasse Horne Kjældgaard (Leiden: Brill, forthcoming).
50 See e. g., Thorvald Stoltenberg, *Nordic Cooperation on Foreign and Security Policy*, Proposals
presented to the extraordinary meeting of Nordic foreign ministers (Oslo, February 2009),
https://www.regjeringen.no/globalassets/upload/ud/vedlegg/nordicreport.pdf.
51 Kazimierz Musiał, "Reconstructing Nordic Significance in Europe on the Threshold of the
21st Century," *Scandinavian Journal of History* 34, no. 3 (2009): 286–306, doi:10.1080/
03468750903134723.
52 A phenomenon examined and exemplified by the multi-million kroner programme UiO:Nor-
dic at the University of Oslo, which facilitates studies of Nordic issues and the Nordic region
from a social science and humanities perspective. See https://www.uio.no/forskning/satsing-
er/norden/forskning.
53 Kristjánsdóttir, "For Equality or Against Foreign Oppression?"; Kristjánsdóttir, "Facing the
Nation – Nordic Communists and Their National Contexts, from the 1920s and into the Cold
War."

often than not this has been overridden by the geopolitical imperative to keep at a safe distance from the eastern neighbour Russia. For example, while Urho Kekkonen, as a young nationalist intellectual of the Agrarian League had been sceptical of associating Finland with Scandinavia, he was, as President of the Republic during the treacherous Cold War years, eager to emphasise Finland's Nordicness.[54]

In the autonomous regions of Greenland, the Faroe Islands, and Åland, the Nordic discourse has at times had the almost reverse function of strengthening autonomy and weakening the relation to the host countries Denmark and Finland. While the Faroe Islands and Greenland remain underdogs within the Kingdom of Denmark, the Nordic context may provide them with an arena for exerting sovereignty. In concrete terms, the Nordic Council, where the Faroe Islands and Åland have been members since 1970 and Greenland since 1984, has become an important institutional arena for (para-)diplomacy for these autonomous regions.[55]

The rhetoric of Nordicness within the region and abroad

The rhetorical appeal of Scandinavia outside the region can be traced to the nineteenth century in certain contexts,[56] but became firmly established from the 1930s on. It has even been argued that the very idea of *Norden* as a distinct region has been produced abroad, or at least in close dialogue with foreign discourses.[57] From the 1980s this was expressed in references to a Scandinavian or

---

54 Koikkalainen, "From Agrarian Republicanism to the Politics of Neutrality."
55 Sarah Stephan, "Making Autonomies Matter: Sub-State Actor Accommodation in the Nordic Council and the Nordic Council of Ministers. An Analysis of the Institutional Framework for Accommodating the Faroe Islands, Greenland and Åland within 'Norden,'" *European Diversity and Autonomy Papers EDAP* 3 (2014), http://www.eurac.edu/edap; Hasan Akintug, "The Åland Islands Meet European Integration: Politics of History and the EU Referendums on Åland" (MA diss., University of Helsinki, 2020), https://helda.helsinki.fi/handle/10138/318984.
56 Andrew Newby, "'One Valhalla of the Free': Scandinavia, Britain and Northern Identity in the Mid-Nineteenth Century," in *Communicating the North*, ed. Jonas Harvard and Peter Stadius (Farnham: Ashgate, 2013), 147–169.
57 Kazimierz Musiał, *Roots of the Scandinavian Model: Images of Progress in the Era of Modernisation* (Baden-Baden: Nomos, 2002); Carl Marklund and Klaus Petersen, "Return to Sender – American Images of the Nordic Welfare States and Nordic Welfare State Branding," *European Journal of Scandinavian Studies* 43, no. 2 (2013): 245–257, doi:10.1515/ejss-2013–0016; Norbert Götz and Heidi Haggrén, eds., *Regional Cooperation and International Organizations: The Nordic Model in Transnational Alignment* (London: Routledge, 2009).

Nordic "model" (or models) available for emulation or export (see Hilson and Hoctor in this volume). Here too, notions of Scandinavia or *Norden* were often used interchangeably with national labels, with close affinities between the Swedish and Scandinavian models in particular.[58] While such images were often positive, they were never exclusively utopian: "Scandinavia" could also be used rhetorically to convey dystopian images, such as high rates of taxation or social control on the one hand, or the decadence of secularism and sexual liberation on the other.

In serving highly local purposes abroad, the rhetoric of Nordicness often refers to pointed ideal types – whether utopian or dystopian – where the actual state of affairs in the Nordic countries is almost irrelevant. It may be argued that external circulation sometimes serves to conserve obsolete ideas of what the Nordic countries are. Examples of this might include references to high rates of suicide or the debates on "Scandinavian socialism" in connection with the 2020 US Presidential elections.[59] The Nordic social democratic welfare state also continues to live on in foreign political debates, despite the fact that its foundations have been transformed in the past decades, particularly in Sweden.[60] Indeed, in our volume, Mary Hilson and Tom Hoctor show how the idea of the Nordic model has been used positively by both the left and the right in UK politics since the 1990s. Sometimes these foreign uses boomerang back to the Nordic countries themselves, becoming part of branding initiatives or political campaigns based on simplified stereotypes of innate Nordic cultural traits. The Swedish centre-right government's initiative *The Nordic Way* at the 2011 World Economic Forum in Davos is a case in point.[61]

While it is self-evident that the images of *Norden* within the region and outside it are not the same, the rhetorical perspective can be a useful way of exploring the connections and interplay between foreign and domestic visions of Nordicness. If notions like the Nordic model are invented to serve particular local purposes in British, German or American contexts, the Nordic appropriation of this rhetoric shows that the reception is not passive and that actors in the region actively use the brands for their own purposes. More recently, terms like Nordic

---

58 Hellenes, "Tracing the Nordic Model."

59 Carl Marklund and Byron Zachary Rom-Jensen, "Vanishing Scandinavian 'Socialism' in the 2020 US Election," 2020, https://nordics.info/show/artikel/scandinavias-vanishing-socialism-in-the-2020-us-election.

60 Jenny Andersson, "Drivkrafterna bakom nyliberaliseringen kom från många olika håll," *Respons*, no. 1, 2020, http://tidskriftenrespons.se/artikel/drivkrafterna-bakom-nyliberaliseringen-kom-fran-manga-olika-hall.

61 Harvard and Stadius, "Conclusion: Mediating the Nordic Brand – History Recycled."

noir and New Nordic Food have gained in popularity in, for example, Britain and Germany, which, in turn has led to an increased awareness of a common genre (and marketing possibilities) among Nordic authors and publishers (see Stougaard-Nielsen and Kelting, both in this volume).

The rhetoric of Nordicness is often used to distinguish particular features of the region, but it can also be an appeal to something higher or universal. Talking about the welfare state as Nordic rather than Norwegian or Swedish gives it the character of being something more eminent than a contingent result of a series of domestic political decisions. It becomes a "model" which, paradoxically, is at the same time culturally anchored and universal, and as such replicable by others (see Hilson & Hoctor in this volume). The recent rhetoric of Nordic values can be seen as a similar attempt to put a partisan position beyond political contestation.[62] The idea that there are values that are commonly shared by people in the region either exaggerates the homogeneity of the populace or speaks of values on such an abstract level that they cannot in any way be regarded as belonging exclusively to *Norden*. Indeed, one would be hard-pressed to tell the difference between Nordic, European or Western values. It seems that all of these three rhetorical tropes evoke an imaginary of shared values that may be threatened by an equally imagined other. Nordic values also seem to be inherent to *Norden* regardless of the conflicted history of the region, the asymmetrical relations between the five countries or their complicated relationship to the three autonomous regions, or indeed the political tensions of contemporary politics (are Nordic values social democratic, neoliberal or national conservative?). Much of the universalising character of the notions of the Nordic model and Nordic values is arguably drawn from the nouns "model" and "values," but the modifier "Nordic" provides a rhetorical edge in placing them outside the realm of national politics.

The historical layers of Nordic rhetoric

This book contains eight case studies purposely chosen in order to give a broad account of the rhetoric of Nordicness in various fields of culture, society and politics, from the nineteenth century to the present. Although they all take their starting point from the common theoretical foundation laid out above, they also represent different scholarly disciplines and offer standalone contributions to debates associated with the individual themes of their chapters. Thus, some of

---

62 Klaus Petersen, "Nordiske værdier: et kritisk reflekterende essay," in *Meningen med föreningen*, ed. Henrik Wilen (København: Föreningarna Norden, 2019), 73–83.

them emphasise analyses of long-term diachronic change in the use of concepts, whereas others are more inclined to analyse rhetoric in individual speech acts or study the political implications of particular discursive frameworks.

In chapter 2, Ruth Hemstad explores the political visions attached to notions of "Scandinavian unity" and "Scandinavian sympathies" in the nineteenth century as well as the conceptual struggles between Swedish and Danish definitions of Scandinavia in the nineteenth century. Merle Weßel, in chapter 3, explores the interplay between American and Nordic uses of the term "Nordic race" in the interwar period. These chapters are followed by investigations of two key notions of Cold War Nordicity. In chapter 4, Mary Hilson and Tom Hoctor discuss the concept of a Nordic model as an interplay between foreign and Nordic discourses from the 1930s onwards, analysing in particular the role of the Nordic model in British politics during the 2000s. Johan Strang examines the shifting implications of Nordic cooperation from 1952 to the 2000s in chapter 5. Chapters 6 and 7 probe more deeply into the 1990s as a turning point for a new rhetoric of Nordicness within Europe. Pirjo Markkola discusses how gender equality became framed and branded as "Nordic" in the 1990s, and Tero Erkkilä describes how openness and transparency were turned into features of Nordic political culture in a period of Europeanisation in the late 1990s and early 2000s, especially in Finland. The final two chapters focus on the recent wave of Nordic branding in the field of culture. In chapter 8 Lily Kelting studies "New Nordic Food" with its references to a primordial and masculine Nordicness, showing how the Nordicness of New Nordic Food paradoxically became de-territorialised and universalised. Jakob Stougaard-Nielsen explores how the Nordicness of Nordic crime fiction became part of the British longing for a lost welfare paradise – a *borealist* nostalgia.

The volume is not intended as a final or complete account. Many additional cases could have been included (e. g., Nordic design, the Nordic welfare state, and Nordic peace/neutrality). Moreover, most of the examples refer to uses of the rhetorics of Nordicness within the region or in English-language contexts outside it, with little attention paid to how the concept is used in other languages. Collectively, however, the book enables us to draw some conclusions regarding not only the main tensions, but also the historical layers present in the Nordic rhetoric. Overall, the rhetorical approach challenges us to rethink earlier chronologies of what makes *Norden* Nordic. Our aim is not necessarily to question the long roots of features that can be seen as Nordic, but to highlight critical moments when these characteristics were conceptualised as Nordic. Discussions of the region's cultural distinctiveness often trace these to the Reformation and the early modern period, culminating with the nineteenth-century Scandinavianist project,[63] but if we consider the contestation and framing of the Nordic from the point of view of discourse, the nineteenth century was the starting point for when the rhetoric of Nordicness became politically and culturally laden. The same goes for many of the key institutions of Nordicness. For example, histories of Nordic cooperation usually begin with references to the nineteenth century or earlier, but the real breakthrough of the rhetoric of Nordic cooperation can arguably be found in the interwar and Cold War eras (see the chapter by Strang). Similarly, scholars disagree over whether the roots of the Nordic welfare state can be traced to early modern Lutheranism or to institutional developments in the short twentieth century, but the rhetoric of the Nordic welfare state originates in the 1990s (see below).[64] Accounts of Nordic openness usually go back to the eighteenth century, but the rhetorical account highlights the post-Cold War period (Erkkilä in this volume).

The nineteenth and early twentieth centuries: Scandinavianism and the making of the rhetoric of exceptionality

There are Scandinavian language examples of *nordisk* used as a denominator for the Scandinavian Peninsula from the seventeenth century on. For instance, the commission dealing with the incorporation of Skåne into the Swedish realm after the Peace of Roskilde in 1658, referred in a letter to the possibility of uniting "the three Nordic (*nordisk*) realms under one crown."[65] The term was also used outside the region. Eighteenth-century British discourse on the Northern powers denoted the Danish and Swedish realms, but often also included Russia and

---

63 For influential examples, see Sørensen and Stråth, *The Cultural Construction of Norden*; Uffe Østergaard, "The Geopolitics of Nordic Identity: From Composite States to Nation States," in *The Cultural Construction of Norden*, ed. Øystein Sørensen and Bo Stråth (Oslo: Scandinavian University Press, 1997), 25–71; Henrik Stenius, "Nordic Associational Life in a European and an Inter-Nordic Perspective," in *Nordic Associations in a European Perspective*, ed. Risto Alapuro and Henrik Stenius (Baden-Baden: Nomos, 2010), 29–86, doi:10.5771/9783845225944–29.

64 Tim Knudsen, ed., *Den nordiske protestantisme og velfærdsstaten* (Århus: Aarhus universitetsforlag, 2000); Robert H. Nelson, *Lutheranism and the Nordic Spirit of Social Democracy: A Different Protestant Ethic* (Aarhus: Aarhus University Press, 2017), doi:10.2307/j.ctv62hgm7; Niels Finn Christiansen et al., eds., *The Nordic Model of Welfare: A Historical Reappraisal* (Copenhagen: Museum Tusculanum Press, 2006).

65 Svenska Akademiens ordbok (SAOB), accessed June 1, 2021, https://www.saob.se/; Lauritz Weibull, "Efter Roskilde fred. Ur skånska kommissionens och Taubenfelts bref till Kungl. Maj: T 1658–1660," *Historisk Tidskrift För Skåneland* 1, no. 4–6 (1901): 239.

Prussia.[66] Nevertheless, the discourse on the Northern realms at this time does not come across as common or particularly charged with connotations other than purely geographical. This holds both for intra-Scandinavian conceptualisations as well as for external descriptions of the North.

It was in the nineteenth century, in the context of intensified nation building, that "Scandinavian" and "Nordic" gained a politicised future orientation.[67] This happened primarily within the region itself and especially from the 1830s onwards, when the rhetoric of Scandinavian and Nordic was geared towards creating Nordic unity in the spirit of Scandinavianism. Meetings with Danish and Swedish students as well as literary projects, such as Frederik Barfod's *Brage og Idun* (from 1839) became outlets for Scandinavian unity. Norwegian voices were seldom as loud as those of Swedish and Danish protagonists, and as shown by Hemstad in this volume, the Norwegians were wary that the rhetoric of Scandinavia was a means to subordinate Norway under Swedish rule. Even in Finland, which was peripheral to the cause, voices for Scandinavianism were heard. Emil von Qvanten's *Fennomani och skandinavism* from 1855 was a critique of political and cultural developments in Finland after its incorporation into the Russian empire in 1809 and proclaimed a Scandinavian orientation. It lamented the Finnish disconnection to "Scandinavian civilization" (*Skandinavisk bildning*), thus rhetorically coupling Finland's Swedish heritage to something larger. Finland had become disassociated from Scandinavia but could be reconnected with it.[68]

It is, however, important to emphasise the complex and intertwined relationship between Scandinavianism and nationalism in the context of nineteenth-century romanticism. "Nordic mythology" was a common legacy of the region and in this way the discourses on *skandinavisk* and *nordisk* became key parts of the national movement, particularly in Denmark and Sweden. Indeed, the Swedish national anthem celebrates "Norden" rather than "Sweden". Similarly, the pastor and educationalist N.F.S. Grundtvig, the central figure in the Danish

---

66 Sophie Holm, *Diplomatins ideal och praktik: Utländska sändebud i Stockholm 1746–1748* (PhD diss., Helsingfors Universitet, 2019).

67 Ruth Hemstad, *Fra Indian Summer til nordisk vinter: Skandinavisk samarbeid, skandinavisme og unionsoppløsningen* (Oslo: Akademisk publisering, 2008); Ruth Hemstad, "Scandinavianism. Mapping the Rise of a New Concept," *Contributions to the History of Concepts* 13, no. 1 (2018): 1–21, doi:10.3167/choc.2018.130102.

68 Emil von Qvanten, *Fennomani och Skandinavism: Om Finland och dess sednaste utveckling* (Stockholm: Zachrish Haeggerström, 1855), 31.

national awakening, was also a spokesperson of Scandinavian and Nordic cultural unity.[69]

For most of the nineteenth century, the terms *nordisk* and *skandinavisk* were usually used interchangeably in Danish, Norwegian and Swedish, but Scandinavian was more commonly used in conjunction with political visions of the period and was therefore the term that had a stronger mobilising effect. This changed gradually towards the end of the century. *Nordisk* became readily more common and gained more political salience.[70] By the early twentieth century *nordisk* had become the more dominant term for inter-Nordic political cooperation and mobilisation, while *skandinavisk* mainly lived on in the names of publications as well as cultural and literary connections.

The terminological shift echoes a distinction sometimes made between the era of Scandinavianism in the nineteenth century and the age of Nordism in the twentieth. In this distinction, the former is seen as a pan-national movement or even an ideology and the latter designated as political and civic cooperation.[71] Nordism was void of attempts to unify the Nordic nations in a federal structure, but was embodied instead in collaboration, first in civil society (e. g., the lawyers' meetings since 1872 and the *Norden* Associations in 1919) and later also at the official state level.[72] The shift from "Scandinavian" to "Nordic" was particularly relevant for Iceland and Finland, because after 1918 both countries found themselves in new positions of autonomy and independence, respectively, and had to explore different foreign policy alternatives. The issue was contested in both countries, with some Finns calling for a Baltic orientation and some Icelanders hoping for a weaker connection to Denmark. Nonetheless, framing Iceland and Finland as Nordic countries provided a balance: emphasising national uniqueness as part of a Nordic family.[73] In Denmark, Sweden and Norway, the

---

69 Østergaard, "The Geopolitics of Nordic Identity"; Eva Danielson and Märta Ramsten, *Du gamla, du friska: Från folkvisa till nationalsång* (Stockholm: Atlantis, 2013); Jes Fabricius Møller, "Grundtvig, Danmark og Norden," in *Skandinavismen*, ed. Ruth Hemstad, Jes Fabricius Møller, and Dag Thorkildsen (Odense: Syddansk universitetsforlag, 2018), 99–120.

70 Hemstad, "Scandinavianism. Mapping the Rise of a New Concept."; see also Hemstad in this volume.

71 Østergaard, "The Geopolitics of Nordic Identity."

72 Monika Janfelt, *Att leva i den bästa av världar: Föreningarna Nordens syn på Norden 1919–1933* (Stockholm: Carlsson, 2005); Peter Stadius, "Trekungamötet i Malmö 1914. Mot en ny nordisk retorik i skuggan av världskriget," *Historisk tidskrift för Finland* 99, no. 4 (December 2014): 369–394; Strang, "Introduction: The Nordic Model of Transnational Cooperation?"

73 Kristjánsdóttir, "For Equality or Against Foreign Oppression?"; Kristjánsdóttir, "Facing the Nation – Nordic Communists and Their National Contexts, from the 1920s and into the Cold War"; Mikko Majander, *Pohjoismaa vai kansandemokratia? Sosiaalidemokraatit, Kommunistit ja*

shift from Scandinavian rhetoric to Nordic rhetoric was less loaded with geo-political connotations, meaning that the terms *nordisk* and *skandinavisk* could be used as interchangeable and distinct notions alike.

The complicated relationship between "Nordic" and "Scandinavian" was not, however, necessarily reflected in usages outside the region. In German, the term *nordisch* was applied much more broadly, often including much of German-speaking Europe, and was consequently also used more commonly than the more specific *skandinavisch*. It was also widely used in National Socialist rhetoric, generating some aversion to describing the Nordic countries as *nordisch* after the Second World War.[74] The ambivalence of the terms *Norden* and *nordisch* in German also meant that they could be used to describe the Nordic countries (as in *die nordische länder*), the Nordic countries and the north German areas together (as was the case in Danish tourist marketing in Germany in the 1930s), or they could be used to refer to the north German areas only. The German state of Schleswig-Holstein in 2020, for example, used the slogan *"Der echte Norden"* (the true north) in its tourist marketing directed to German travellers – much to the amusement of visitors from the Nordic countries who might well have thought that they had monopoly on the term.[75]

In English the story is different, as the term Scandinavian has clearly been the preferred descriptor and for much of the twentieth century the preferred translation for *nordisk* was Scandinavian. For instance, the Nordisk Andelsforbund founded in 1918 was referred to in contemporary sources from the 1920s and 1930s as the Scandinavian Co-operative Wholesale Society.[76] The reference work *Annual Register* (founded 1758) mentions "the so-called Nordic countries" in the 1920s in relation to US migration policies. Writing in 1958, geographer W. R. Mead noted that the term *Norden* was used within the region, but "is unsatisfactory for world currency." He also noted that different UK institutions used different terms – the Foreign Office had a Northern Department for example,

---

Suomen kansainvälinen asema 1944–1951 (Helsinki: Suomalaisen Kirjallisuuden Seura, 2004); Kurunmäki and Strang, "Introduction: 'Nordic Democracy' in a World of Tensions."

74 Malte Gasche, *Der "Germanische Wissenschaftseinsatz" des "Ahnenerbes" der SS, 1942–1945: Zwischen Vollendung der "Völkischen Gemeinschaft" und dem Streben nach "Erlösung,"* (Bonn: Verlag Dr. Rudolf Habelt GmbH, 2014); Hans-Jürgen Lutzhöft, *Der Nordische Gedanke in Deutschland 1920–1940* (Stuttgart: E. Klett, 1971).

75 Frederik Forrai Ørskov, "In Ideological Transit: German Tourism to Denmark in the 1930s," *Journal of Tourism History* 11, no. 3 (September 2, 2019): 243–262, doi:10.1080/1755182X.2019.1650127; "Urlaub in Schleswig-Holstein – Offizielle Tourismusseite," www.sh-tourismus.de, August 25, 2016, https://www.sh-tourismus.de/.

76 Mary Hilson, *The International Co-operative Alliance and the Consumer Co-operative Movement in Northern Europe, c. 1860–1939*, (Manchester: Manchester University Press, 2018).

while the BBC's "Scandinavian section" included Finland – but concluded that the name of the region in English was still largely unresolved.[77] The term Nordic really caught on in English only after the establishment of the Nordic Council in 1952. A search of the Google Books dataset shows that "Nordic countries" soon surpassed the earlier term "Northern countries" and has gradually increased ever since. Even so, "Scandinavian countries" was more widely used than "Nordic countries" for much of the twentieth century and up to the 1980s.[78] One possible explanation of why "Nordic" did not immediately catch on in English, apart from the concept's general unfamiliarity, was its tainted associations from the past: the concept of a "Nordic race" was prevalent in American eugenics discourse in the interwar period, and, of course, in German National Socialism.[79] Today, these (explicitly) racist connotations have largely been lost. While "the Nordics" in the 1920s and 1930s was used practically exclusively in order to talk about persons assumed to belong to a Nordic race (for example, in the 1939 volume *The Races of Europe*), the term has in the 2000s returned as a friendly short-hand for the Nordic countries, often used for branding purposes.[80]

Although the discourse of a Nordic race was also present in *Norden* in the interwar period – for example in the work of Herman Lundborg – its echoes were largely pushed to the margins of the radical right. Indeed, the 1920s and 1930s form a critical juncture when "the Nordic" became politicised and temporalised even more strongly than before, even to the extent that it was the object of political struggles for ownership. Whereas Scandinavianism and *Nordism* had been largely a liberal bourgeois discourse, the rhetoric of Nordicness in the 1930s was claimed by the labour movement, who used it to provide historical and national legitimacy to their political project. It formed a bridge between the space of experience and the horizon of expectation. If Nordic democracy had strong roots in the age-old traditions of peasant freedom and in popular mobilisation, it was the task of the labour movement to carry the project into its fruition as a social democracy.[81]

---

77 W. R. Mead, *An Economic Geography of the Scandinavian States and Finland* (London: University of London Press, 1958), 6.

78 For an indicator of this, see https://books.google.com/ngrams.

79 Merle Weßel, "The Concept of the 'Nordic Race' in German and Nordic Racial-Theoretical Research in the 1920s," *NORDEUROPAforum – Zeitschrift Für Kulturstudien* (2016): 29–49, doi:10.18452/8186; See also Weßel in this volume.

80 Carleton Stevens Coon, *The Races of Europe* (New York: Macmillan, 1939); see e.g., https://thenordics.com.

81 Ruth Hemstad, "Scandinavianism, Nordic Co-operation and 'Nordic Democracy,'" in *Rhetorics of Nordic Democracy*, ed. Jussi Kurunmäki and Johan Strang (Helsinki: Finnish Literature So-

This was also a time when it was important to mark a difference between *Norden* and Europe, the old continent being plagued by economic, social and political troubles. This view was presented, for example, by Danish Social Democrat Hartvig Frisch in his book *Pest over Europa* (Plague over Europe).[82] In 1935, the Swedish Social Democratic Youth organised a "Day of Nordic Democracy" in Malmö, where the Nordic prime ministers gave speeches under the heading of "Nordic democracy" to rally support for democracy against its internal and external threats. Swedish Prime Minister Per Albin Hansson in particular saw an international call for the Nordic democracies as models for other countries.[83] Thus, referring to the Nordic countries as Nordic became a way of extending the description of national culture and politics. It reframed domestic affairs in a larger Nordic context and, potentially at least, made them more interesting for those outside the Nordic sphere.[84]

The rhetoric of Nordic democracy, freedom, and unity also played an important role during the Second World War.[85] The threats to the Nordic countries were, however, very different, so when the Finnish philosopher Georg Henrik von Wright in 1941 wanted to frame Finland's alliance with Nazi-Germany and the revenge war against the Soviet Union as a "Nordic struggle," he might have received some sympathies from Swedish conservatives, but very little from Nazi-occupied Denmark and Norway.[86]

Cold War *Norden* and beyond

Political developments in the decades after the Second World War left the region divided on crucial issues like defence (NATO members versus non-aligned) and

---

ciety, 2010), doi:10.21435/sfh.17; Kurunmäki and Strang, "Introduction: 'Nordic Democracy' in a World of Tensions."

82 Hartvig Frisch, *Pest over Europa: Bolschevisme – Fascisme – Nazisme* (Copenhagen: Henrik Koppels Forlag, 1933).

83 Jussi Kurunmäki, "'Nordic Democracy' in 1935: On the Finnish and Swedish Rhetoric of Democracy," in *Rhetorics of Nordic Democracy*, ed. Jussi Kurunmäki and Johan Strang (Helsinki: Finnish Literature Society, 2010), doi:10.21435/sfh.17.

84 Kurunmäki and Strang, "Introduction: 'Nordic Democracy' in a World of Tensions."

85 Jan Hecker-Stampehl, *Vereinigte Staaten des Nordens: Integrationsideen in Nordeuropa im Zweiten Weltkrieg* (München: Oldenbourg, 2011).

86 Georg Henrik von Wright, "Sverige och Ryssland," *Finsk Tidskrift* (1941): 193; Johan Strang, "Georg Henrik von Wright och Ingemar Hedenius: Rollen som intellektuell och analytisk filosof i Finland och Sverige," in *Tankens utåtvändhet: Georg Henrik von Wright som intellektuell*, ed. Johan Strang & Thomas Wallgren (Helsingfors: Svenska litteratursällskapet 2016).

the economy (repeated failures to create a Nordic customs union and different policies towards European economic cooperation), but this only served to strengthen the rhetoric of Nordicness as a means to display regional unity and to push the institutionalisation of Nordic cooperation forward. Indeed, as noted by Norbert Götz and Heidi Haggren, divisive as it was, the Cold War constellation was in many respects particularly supportive of Nordic affiliation.[87]

The discourse on Nordic cooperation was at the heart of this development, bridging the tension between the idea that the Nordic countries are part of Europe and the idea that they are, simultaneously, distinct from it (Strang in this volume). Nordic rhetoric burgeoned particularly in the names of different institutions and organisations with a transnational Nordic scope and mission – the Nordic Culture Commission (1946), the Nordic Council (1952), Nordisk journalistkursus (1958), Nordisk utredningsserie (1960), the Nordic Culture Fund (1967), the Nordic Council of Ministers (1971), the Nordic Investment Bank (1976), and Nordiska nämnden för alkohol och narkotikafrågor (1978), to name just a few from an abundance of examples. Even if the adjective "Nordic" undoubtedly carried with it many (positive) connotations, it was usually used primarily as a signifier of the geographical domain of the initiatives (see also Markkola in this volume). Indeed, the representative transnational dimension of Nordicness was arguably particularly important during the Cold War period – it was hard for one country to use Nordic or Scandinavian unless the others were also represented. While difficult to prove, this also seems to hold for non-state initiatives in the cultural sector as well as commercial enterprises that were labelled Nordic or Scandinavian in this period, like the Scandinavian Airlines System (SAS) founded in 1946.

The representative transnational dimension of Nordicness was important also in the joint Nordic branding efforts abroad, most notably regarding Scandinavian design.[88] From the 1950s onwards we find several examples of this which involved an active push by design practitioners and marketers from within the Nordic region as well as a pull particularly from the English-speaking world. Catalogues and marketing items with "Scandinavian design" as a heading were published in Copenhagen, Helsinki and New York.[89] Although these consis-

---

87 Götz and Haggrén, *Regional Cooperation and International Organizations*, 2.

88 Frantz Wilhelm Wendt, *Cooperation in the Nordic Countries: Achievements and Obstacles* (Stockholm: Almqvist & Wiksell International, 1981), 330–331.

89 Viggo Sten Møller, ed., *Scandinavian Design: Directory of Arts and Crafts Resources in Denmark, Finland, Norway, Sweden, Copenhagen, 1953* (Copenhagen: Langkjærs bogtrykkeri, 1953); Ulf Hård af Segerstad, Eward Maze, and Nancy Maze, *Scandinavian Design* (Helsinki: Otava,

tently included items of Finnish design, the label "Nordic design" seemed to be used to a much lesser degree, which may be explained by the fact that designers were adapting to English-speaking marketing. In any case, design comes across as an early example of how Nordic brands could be used to make profits outside of the Nordic region, half a century before the rhetoric of New Nordicness.

The end of the Cold War and the accompanying shift in the dynamics between intra-Nordic and extra-Nordic relations was a period of reorientation and even crisis for the notion of *Norden* as a distinctive region and a turning point in discourses about *Norden*. The 1990s was a point in time when the rhetoric of Nordicness proliferated as a designation for many things that were being left behind. Rhetorical uses of "the Nordic" surged as a discourse of nostalgia.[90] The potent example of this is arguably "the Nordic welfare state." While it is well established in both social scientific and historical research that there was something distinctive in the way that the welfare state took shape in the region in the mid-twentieth century, it was actually very rare that the phrase "welfare state" (*välfärdsstat, velferdsstat, hyvinvointivaltio*) was combined with the adjective "Nordic." In 1978, Stein Kuhnle wrote an article about "the Nordic Welfare States," but that was more an intra-Nordic comparison than an attempt to crystallise a common essence.[91] In fact, it was not until the 1990s that the phrase "the Nordic welfare state" was propelled into the centre of both academic and political discourse. This followed the publication of Gøsta Esping-Andersen's highly influential study *The Three Worlds of Welfare Capitalism*.[92]

The same argument could be made for the notions of "Nordic peace" or "Nordic neutrality", which also mushroomed rhetorically precisely when their political relevance was cast in doubt.[93] While it is certainly true that the Nordic

1961); Erik Höglund et al., "The Revolution in Scandinavian Design," *Craft Horizons* 18, no. 2 (April 1958), https://digital.craftcouncil.org/digital/collection/p15785coll2/id/4711.

90 Ole Wæver, "Nordic Nostalgia: Northern Europe after the Cold War," *International Affairs* 68, no. 1 (1992): 77–102, doi:10.2307/2620462.

91 Stein Kuhnle, "The Beginnings of the Nordic Welfare States: Similarities and Differences," *Acta Sociologica* 21 (1978): 9–35.

92 Gøsta Esping-Andersen, *The Three Worlds of Welfare Capitalism* (Cambridge: Polity Press, 1990).; see also the chapter by Hilson and Hoctor in this volume. We would like to thank Nils Edling for pointing this out to us.

93 Clive Archer and Pertti Joenniemi, *The Nordic Peace* (Aldershot: Ashgate, 2003); Hans Mouritzen, "The Nordic Model as a Foreign Policy Instrument: Its Rise and Fall," *Journal of Peace Research* 32, no. 1 (1995): 9–21, doi:10.1177/0022343395032001002.; see also Douglas Brommesson, "Introduction to Special Section: From Nordic Exceptionalism to a Third Order Priority – Variations of 'Nordicness' in Foreign and Security Policy," *Global Affairs* 4, no. 4–5 (2018): 355–362, doi:10.1080/23340460.2018.1533385; Browning, "Branding Nordicity"; Adrian Hyde-Price, "Epi-

countries collaborated with each other in the League of Nations and the United Nations,[94] it was arguably not until the 1990s that the speech act of calling their engagements for world peace or third world development "Nordic" burgeoned. The notion of a "Nordic balance" gained some traction as a justification for Swedish neutrality, but it was mostly used by scholars to describe the Cold War security configuration in the region with the three Nordic NATO members, Swedish neutrality and the special Finnish relationship with the Soviet Union.[95] The 1963 Finnish initiative of a "Nordic nuclear-weapon-free zone" can be seen as a partisan attempt at utilising the peace connotations of "the Nordic," which largely failed to gain support among the Nordic NATO members.

What accounts for this proliferation of "the Nordic" as a projection backwards in the 1990s? The obvious explanation, highlighted in the chapters by Markkola, Erkkilä and Strang, is that in the 1990s context of Europeanisation, "the Nordic" functioned as a way of articulating a difference from, and later a distinction within, Europe. But another reason is surely the urge to defend something that was perceived as being on the verge of being lost. As the welfare state became challenged, both as an economically viable system during the economic depression, particularly in Finland and Sweden, and as a semi-socialist ideology in a period of liberalisation and marketisation, the adjective "Nordic" turned the welfare state into something more than the result of contingent policies: it became a national and regional legacy that carried obligations into the future. Conversely, however, the rhetoric of Nordicness also served the purpose of concealing change. If Hilson and Hoctor in their chapter show how the pleasant rhetoric of the Nordic model was used by British conservatives to legitimise neoliberal reforms, similar uses of "the Nordic" are also easy to find within the Nordic region itself (see Strang's chapter). The rhetoric of Nordicness also continued to be used in foreign policy, for example as part of campaigns for seats in the United Nations Security Council, even though many scholars point to a significant change of policy.[96] In 2015, cuts in Finnish foreign aid and tightened refugee policies were legitimised by reference to similar changes in the other Nordic countries. Indeed, as Finnish political scientists Hanna Ojanen and Tapio Raunio ob-

――――――

logue: 'Nordicness' – Theory and Practice," *Global Affairs* 4, no. 4–5 (2018): 435–443, doi:10.1080/23340460.2018.1497451.

94 Götz and Haggrén, *Regional Cooperation and International Organizations.*

95 Erik Noreen, "The Nordic Balance: A Security Policy Concept in Theory and Practice," *Cooperation and Conflict* 18, no. 1 (1983): 43–56, doi:10.1177/001083678301800104.

96 Anders Wivel, "What Happened to the Nordic Model for International Peace and Security?," *Peace Review* 29, no. 4 (2017): 489–496, doi:10.1080/10402659.2017.1381521.

serve, "we can see signs of 'Nordicness' turning into a way of legitimizing policies that deviate from the classic picture of what Nordic is."[97]

If the 1990s stand out as one of the key turning points in the history of the
rhetoric of Nordicness, several articles in this volume suggest that we have experienced another recent juncture, which started around 2005 with the reinvention
and redefinition of the Nordic model as discussed by Hilson and Hoctor, and the
coinage of "New Nordic" brands within the field of culture and commerce as analysed by Kelting (New Nordic Food) and Stougaard-Nielsen (Nordic Noir). This
new rhetoric of Nordicness signifies a turn to a logic of branding where the
aim is no longer to overcome regional differences, to learn from each other, or
to create a Nordic community, but rather to promote the region and its products
through simplified and essentialised notions of "Nordicness". The rise of the
Nordic brand has to be understood as part of the growing international interest
in nation branding during the first decades of the early twenty-first century,
when nation states embraced the idea of having to compete with their reputation
in a globalised world economy. Commercial, political and cultural spheres were
hybridised in national branding programmes aiming to attract investments and
promote export.[98] With the success of the Nordic countries in various international rankings, and by virtue of its inherent flexibility, the rhetoric of New Nordicness proved a powerful addition to the national brands. Accordingly, the Nordic governments urged the Nordic Council of Ministers to adopt a strategy of
region branding to capitalise on a rising global interest in the Nordic region,
for example through its promotion of New Nordic Food, as described in Lily Kelting's chapter.[99]

The rise of the Nordic brand and the rhetoric of "New Nordicness" was also
the latest example of the "return to sender" phenomenon described by Carl Marklund and Klaus Petersen in relation to mid-twentieth-century discussions about
the global circulation of the Nordic welfare state.[100] The Nordic brand was born
from foreign interest in the Nordic region, and as a Nordic domestication of for-

---

97 Hanna Ojanen and Tapio Raunio, "The Varying Degrees and Meanings of Nordicness in Finnish Foreign Policy," *Global Affairs* 4, no. 4–5 (2018): 415, doi:10.1080/23340460.2018.1533386.
98 E. g., Simon Anholt, *Competitive Identity: The New Brand Management for Nations, Cities and
Regions* (London: Palgrave Macmillan, 2007), doi:10.1057/9780230627727.; see Mads Mordhorst,
"Nation-Branding og nationalstaten," *Den Jyske Historiker* 126 (2010): 16–39; Angell and Mordhorst, "National Reputation Management and the Competition State."
99 See also Anna Kharkina, *From Kinship to Global Brand: The Discourse on Culture in Nordic
Cooperation after World War II* (Huddinge: Södertörns högskola, 2013).
100 Marklund and Petersen, "Return to Sender."

eign discussions about "the Nordic." In this translation process, within the region itself "the Nordic" became increasingly decoupled from the idea of a regional community, instead it became an international label for various phenomena related to the region. Indeed, it was no longer as relevant whether "the New Nordic" represented the whole of the region, an average of the region, or even whether it gave an accurate description of the region. It became a marker of quality instead of location; something prescriptive or even aspirational.[101]

Conclusion: from community to branding?

The central argument of this book is that the essential features and historical foundations of "Nordicness" are subject to constant deliberation and debate. While there is a lot of valuable constructivist literature describing the political cultures of the Nordic region, very little has been said from a conceptual-rhetorical perspective about "the Nordic" itself. Such a shift in perspective is motivated particularly by the proliferation and fragmentation of the rhetoric of Nordicness during the 2010s. In examining the historical layers of "the Nordic," our book contributes to a historical understanding of the increasing frequency and ambiguity of the current rhetoric of Nordicness. Intended neither as a complete nor a final account, our book allows us to identify some general trajectories and topics for further research.

Crudely put, it seems to us that the Nordic discourse has mutated from one about cultural community to one about political cooperation, and more recently to one about branding. This transformation needs to be analysed in close relation to the complex and often poorly understood interplay between foreign and intra-Nordic uses of "the Nordic." In relation to the former, the English-language context is especially important, not only because of the global significance of English but also because English is so widely used within the Nordic region. A strict division between the outside and inside is not that useful, as many active in the field of discussing and redefining "the Nordic" move across such distinctions with ease. (That includes, of course, the academics who have contributed to this book.) Still, it seems beyond doubt that the dynamic between outside impulses and internal innovations has been crucial for the rhetoric of Nordicness since at least the First World War. It was central to the discourse

---

101 Pauli Kettunen, "The Conceptual History of the Welfare State in Finland," in *The Changing Meanings of the Welfare State: Histories of a Key Concept in the Nordic Countries*, ed. Nils Edling, (New York: Berghahn Books, 2019), 225–275; see also Strang in this volume.

on Nordic democracy in the inter-war era and to the project of building political and institutional cooperation during much of the twentieth century.

It also holds the key for understanding the special nature of the recent wave of New Nordicness associated with the export of Nordic models and brands in the first decades of the new millennium. The first attempts at marketing Scandinavian design or the Nordic social systems were based on a representation of all five countries. As such, the aim was to create and display a cultural-political community and the rhetoric was thus closely related to that of Nordic cooperation. In global circulation, however, this idea of representativity was less important and "the Nordic" was turned instead into a name and brand for various things associated with the Nordic region. It became a quality rather than a regional marker. This usage has been picked up in the region itself, as "the Nordic" has become used with exponential plurality. The New Nordic is no longer about creating something transnationally Nordic, but about highlighting a quality or a special aspect of something local or national. As such, the global success of the Nordic brand has transformed the purpose of the rhetoric of Nordicness within the region: from creating a cultural or political community, to creating an attribute or quality to be used in global markets.

While the interplay between intra-Nordic and extra-Nordic conceptualisations creates a lot of variance in language use, our concern is not to expose or correct misguided images of the Nordic at different times and in various parts of the world. Nor do we partake in a nostalgic attempt to recreate a past when "the Nordic" stood for something simpler than today. Studying the historical layers of current uses of "the Nordic" is important for recognising that the future is ultimately open ended and dependent on political struggles over the key features of what is Nordic. Scholars, politicians and cultural or commercial actors have to appreciate that they have very limited possibilities of managing the ways in which "the Nordic" is used around the world. But more knowledge is certainly needed in order to understand the triggers, logics, and historical layers of the rhetoric of Nordicness in various parts of the world, especially outside Europe and North America.

Ruth Hemstad

Scandinavian Sympathies and Nordic Unity: The Rhetoric of Scandinavianness in the Nineteenth Century

The history of "Nordic" and – in particular – "Scandinavian" as flexible and contested concepts may be traced back at least to the early nineteenth century. This history is strongly connected with competing national and pan-national projects within the Nordic region. This chapter seeks to explore the emergence and transformation of "Scandinavian" and the related and more widespread term "Nordic" as appealing and contested rhetorical concepts during the long nineteenth century. The pan-Scandinavian movement, it will be argued, played a key role in this development by stimulating a widespread rhetoric of "Nordicness" – or rather of "*Scandinavianness*" – in the 1840s, thus adding significant dimensions of meanings to these concepts.[1]

With the introduction of a range of new phrases with rhetorical power, such as "Scandinavian sympathies" and the "Scandinavian idea," the usage of the term "Scandinavian" rose rapidly from the mid-nineteenth century onwards. An emergent public sphere and print culture, increasingly influenced by what was to be known as "Scandinavianism," stimulated this tendency. Civil society initiatives further contributed to the development. A range of new pan-Scandinavian associations that termed themselves "Scandinavian" and later "Nordic" was established within as well as beyond the Scandinavian region.[2]

In mapping the usage of these terms, a combination of quantitative and qualitative analysis, of distant and close readings is employed. Distant readings of Nordic newspaper corpora, from Norway, Sweden, Denmark and Finland respectively,[3] gives a reasonable idea of key word frequencies and collocational re-

---

[1] There are examples, although scarce, of the use of the terms "Nordicness" (*Nordiskhed*) and "Scandinavianness" (*Skandinaviskhed*) from the mid-1840s.

[2] Ruth Hemstad, "Organizational Scandinavianism Abroad: Literature, Sociability and Pan-Scandinavian Associational Life in German-speaking Europe 1842–1912," in *Mit dem Buch in der Hand: Beiträge zur deutsch-skandinavischen Buch- und Bibliotheksgeschichte/A Book in Hand: German-Scandinavian Book and Library History*, ed. Marie-Theres Federhofer and Sabine Meyer, Berliner Beiträge zur Skandinavistik 31 (Berlin: Norderopa-Institut, 2021), 159–183; Ruth Hemstad, *Fra Indian summer til nordisk vinter: Skandinavisk samarbeid, skandinavisme og unionsoppløsningen* (Oslo: Akademisk Publisering, 2008).

[3] The following Nordic newspaper databases are used in this study: Nasjonalbiblioteket, Norway, www.nb.no; Mediastream, Denmark, www2.statsbiblioteket.dk; Svenska Dagstidningar,

lationships – words that are frequently used in combination with the key words. By comparing the frequency of the terms "Nordic" and "Scandinavian" in newspapers in the Nordic countries during the nineteenth century (1790–1900), made possible through the significant amount of digitized material available, some interesting patterns appear. Although the analysis will seek to identify and explore changes throughout the century, some periods will be of particular interest.

The emergence of a specific pan-Scandinavian vocabulary and the rhetorical use of certain phrases based on the adjectives "Scandinavian" and "Nordic" is evident from the mid-1840s. In order to understand the contested character of these notions, which is particularly apparent in parts of the Norwegian national discourse, it is, however, necessary to examine the conceptual transformations of the previous period, especially since 1814. In the 1840s there was an interesting shift not only in the frequency but also – as close reading reveals – in the meaning of the terms "Scandinavia" and "Scandinavian". Following the 1840s, pan-Scandinavian rhetoric had a lasting influence and around 1900, a renewed rhetoric of Scandinavianness emerged followed by a rejection of related concepts in parts of the Swedish public sphere.[4]

In addition to mapping the frequency during the century through key word searches, collocate searching is employed in order to identify and map relevant phrases.[5] Certain phrases are significant and were extensively used, especially in the period between the 1840s and the 1860s – including "Scandinavian sympathies." Close readings of additional relevant sources, such as pamphlets, books, journal and newspaper articles, are used to analyse and place the main results in their relevant discursive and political contexts.

A first main point is that the term "Nordic" is older and more frequently used than "Scandinavian" until the first decades of the nineteenth century.[6] Key word searches of the digital newspaper corpora in the Scandinavian national libraries show that "Nordic" is used throughout the eighteenth century.[7] There are only

---

Sweden, tidningar.kb.se; DIGI–Nationalbibliotekets digitala samlingar, Finland, digi.kansallis-kirjasto.fi.

4 Hemstad, *Fra Indian summer*, 297–359.

5 Collocate searching was applied on the text corpus at the National Library of Norway in cooperation with Lars G. Johnsen at the Norwegian Language Bank at the National Library.

6 In the Nordic newspaper databases, the oldest reference to "Scandinavian" is in a Danish newspaper in 1781. Full text searches for "skandinavisk*" and "scandinavisk*" in the comprehensive Norwegian book corpus at the National Library of Norway and searches for the same words in titles in the national library catalogues in Norway, Sweden, and Denmark, support this result.

7 The use of "Nordic" and "Norden" in the eighteenth century often reflected a wide concept of the North that included Russia, Poland and Prussia. Henriette Kliemann-Geisinger, "Mapping

few examples, however, of "Scandinavian" from the last part of the century. Several of them refer to the association Skandinavisk Literatur-Selskab (Scandinavian literary society), established 1796, and its journal *Skandinavisk Museum*.[8] The society aimed at promoting literary connections between the "Scandinavian realms" by facilitating closer contacts between Danish and Swedish intellectuals and improving knowledge of "Scandinavian literature" – a new phrase at this time.

"Scandinavia" was originally a Latin term, derived from "Scania" in the south-eastern part of Sweden. Early examples from the mid and late eighteenth century point towards a growing awareness of Scandinavia as a potential cultural-political entity consisting of Denmark, Norway, and Sweden.[9] The use of the term also reflected the renewed interest in Old Norse culture at the time. "Scandinavia" and "the old Scandinavians" were terms used to describe the area and its inhabitants in the ancient era. These terms did not stem from Saga literature but from Greek and Roman sources, an aspect frequently pointed out by nationally-minded Norwegian scholars arguing against the unhistorical and "false" use of these terms by Danish and Swedish scholars.[10]

Norwegian newspapers and journals in the 1820s and 1830s regularly stated that "Scandinavian," "Scandinavians," and "Scandinavia" were recent terms. "A *Scandinavian* is a fresh new word," the newspaper *Morgenbladet* stated in 1829.[11] In 1835, it was commented that "Scandinavia" had recently became popular – in Denmark as a common name for the three Nordic countries, and in Sweden as a common name for Norway and Sweden.[12] Two years later, during a period of increased political tension between the two union partners Norway and Sweden,

---

the North – Spatial Dimensions and Geographical Concepts of Northern Europe," in *Northbound: Travels, Encounters, and Constructions 1700–1830*, ed. Karen Klitgaard Povlsen (Aarhus: Aarhus University Press, 2007), 70–76.

8 *Skandinavisk Museum* (1798–1803), followed by the book series *Det Skandinaviske Literaturselskabs Skrifter* (1805–1832).

9 Erik Bodensten, "Scandinavia Magna: En alternativ nordisk statsbildning 1743," in *Nordens historiker: Vänbok till Harald Gustafsson*, ed. Erik Bodensten et al. (Lund: Historiska Institutionen, Lunds Universitet, 2018), 61–75; Frederik Sneedorf, "Vigtigheden af de tre nordiske Rigers Forening. En Tale af afgangne Professor F. Sneedorf, holden i det nordiske Selskab i London i Foraaret 1792," *Skandinavisk Museum* 2 (1798): 122–134.

10 Historians such as Peter Andreas Munch and Jens Christian Berg presented this sort of argument. See Ruth Hemstad, "'Norden' og 'Skandinavien.' Begrepsbruk i brytningstid," in *Nordens historiker*, ed. Erik Bodensten et al., 45–60.

11 "En *Skandinaver* er et nybagt Ord," published as part of the poem "Forsvar for Rævbælgmakeren" (anon.) in *Morgenbladet*, 28 August 1829, reprinted in *Tillæg til Morgenbladet*, 9 April 1833.

12 "Norge," *Morgenbladet*, 10 January 1835. The article reprints parts of an article by Jens Christian Berg published in the series *Samlinger til det norske Folks Sprog og Historie*.

another Norwegian newspaper criticized the widespread Swedish usage of such "disgusting" terms as "Scandinavia," "Scandinavians," and "Scandinavian" in books and maps.[13] In 1839, another writer argued against Danish utilization of "the blurred and ambiguous terms '*Nordic*' [...] and the later invented favourite expressions '*Scandinavians*,' *Scandinavian*" as common denominators for the three Nordic nations by those "who want to appropriate what belongs to Norwegian history only," hinting at Danish efforts of appropriation of Old Norse heritage.[14]

The Norwegian wariness towards the use of the adjective "Scandinavian" and the related terms "Scandinavians" and "Scandinavia," particularly prominent from the late 1830s, had at least two sources. Two different notions of "Scandinavia" and "Scandinavians" were put forward during the first decades of the century, from Swedish and Danish agents respectively, characterized by a seemingly similar rhetoric. As a consequence, the significance of being "Scandinavian" changed remarkably. The transformation was part of the rhetorical struggle of what was to be understood more precisely as "Scandinavian" and "Scandinavia."

The following sections will concentrate on these two projects – a Swedish-initiated state-building program from above and a Danish-driven pan-national, nation-building project from below – and their rhetorical uses of the concepts in question. The Norwegian nation-building project, in the making since around 1814 was conversely directed towards Danish cultural and Swedish political dominance, while stressing the principle of reciprocity.

The Swedish Scandinavian Rhetoric

A second main point regarding the history of "Scandinavian" as a contested concept in the nineteenth century is the significant shift in the use of the term, especially in Swedish newspapers, in 1814. The early Swedish rhetoric of Scandinavianness exploded in 1814, reflecting the establishment of the Swedish-Norwegian union that year.[15] This rhetoric continued into the 1820s and 1830s.

---

13 *Den Constitutionelle*, 19 February 1837 (editorial article on the front page).

14 "Hartkorn. III," *Morgenbladet*, 24 November 1839.

15 In Swedish newspapers, there are only 3 examples of the use of "Scandinavian" during the period 1811–1813, but 62 examples in 1814. I have used the word search facilities using the key word followed by an asterisk, to ensure the inclusion of different variants ("skandinavisk*"/ "scandinavisk*" and "nordisk*"). The search is case-insensitive. Svenska dagstidningar, accessed 13 September 2020, tidningar.kb.se.

Frequently used phrases were, in particular, the "Scandinavian Peninsula" and the "Scandinavian realms" alongside "Scandinavian peoples" and "Scandinavian nations." The recurrent use of the term "Scandinavian" mirrored a discourse and a print culture reflecting the union, one way or another, as part of a growing Swedish public sphere.The term did not, however, refer to the wider Scandinavian region.[16]

The French Marshal Jean Bernadotte, who became Crown Prince Charles John in Sweden in 1810, was pivotal in introducing "Scandinavia" and "Scandinavian" as rhetorical and geo-political terms after 1812.[17] He made the older imperial Swedish vision of uniting Norway with Sweden his own primary goal. Based on the Treaty of 1812 with Russia, the policy of turning the Scandinavian Peninsula into a Swedish Scandinavian empire was a means to consolidate Sweden after the loss of Finland in 1809.

In Charles John's view and in his rhetoric, "Scandinavia" was therefore delimited to include Sweden and Norway exclusively. This meant to actively forget about Finland and exclude Denmark from the region. Both countries had been included in the definition of "Scandinavia" in Swedish textbooks as late as 1805.[18] Bernadotte's favourite geopolitical concept was hence that of the "Scandinavian Peninsula," or "what may be termed the Scandinavian Peninsula", as it was framed in one of the key pamphlets distributed throughout Europe, written by August Wilhelm Schlegel in cooperation with Madame de Staël.[19] The expression suggests that the term was not settled, an impression strengthened by the following Danish reactions, which underlined the neologistic aspect of the con-

---

16 "Scandinavian," in Sweden at this time referred to the Scandinavian peninsula. An example of this usage is the "*Skandinavisk*" in Sven Nilsson's *Skandinavisk Fauna: En handbok för jägare och zoologer*. This publication, among others, contributed to the high prevalence of "Scandinavian" in the Swedish newspapers in 1820s and 1830s. It was first published in 1820 and had three volumes, with additional publications of illustration charts, and was frequently advertised in Swedish newspapers.

17 Ruth Hemstad, *Propagandakrig: Kampen om Norge i Norden og Europa 1812–1814* (Oslo: Novus forlag, 2014).

18 Gustaf Abraham Silverstolpe, *Lärobok i Svenska Historien* (Stockholm: H.A. Nordström, 1805), 12.

19 Mme de Staël, *An Appeal to the Nations of Europe against the Continental System* (London: J.M. Richardson, 1813), 58. See also Ruth Hemstad, "Madame de Staël and the War of Opinion Regarding the Cession of Norway 1813–1814," *Scandinavica* 54, no. 1 (2015): 100–120.

cept: "what may be termed (according to Madame de Staël Holstein's new Geographical Nomenclature) the Scandinavian Peninsula".[20]

In labelling and naming the new political union of 1814, Swedish authorities utilised both substantivation and adjectivation, introducing the terms "Scandinavia" and "Scandinavians" as common denominators to construct a common identity within the union. Adjectives, it is emphasized, "apply a common denominator to phenomena whose diversity is recognized; substantival labelling, on the contrary, tends to do away with these differences."[21] The Swedish "Scandinavia" was an alternative name for Sweden and Norway. "Scandinavians" were accordingly the inhabitants of "Scandinavia," i. e., Swedes and Norwegians. These terms were widely used in books, pamphlets, poems, in newspapers and journals, in geographical textbooks, statistics, encyclopaedias and maps, in official proclamations and published speeches in Sweden.[22] In one elementary textbook in geography from 1815, "Scandinavia" was even more narrowly defined, as "Sweden in a broad meaning" – meaning "Sweden proper" and Norway, as Daniel Djurberg writes in *Geographie för Begynnare*.[23] Norwegians later reacted against this book and its "false" concepts.[24] However, Djurberg's textbook was commonly used in Swedish elementary schools. This narrow definition was sometimes commented on in Swedish publications, acknowledging that "Scandinavia" usually denotes the three Nordic realms – Sweden, Denmark, and Norway – to provide balance to Swedish authors who had limited the meaning of the term to include only Sweden and Norway.[25]

---

20 Andreas Andersen Feldborg, *Cursory Remarks on the meditated Attack on Norway; Comprising Strictures on Madame de Staël Holstein 'Appeal to the Nations of Europe'* (London: Hamblin & Seyfang, 1813), 82.

21 Marnix Beyen, "Who is the Nation and What Does It Do? The Discursive Construction of the Nation in Belgian and Dutch National Histories of the Romantic Period," in *The Historical Imagination in Nineteenth-Century Britain and the Low Countries*, ed. Hugh Dunthorne and Michael Wintle (Leiden: Brill, 2013), 69, 76. See also Ruth Hemstad, "The United Kingdoms of Norway and Sweden and the United Kingdom of the Netherlands 1814–1830: Comparative Perspectives on Politics of Amalgamation and Nation Building," *Scandinavica* 58, no. 2 ([2019] 2020): 76–97.

22 Ruth Hemstad, "Geopolitikk og geografibøker for folket: Den norsk-svenske unionens besværlige beskrivelser," in *Sann opplysning? Naturvitenskap i nordisk folkeopplysning 1650–2016*, ed. Merethe Roos and Johan Tønnesson (Oslo: Cappelen Damm, 2017), 101–126.

23 Daniel Djurberg, *Geographie för Begynnare*, 6th edition (Örebro: N.M. Lindhs förlag, 1815).

24 Carl B. Roosen, *Alvorstale i Anledning den i Sverig udgivne Bog: Geographie eör [sic] Begynnare, författad af Daniel Djurberg* (Fredrikshald: H. Gundersen & H. Larsen, 1833).

25 Hemstad, "Geopolitikk og geografibøker for folket."

In Norway, being forced into this new union with Sweden after leaving the dual monarchy with Denmark after 400 years, there was, as has already been shown, a resistance among parts of the population to these definitions of "Scandinavia," and "Scandinavians." They were interpreted as Swedish rhetorical devices used in order to strengthen the common union, potentially threatening the traditional terms "Norway" and "Norwegians". There was, it may be argued, an enduring awareness against what could be suspected of being Scandinavian imperialistic plans – under disguise of the rhetoric of Scandinavianness – be it from the side of Sweden or Denmark.

Between 1814 and the early 1840s "Scandinavia" was, in Sweden – not in Norway or Denmark – usually used in a narrow sense, equivalent to the term the "Scandinavian Peninsula." The Danish author Christian Molbech also notes in his travel book after a visit to Sweden that this was the common usage in Sweden until around 1840.[26] By 1848, however, "Scandinavia" was still defined in a Swedish encyclopaedia as an old name for Sweden and Norway, as an originally Latin, historic-poetic denomination of these two countries.[27] "Scandinavia" was never the name of a political entity, it is underlined. The existing union between Norway and Sweden is, quite strikingly, not mentioned in this entry.

There was a significant increase in the frequency of the term in Swedish newspapers – following a common Nordic pattern – in the 1840s, when the concept is broadened considerably.

The Danish Scandinavian Rhetoric

In Denmark, as in Sweden and Norway, "Scandinavian" was used to an increasing degree from the beginning of the nineteenth century, along with the traditional and more widespread use of "Nordic." However, "Scandinavia" and "Scandinavian" had a broader meaning in Denmark and Norway compared to Sweden after 1814. As a result of a new orientation towards the neighbouring Scandinavian countries and their common ancient cultural heritage, from the late eighteenth century onwards, journals, books, pamphlets and poems, associations, meetings, and events were using "Scandinavian" as part of their name or title and gradually "Scandinavian" became a widespread adjective. The revival of

---

26 Christian Molbech, *Lund, Upsala og Stockholm i Sommeren 1842: Nogle Blade af en Dagbog med et Tillæg om "den skandinaviske Eenhed"* (Copenhagen: Gyldendalske Boghandling, 1844), 283–320.
27 *Svenskt konversationslexikon*, 3rd ed. (Stockholm: Gustaf Berg, 1848), 547–548.

interest in Old Norse literature, manuscripts, and monuments contributed to illuminating an ancient common "Nordic" history and culture and at the same time stimulating national consciousness in Denmark, Norway, Sweden – and Iceland. While "Nordic" was the traditional, and usually preferred, term to describe Old Norse culture, indicating a backward-looking cultural orientation, "Scandinavian" more explicitly included Sweden and Norway and had, at least from the 1830s and 1840s, stronger political connotations. It represented a distinct orientation northward as a way of securing the ancient heritage from German appropriation of the Old Norse legacy.[28]

An early example of a Danish rhetoric of Nordicness was the dissemination of semi-official pamphlets in southern Sweden from 1808 to 1810, propagating the candidacy of the Danish King as King of Sweden. In these pamphlets, the preferred term was "Nordic" rather than "Scandinavian," even if both terms were frequently used.[29] The choice of Bernadotte as Swedish Crown Prince in 1810 changed the condition for dynastic pan-Scandinavian activities, at least until the 1850s.[30]

During the 1830s, "Scandinavian" gradually accrued connotations of "newness," and "new ideas," and "Scandinavia" was transformed into the land of the future – a common future for Danes, Swedes, and Norwegians. Old Norse enthusiasm merged with liberal and national reactions to absolute rule and a developing Danish-German conflict over the Duchies Schleswig and Holstein in the divided borderland. The Danish rhetoric of Scandinavianness from the mid-1830s was thus a new kind, in opposition to the authorities and not directed by them. Furthermore, it was influenced by, while at the same time being opposed to, the German national movement at the time. A transnational pan-Scandinavian movement was in the making from the late 1830s, gaining support from liberal-oriented groups and individuals, including publicists, writers, and students, mainly in Denmark and Sweden, during the 1840s.

---

28 See also Tim van Gerven on the use of this legacy in national consciousness-raising projects: "Scandinavism: Overlapping and Competing Identities in the Nordic World 1770 – 1919" (PhD diss., University of Amsterdam, 2020, forthcoming Brill, 2022).

29 Ruth Hemstad, "Fra 'det förenade Scandinavien' til 'Nordens Tvillingrige': Skandinavistisk propaganda før skandinavismen, 1808 – 1814," in *Skandinavism: En rörelse och en idé under 1800-talet*, ed. Magdalena Hillström and Hanne Sanders (Göteborg: Makadam förlag, 2014), 56 – 58.

30 Morten Nordhagen Ottosen, "Den dynastiske skandinavismens grobunn og grenser, ca. 1845 – 1870," in *Skandinavismen*, ed. Ruth Hemstad, Jes Fabricius Møller and Dag Thorkildsen (Odense: Syddansk Universitetsforlag, 2018), 257 – 286.

The pan-Scandinavian movement developed from regional Danish and Swedish collaboration across the Öresund Sound from around 1800, to gradually more institutionalized collaboration between devoted groups in Denmark, Sweden and, more hesitantly, Norway and Finland. The movement sought to construct a common Scandinavian identity by highlighting the common Old Norse heritage, the kindred languages, and cultural similarities among "Scandinavians." In addition, it focused on the strategic political need to stand up to Prussia and Russia.[31] The movement gained momentum and spread from Denmark to the other Scandinavian countries foremost through the spectacular social and political student events taking place from the early 1840s, the so-called "Scandinavian student voyages," which were media events at the time.[32] Influenced by these impulses, to be a "Scandinavian" in Swedish rhetoric gradually also included the Danes.

Meetings, associations, and events led to new and strengthened transnational networks. Through a comprehensive and conscious use of journals, newspapers, pamphlets, books of different kinds, songs, poems, and speeches, a new pan-Scandinavian vocabulary was widely spread and circulated to the Nordic countries and beyond.[33] The effect this had in increasing the frequency of the term "Scandinavian" in the newspapers, not only in Denmark but in all the Nordic countries, is striking.

In 1843, after a student meeting in Uppsala, the publicist and scholar Ludvig Kristensen Daa, one of the few Norwegians publicly and positively oriented towards the new "Scandinavian ideas," wrote in his journal *Granskeren* about the current movement: "Lately, the youth of our neighbours and brothers, the Swedish and Danish youngsters, have also [as among the Italian and German youth] found their great idea, namely the Scandinavian idea of Nordic

---

31 Åke Holmberg, *Skandinavismen i Sverige vid 1800-talets mitt* (Göteborg: Elanders boktryk-keri, 1946); Erik Møller, *Skandinavisk stræben og svensk politik omkring 1860* (Copenhagen: Gad, 1948); Henrik Becker-Christensen, *Skandinaviske drømme og politiske realiteter: Den politiske skandinavisme i Danmark 1830–1850* (Aarhus: Arusia, 1981); Rasmus Glenthøj, *1864: Sønner av de slagne* (Copenhagen: Gad, 2014), Rasmus Glenthøj and Morten Nordhagen Ottosen, Union eller undergang. Kampen for et forenet Skandinavien (Copenhagen: Gads Forlag, 2021).

32 Jonas Harvard and Magdalena Hillström, "Media Scandinavianism: Media Events and the Historical Legacy of Pan-Scandinavianism," in *Communicating the North: Media Structures and Images in the Making of the Nordic Region*, ed. Peter Stadius and Jonas Harvard (Farnham: Ashgate Publishing, 2013), 75–98.

33 Ruth Hemstad, "'En skandinavisk Nationalitet' som litterært prosjekt: 1840-årenes transnasjonale offentlighet i Norden," in *Nation som kvalitet: 1800-talets litterära offentligheter och folk i Norden*, ed. Anna Bohlin and Elin Stengrundet (Bergen: Alvheim & Eide akademisk forlag, 2021).

unity."[34] The Norwegian youth were, however, more hesitant. The discussions in the Norwegian Student association after this meeting were predominantly critical of the new ideas.[35]

The "Scandinavian idea of Nordic unity" was only one out of a great many similar phrases and frequently used expressions that were consciously employed by pan-Scandinavian activists. These phrases may be seen as part of a renewed Scandinavian political language, disseminated in different ways, that was used as a means to achieve political goals.[36] Based on the reformulated, rhetorical concept of a "Scandinavian" as someone supportive of the "Scandinavian idea" and the broader understanding of "Scandinavia" – being the land of the common prosperous future – the concept of "Scandinavianism" emerged. This new ism, which mirrored other pan-national movements of the day, was commonly in use after 1844.[37]

In 1839, Fredrik Barfod's quarterly journal *Brage og Idun,* the first transnational journal with an explicit pan-Scandinavian agenda, was published and circulated to Scandinavian, mainly Danish and Swedish, subscribers. The term "Scandinavian" was regularly used in the five volumes published between 1839 and 1842, when Barfod's enterprise was stopped due to censorship restrictions. Examples are phrases like "a Scandinavian soul", "Scandinavian endeavours", "Scandinavian nations", "Scandinavian sympathies", a "Scandinavian mindset" and "the Scandinavian North". The dominance of the term "Nordic" in the journal however outnumbers that of "Scandinavian" by a wide margin.[38]

Significant is also the first "Scandinavian Meeting of Natural Scientists" held in Gothenburg in 1839. Inspired by German, British, and Swiss examples, it was the first in a range of regularly held transnational meetings within different professions and groups across the Nordic region. Advocates of the "Scandinavian idea," attending the meeting in 1839, claimed that it was the first proof of "a scientific union of the North."[39] It was interpreted as a sign of Scandinavian recon-

---

34 "Om Skandinavien," *Granskeren,* 15 June 1843.
35 See also Frederik Wallem, *Det norske Studentersamfund gjennom hundrede aar: 1813–1913,* vol. 1 (Kristiania: Aschehoug, 1916), 272–281; John Sannes, *Patrioter, intelligens og skandinaver: Norske reaksjoner på skandinavismen før 1848* (Oslo: Universitetsforlaget, 1959).
36 For more on the languages of politics – including their role in shaping citizens' actions and constituting their worldviews, see David Craig and James Thomson, eds., *Languages of Politics in Nineteenth-Century Britain* (London: Palgrave Macmillan, 2013), 1–20.
37 Ruth Hemstad, "Scandinavianism: Mapping the Rise of a New Concept," *Contributions to the History of Concepts* 13, no. 1 (2018): 1–21.
38 In the five published and digitized volumes there are 36 mentions of "Scandinavian" and 300 of "Nordic" (table of contents and register not included).
39 See Hemstad, *Fra Indian summer,* 49.

ciliation and the necessity of closer collaboration. Numerous speeches during the meeting – published in Scandinavian newspapers and journals such as *Brage og Idun*, and as part of the published account of the meeting – demonstrated an eager use of the rhetoric of Scandinavianness. Several similar meetings and related associations termed themselves "Scandinavian" from the 1840s onwards.[40]

After the first grand student meeting in Uppsala in June 1843, associations with a pan-Scandinavian goal were established in Copenhagen and Uppsala. The aim was to strengthen the cultural connections between the three Scandinavian countries. In Denmark, the new Skandinavisk Samfund [Scandinavian society], established by students and leaders of the pan-Scandinavian movement, was prohibited by the authorities, due in part to its name. The prohibition caused a sharp debate in the public sphere and probably only helped to strengthen the movement. The Copenhagen cultural elite soon established another association, Skandinavisk Selskab, in September 1843. This time, the association got the necessary approval on the explicit precondition that their meetings would not be used for political discussion. A similar association, Skandinaviska Sällskapet, was established in Uppsala in October 1843.

The pan-Scandinavian profile of these new associations is emphasized in a Swedish encyclopaedia published 1848, in a separate entry on "Scandinavian association."

> *Scandinavian societies* is the name of the associations, which in recent years have been established within as well as outside Scandinavia, in order to contribute to the development of the common Swedish, Norwegian and Danish nationality. The purpose of these associations is to stimulate the feeling of one nationality, not Swedish, Norwegian or Danish, but Scandinavian.[41]

The encyclopaedic definition is illuminating regarding the use of the term "Scandinavian," and phrases like "the Scandinavian idea" and "the Scandinavian nationality," and the perceived role of "Scandinavian associations" in this pan-national project. "Scandinavian" associations abroad were part of this picture. Pan-Scandinavian diaspora associations abroad, by and for Scandinavians working in or travelling to other parts of the world, were usually open to all "Scandinavians" in a certain city and commonly termed themselves a "Scandinavian association." They were established in a range of European cities from the 1840s on-

---

40 A list of meetings held in the Nordic region from 1839 to 1929 is included as an appendix in Hemstad, *Fra Indian summer.*
41 Translation by the author. *Svenskt konversationslexikon* 3: 547–548.

wards, and among emigrants in the United States, Australia, and Africa.[42] Several of the new associations abroad stayed in contact with the Scandinavian associations back home, which helped to build up "Scandinavian libraries" abroad by sending "Scandinavian literature," including books, journals, and newspapers. News from these diaspora associations were reported on regularly in newspapers in Denmark, Norway, and Sweden, contributing to a transnational discourse.

An interesting, revealing discussion suggesting that "Scandinavian" was assumed as a potentially more political term than "Nordic" in the 1840s took place in Hamburg when a cultural-literary association was established in late 1842 by Scandinavians – predominantly Danes – as the first of its kind in the nineteenth century. The discussions reached the Scandinavian newspapers, which reported that the Swedish-Norwegian and Danish diplomatic representatives in Hamburg were informed about the new association, which had termed itself a "Scandinavian association."[43] This was not a problem for the Swedish diplomats. The Danish envoy, however, protested, fearing potential political reactions to the use of the term "Scandinavian," including, in particular, the potential reaction of the Russian court. As a result, the association chose the apparently more neutral term "Nordic," calling itself Nordisk Læseforening [the Nordic reading society]. The following spring, however, the original name was restored. The "Scandinavian association" in Hamburg continued until 1912 and was regularly reported on in the Scandinavian press as an example of Scandinavian sentiments and cooperation abroad. This picture changed totally, however, due to the dissolution of the Norwegian-Swedish union in 1905, causing a renewed quarrel regarding the naming of the association after the Swedish members demonstratively left the association.

The Scandinavian Vocabulary Turn

A third point in the history of the rhetoric of Scandinavianness is the sharp rise in the frequency of the term "Scandinavian" from the mid-1840s. This applies to

---

42 Ruth Hemstad, "Organizational Scandinavianism Abroad"; Ruth Hemstad, "Literature as Auxiliary Forces: Scandinavianism, Pan-Scandinavian Associations and Transnational Dissemination of Literature," in *Culture and Conflict: Nation-building in Denmark and Scandinavia 1800 – 1930*, ed. Sine Krogh, Thor Mednick and Karina Lykke Grand (Aarhus: Aarhus University Press, 2022), 161–164.
43 Originally referred to in *Aalborg Stiftstidende og Adresse-Avis*, 27 January 1843. On the association in Hamburg, see also Hemstad, "Organizational Scandinavianism Abroad."

newspapers in Denmark, Sweden, and Norway – and to a certain degree in Finland – indicating the emergence of what could resemble a Nordic public sphere. There are different limitations regarding the scope and quality of the digitized material in the various Nordic newspaper corpora, especially when it comes to older printed publications, and there is still a lack of digitized journals and other printed material. The newspaper databases give, however, a clear indication of the changes in the vocabulary and of the frequencies of terms such as "Scandinavian" and "Nordic."[44]

In Danish newspapers, there was a gradual rise in the use of the term "Scandinavian" since 1800, but this changed dramatically in the 1840s. From a relatively low frequency during the 1830s the frequency increased by a factor of twenty in the 1840s.[45] Almost a quarter of these mentions originates from the pro-Scandinavian newspaper *Fædrelandet*.[46] This is almost as many occurrences as the overall more frequent term "Nordic" in Danish newspapers during this decade.[47] After a gradual rise in the 1850s, there was another sharp rise in the use of "Scandinavian" in the 1860s.[48] From the 1870s, the gradual rise of "Scandinavian" continued, while "Nordic" again became clearly more dominant (fig. 1).

This development corresponds partly – and especially for the period between the 1830s and the 1860s – with the Swedish, Norwegian, and Finnish results. The comparison also reveals an interesting difference between a dominant frequency of "Nordic" in Denmark and Finland, and a relatively more frequent use of "Scandinavian" in Sweden and Norway for the period between the 1870s and the 1890s. In Swedish newspapers, "Scandinavian" rises markedly from the 1830s to the 1840s, even surpassing the frequency of the term "Nor-

---

44 This is valid also when the frequency is measured in absolute numbers of hits/mentions (the number of hits in the newspaper databases reflects the amount of newspaper issues with mentions of "Scandinavian" or "Nordic", not the total amount of mentions in each issue put together). For the Norwegian material, relative frequency supports the findings in this study.

45 The frequency of the term "Scandinavian" in Danish newspapers rose from 161 mentions during the 1830s to 3,795 mentions during the 1840s. (An asterisk ["skandinavisk*"] was added to the keyword search to ensure the inclusion of different variants. The search is case-insensitive.) Mediestream, accessed 13 September, 2020, www2.statsbiblioteket.dk/mediestream.

46 There were 885 mentions of "Scandinavian" in *Fædrelandet* during the 1840s.

47 The frequency of the term "Nordic" ("nordisk*") rose from 2,046 mentions during the 1830s to 4,038 mentions during the 1840s.

48 There are 13,253 mentions of "Scandinavian" during the 1860s compared to 18,807 mentions of "Nordic" during the same period.

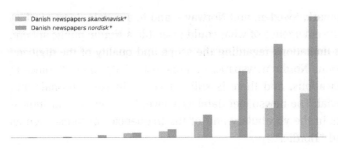

▓ Danish newspapers *skandinavisk**
▓ Danish newspapers *nordisk**

Figure 1: Frequency of the terms "Scandinavian" and "Nordic" in Danish newspapers 1810 – 1899.
Source: Mediestream, accessed 13 September, 2020, www2.statsbiblioteket.dk/mediestream.
Illustration copyright Lars G. Johnsen, National Library of Norway.

dic."[49] After a gradual rise in the 1850s, the use of "Scandinavian" again rose considerably in the 1860s.[50] In the 1870s, there was a gradual rise of both terms, with "Nordic" only again slightly surpassing "Scandinavian" in the decade between 1890 and 1899 (fig. 2).

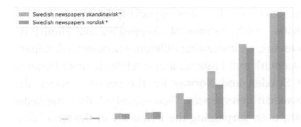

▓ Swedish newspapers *skandinavisk**
▓ Swedish newspapers *nordisk**

Figure 2: Frequency of the terms "Scandinavian" and "Nordic" in Swedish newspapers 1810 – 1899. Source: Svenska dagstidningar, accessed 13 September 2020, tidningar.kb.se. Illustration copyright Lars G. Johnsen, National Library of Norway.

---

49 The frequency of the term "Scandinavian" ("skandinavisk*") in Swedish newspapers rose from 710 mentions during the 1830s to 5,967 mentions during the 1840s. The frequency of the term "Nordic" ("nordisk*") rose from 1,718 mentions during the 1830s to 5,551 during the 1840s. (A search on "scandinavisk*" gave 32 additional hits during the 1830s, and 83 hits during the 1840s. The search is case-insensitive). Svenska dagstidningar, accessed 13 September 2020, www.tidningar.kb.se.
50 There are 25,688 mentions of "Scandinavian" during the 1860s compared to 19,524 of "Nordic" during the same period. Included in this result are also advertisements for the bank Skandinaviska Kreditaktiebolaget, founded in 1864.

In the Norwegian digitized newspaper corpus, the same tendency is prevalent, even if the contemporary number of newspapers was considerably less in Norway than in the established Danish and Swedish print cultures. "Scandinavian" was used moderately in the 1830s before its usage rose significantly in the 1840s (cf. fig. 3).[51] In the same period, the term "Nordic" also rose, but comparatively less.[52] The 1850s represented a relative rise in the frequency of "Scandinavian", surpassing that of "Nordic." From the 1870s to the 1880, "Nordic" was slightly more widespread. During the 1890s, "Scandinavian" again surpassed "Nordic," but since 1900, "Nordic" has gradually become the most dominant term again.

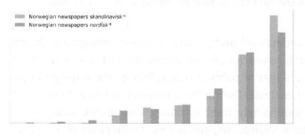

Norwegian newspapers *skandinavisk**
Norwegian newspapers *nordisk**

Figure 3: Frequency of the terms "Scandinavian" and "Nordic" in Norwegian newspapers 1810–1899. Source: National Library of Norway, accessed 13 September 2020, www.nb.no. Illustration copyright Lars G. Johnsen, National Library of Norway.

Swedish language newspapers in Finland also reflect the same development. The newspaper corpus displays an increase in the term "Scandinavian" from the 1830s to the 1840s compared to that of "Nordic".[53] There is a gradual increase of both terms in the 1850s and 1860s with a clear increase of "Nordic" in the 1870s and of both terms in the 1880s followed by a minor decrease of "Scandinavian" in the 1890s. The term "Nordic" is overall more frequent in this corpus during the whole period from 1810 to 1900 (fig. 4).

---

51 The frequency of the term "Scandinavian" ("skandinavisk*") in Norwegian newspapers rose from 79 mentions during the 1830s to 1,209 mentions during the 1840s. (The search is case-insensitive). National Library of Norway, accessed 13 September 2020, www.nb.no.
52 The frequency of the term "Nordic" ("nordisk*") rose from 486 mentions during the 1830s to 1,954 mentions during the 1840s.
53 The frequency of the term "Scandinavian" ("skandinavisk"*/"scandinavisk*") in Swedish language newspapers – and advertisements in Swedish in Finnish language newspapers – in Finland rose from 95 mentions during the 1830s to 227 mentions during the 1840s. The frequency of the term "Nordic" ("nordisk*") rose from 218 mentions during the 1830s to 457 mentions during the 1840s. (The search is case-insensitive). DIGI, accessed 16 September 2020, digi.kansalliskirjasto.fi.

Figure 4: Frequency of the terms "Scandinavian" and "Nordic" in Swedish-language newspapers in Finland 1810–1899. Source: DIGI, accessed 16 September 2020, digi.-kansalliskirjasto.fi. Illustration copyright Lars G. Johnsen, National Library of Norway.

The references to "Scandinavian" and "Nordic" in Nordic newspapers in general covers editorial content, as articles and submitted letters, but also advertisements, announcements, and lists of publications, reflecting the widespread use of these terms in different contexts. During the nineteenth century "Scandinavian" and "Nordic" were increasingly used in names of journals, newspapers, firms, organizations, cultural institutions, and different enterprises of a transnational character. This tendency reflects a general transnational development and indicates that a Scandinavian/Nordic orientation had become an integrated, "ambient" part of cultural and social life across the region and could also be utilised for branding purposes.[54] Part of this picture is the rising number of meetings and associations using "Scandinavian" or "Nordic" in their names.[55]

Scandinavian Sympathies and Related Phrases

The sharp rise in the frequency of the term "Scandinavian" in Nordic newspaper corpora also reflects the range of new phrases entering the new pan-Scandinavian vocabulary. Illustrative is the critical discussion by Christian Molbech in his travel account published in 1844 where he added an almost forty-page long, highly critical appendix regarding what he called "the Scandinavian

---

54 Tim van Gerven uses the phrase "ambient Scandinavism" to describe how markers of a pan-Scandinavian identity (such as literature, monuments, and street-names) became an unobtrusive background of daily life during the late nineteenth century. Van Gerven, "Scandinavism," 264, 327.

55 See appendix in Hemstad, *Fra Indian summer*.

idea" or "the Scandinavian idea of unity."[56] The text demonstrates how the term "Scandinavian" was used in an already flourishing amount of new expressions and phrases, among them a "new Scandinavianness," a "Scandinavian connection," the "Scandinavian North," the "new Scandinavia," "the first sudden Scandinavian enthusiasm," "Scandinavian sympathies," and "the Scandinavian issue."

In Sweden, the term "Scandinavian" was redefined in the 1840s, even if, as we have seen, the previous narrower use and understanding continued alongside the new interpretation. Newspapers and journals naming themselves "Scandinavian" in the 1840s hence referred explicitly to another, larger, and future-oriented "Scandinavia" than what had hitherto been the case.[57]

Along with the marked increase in the term "Scandinavian," there was a renewed interest in "Nordic" as part of the new political-cultural vocabulary. A key phrase here is *Nordens Eenhed* [Nordic unity/unity of the North], sometimes specified as a spiritual, cultural, or even political, unity.

Some specific phrases are used throughout the century, with periods of increasing and decreasing usage. Other phrases, interestingly, only turn up during limited time periods. Some of these word combinations are seemingly quite neutral, while others are ambiguous, charged with meaning and clearly rhetorical. It is possible to identify and analyse through a combination of close and distant readings phrases of interest, frequently used expressions, and term co-occurrences. By counting the frequencies of certain bigrams in the text corpus at the National Library of Norway and searching for key words and specific phrases in Nordic newspaper databases, as well as conducting close readings of relevant material, one can begin to see several patterns appear.[58]

Several of the new phrases found in this research were coined by pan-Scandinavian activists. Some of the phrases with the term "Nordic" are integrated

---

56 Christian Molbech, "Om 'den skandinaviske Eenhed,'" in Molbech, *Lund, Upsala og Stockholm*, 28. Molbech's list also demonstrates a contemporary use of the term "Scandinavianness," see page 297. See also Hemstad, "Scandinavianism," 11.

57 "Anmälan," *Tidning för Skandinavien*, 30 December 1843.

58 Bigram collocations based on newspaper and books, 1790–1920 are made available for this study by Lars G. Johnsen. N-gram resources at the National Library of Norway: https://www.nb.no/sprakbanken/ressurskatalog/oai-nb-no-sbr-35/. For descriptions of data resources at NBdigital, see Magnus Breder Birkenes et al., "From Digital Library to N-Grams: NB N-gram," in *Proceedings of the 20th Nordic Conference of Computational Linguistics* (Linköping, 2015), 293–295. See also Lars Johnsen, "Eldre bøker i den digitale samlingen: Et elektronisk blikk på tekster fra perioden 1650–1850," in *Litterære verdensborgere: Transnasjonale perspektiver på norsk bokhistorie 1519–1850*, ed. Aasta Marie Bjorvand Bjørkøy et al. (Oslo: National Library of Norway, 2019), 190–214.

parts of the pan-Scandinavian rhetoric, having clear political implications and connotations, such as "Nordic unity," "Nordic spirit/volksgeist," and "Nordic union/federation/alliance." More frequent in the rhetoric applied by the pan-Scandinavian movement, and used mainly from the 1840s until the 1860s, were phrases such as "Scandinavian sympathies"; the "Scandinavian idea" or the "Scandinavian idea of unity"; the "Scandinavian issue/question"; the "Scandinavian union"; and "Scandinavian efforts/endeavours." Other frequent phrases are the "Scandinavian people(s)," "Scandinavian nation(s)/nationality," and "Scandinavian aims/purposes." Widespread are also phrases including "Norden" or "Scandinavia," as the "Scandinavian North," the "spiritual unity of the North," "Our Norden/Scandinavia," and "the unity of Norden/Scandinavia." Even "Scandinavian associations," as we have seen, could be understood as a specific form of association, meant to propagate "Scandinavian ideas" and promote the knowledge of "Scandinavian literature." Many of these phrases were used in all three Scandinavian countries, as a transnational pan-Scandinavian vocabulary with shared key concepts, others were mainly used in one or two countries, like the "Scandinavian fatherland," which was mostly a Danish invention. All these phrases should be seen as part of the discursive, semantic context surrounding the pan-Scandinavian movement.

"Nordic" and "Scandinavian" were to a certain extent interchangeable concepts during most of the nineteenth century, which the bigram counts also support. In many instances, and out of esthetical-poetical reasons, there was a question of using alternatives in the descriptions used. The term "Nordic" is overall clearly more dominant during the whole century, but "Scandinavian" increased to a certain point in Denmark in the 1860s and early 1870s, and in Norway and Sweden until the 1890s, followed by a relative decline. Some phrases were usually, or only, used in combination with either "Nordic" or "Scandinavian." Typically, descriptive phrases of the area and territory used these terms interchangeably, for example: "Scandinavian/Nordic countries," "Scandinavian/Nordic Kingdoms/realms," and "Scandinavian/Nordic states" – an exception to this tendency is the description of the peninsula, "Scandinavian Peninsula" predominates with only a few, mainly Norwegian, examples of the phrase "Nordic Peninsula." Phrases that refer to the inhabitants of territory follow the same logic: "Scandinavian/Nordic peoples" and "Scandinavian/Nordic nationalities/nations". Some of these terms could also be used in singular, rhetorically underlining the unity among the Scandinavians, such as "*the* Scandinavian people/nationality/nation". Some phrases changed gradually from "Scandinavian" to "Nordic" during the century, such as "Scandinavian/Nordic cooperation," and related to this, "Scandinavian/Nordic meetings/associations".

Some phrases could change their meaning, depending on the context, as part of a Swedish or a Danish rhetoric. The "Scandinavian union" could mean Sweden and Norway *or* Denmark, Sweden, and Norway, and the inhabitants in question – the "Scandinavians" – could mean the Swedish and Norwegian people *or* the Danish, Swedish, and Norwegian people *or* even, more explicitly, the Danish, Swedish and Norwegian supporters of the "Scandinavian idea." A "Scandinavian song" could be praising the union between Sweden and Norway, especially when written around 1814 *or* it could, later on, be one of the hundreds of songs distributed during the "Scandinavian/Nordic student meetings."

Some phrases are predominantly "Nordic," like the ones describing Old Norse heritage.[59] Old Norse history, language, and antiquities were dominantly termed "Nordic," not "Scandinavian." In the Sagas themselves, "Scandinavian" was not used, as was emphasized in the Norwegian critique against Danish attempts to claim part of the ownership to this heritage. "Nordic" was preferred as well when speaking of Vikings, pagans, Gods and runes, as well as tribes. History was also dominantly "Nordic." There are "Nordic mythology/legends," as well as "Nordic folk songs/fairy-tales/poetry/art/authors," but "literature" could either be described as "Scandinavian" or "Nordic." And although countries, states, and realms are interchangeably "Nordic" or "Scandinavian," there are seemingly only "*Nordic* powers" and a "*Nordic* force."

The rhetoric of Scandinavianness around 1840 was soon met by counter concepts clearly indicating the ambiguity embedded in these concepts. One of these, although quite rare, was "Unscandinavian." Another, more frequently used, was "antiscandinavian." There were also "antiscandinavians," referring negatively to "Scandinavians," or "so-called Scandinavians," referring to someone who was in favour of the "Scandinavian idea." "Unscandinavian" was used in an article in the Danish satirical and political magazine, *Corsaren*, while mocking the incredible number of speeches and toasts being held at the huge "Nordic" student meeting in Copenhagen during the summer of 1845. The author claims there were "247 Scandinavian speeches... always about one and the same thing, that Denmark, Norway and Sweden had been in disagreement, but now were the best of friends – that is simply too much... that is unscandinavian."[60]

---

59 See also J.J.A. Worsaae, "Om vigtigheden af et centrum for Nordisk Oldforskning," *Annaler for Nordisk Oldkyndighed og Historie*, 1846: 3–20. In Sweden, "Scandinavian" was also used to describe this past history. "Nordic race" is, however, seemingly not commonly used (on humans) until the 1920s. See also Merle Weßel in this volume.

60 *Corsaren*, 4 July 1845, cited after Julius Clausen, *Skandinavismen historisk fremstillet* (Copenhagen: Det Nordiske Forlag, 1900), 101. Corsaren was edited by M.A. Goldschmidt.

The development in the rhetorical use of "Scandinavian" in the 1840s cannot be understood without considering the impact of the pan-Scandinavian movement. The usage culminated with the two German-Danish wars on the Duchy of Schleswig, 1848–51 and 1864, resulting in the Danish loss of Schleswig. During the 1870s, the 1880s, and most of the 1890s the rhetoric of Scandinavianness was less outspoken, but still not completely forgotten.

From the Rhetoric of Scandinavianness to the Rhetoric of Nordicness

A fourth point regarding the rhetoric of Scandinavianness in the nineteenth century is the renewed interest at the turn of the century followed by a rejection of these concepts in conservative parts of the Swedish public sphere. This development probably contributed to strengthening another tendency, which is the final main point, namely, that the rhetoric of Scandinavianness gradually transformed into a rhetoric of Nordicness from the last part of the nineteenth century onwards. This last section will briefly look into this development.

The period of specific interest is around the year 1900, which saw a revival of pan-Scandinavian sentiments stimulated by what was termed "neo-Scandinavianism."[61] A range of "Scandinavian" and "Nordic" associations and meetings filled the air, many of them using a rhetoric reminiscent of earlier periods. This Indian summer period, also reflecting Russian and German pressure against Finland and the Danish borderlands respectively, turned, however, into a cold Nordic winter after the dissolution of the Norwegian-Swedish union in 1905. Swedish "neo-Scandinavianists" openly declared the final death of "Scandinavianism" caused by Norway unilaterally leaving the union. Swedish reactions hence turned against the flourishing Nordic cooperation at the time, including the many Scandinavian associations established abroad, such as the one in Hamburg. The terms "Scandinavia" and "Scandinavian" were no longer appealing but rather contested and were rejected as inappropriate and in conflict with Swedish national interests in conservative parts of the Swedish public sphere.[62]

The pan-Scandinavian associations abroad, usually termed "Scandinavian," not "Nordic," continued to celebrate "Scandinavian" culture, traditions, and spirit, along with "Nordic Christmas" and "Scandinavian friendship" until the dis-

---

61 Hemstad, *Fra Indian summer*, 87–229.
62 "De 'skandinaviska' sjömanshemmen utomlands," *Göteborgs Aftonblad*, 17 July, 1908.

solution of the union in 1905. In 1906 and 1907, following the dissolution, and the subsequent anti-Scandinavian sentiments in Sweden, many associations, especially in European cities, were terminated.[63] The Scandinavian Association in Rome, established 1860, was one of the few older associations to survive 1905, and it is still in operation today.

An encyclopaedic entry in the Swedish *Nordisk Familjebok* – not an untypical name at the time – illuminates the conceptual changes within this field. The entry for "Scandinavian associations abroad" was still included in the 1917 volume, but without any definition, only a reference to another entry: "see Swedes living abroad."[64] *Utlandssvenskar* was then defined as "Swedish speaking citizens of Swedish origin" (including former Swedish territories), living in a state other than Sweden.[65] Several of the pan-Scandinavian associations abroad had been dissolved and new, nation-based clubs were established instead, backed by national umbrella organizations in the home countries.

The naming of transnational meetings within Scandinavia illustrates the transformation from "Scandinavian" to "Nordic" during the last part of the nineteenth century. Beginning with the first meeting series, that started in 1839, and in the decades following, associations and meetings across the region were termed "Scandinavian." During the 1860s, new meetings were either called "Scandinavian" or "Nordic." Starting with the 1870s, however, new meetings and conferences were primarily called "Nordic" rather than "Scandinavian," in part reflecting a growing number of Finnish participants. After 1900, there are only rare exceptions still using the adjective "Scandinavian" for these kinds of transnational activities.[66]

The same pattern can be seen in the names of the pan-Scandinavian oriented networks of associations. Within Scandinavia, associations with pan-Scandinavian ambitions, although nationally based, were established in three different, short-lived rows during the nineteenth century. The naming of them changed over time following the main transformation from "Scandinavian" to "Nordic." A forerunner was the above-mentioned Scandinavian Literary Society, established in 1796. During the 1840s, the associations were, as we have seen, termed "Scandinavian." When new associations were established after the second Ger-

---

63 Hemstad, "Organizational Scandinavianism Abroad"; Hemstad, *Fra Indian summer*, 345–359.

64 "Skandinaviska föreningar i utlandet: Se Utlandssvenskar," *Nordisk Familjebok* 25, 2nd ed. (Stockholm, 1917), 876.

65 *Nordisk Familjebok* 31 (Stockholm, 1921), 111.

66 Among the exceptions are "Scandinavian Labour Congresses," "Scandinavian Dentists Meetings," and "Scandinavian Woman Conferences". See appendix in Hemstad, *Fra Indian summer*.

man-Danish war in 1864, they were termed "Nordic" in Sweden and Denmark. The first association of this kind in Norway, established during the war, termed itself however "Scandinavian" [Skandinavisk Selskab]. As part of the revival of pan-Scandinavian notions after 1899, new associations were founded, using a common name: Nordisk Forening [Nordic association]. After a period of reduced cooperation and contact after 1905, the First World War reactivated Nordic cooperation, meetings, and transnational associational life. Foreningene Norden [Norden associations] were established not only in the Scandinavian countries in 1919, but also in Iceland in 1922, in Finland in 1924, and later in the Baltic area. They proved to have a longer life than their predecessors did. They have represented, and still represent, an enduring rhetoric of Nordicness.

Conclusion

This chapter has explored the emergence, rise, and decline of the term "Scandinavian" as a flexible and contested concept in newspapers published in Denmark, Sweden, Norway and Finland in the long nineteenth century. Based on an approach combining close and distant reading, through key word and collocate searching of Nordic newspapers, and additional readings of journals, books, and pamphlets, it argues that the use of the term "Scandinavian," along with a revived use of the older and more common term "Nordic," increased rapidly in the Nordic countries in the 1840s. The study demonstrates how different groups have sought to claim the term "Scandinavian" for their own purposes, leading to rhetorical struggles. A rhetoric of Scandinavianness – utilising the relatively rare and unsettled term "Scandinavian" compared to that of "Nordic" around 1800 – was used in competing Swedish and Danish pan-national projects. The use of the term "Scandinavian" exploded within the new Scandinavian public sphere that emerged in the 1840s, with associations, journals, and newspapers promoting the "Scandinavian idea." New connotations were attached to established terms, and a range of conceptual innovations with rhetorical power led to conceptual contests and disputes.

While the Swedish interpretation of "Scandinavia" and "Scandinavian" – as restricted to the Scandinavian Peninsula – used in the decades following 1814 has more or less faded into oblivion, the pan-Scandinavian movement of the mid-nineteenth century, it may be argued, had an enduring influence on the contested rhetoric of Scandinavianness and Nordicness throughout the century –

and well beyond.[67] The re-politicization of this concept around 1900 – 1905, and the national tensions and anti-Scandinavian sentiments after 1905, contributed to making it even more contested. When the transnational cooperation started up again around 1918, and with Finland and Iceland as integrated parts of it, the term "Nordic" was the most appropriate adjective to use, although it continued to be flexible, appealing, and contested, as the following chapters of this volume demonstrate.

---

67 Hemstad, *Fra Indian summer*, 394 – 418; Hemstad, "Scandinavianism, Nordic Co-operation and 'Nordic Democracy,'" in *Rhetorics of Nordic Democracy*, ed. Jussi Kurunmäki and Johan Strang (Helsinki: Finnish Literature Society, 2010), 179 – 193.

Merle Weßel

The Nordic in the Scientific Racial Discourses in the United States and Northern Europe in the Interwar Period: The Passing of Greatness

Introduction

The term *Nordic* in relation to race science was introduced in the early twentieth century in the United States by Madison Grant. Though the notion of the supremacy of the races of Northern Europe was frequently discussed in the nineteenth century, the prominent terms in this discussion were *Aryan* or *Teutonic*, rather than *Nordic*. The shift from Aryan to Nordic was a gradual one. Between 1853 and 1855, the term *Aryan race* was first used by the French author Arthur de Gobineau to describe what he regarded as the superior race of Northern Europe.[1] In 1899, the economist William Ripley introduced the term *Teutonic race*, which, according to him, was based mainly in the United States, Great Britain and Germany.[2] He did not specifically consider Scandinavia in his definition.

Madison Grant then introduced the term *Nordic* and put the Nordic countries – or to be more precise, Scandinavia (Denmark, Sweden and Norway) – on the racial map as the core of civilisation and political order.[3] In the young historian and journalist Lothrop Stoddard (1883–1950) Grant found a protégée who continued his legacy of scientific racism well into the 1930s with books like *The Rising Tide of Color against White World-Supremacy* (1922) and *The Racial Realities in Europe* (1924).[4] Both were convinced that the Nordic race was superior and the most civilised of all races, the race that led any great nation to success. They argued that only with a high degree of Nordic blood could a society be politically,

---

1 Arthur de Gobineau, *Essai Sur l'inégalité Des Races Humaines*, 3 vols (Hanover: Rumpler, 1853).

2 William Zebina Ripley, *The Races of Europe: A Sociological Study* (New York: D. Appleton and Company, 1899).

3 John P. Jackson and Nadine M. Weidman, "The Origins of Scientific Racism," *The Journal of Blacks in Higher Education* 50 (2005): 66–79.

4 Lothrop Stoddard, *The Rising Tide of Color against White World Supremacy* (New York: Scribner, 1920); Lothrop Stoddard, *The Racial Realities in Europe* (New York: Scribner, 1924).

economically, and socially successful. If the degree of Nordic blood decreased in a society, civilisation would likewise decline.[5]

This terminological shift was connected to an interplay of scientific and political changes. The increasing interest of racial scientists and anthropologists in the understanding of human races was related to the political climate in the United States This was influenced by fears of poorer European immigrants seeking their fortunes in the new world and the impact of this on US society.[6] There was a consolidation of racial discourse in science especially after the turn of the century, and after the Great War this discourse found its way into politics and society. This discussion peaked in the Immigration Act of 1924, which regulated immigration to the United States on racial grounds. The Act favoured people from Northern Europe and prevented Southern and Eastern Europeans from entering the United States.[7]

However, the idea of a superior Nordic race found support not only in the United States but also in many Northern European countries. In Germany, for example, leading racial scientists like Eugen Fischer, Fritz Lenz, and Hans F.K. Günther discussed notions of a superior *nordische Rasse* and its possible decline through race mixing.[8] In the Nordic countries, racial biologists, such as the Swede Herman Lundborg, adopted the term *nordisk* in their race studies in the early twentieth century, though its use did not originate there. The adoption of Nordic terminology in the Nordic countries followed a pattern familiar from other usages of the rhetorics of Nordicness – it was largely an adoption of US uses.[9]

The term "Nordic" [*nordisch/nordisk*] was the key term in racial science and the conceptualization of racial superiority and hierarchy in early twentieth-century Germany and Sweden. In Germany, the racial theorists Erwin Baur, Eugen Fischer, and Fritz Lenz published their book *Menschliche Erblichkeitslehre und*

---

5 Madison Grant, *The Passing of the Great Race or the Racial Basis of European History* (New York: C. Scribner, 1936); Jonathan Peter Spiro, *Defending the Master Race: Conservation, Eugenics, and the Legacy of Madison Grant* (Burlington: University Press of New England, 2009).
6 Kristofer Allerfeldt, "'And We Got Here First': Albert Johnson, National Origins and Self-Interest in the Immigration Debate of the 1920s," *Journal of Contemporary History* 45, no. 1 (January 2010): 7–26, doi:10.1177/0022009409348019.
7 Allerfeldt, "'And We Got Here First.'"
8 Hans F.K. Günter, *Ritter, Tod und Teufel. Der heldische Gedanke* (Munich: J. F. Lehmann Verlag, 1920); Erwin Baur, Eugen Fischer, and Fritz Lenz, *Menschliche Erblichkeitslehre und Rassenhygiene* (München: J.F. Lehmann, 1931), 547.
9 Carl Marklund and Klaus Petersen, "Return to Sender – American Images of the Nordic Welfare States and Nordic Welfare State Branding," *European Journal of Scandinavian Studies* 43, no. 2 (January 2013), https://doi.org/10.1515/ejss-2013–0016.

Rassenhygiene (1921/1931) in which they claimed that the members of the *nordische Rasse* were the bravest and most intelligent.[10] Here *nordisch* refers to a geographical area occupied mainly by people of the *nordische Rasse* – Northern Europe, Northwest Europe, and the coastal areas of the North and Baltic seas.[11] These theorists declared the term *germanisch* to be a term of the past, used because the *nordische Rasse* had its origin in the German *Kaiserreich* of the Middle Ages and had developed from there.[12] The term *Aryan*, as used by Ripley in 1899, was for them a purely linguistic term that did not relate to the cultural context.[13] While the German racial scientists saw the origin of the Nordic race in Germany, the Swedish researchers, such as the racial biologist Herman Lundborg, understood Sweden as the geographical centre of the *nordisk ras*. He, as with Grant and the German colleagues, used the term *nordisk* to refer to a geographical location its inhabitants. Yet, he argued that the *nordisk ras* was mainly defined by an anthropological bond and that no racial hierarchies could be detected between the Nordic race and other European races.[14] The different conceptualisation and nationally defined use of the terms *Nordic*, *nordisch*, and *nordisk* had an effect on the racial implications made by the different researchers as well as the racialist results of their research.

This chapter discusses Grant and Stoddard's conceptualisation of the Nordic race as a superior race. The primary question is: how did Grant and Stoddard form the notion of Nordicness in their racial theory? Why did Grant and Stoddard use the term Nordic rather than following William Ripley's conceptualisation of the Teutonic or Germanic race?[15] Since the discourse of the Nordic race was not limited to the United States but similar ideas emerged at the same time in Europe, I compare how the concept of Nordicness and Nordic race can be understood in the context of similar ideas, taking Sweden and Germany as case studies. I chose Sweden as the exemplary case for the Nordic countries because in Nordic racial theory the Nordic countries constituted the core area of the Nordic race with the "purest" Nordic people. Yet, though the Nordic race discourse was very active in Sweden in the interwar period, no political radicalisation resulted from it. As the second case, I selected Germany because German racial theorists considered Germany to be a country with a significant number of Nordic people

---

10 Baur, Fischer, and Lenz, *Menschliche Erblichkeitslehre und Rassenhygiene*, 547.
11 Baur, Fischer, and Lenz, *Menschliche Erblichkeitslehre und Rassenhygiene*, 147.
12 Baur, Fischer, and Lenz, *Menschliche Erblichkeitslehre und Rassenhygiene*, 541.
13 Baur, Fischer, and Lenz, *Menschliche Erblichkeitslehre und Rassenhygiene*, 542.
14 Herman Lundborg, *The racial Characters of the Swedish Nation* (Uppsala: Almquist & Wiksell, 1926); Herman Lundborg, *Rassenkunde des schwedischen Volkes* (Jena: Fischer, 1928).
15 Ripley, *The Races of Europe: A Sociological Study.*

and the idea of Nordic superiority was politically radicalised in the 1930s. I show how the geographical and political environment shaped the concept of the Nordic race, despite the cross-national similarities of the discourse. Here, notions of a transnational transfer of culture and knowledge are relevant to demonstrate how the knowledge and understanding of the concept of the Nordic race travelled across the Atlantic Ocean and within Europe in the early twentieth century.[16]

In 2011, Johannes Burgers compared Grant's racial theory to the theories of Hungarian Zionist Max Nordau.[17] I build on this comparative literature. The emphasis here is not on Grant's biography, rather it is on Grant's conceptualization of the Nordic race and his contribution to the development of a movement proclaiming Nordic and White supremacy in the United States during the 1920s.

Many thinkers engaged in discussions about the concept of a Nordic race in Europe during the 1920s and 1930s. In what follows, I draw on studies of these debates by Nikola Karcher, Hans-Jürgen Lutzhöft, and Gunnar Broberg with Nils Roll-Hansen, as well as my own work, and for the Swedish context, on studies by Mattias Tydén and Maria Björkman to show the similarities and differences between the Northern European and US Nordic discourse.[18]

The chapter is divided into three parts. The first part discusses the development of scientific racism and the conceptualization of the Nordic race as a superior race in the United States, with a particular focus on the works of Grant and Stoddard. I show why Grant and Stoddard favoured the term *Nordic* over the previous terms *Germanic* or *Teutonic* and how this conceptual turn took place. In the second part, I place the US discourse in relation to similar discourses in Germany and Sweden. I show that despite common fears about the degeneration of the

---

16 Stefan Nygård and Johan Strang, "Facing Asymmetry: Nordic Intellectuals and Center-Periphery Dynamics in European Cultural Space," *Journal of the History of Ideas* 77, no. 1 (25 February 2016): 75–97, doi:10.1353/jhi.2016.0006.

17 Johannes Hendrikus Burgers, :Max Nordau, Madison Grant, and Racialized Theories of Ideology," *Journal of the History of Ideas* 72, no. 1 (2011): 119–140.

18 Maria Björkman, *Den anfrätta stammen: Nils von Hofsten, eugeniken och steriliseringarna 1909–1963*, Pandora-serien xviii (Lund: Arkiv förlag, 2011); Gunnar Broberg, "Scandinavia: An Introduction," in *Eugenics and the Welfare State: Norway, Sweden, Denmark, and Finland*, ed. Gunnar Broberg and Nils Roll-Hansen (East Lansing: Michigan State University Press, 2005), 1–8; Nicola Karcher, "Schirmorganisation der Nordischen Bewegung: Der Nordische Ring und seine Repräsentanten in Norwegen," *Nordeuropaforum* 1, no. 19 (13 July 2009): 7–36, doi:10.18452/7996; Mattias Tydén, *Från politik till praktik: de svenska steriliseringslagarna 1935–1975*, 2nd ed., Acta Universitatis Stockholmiensis, Stockholm studies in history 63 (Stockholm: Södertälje, 2002); Merle Weßel, "Concept of 'Nordic Race' in German and Nordic Racial-Theoretical Research in the 1920s," *Nordeuropaforum*, 2016, 29–49; Hans-Jürgen Lutzhöft, *Der Nordische Gedanke in Deutschland 1920–1940* (Stuttgart: E. Klett, 1971).

Nordic race and the impact of this on civilisation, the conceptualisation of the Nordic race differed, geographically and conceptually, across the Atlantic Ocean. In the third part, I focus on the transnational transfer of knowledge and discourse about the Nordic race. I discuss whether this undertaking can be considered a transnational movement in the rhetorical uses of Nordicness and what aims and effects were connected within the different strains. I show that Germany was a centre for research about the Nordic race, since Grant and Lundborg had extensive connections to German race scientists although no direct link between Grant and Lundborg themselves can be detected.

Scientific Racism in the United States

The idea of a hierarchy of human races was not invented by Grant or Stoddard. Charles Darwin argued in his evolutionary theory that no race was superior to the others. In the decades after the publication of his work, however, the French writer Arthur de Gobineau, the American economist William Ripley, and the British philosopher and biologist Herbert Spencer, among others, contributed to the idea that evolution was indeed the struggle between the races. This thinking grew into the ideology of scientific racism.

Whereas Darwin argued against the supremacy of the Northern races and argued that environment had no effect on genes, de Gobineau argued that in Northern parts of Europe there developed a superior race due to its context of a harsh climate. They suggested that civilisation was a product of race and that the Nordic race produced the highest form of civilisation. They also argued that race, not nation or political order, was the foundation for social order.[19] While the late nineteenth-century, racial theorists, such as William Ripley, had focused mainly on anthropological issues in the context of race, racial theorists such as Madison Grant and Lothrop Stoddard introduced social and political ideas into the discussion. In this way, they turned racial discourse away from anthropology and biology and towards social and political discourse.

Grant was born in 1865 into a wealthy, upper-class family in New York. He studied at Yale University as an undergraduate and received a law degree from Columbia University in 1890. Yet, his legal career was short-lived as he pursued his interests in zoology, genealogy, and anthropology.[20] Grant developed a spe-

---

19 Jackson and Weidman, "The Origins of Scientific Racism," 66.
20 Charles C. Alexander, "Prophet of American Racism: Madison Grant and the Nordic Myth," *Phylon (1960-)* 23, no. 1 (1962): 73–74, doi:10.2307/274146.

cial interest in the conservation of American wildlife. He was member of the prestigious Boone and Crocket Club, a conservation and hunting club with other prominent members, such as future president Theodore Roosevelt. He shaped various other nature-focused associations, like the National Parks Association and the New York Zoological Society, and he was a founder of the Bronx Zoo in New York in 1899.[21] Furthermore, he was vice-president of the Immigration Restriction League and member of the Eugenics Research Association. His ideas influenced the drafting of the Johnson Immigration Act of 1924, which regulated immigration to the United States on racial grounds.[22] On top of this, Grant published numerous articles about wildlife conservation, nature, and anthropology, as well as the danger of the downfall of civilisation in Europe and its threat to society in the United States. He was a strong advocate for eugenics and placed himself in the popular discourse about degeneration and the decline of civilisation.[23]

Grant created a group of followers during his active years. One of his most vocal protégées was the journalist and historian Lothrop Stoddard. In his biography of Grant, Jonathan Spiro calls Stoddard the second most influential racist of the United States.[24] His background was similar to Grant's. Stoddard came from an old and wealthy New England family and he also trained, like Grant, as a lawyer but never actually practised law. He studied history at Harvard University and worked as a journalist and an author. Stoddard was considered the apostle of Grant, who was considered the prophet of scientific racism.[25] He published 22 books and numerous articles, the most significant of which were *The Rising Tide of Color against White World-Supremacy* (1920), *The Revolt against Civilisation* (1922) and *The Racial Realities in Europe* (1924).[26] The central theme, following Grant, was the supremacy of the Nordic race, its contribution to civilisation and its feared downfall in the near future. Stoddard was well known in intellectual circles and influenced the intellectuals and authors of his time. The writer F. Scott Fitzgerald alluded to Stoddard and his works in his book *The Great Gatsby* (1925), where his character Tom Buchanan refers to a book on the subject.

---

21 Spiro, *Defending the Master Race*, 75.
22 Alexander, "Prophet of American Racism," 75.
23 Alexander, "Prophet of American Racism," 89.
24 Spiro, *Defending the Master Race*, 171.
25 Spiro, *Defending the Master Race*, 173.
26 Stoddard, *The Rising Tide of Color against White World Supremacy*; Lothrop Stoddard, *The Revolt against Civilization: The Menace of the under Man* (New York: Scribner, 1922); Lothrop Stoddard, *The Racial Realities in Europe*.

"Civilization's going to pieces," broke out Tom violently. "I've gotten to be a terrible pessimist about things. Have you read *The Rise of the Colored Empires* by this man Goddard? [...] It's a fine book, and everybody ought to read it. The idea is if we don't look out the white race will be – will be utterly submerged. It's all scientific stuff; it's been proved. [...] This fellow has worked out the whole thing. It's up to us, who are the dominant race, to watch out or these other races will have control of things. [...] This idea is that we're Nordics. I am, and you are, and you are, and [...] we've produced all the things that go to make civilization – oh, science and art, and all that. Do you see?"[27]

The casual allusion to Stoddard's book and the topic of the presumed downfall of civilisation in a popular novel show that scientific ideas about race were not marginalised but that the discourse about races and civilisation was very much part of intellectual discussions. Books by Stoddard and others were widely read and became so well known that they appeared in literature as part of the zeitgeist.

However, the careers of both Grant and Stoddard were short lived, peaking in the time after the Great War in the 1920s. Yet both left behind extensive material that enlightens us about the conceptualisation of the Nordic race in the United States in the interwar period. Grant's book *The Passing of the Great Race* (1916/ 1936) was dedicated to the history of the Nordic race and its achievements, but also prophesied its downfall in the next decades. In the preface to the second edition, the US-anthropologist Henry Fairfield Osborn stated that recent history had shown that the Nordic race was the race that countries needed to rely on for leadership.[28] In the preface to the first edition Osborn stated: "if I were asked: What is the greatest danger which threatens the American republic today? I would certainly reply: The gradual dying out among our people of those hereditary traits through which the principles of our religious, political and social foundations were laid down and their insidious replacement by traits of less noble character."[29] The strong interest in the Nordic race and Nordic supremacy started shortly before the Great War and increased significantly in the interwar period. The political and social changes that came with the experience of the war, not only in the United States but also in Germany, were shaped by a sense of loss of the world as it had been known and the subsequent uncertainty of the future.

Grant emphasised repeatedly in his works that he objected to the classification of some races as superior to others, but at the same time he contradicted his statement by declaring that the human races were not equal and alike.[30] In his

---

27 Fitzgerald, F. Scott, *The Great Gatsby* (Cambridge: Cambridge University Press, 1993), 14.
28 Grant, *The Passing of the Great Race or the Racial Basis of European History*, xi.
29 Grant, *The Passing of the Great Race or the Racial Basis of European History*, ix.
30 Madison Grant, *The Conquest of the Continent* (New York: C. Scribner, 1933), ix.

books, he discussed the races of the world and especially the three races he defined as European races: the Nordic, the Alpine, and the Mediterranean. Here my focus is on the conceptualization of the Nordic race. Grant's description of the physical characteristics of the Nordic race was no different to descriptions by other international racial theorists, such as Fischer, Lenz, or Lundborg. The members of the Nordic race were long-skulled with fair skin, blond or brown hair, and light-coloured eyes. He described them as "a race of soldiers, sailors, adventurers and explorers, but above all, of rulers, organizers and aristocrats in sharp contrast of the essentially peasant and democratic character of the Alpines. The Nordic race is domineering, individualistic, self-reliant and jealous of their personal freedom both in political and religious systems and as a result they are usually Protestant."[31]

Grant argued that the superiority of the Nordic race was defined by its environment. He demarcated the core area of the Nordic race as the areas surrounding the North and Baltic seas, though this area was not fixed but changed over time.[32] He supported the neo-Malthusian notion that the environment influenced genes and that genes changed due to environmental circumstances over time and generations. Grant argued that the harsh living conditions of the North – the long winters, the lack of daylight, and the bad weather – had a positive influence on people of the Nordic race, even though the weather was endured rather than enjoyed.[33] The fair environment of Southern Europe where the Mediterranean race was dominant did not force the people to strive for survival. Grant stated that good weather made people mentally and physically weak.[34]

Grant created a complex network of the human race structure. On top were the three main species: the Caucasians, the Mongols, and the "Negroids". Secondly, he divided them into subspecies or races. The Caucasians, for example, were divided into Nordic, Alpine, and Mediterranean – the three European races. Thirdly, Grant introduced varieties. Here, the Nordic race was split into Teutonics, Scandinavians, and other varieties based on the region they inhabited. The Teutonics, for example, were based in Great Britain and Northern Germany, and the Scandinavians in Norway, Sweden, Denmark, and the coastal area of Finland.[35] Sweden was considered by Grant the core area of the Nordic race, where the purest types could be found. In Germany or Great Britain, the Nordic

---

31 Grant, *The Passing of the Great Race or the Racial Basis of European History*, 228.
32 Grant, *The Passing of the Great Race or the Racial Basis of European History*, 20.
33 Grant, *The Passing of the Great Race or the Racial Basis of European History*, 38.
34 Grant, *The Passing of the Great Race or the Racial Basis of European History*, 38 – 39.
35 Grant, *The Passing of the Great Race or the Racial Basis of European History*, 65 – 66; Spiro, *Defending the Master Race*, 96.

race mixed with other races but the high percentage of Nordic blood within the people ensured their high quality.[36]

Stoddard echoed in many ways the thoughts of his mentor Grant and contributed little new to racial theories of the early twentieth century. He also divided European races into Nordic, Alpine, and Mediterranean. He located the areas of settlement the same way Grant did and followed Grant and most other racial theorists of his time in the physical description of the Nordic race.[37] Stoddard argued that the terms *Aryan, Indo-European,* and *Germanic* were to be considered purely linguistic. Only *Nordic* could be considered a term that defined the racial uniqueness and superiority of the group of people living in Northern Europe and belonging to the Nordic race, according to Stoddard.[38] Here Ripley's terminology of the Teutonic race clearly shifts to Grant and Stoddard's Nordic race.

The term *Caucasian,* according to Grant, was used to distinguish White from Black people in the United States but could not be used in other contexts.[39] *Teutonic,* as Grant claimed, was also a linguistic term that distinguished the latecomers of the Nordic race from the early Celtic-speaking Nordic tribes.[40] Grant and Stoddard agreed that all other terms previously used to describe the Nordic race, such as *Aryan, Germanic,* or *Teutonic,* actually referred to linguistic differences but not to racial differences – physical and mental traits. Grant stated:

> Just as the classification of man according to race needs revision in the light of recent discoveries, so the definition of race must be understood anew in the light of genetics. Thirty years ago, we talked glibly about the Aryan or Indo-European race, or the Caucasian or Germanic race. All these terms must be discarded. Aryan, Indo-European, and Germanic are only linguistic terms and Caucasian has no meaning except as used in America to distinguish between whites and colored. [41]

Yet, Stoddard started to use the term "White race," which comprised the Nordic, Alpine, and Mediterranean races. Grant was not convinced at this time that these three races could be grouped together but Stoddard considered them all to be races of "good" stock and genetically at least above the "colored races" [*sic*]. Nevertheless, Stoddard agreed with Grant that the Nordic race was the most val-

---

36 Grant, *The Passing of the Great Race or the Racial Basis of European History,* 68, 169, 211.

37 Stoddard, *The Rising Tide of Color against White World Supremacy,* 5–7.

38 Stoddard, *The Rising Tide of Color against White World Supremacy, 162.*

39 Grant, *The Conquest of the Continent,* 21–22.

40 Grant, *The Conquest of the Continent,* 43.

41 Grant, *The Conquest of the Continent,* 21–22.

uable one.[42] While people from the Nordic countries had not previously been considered White, Stoddard connected Nordicness to Whiteness.[43]

The fear for the future of the Nordic race was a central theme for Stoddard. Whereas Grant had already anticipated a grim future for the Nordic race, Stoddard argued that "it is the Nordics who are most affected by the dysgenic [sic] aspects of our civilization."[44] He gave two examples of the decline of the Nordic race. With the first he directed the view to the United States. Stoddard argued that "our country, originally settled almost exclusively by Nordics, was toward the close of the nineteenth century invaded by hordes of immigrant Alpines and Mediterraneans, not to mention Asiatic elements like Levantines and Jews."[45] Stoddard refers to "Nordics" here because in his mind the first settlers in America came exclusively from countries with a high concentration of the Nordic bloodline, such as Great Britain, parts of Germany, and Sweden. He continued: "as a result, the Nordic native American has been crowded out with amazing rapidity by these swarming, prolific aliens, and after two short generations he has in many of our urban areas become almost extinct."[46] He drew a direct line between rising social and economic problems in the United States after the turn of the century and the geographical change in the migration structures he appeared to have recognized.

According to Stoddard, following Grant's argument, the Nordic race was endangered not only in the United States but also in Europe, its area of origin. He claimed that it was mainly the Nordic race that had suffered during the Great War: "the Nordic went forth eagerly to battle, while the more stolid Alpine and, above all, the little brunet Mediterranean either stayed at home or even when at the front showed less fighting spirit, took fewer chances, and oftener saved their skins."[47] The Great War thus weakened White solidarity, which have previously been a unifying force.[48] Stoddard's line of logic was that in the Great War the White races fought each other and other races were less involved, which meant that mainly members of the White races, in particular

---

42 Grant, *The Conquest of the Continent*, 157; Stoddard, *The Rising Tide of Color against White World Supremacy*, 162–63.

43 Catrin Lundström and Benjamin R. Teitelbaum, "Nordic Whiteness: An Introduction," *Scandinavian Studies* 89, no. 2 (2017): 151, doi:10.5406/scanstud.89.2.0151.

44 Stoddard, *The Rising Tide of Color against White World Supremacy*, 163.

45 Stoddard, *The Rising Tide of Color against White World Supremacy*, 165.

46 Stoddard, *The Rising Tide of Color against White World Supremacy*, 165.

47 Stoddard, *The Rising Tide of Color against White World Supremacy*, 183.

48 Stoddard, *The Rising Tide of Color against White World Supremacy*, 169.

the Nordic race, lost their lives in the war. According to him this affected not only the current generation but also the future ones.[49]

Grant and Stoddard's scientific racism was based on their experiences of change in American culture after the turn of the century and the Great War. They perceived a degeneration of the society and as a result felt that the world they knew was changing. Their concerns about an increase in low quality immigrants – as they perceived them – triggered their interest in race mixtures and trying to preserve the status quo.

Grant and Stoddard, as wealthy, educated men of their time with a strong belief in science, used scientific argumentation to support non-scientific claims regarding hierarchies of human races as determinate of historical developments. It is significant how much influence amateur scientists like Grant and Stoddard could gain in politics and the scientific community. They were even able to influence legislation, for instance, the development of the Johnson Act in 1924. The Nordic race and being Nordic became a main identity marker for these men. They used it to proclaim their superior position in society and ensure the preservation of their power in the United States.

Nordisk Ras in Sweden Racial Theory

Enthusiasts for the Nordic race and racial scientists spanned across the Western world, creating an informal network.[50] In the early twentieth century, the Nordic race concept was popular in most Western countries. It was frequently used to define hierarchies of people, especially to make distinctions between native inhabitants of a nation and immigrants. The discourse, however, was not the same on both sides of the Atlantic. In the United States, as we have seen in the previous section, the focus was to protect the nation from immigrants arriving from Europe, in particular Southern Europe, and changing the societal and racial map of the United States. In Europe the discussion was different. The decline of the population quality and the fear of racial degeneration constituted the core of the discourse, but in Sweden, it was not immigration but emigration

---

49 Stoddard, *The Rising Tide of Color against White World Supremacy*, 169, 198.
50 Maria Björkman and Sven Widmalm, "Selling Eugenics: The Case of Sweden," *Notes and Records of the Royal Society* 64, no. 4 (20 December 2010): 379–400, https://doi.org/10.1098/rsnr.2010.0009.

that was the main concern.[51] In the interwar period in Sweden, racial biologists raised concerns that people of a so-called "high-quality" racial make-up would emigrate, and that so-called "degenerate" people would stay behind.[52]

Racial research in Sweden was less directed toward external influence and instead was concerned with the internal race structure of the Swedish nation. The Swedish racial biologist and leader of the state institute for racial biology Herman Lundborg published several books analysing the racial characters of the Swedish nation.[53] In his more general publications on a theory of race, such as *Rasfrågor i modern belysning* (1919) and *Rasbiologi och rashygien: Nutida kultur- och rasfrågor i etisk belysning* (1922), his focus was primarily on Northern Europe and he did not take the global approach as Grant and Stoddard did.[54] However, like his US colleagues, Lundborg argued that nations consist of race mixtures. For example, the German nation had traces of the *nordisk ras* but also others. The *nordisk ras*, according to Lundborg, could be found in most races, but in a lower quantity.[55] Lundborg also highlighted the difference between the terms *race* and *folk*, which had an influence on the use of the word *Nordic* in his work. He argued that a *folk* was a group of people joined by culture and *race* constituted a group of people with shared physical and mental characteristics that were inherited.[56] For example, the German *folk* included the Nordic race as well as other races and the Nordic race could also be found among Roman or Slavic *folk*.[57] He argued that every *folk* was actually a mixture of races and never exclusively consisted of one race, but the quantity of *nordisk* traces in a *folk* defined its quality.[58] The term *nordisk* did not itself have a racist connotation in Lundborg's racial theory; it was a descriptive term, which did not say much about the quality of the race or create strict hierarchies between races, as in US or German racial research. He was much vaguer in his publications,

---

51 Hofsten, Nils von, *Ärftlighetslära* (Uppsala: P.A. Norstedt & Söner, 1919); Herman Lundborg, *Rasfrågor i Modern Belysning* (Stockholm: P.A. Norstedt, 1919); Broberg, "Scandinavia: An Introduction."

52 Hofsten, Nils von, *Ärftlighetslära*, 490; Lundborg, *Rasfrågor i Modern Belysning*, 126; Broberg, "Scandinavia: An Introduction," 3–4.

53 Björkman, *Den anfrätta stammen*; Tydén, *Från politik till praktik*; Maja Hagerman, *Käraste Herman: Rasbiologen Herman Lundborgs gåta* (Stockholm: Norstedts, 2015).

54 Herman Lundborg, *Rasbiologi Och Rashygien: Nutida Kultur-Och Rasfrågor i Etisk Belysning* (Stockholm: P.A. Norstedt, 1922); Lundborg, *Rasfrågor i Modern Belysning*.

55 Lundborg, *Rassenkunde des schwedischen Volkes*, 1.

56 Lundborg, *Rassenkunde des schwedischen Volkes*, 1.

57 Lundborg, *Rassenkunde des schwedischen Volkes*, 1.

58 Lundborg, *Rassenkunde des schwedischen Volkes*, 119.

though more precise about his racist ideas in private.[59] Since he published his research in German, Swedish, and English, it cannot be clearly stated how the term *nordisk* might differ from *Nordic* and *nordisch* in regard to his American and German colleagues. However, it can be stated that Lundborg used *nordisk* not as a cultural or political term, like Grant did, but as a biological one.

In the context of neo-Malthusian ideas of genetic heritage, Lundborg argued that although the environment influenced physical development – such as body size – not all differences in physical appearances could be related to the environment, as many were attributable to racial differences.[60] In many ways Lundborg shared Grant's ideas on the influence of the environment on the racial constitution but he indicated a certain conceptual uncertainty about how the environment exactly influenced the development of genes. This may have been due to his scientific education as a biologist, which gave him a deeper understanding of genetics. Since Lundborg was a biologist focusing on Sweden, his research on the *nordisk ras* was strongly influenced by his academic background and by his own studies of the races in Sweden that he mapped extensively in the early twentieth century. Direct contact between Grant and Lundborg has not been found. Lundborg's main contacts in the United States were with more established and professional racial scientists, such as Charles Davenport, the leader of the Cold Spring Harbor Eugenics Record Office, and not with amateur scientists like Grant.

Though Lundborg did not have a direct connection with Grant, he had very direct connections with Grant's German colleagues Lenz, Baur, and Fischer as well as racial theorist Hans F.K. Günther who played a leading role in National Socialist racial theory.[61] Günther lived in Sweden in the 1920s and lectured at Lundborg's institute.[62] The Swedish Racial Biology Institute was modelled after the German Kaiser Wilhelm Institute.[63] Lundborg is described as a radical conservatist who helped introduce German racial theory to Sweden.[64] Although his research was influenced by the idea in radical German racial theory that the Nordic race sits at the top of a racial hierarchy, it was also influenced by theories from scholars in the Nordic region. In that sense, *nordisk* had a double meaning in race science in Sweden. It constituted the research subject but also the context in which the research took place. Nordic scholars cooperated in their efforts in

59 Björkman, *Den anfrätta stammen*; Björkman and Widmalm, "Selling Eugenics."
60 Lundborg, *Rassenkunde des schwedischen Volkes*, 1.
61 Björkman, *Den anfrätta stammen*; Hagerman, *Käraste Herman*.
62 Björkman and Widmalm, "Selling Eugenics."
63 Björkman and Widmalm, "Selling Eugenics."
64 Björkman and Widmalm, "Selling Eugenics."

racial research and shared their ideas in meetings and conferences within a closed network.[65]

Grant and Stoddard's Connections to Germany

Grant did have extensive and direct contacts to German racial theorists, especially to Eugen Fischer, the German medical doctor, anthropologist, and racial hygienist, who studied race mixtures in the German colonies in Africa. In 1937, Fischer wrote the foreword to the German translation of *Conquest of the Continent*.[66] The arguments of Fischer, Baur, and Lenz harmonised with those of Grant. They praised the physical, mental, and social superiority of the *nordische Rasse*, which according to them made representatives of the *nordische Rasse* leaders of civilisation and the world. Fischer, Baur, and Lenz were not as conceptually clear with their terms as Grant and Stoddard but used both *germanisch* and *nordisch*. Lenz argued that "die Germanenreiche, welche aus der sogenannten Völkerwanderung hervorgingen, wurden gegründet von Stämmen nordischer Rasse. Das deutsche Kaiserreich des Mittelalters ruhte ganz und gar auf den Schultern von Germanen."[67] The interchangeable use of *germanisch* and *nordisch* could be because Germany was not part of the core area of the Nordic race, which was mostly located in Sweden. However, the German racial scientists wanted to ensure that Germans could be considered Nordic, so they expanded the historical core area of the Nordic race to the Germanic Reich of the Middle Ages and claimed *germanisch* as a prehistoric term for *nordisch*. Similarly to Grant and Stoddard, Lenz surveyed European history proclaiming any major historical event, such as the Reformation or the Renaissance, to be an achievement made through the contribution of the members of the *nordische Rasse*.[68] He also agreed with Grant and Stoddard that *Aryan* was not a term to describe the *nordische Rasse* but had to be considered a linguistic term. He concluded that it was not an exaggeration to state that the countries of north-western Europe had the most developed civilisation due to the high concentration of the *nordische Rasse*, since the *nordische Rasse* was the most intelligent race.[69]

---

65 Björkman and Widmalm, "Selling Eugenics."
66 Spiro, *Defending the Master Race*, 359.
67 Fritz Lenz, "Die seelischen Unterschiede der großen Rassen," in *Menschliche Erblichkeitslehre Und Rassenhygiene*, ed. Erwin Baur, Eugen Fischer, and Fritz Lenz (Munich: J.F. Lehmann, 1931), 541.
68 Lenz, "Die seelischen Unterschiede der großen Rassen," 542.
69 Lenz, "Die seelischen Unterschiede der großen Rassen," 542.

In Germany, Grant's second important contact was the philologist and racial theorist Hans F.K. Günther, who was a Nordic enthusiast and a member of the Nordische Bewegung. This was a network of German race and 'folkish' (*völkische*)[70] enthusiasts that included several general organisations such as Nordischer Ring and *völkische* youth organizations such as Jungnordischer Bund or Artamanen.[71] Later, Günther was the leading Nordic expert of the National Socialists and a close friend of Adolf Hitler. He cited Grant frequently in his publications.[72] Herman Lundborg was also in touch with Günther, who visited Uppsala and Lundborg's racial institute in 1923.[73]

Grant's ideas were met with great enthusiasm in Germany from the time of the Weimar Republic onwards. *The Passing of the Great Race* was translated by the Austrian professor Rudolf Pollard with the title *Der Untergang der großen Rasse* (1929), who concluded that the book should be a warning to the German people. Stoddard, too, did not shy away from being in contact with the German National Socialists and even visited Germany in 1940.[74]

Germany was a meeting point for racial scientists. In the Weimar Republic and especially later under the National Socialists, Germany became central for people interested in the Nordic race and concerned with its condition. The overlap between the ideas of Grant and Stoddard and those of their colleagues in Northern Europe was significant. It might not be too far-fetched even to suggest a global interest in the Nordic race with certain differences occurring between networks of scholars. The intellectual intersections between Grant and Stoddard and their German colleagues were, however, far more direct. Fischer, Lenz, and Baur made, in many ways, the same claims as Grant and Stoddard about Nordic intellectual superiority. It can be assumed they were more influenced by Grant and Stoddard than the other way around, because Grant's books were published in Germany in the 1920s. Nevertheless, Fischer, Lenz, and Baur were not as conceptually clear as Grant and Stoddard. They used *nordisch* and *germanisch* as interchangeable terms, on the basis that *Germanen* had originated in the *nordische*

---

70 *Völkisch*, was often used by racial theorists and within racist movements, especially National Socialism, to define their own racial superiority.

71 Karcher, 'Schirmorganisation der Nordischen Bewegung'; Lutzhöft, *Der Nordische Gedanke in Deutschland 1920–1940*, 55.

72 Spiro, *Defending the Master Race*, 359.

73 Hagerman, *Käraste Herman*; Gunnar Broberg and Mattias Tydén, "Eugenics in Sweden: Efficient Care," in *Eugenics and the Welfare State: Norway, Sweden, Denmark, and Finland* (East Lansing: Michigan State University Press, 2005), 90.

74 Burgers, "Max Nordau, Madison Grant, and Racialized Theories of Ideology," 139–140.

Rasse.[75] For them, the term *Germanen* referred to a population that was part of the *nordische Rasse* in the Middle Ages. They all agreed however that *Aryan* was only a linguistic term and that the Aryan race had died out a very long time ago. Conversely, Stoddard and Grant especially, argued that *Nordic* was the correct term rather than the obsolete term *Germanic*.

Transnational Movement of Nordic Enthusiasts?

Following on from the previous section, a question arises whether rising interest in the Nordic race as a key feature to conceptualising civilisation and superiority in the United States and Northern Europe can be considered a transnational movement. Before this question is answered two points need to be discussed: firstly, why the term "Nordic" [*nordisch/nordisk*] became so popular in scientific discourse; and secondly, how it could later enter social and political discourse and influence legislation like the Johnson Act in the United States or the German race laws in 1933.

In the context of the United States, Matthew Guterl argues that a Nordic movement was used after the Great War to try to solve many political problems.[76] He argues that a Nordic vogue swept over American popular culture in the 1920s, particularly in New York.[77] Leading authors of the time like Ernest Hemingway, Sinclair Lewis, and, as already cited, F. Scott Fitzgerald, showed interest in Nordic subjects and referred to them in their work.[78] The Nordic vogue also strongly influenced the political sphere. Visual differences between so-called races became more important than before. Whereas in the nineteenth century Irish immigrants were unwanted, now they were able to climb the race ladder due to their Whiteness, while immigrants with darker skin from Southern Europe and Black Americans, with their rising liberation movement, became targets of racism.[79] Whiteness, together with Nordicness, became a leading force within politics

---

75 Baur, Fischer, and Lenz, *Menschliche Erblichkeitslehre und Rassenhygiene*, 541.
76 Matthew Pratt Guterl, *The Color of Race in America, 1900–1940* (Cambridge, MA: Harvard University Press, 2001), 41. I do not think the Nordic trend was limited to the US context. It can also be seen in the Nordic countries with their renewed interest in their region that led to meetings between Nordic scientists and eventually resulted in political and cultural institutions like the Nordic Council. See Björkman and Widmalm, "Selling Eugenics."
77 Guterl, *The Color of Race in America, 1900–1940*, 42.
78 Guterl, *The Color of Race in America, 1900–1940*, 42.
79 Guterl, *The Color of Race in America, 1900–1940*, 75, 140.

and the two were strongly interconnected. The framing of the Nordic race and Nordic supremacy led to a redefinition of Whiteness.

Although the general interest in the Nordic race and Nordicness was rooted in the ideas of Grantian eugenics, in the interwar period, according to Guterl, it turned into racial fear.[80] This was then connected to ideas regarding the social worth of individuals, with attendant cultural, social, and political implications. Being Nordic meant being White and Whiteness became an integral part of American popular culture. Class formation and race consciousness worked hand in hand.[81] This connotation was rooted particularly in the Anglo-American scientific race discourse and from there entered the social debates of the early twentieth century – previously, only immigrants from Germany and England were considered to be White in the United States.[82] People with fairer skin began to be perceived as valuable members of American society, because – according to scientific and political theories of the time – their skin colour guaranteed that they possessed the characteristics of the Nordic race, such as intelligence, bravery, and morality.[83] Whiteness and Nordicness were brought together as concepts by racial theorists and biologists to describe the most desirable people of the American nation. Before this connection was made, people from Nordic countries were not labelled as White.[84]

In Germany, a similar strong turn – what could be called a movement – to Nordicness can be observed. In the early twentieth century, several clubs and committees were founded in Germany, for the purpose of advancing the Nordic idea, for example Nordischer Ring/ Deutscher Widerbund, Bogenclub or the Deutscher Bund für Volksaufartung und Erbkunde. These clubs were non-professional and non-scientific but interacted with the community of racial theorists, some of whom, such as Fritz Lenz or Eugen Fischer, were even members.[85]

The greatest difference between the German and the US Nordic movements was, however, their respective eras. The prime era of Nordicness in the United States was in the 1920s, peaking in 1924 with the Johnson Immigration Act. After 1930, interest in the Nordic race and Nordic superiority decreased again. This did not mean that racial segregation was no longer a salient issue, but the focus on Nordicness in the discourse declined and Whiteness became a

---

80 Guterl, *The Color of Race in America, 1900–1940*, 41.
81 Guterl, *The Color of Race in America, 1900–1940*, 41.
82 Catrin Lundström and Benjamin R. Teitelbaum, "Nordic Whiteness," 151–52.
83 Grant, *The Conquest of the Continent*, 165.
84 Catrin Lundström and Benjamin R. Teitelbaum, "Nordic Whiteness," 151.
85 Merle Weßel, *An Unholy Union? Eugenic Feminism in the Nordic Countries, ca. 1890–1940* (Helsinki: Unigrafia, 2018), 34; Karcher, "Schirmorganisation der Nordischen Bewegung," 11–21.

more crucial category. Furthermore, Grant and Stoddard's prominence decreased dramatically in the 1930s. Grant started to focus more on his work on animals, and for the New York Zoo, before his death in 1937.[86] Stoddard's presence in New York society also declined at the same time. This might be related to the rise of fascism in Europe and their claim to the Nordic concept, which was not compatible with US democracy. However, as the Nordic movement ended in the United States it was only beginning in Germany. With the rise to power of the National Socialists in 1933, Germany's government and political elite were heavily invested in the concept of the superiority of the *nordische Rasse*. In 1933, the Nordic club Nordische Gesellschaft was put under National Socialist leadership. In this way, it was transformed from an independent and open club to an instrument of the right-wing party. The club had a double task: to lead the propaganda on the *nordische Idee* in Germany and to establish and nurture close relationships to other Nordic groups.[87]

The leading Nordic enthusiasts of the 1920s became central figures in National Socialist politics. From 1927 until 1942, Eugen Fischer was the leader of the Kaiser-Wilhelm-Institut für Anthropologie, menschlichen Erblehre und Eugenik, which was the state institute for eugenics and racial theory during the Weimar Republic and later.[88] As rector of the university in Berlin between 1933 and 1934, he facilitated the dismissal of many of the Jewish staff members, though he only became a member of the National Socialist Party in 1940. From 1933 onwards, his colleague Fritz Lenz led the eugenics department of the Kaiser-Wilhelm-Institute. Fischer was an expert adviser for the development of the *Gesetz für die Verhütung erbkranken Nachwuchses* (1933), and he became a member of the NSDAP in 1937.

In Sweden, the connections between the Nordic idea and racial politics were not as clear. Herman Lundborg retired as leader of the institute for racial biology in 1935. The physician and racial biologist Gunnar Dahlberg became the next leader. In 1934, Sweden implemented legislation that allowed the voluntary sterilization of so-called unfavourable individuals.[89] Though at first glance the sterilization law in Sweden might have shown similarities with the German laws of 1933 and 1935, the Swedish law did not have an explicit racial background.[90] It

86 Alexander, "Prophet of American Racism," 90.
87 Lutzhöft, *Der Nordische Gedanke in Deutschland 1920–1940*, 62.
88 Paul Weindling, "Weimar Eugenics: The Kaiser Wilhelm Institute for Anthropology, Human Heredity and Eugenics in Social Context," *Annals of Science* 42, no. 3 (1 May 1985): 303–318, doi:10.1080/00033798500200221.
89 Tydén, *Från politik till praktik*.
90 Tydén, *Från politik till praktik*.

was not based on notions of race as such, especially not on a conceptualization of Nordic supremacy, but it was structurally infused with class, gender and racial bias as part of the population question in the establishment of the welfare state.[91] However, racial repercussions cannot be denied, for example in context of the Sámi people or Travellers.[92]

Enthusiasm for the Nordic race did not take off in its core country in the same way it did in Germany and the United States. The reasons for this were manifold. From the 1930s onwards, Sweden had a rather stable social democratic government, which steadily modernised the country. The standard of living of the Swedish people increased, and welfare was distributed more equally. Sweden did not see the same political and social issues that were rising in Germany and the United States. Furthermore, the Social Democrats began using the term *Nordic*, resulting in the term being associated with the liberal left. Its political meaning changed with increased usage of terms such as "Nordic democracy" and the "Nordic welfare state."[93] In this way it was not exclusively discussed in racial terms anymore, which made it difficult for right-wing groups and fascists to take over the term, as happened in Germany, for example.

To sum up, Nordicness and Nordic enthusiasm spread in several countries in the 1920s and 1930s, but the results were very different and very much influenced by the political and social environment. In countries like Germany, that had a right-wing government, it would gain social and political ground in the 1930s. More moderate countries like Sweden did not experience a political movement of Nordicness but rather a vital interest. Enthusiasm for Nordicness in the United States was short but intense and far-reaching because the idea was able to gain ground in politics and influence law-making. Despite the Nordic enthusiasts sharing their ideas across borders, it might be an overstatement to suggest it was a transnational movement. In the context of the term "Nordic race," however, one can trace the emergence of a trend towards degeneration, extremism, and racism that originated in the United States and then spread to Europe.

Conclusion

As prominent and important as they were during their lifetimes, it is remarkable how the legacies of Madison Grant and Lothrop Stoddard, in racial science as

---

91 Weßel, *An Unholy Union?*
92 Broberg and Tydén, "Eugenics in Sweden: Efficient Care," 130–33.
93 Jussi Kurunmäki and Johan Strang, *Rhetorics of Nordic Democracy* (Helsinki: Finnish Literature Society, 2010), doi:10.21435/sfh.17.

well as politics, are forgotten today. Both developed ideas about scientific racism, hierarchies of races, and especially, the supremacy of the Nordic race. These ideas were transformed from scientific constructs to political instruments. Grant and Stoddard contributed significantly to the development of the concept of a Nordic race and its global distribution in the early twentieth century. Neither man was a scientist himself, but both were influential society people who built a bridge between science and society. They popularised the idea that the appearance of people as well as their mental characteristics were based on their race. Most of the ideas Grant and Stoddard proclaimed were not new as such, but Grant especially shaped the term "Nordic race." This term was later used and developed within the global trend towards Whiteness and racial segregation. The invisibility of Grant and Stoddard's Nordic race discourse in the United States can mostly be explained by the irrevocably changed political sphere following the events of the Second World War. The discourse never gained large-scale political ground after the Second World War, however it prevails among far-right and fascist movements who romanticise the Third Reich and continue to discuss the Nordic race in the context of White supremacy.

As I have shown, ideas about the superiority of the Nordic race were discussed in several Western countries and across nations.[94] In the end, it is difficult to estimate who influenced whom because many publications were written and published at the same time. They contain the same ideas and descriptions regarding racial hierarchies and the composition of individual races. However, two conclusions can be made. Firstly, that "Nordic" [nordisch/nordisk] was a key term of early twentieth century racial theory and science. Secondly, its spread did not originate in the Nordic countries, but was first made popular in the United States and then spread to Europe.

None of the race theorists seemed to doubt that the Nordic race was the most superior race of all and the guarantee for civilisation and progress. Usually, they counted themselves as members of this race and their negative view of the future of the Nordic race might be linked to an expectation of a grim future of their own position in society. The modernisation of societies, and the rise of new democratic ideals as well as communism and fascism in the 1920s and 1930s, challenged the world as they knew it. Grant considered democracy to be an instrument of the weak and did not agree that everyone should have the same voice in society. For Grant, democracy was the end of civilisation.[95]

---

94 Björkman and Widmalm, "Selling Eugenics."
95 Grant, *The Passing of the Great Race or the Racial Basis of European History*, xx, 5–8, 227–30.

The passing of greatness also seemed to be at the core of racial theory in the other countries discussed here. Germany feared the disintegration of its nation after their loss in the First World War. The focus on the *nordische Rasse* was one of the methods of the racial scientists of the Weimar Republic and got picked up in the 1930s by the National Socialists. Racial hierarchy became the method to prove the greatness of the German nation and bring it back to the centre of the world stage. This resulted in the long-term bastardisation of the term *nordisch* in Germany. The connotations of racial supremacy and National Socialism created a problematic connection that put *nordisch* forever in the corner of right-wing politics and fascism. When talking about the Nordic countries, Scandinavia is the term most used in Germany today. The term *Nordische Länder* is basically unknown and rarely used. *Nordisch* has been replaced with *skandinavisch* and has connotations connected to the Nordic welfare state and Nordic lifestyle.

Racial scientists argued that Sweden likewise saw the passing of greatness, as parts of its population vanished through emigration. As small country at the periphery, Sweden always had to fight for its significance in the world. To be at the core of the Nordic discourse and be identified as the core area settled by the Nordic race gave it significance. Additionally, the notion of Sweden as a country in between the political extremes of the time might have proven the point for racial theorists about the great virtue of the members of the Nordic race. However, as discussed, Nordic enthusiasts did not gain support in Sweden in the same way they did in Germany and the United States. Yet that does not mean that in Sweden the term *nordisk* remains free of racist connotations. On the one hand, *nordisk* was used as political term to describe institutions of the region like the Nordic Council, Nordic cultural institutions like Nordiska museet, or political concepts such as the Nordic welfare state. On the other hand, there is today an ongoing battle with right-wing and fascist organizations, such as Nordiska motståndsrörelsen, who try to reclaim the term *nordisk* for racist and White supremacist ideas.

To conclude, the concept of a Nordic race was an international concept based on a glorification of the past and the fear of the future. It was founded on the idea that people identify themselves according to physical appearance and skin colour and that human races can be divided into race hierarchies. The ideas about the Nordic race combined science and politics and brought racial ideas to the forefront of Western societies. Its significance was strongly shaped by national and political circumstances that defined the grounds on which ideas of Nordic supremacy could grow and on which today's extremist movements for White supremacy, like the Nordic resistance movement, still rest.

Mary Hilson and Tom Hoctor

From the "Middle Way" to *The Nordic Way:* Changing Rhetorics of the Nordic Model in Britain[1]

Introduction

The Economist's special report on "Why the world should look at the Nordic countries," published in February 2013 with a Viking on the front cover, is just one well-known example of references to the Nordic model since 2010.[2] Indeed, the "Nordic model" is possibly one of the most widely recognized examples of the rhetorical use of the adjective "Nordic." At the same time, it is also a highly contested concept, within the region and outside it. There is a well-established field of research on images of the Nordic region and their circulation. Scholars acknowledge that foreign images or xenostereotypes of Nordic practices and policies have been shaped in reflexive interaction with self-images or auto-stereotypes produced in the Nordic countries themselves.[3] Moreover, positive stereotypes of the region have frequently been counter-balanced by more negative ones. The Nordic countries have been described as dystopian warnings against the perils of high taxation and an all-powerful state, sometimes caricatured with references to high levels of drunkenness and suicide.[4]

Although it is possible to trace some continuity in the ways in which the Nordic model has been referred to over time, its meaning has generally been unstable, both internally and externally. International interest in the Nordic region has

1 Mary Hilson's research is part of the project "Nordic Model(s) in the global circulation of ideas, 1970–2020," supported by Independent Research Fund Denmark (grant number 8018–00023B). We would like to thank the other members of the project team Andreas Mørkved Hellenes, Carl Marklund and Byron Rom-Jensen for valuable comments on an earlier draft of the chapter.
2 Adrian Wooldridge, "The next supermodel: Why the world should look at the Nordic countries," *The Economist*, February 2, 2013, https://www.economist.com/leaders/2013/02/02/the-next-supermodel.
3 Kazimierz Musiał, *Roots of the Scandinavian Model: Images of Progress in the Era of Modernisation* (Baden-Baden: Nomos Verlag, 2002).
4 For example Roland Huntford, *The New Totalitarians* (London: Allen Lane, 1971); see also Frederick Hale, "Brave New World in Sweden? Roland Huntford's *The New Totalitarians*," *Scandinavian Studies* 78, no. 2 (2006).

intensified during particular historical periods. One such moment was the 1930s, when the region was famously celebrated as a "middle way" between the extremes of authoritarianism and democracy, capitalism and communism.[5] According to historian Bo Stråth, the earliest references to the "Nordic model" as such date from the 1960s, when the term was used by political scientists referring to Nordic co-operation within the United Nations.[6] As Stråth puts it, the widespread use of the term "Nordic model" from the 1990s should be seen in the context of "the search for new identities, communities and interpretative frames... in order to rescue something perceived to be under threat."[7]

Studies of different aspects of the Nordic model have proliferated during the 2000s and 2010s, though there have been, as far as we know, few attempts to explore the history of the term and its rhetorical uses, beginning with its emergence in the 1960s and charting its fluctuating meanings through subsequent years.[8] This chapter has two parts. In the first part, we explore how the term "Nordic model" was used by scholars in comparative analyses of the historical development of the Nordic countries during the post-war period, paying attention to the idea of a Nordic political model and the Nordic model of the welfare state. The focus is on English-language scholarship, especially that produced within the UK.

The distinction between the Nordic model as analytical category and as a normative policy model for emulation elsewhere has never been watertight, however. In the second part of the chapter, we consider how the Nordic model concept has been applied to politics and policy programmes, taking recent political debates in the UK as a case study. Despite fundamental similarities in European

---

5 The most famous example of this is Marquis Childs, *Sweden – the Middle Way* (New Haven: Yale University Press, 1936). See Carl Marklund, "The Social Laboratory, the Middle Way and the Swedish Model: Three Frames for the Image of Sweden," *Scandinavian Journal of History* 34, no. 3 (2009); Peter Stadius, "Happy Countries: Appraisals of Interwar Nordic Societies," in *Communicating the North*, ed. Jonas Harvard and Peter Stadius, (Farnham: Ashgate, 2013).

6 Bo Stråth, "Den nordiska modellen. Historisk bakgrund och hur talet om en nordisk modell uppstod," *Nordisk Tidskrift* (1993); see also Musiał, *Roots of the Scandinavian Model*, 32.

7 Stråth, "Den nordiska modellen," 55.

8 See however Anu Koivunen, Jari Ojala, and Janne Holmén, "Always in Crisis, Always a Solution? The Nordic Model as a Political and Scholarly Concept," in *The Nordic Economic, Social and Political Model: Challenges in the 21st Century*, ed. Anu Koivunen, Jari Ojala, and Janne Holmén, 1–19 (New York: Routledge, 2021) doi:10.4324/9780429026690 – 1; Byrkjeflot, Haldor, Lars Mjøset, Mads Mordhorst and Klaus Petersen, eds. The Making and Circulation of Nordic Models, Ideals and Images (London: Routledge, 2021) doi:10.4324/9781003156925. Work in progress by Andreas Mørkved Hellenes, Mary Hilson, Carl Marklund, and Byron Rom-Jensen as part of the IFRD-funded project "Nordic model(s) in the global circulation of ideas, 1970 – 2020" also tracks the changing meanings of the Nordic model.

approaches to politics and governance, there is nonetheless a pronounced tendency to make the central contradictions of foreign political projects and the antagonisms of other societies intelligible through a process of domestication. In this process, these contradictions and antagonisms are played out through the familiar contradictions of domestic politics and the antagonisms and social conflicts of the "watching" society, rather than the "watched." In this chapter, the "watching" domesticating society will generally be the UK and the "watched" societies Nordic. The adoption of political ideologies in the Nordic countries and the UK, which were justified in terms of a particular "Nordic" way (or "model") of doing politics, were heavily dependent on the academic studies discussed in the first part of the chapter.

We argue in this section that the adoption of Third Way political logic *and* strategy by social democrats in Europe created a rhetoric which was easily imitable by liberal and conservative parties in the UK and the Nordic countries, and which was also used to re-articulate the meaning of the "Nordic" in Norden and abroad. This manifested itself concretely in two areas: the broad idea of the "radical centre,"[9] – an approach to politics characterised by the rejection of traditional economic divisions between left and right[10] – and the related attempt to position existing social democratic, and later liberal conservative politics, especially those of the Nordic countries, within the parameters of this "radical centre." This case study will suggest answers to two questions: Why and how were "radical centrist" political strategies adopted in the UK and Sweden from the late 1990s until the 2010s? And how did this process alter the rhetoric of the "Nordic model"?

The terms "Scandinavian model" and "Nordic model" are treated as synonyms here, though it is our impression that the term "Nordic model" has become more prominent since 2010, at least in English-speaking contexts. Use of the Nordic or Scandinavian model also has to be understood in relation to references to national models, especially the Swedish model. This term was established earlier and until the 1990s at least often stood as a proxy for the region as a whole, though never exclusively.[11]

---

9 Jenny Andersson, *The Library and the Workshop: Social Democracy in the Knowledge Age* (Stanford: Stanford University Press, 2010).

10 Chantal Mouffe, "The Radical Centre: A Politics without Adversary", *Soundings* no. 9 (Summer 1998), 11–23.

11 Carl Marklund has traced an early usage of the term "Swedish model," in an American source from 1941, where it referred to collective bargaining arrangements. See Marklund, "The Social Laboratory," 272; Andreas Mørkved Hellenes, "Tracing the Nordic Model: French Crea-

The Nordic model before the 1990s

In his textbook *Scandinavian Politics Today*, first published in 1999, political scientist David Arter identified two ideal-type Nordic models. The Nordic model of government referred to "the political institutions, structures and policy measures in [the Nordic] countries;" while the Nordic welfare model was "in large part the legislative product of the former."[12] Distinctive features of the Nordic political model included: the strength and dominance of social democratic parties within stable multi-party systems; a consensual approach to policy making involving formal consultation of corporatist interests; centralised collective bargaining; strong state regulation and the importance of personal relations among elites in relatively small states.[13] Arter's list of features was similar to those found in other formal definitions of the Nordic model, for example in the Danish encyclopaedia *Den Store Danske*, which referred to the universal welfare state, tax-financed and state-run; the influence of social democratic parties within a consensual political culture; and women's high levels of economic activity.[14]

In defining a Nordic political model Arter was drawing on the established literature in political science that treated the small Nordic countries as a natural unit for comparative analysis. Such comparisons could emphasise similarities – between the Nordic region and other countries or regions – but also internal differences within the region.[15] In an earlier study from 1982, Arter and his three co-

---

tions, Swedish Appropriations and Nordic Articulations," in *Making and Circulation of the Nordic Model*, ed. Haldor Byrkjeflot et al. (London: Routledge, 2021), 83–101.

12 David Arter, *Scandinavian Politics Today* (Manchester: Manchester University Press, 1999), 147.

13 Arter, *Scandinavian Politics Today*, 147–49.

14 Allan Karker, "Den nordiske model," *Den Store Danske, lex.dk*, Accessed 27 May 2021, https://denstoredanske.lex.dk/den_nordiske_model. See also Knut Heidar, "Comparative Perspectives on the Northern Countries," in *Nordic Politics: Comparative Perspectives*, ed. Knut Heidar, (Oslo: Universitetsforlaget, 2004); Nicholas Aylott, "A Nordic Model of Democracy? Political Representation in Northern Europe," in *Models of Democracy in Nordic and Baltic Europe: Political Institutions and Discourse*, ed. Nicholas Aylott (Farnham: Ashgate, 2014); Mary Hilson, *The Nordic Model: Scandinavia since 1945* (London: Reaktion, 2008). On Nordic gender equality, see Pirjo Markkola's chapter in this volume.

15 Examples include: Dankwart A Rustow, "Scandinavia: Working Multi-Party Systems," in *Modern Political Parties: Approaches to Comparative Politics*, ed. Sigmund Neumann (Chicago: University of Chicago Press, 1956); Nils Andrén, *Government and Politics in the Nordic Countries. Denmark, Finland, Iceland, Norway and Sweden* (Stockholm: Almqvist & Wiksell, 1964); Peter Essaiasson and Knut Heidar, eds., *Beyond Westminster and Congress: The Nordic Experience* (Columbus: Ohio State University Press, 2000).

authors – all academics from British universities – had asked whether the Scandinavian (Nordic) states could be regarded as "a separate species of the West European genus of parliamentary democracies." If they were, could they be classified as "consensual" democracies, in contrast to other more adversarial or confrontational ways of doing politics?[16] Drawing on Arendt Lijphart's work on consensual democracies, Elder, Thomas, and Arter defined the term in terms of a) the broad acceptance of the political system and low levels of opposition to its rules; b) low levels of political conflict; c) a process of public policy making based on consensus and compromise.[17] They found that politics in the Nordic countries largely corresponded to the first two criteria, but in the context of the early 1980s they noted that consensus seemed to be waning with the rise of new political issues and parties. They also questioned the distinctiveness of aspects of policy making in the Nordic context, such as the widespread use of commissions of enquiry.[18]

As reviewer John Logue noted, the notion of consensual democracy functioned here as an analytical "model," against which the empirical realities of the Nordic democracies could be studied. The book's authors also used the term "Nordic political model" to refer to the five-party system of Scandinavian politics. Logue's own textbook on Scandinavian politics, co-authored with fellow US academic Eric Einhorn, appeared in 1989. Einhorn and Logue were interested in analysing the "central policy areas of the Scandinavian model," above all the provision of social services as part of a mixed capitalist economy, or in other words the welfare state. They also posed the question, "is there a Scandinavian democratic model?" analysing the evolution of Scandinavian political institutions and democratic culture in three stages: political democracy, social democracy, and economic democracy. As the book's subtitle suggested, a central thesis was that the "key to the 'Scandinavian model'" was the expansion of the public sector under the stewardship of strong social democratic parties, although the authors also insisted that it was a fallacy to regard the Scandinavian countries as "socialistic."[19]

---

16 Neil Elder, Alastair H Thomas, and David Arter, *The Consensual Democracies? The Government and Politics of the Scandinavian States* (Oxford: Martin Robertson, 1982), 8. See also John Logue, review of *The Consensual Democracies?* by Neil Elder et al., *Scandinavian Studies* 55, no. 3 (Summer 1983).

17 Elder, Thomas, and Arter, *The Consensual Democracies?* 9–11.

18 Elder, Thomas, and Arter, *The Consensual Democracies?*

19 Eric Einhorn and John Logue, *Modern Welfare States: Politics and Policies in Social Democratic Scandinavia* (New York: Praeger, 1989). "Scandinavia" in this book referred to Denmark, Norway, and Sweden.

As with the Nordic political model, the notion of a Nordic welfare model drew on an established tradition of analysing some or all of the Nordic countries as a natural unit in comparative studies, even if such studies were not explicitly theorised as an ideal-type "model."[20] A particularly influential contribution was Gøsta Esping-Andersen's *Three Worlds of Welfare Capitalism* (1990), which was to become the standard reference in the field for a generation.[21] Drawing from a comparison of eighteen welfare states, Esping-Andersen characterized the three Scandinavian countries as a distinctive "social democratic regime," based on the extent to which these countries had decommodified social relations or in other words the extent to which citizens were freed from dependence on the market for their welfare. Through the comprehensive and universal provision of social rights, the welfare state had contributed to forging social relations in Scandinavia that were relatively egalitarian, in contrast to the more stratified systems of the other two "worlds," the liberal Anglo-Saxon countries or the corporatist welfare states of central Europe. The unique feature of the "peculiarly 'Scandinavian model,'" according to Esping-Andersen and Walter Korpi, was "the extent to which social policy has become comprehensive and *institutional.*"[22]

As an ideal type, the Nordic model therefore functioned as a heuristic category for testing the empirical realities of Nordic politics and society, both within the region and in broader comparisons with other units. Used in this way, the term was certainly present in English-language scholarship during the 1980s, implying comparative analyses structured around the question "is there a Nordic model?" Often, the conclusion was that there was not. Writing in 2001, Niels Finn Christensen and Klaus Petersen noted how the Nordic model had become a standard concept in comparative welfare state research, but they coined the phrase "one model – five exceptions" to sum up the historical differences between the five Nordic countries.[23] A decade earlier, sociologist Lars Mjøset had

---

20 For example: George R. Nelson, ed., *Freedom and Welfare: Social Patterns in the Northern Countries of Europe* (Copenhagen: Ministries of Social Affairs of Denmark, Finland, Iceland, Norway, Sweden, 1953); Stein Ringen, "Welfare Studies in Scandinavia," *Scandinavian Political Studies* 9 (1974).

21 Gøsta Esping-Andersen, *The Three Worlds of Welfare Capitalism* (Cambridge: Polity Press, 1990). For an assessment of the significance of Esping-Andersen's study in welfare research see Patrick Emmenegger et al., "*Three Worlds of Welfare Capitalism:* The Making of a Classic," *Journal of European Social Policy* 25, no. 1 (February 2015): 3–13, doi:10.1177/0958928714556966.

22 Gøsta Esping-Andersen and Walter Korpi, "From Poor Relief to Institutional Welfare States: The Development of Scandinavian Social Policy," in *The Scandinavian Model: Welfare States and Welfare Research,* ed. Robert Erikson et al. (Armonk: M E Sharpe, 1987), 42.

23 Niels Finn Christiansen and Klaus Petersen, "Preface," *Scandinavian Journal of History* 26, no. 3 (2001); Mikko Kautto, "The Nordic Countries," in *The Oxford Handbook of the Welfare*

concluded that "comparative research has so far only demonstrated a number of Nordic peculiarities... [which] do not, it seems, form a comprehensive and coherent model with common mechanisms."[24] On the other hand, Mjøset also concluded that the Nordic model could form the basis for a renewal of regional identity at a time of considerable uncertainty for the region. This was an assessment which has shown itself, in retrospect, to be a remarkably accurate prophecy. Ideal types never exist in political vacuums, but are always, in J Magnus Ryner's words, "decisively shaped by pre-understandings and assumptions, that in turn reflect particular social concerns and purposes."[25] The history of the Nordic model as an analytical category cannot be considered independently from more normative understandings of the region, the shared characteristics of which were exportable and worth emulating.

As Mjøset predicted, this use of the Nordic model was to become widespread from the 1990s, but it was also present before then. In reviewing Elder, Thomas, and Arter's study of consensual democracy, John Logue noted how this was a "timely theme, particularly in Thatcher's Britain" of the early 1980s.[26] In 1990, Stein Kuhnle observed that "[t]he so-called 'Scandinavian model' now appears to attract attention from all political corners of the world, particularly from representatives of the failed communist systems of Eastern Europe," for whom Scandinavian social democratic capitalism was more attractive than 'Western capitalism.'[27] Another reviewer of Einhorn and Logue's book argued that Scandinavia "may well serve as a model" in changing times, "with a confused world seeking answers to the riddle of economic and political well being."[28] An early example of a book that referred to "the Nordic model" in its title was an anthology edited by two academics from Scottish universities, which appeared in 1980. Subtitled *Studies in public policy innovation*, the book posed the direct question "What can

---

State, ed. Francis G. Castles et al. (Oxford: Oxford University Press, 2010). An outline of the characteristics of the Nordic welfare model and a summary of the literature on this topic can be found in Niels Finn Christiansen and Pirjo Markkola, "Introduction," in *The Nordic Model of Welfare: A Historical Reappraisal*, ed. Niels Finn Christiansen et al. (Copenhagen: Museum Tusculanum Press, 2006).

24 Lars Mjøset, "The Nordic Model Never Existed, but Does It Have a Future?," *Scandinavian Studies* 64, no. 4 (1992): 663.

25 J. Magnus Ryner, "The Nordic Model: Does It Exist? Can It Survive?," *New Political Economy* 12, no. 1 (March 2007): 64, doi:10.1080/13563460601068644.

26 Logue, review of *The Consensual Democracies?*

27 Stein Kuhnle, review of *Modern Welfare States*, *The Journal of Politics* 52, no. 3 (1990), https://doi.org/10.2307.

28 Charles H Zwicker, review of *Modern Welfare States*, *Presidential Studies Quarterly* 21, no. 1 (1991), 197–98.

we learn from Scandinavian society?" in its opening line. The policy models presented – on topics including the role of women, land ownership, the use of oil revenues, and state support for the arts and media – were based on national examples from across the region.[29] The volume also included a chapter by Clive Archer on "Nordic co-operation: a model for the British Isles," which addressed explicitly the possibility that the Nordic Council could function as a model for relations between the nations of the British Isles, following a decade of conflict in Northern Ireland and an upsurge of nationalism in Scotland and Wales.[30] Tom Nairn's book on the same theme *The Break Up of Britain*, first published in 1977, had also asked rhetorically whether an independent Scotland could be "a candidate for membership of an enlarged Nordic Union?" but argued that it "does not possess the homogeneity of the Scandinavian models."[31]

The Nordic model since the 1990s

The term "Nordic/Scandinavian model" was used in English-language academic scholarship during the 1980s. It functioned as an analytical concept for studying the region with a comparative perspective, most notably in the disciplines of history, political science and welfare studies, and it was also used in the normative sense to refer to elements of Scandinavian policies and politics that were seen as attractive and potentially worthy of emulation, at least in the UK. In this context, references to the Scandinavian or Nordic model were often understood – at least implicitly – as synonyms for the Swedish model.[32]

As discussed in the introduction to this volume, the early 1990s was an important watershed for the Nordic region. External shocks – the end of the Cold War, the fall of the Soviet Union, and a new dynamic phase in European integration – combined with significant domestic changes to challenge ideas of Nordic

---

29 Clive Archer and Stephen Maxwell, eds., *The Nordic Model: Studies in Public Policy Innovation* (Farnborough: Gower, 1980).

30 Clive Archer, "Nordic Co-operation: A Model for the British Isles," in *The Nordic Model: Studies in Public Policy Innovation,* ed. Clive Archer and Stephen Maxwell (Farnborough: Gower, 1980).

31 Tom Nairn, *The Break-up of Britain: Crisis and Neo-Nationalism*, rev. ed. (1977; repr., London: Verso), 182, 193. For a discussion of Nordic models in the context of Scottish devolution debates, see Andrew G. Newby, "'In Building a Nation Few Better Examples Can Be Found': Norden and the Scottish Parliament," *Scandinavian Journal of History* 34, no. 3 (September 2009): 307–329, doi:10.1080/03468750903134749.

32 An example of this is found in Archer and Maxwell, *The Nordic Model,* where the literature cited referred exclusively to Sweden. See also Hellenes, "Tracing the Nordic Model."

exceptionalism. Taking stock of these changed circumstances in 1992, international relations scholar Ole Wæver was not optimistic about the long-term prospects for "Nordicity," suggesting that the Baltic Sea offered a more dynamic alternative for building a regional identity.[33] For Wæver, "the crisis of the Scandinavian or Swedish model" – "Scandinavian or Swedish model" here refers to the social democratic welfare state – was triggered partly by deeper cultural shifts, meaning that, "the Nordic or Swedish model has been hit by the general questioning of modernity and enlightenment values." The attractiveness of the Nordic model was also undermined by the end of the ideological conflict between capitalism and communism, which meant that for the former communist countries of Eastern Europe, the "German model of economy and society" was likely to be more attractive.[34]

Wæver's use of the Nordic model in this context refers to the social democratic welfare state, of which the foremost representative was Sweden. The Social Democratic Party lost the general election of 1991, and the new centre-right coalition government, led by the conservative Moderate Party, explicitly distanced itself from the Nordic model in favour of an agenda of economic reform and European integration. According to Hans Mouritzen, domestic debates focused mainly on the *Swedish* model, while the accompanying rejection of the *Nordic* model was largely a "silent revolution."[35] Mouritzen himself, like Lars Mjøset, remained more sanguine about the continued possibility for the Nordic countries to build a specific regional identity around the Nordic model within an expanding EU.[36]

A decade later there was little evidence that the vision of a revitalized Norden within the EU materialized, with signs instead that the Nordic governments were becoming more reluctant to promote the idea of regional exceptionalism.[37] But at the same time, the use of the term Nordic model to refer to political or social developments in the region became ever more widely used. In the second part of this chapter, we explore how the rhetorics of the Nordic model was ap-

---

33 Ole Wæver, "Nordic Nostalgia: Northern Europe after the Cold War," *International Affairs* 68, no. 1 (January 1992): 77–102, doi:10.2307/2620462.

34 Wæver, "Nordic Nostalgia," 86. In this article Wæver used the terms "Scandinavian model" and "Nordic model" as synonyms.

35 Hans Mouritzen, "The Nordic Model as a Foreign Policy Instrument: Its Rise and Fall," *Journal of Peace Research* 32, no. 1 (February 1995): 14, doi:10.1177/0022343395032001002.

36 Mjøset, "The Nordic Model Never Existed;" Mouritzen, "The Nordic Model as a Foreign Policy Instrument."

37 Christopher S. Browning, "Branding Nordicity: Models, Identity and the Decline of Exceptionalism," *Cooperation and Conflict* 42, no. 1 (March 2007): 27–51, doi:10.1177/0010836707073475.

plied to politics and policy programmes during the 1990s and after, taking recent debates in the UK as a case study.

Britain's "radical centre" and its relationship to the Nordic model

The Third Way

The late 1990s saw a period of resurgence of social democracy in Europe and the creation of a detailed formal framework, typically glossed as the "Third Way." The process of transmission and circulation of Third Way ideas is resistant to any simple chronological narrative, and the Third Way should not be considered a homogenous force across Europe, even though some of its implications were homogenising.[38] Here, the focus will be the development of a new social democratic logic by sociologist Anthony Giddens and its propagation by Tony Blair in the United Kingdom, following the latter's election as leader of the Labour Party in 1994 and the election of the "New Labour" government in 1997.[39] Some of New Labour's ideas were adopted in Europe, including the idea of "radical centrism," which we will return to later in this section.

Third Way thinkers presented their ideas as novel, positioning them ideologically between social democracy and neoliberalism rather than capitalism and communism as previous social science and political models had done. However, Anthony Giddens, the chief intellectual force behind the Third Way, fits comfortably into a tradition of gradualist political interest in the Nordic countries stretching back to the 1930s. Early socialist reformers were concerned as much with co-operatives and agricultural reform as the democratic institutions and welfare systems which would come to characterise later incarnations of the Nordic model.[40]

---

[38] John Callaghan, "Old Social Democracy, New Social Movements and Social Democratic Programmatic Renewal, 1968–2000,' in *Transitions in Social Democracy: Cultural and Ideological Problems of the Golden Age*, ed. John Callaghan and Ilaria Favretto (Manchester: Manchester University Press, 2006), 177–93; Andersson, *The Library and the Workshop*.

[39] Anthony Giddens, *The Third Way and Its Critics* (Cambridge: Polity, 2000), 43; Tony Blair, "Leader's Speech," Blackpool, 1996, British Political Speech, http://www.britishpoliticalspeech.org/speech-archive.htm?speech=202.

[40] Kazimierz Musial, *Roots of the Scandinavian Model: Images of Progress in the Era of Modernisation* (Baden-Baden: Nomos Verlag, 2000); Mary Hilson, "Consumer Co-operation and Economic Crisis: The 1936 Roosevelt Inquiry on Co-operative Enterprise and the Emergence of the

In British political terms, Giddens should be seen as the intellectual heir to a revisionist tradition most associated with Tony Crosland, a Labour MP and minister, whose 1956 book *The Future of Socialism* established Sweden, rather than Scandinavia or Norden, as a place which had achieved the basic goals of socialism. Crosland set out the political goals of socialism as follows:

1) the amelioration of "material poverty and physical squalor"
2) the promotion of general "social welfare" for those oppressed or in need
3) belief in equality and the "classless society," as well as "just" rights for workers, and
4) rejection of "competitive antagonism" and its replacement with the ideals of solidarity and collaboration.[41]

According to Crosland, Sweden had achieved the first and fourth of these goals in the 1940s, a full ten years before Britain, and was well on the way to achieving the second and third in consensual fashion through mechanisms like "joint enterprise councils," public investment, and strict controls on share dividends and reinvestment of profits. This view did not go unchallenged and Crosland's rather uncritical admiration of Sweden led Perry Anderson, a leading thinker of the British New Left, to state that the country was "not so much a normal object of real knowledge as a didactic political fable."[42] Broadly speaking, however, it was Crosland's image of Sweden that prevailed on the Anglophone Left.[43]

While Giddens' articulation of the Third Way sits within this revisionist tradition, it nonetheless breaks from it in important ways. Notably, while Crosland envisioned *Swedish* society as comprised of social and political institutions which intervened in and regulated markets, Giddens envisaged *Nordic* social policy as ameliorating the excesses of basically unregulated free markets. It is therefore characteristic of the period that the Nordic policies of greatest interest to the Labour Party were those which offered social protection in ways which were consistent with free markets.

Nordic 'Middle Way,'" *Contemporary European History* 22, no. 2 (May 2013): 181–98, doi:10.1017/S0960777313000040.

41 C.A.R. Crosland, *The Future of Socialism* (London: Jonathan Cape, 1980), 67.

42 Perry Anderson, "Mr Crosland's Dreamland," *New Left Review* 1, no. 7 (1961): 4.

43 Peter Aimer, "The Strategy of Gradualism and the Swedish Wage-earner Funds," *West European Politics* 8, no. 3 (July 1985): 43–55, doi:10.1080/01402388508424540; Andrew Scott, "Social Democracy in Northern Europe: Its Relevance for Australia," *Australian Review of Public Affairs* 7, no. 1 (2006): 1–17; Andrew Scott, "Looking to Sweden in Order to Reconstruct Australia," *Scandinavian Journal of History* 34, no. 3 (September 2009): 330–352, doi:10.1080/03468750903134756.

This was particularly true of flexicurity: the Danish political economic and labour market reforms of the 1990s and measures to introduce market structures into the British National Health Service (NHS).[44] In his book *The Third Way and Its Critics* Giddens, for example, claimed that:

> the Nordic welfare states have long since concentrated upon active labour market policies, now making a delayed appearance in an Anglo-Saxon context under the label of "welfare to work." Nordic social democracy has been characterised by a willingness to introduce reforms on a pragmatic basis with the aim of finding solutions that are effective.[45]

New Labour's retrenchment of unemployment payments was, according to Giddens, as much influenced by Swedish and Danish approaches to the labour market as they were by the US Democrats' attacks on "welfare queens."[46] Formally, the Nordic states functioned as a place where the problems facing industrial societies had already been solved through innovative political economic and welfare policy. The Nordic "pragmatic" approach to this policy captured the essence of Giddens' and Ulrich Beck's shared framework of "reflexive modernization."

Perhaps the most significant innovation was the gradual association of market ideas with the Nordic countries, especially Sweden. Large portions of New Labour's policy on health and social care were articulated in terms of Swedish and Danish public health care systems. This was primarily achieved by positioning the Nordic systems as sites of consumer choice. The Department for Health's 2002 *Delivering the NHS Plan*, for example, noted that "[I]n Sweden and Denmark patients have access to information on waiting times and options for treatment, and patients who have been waiting for treatment have the choice of an alternative provider."[47] This served the immediate strategic imperative of defending a taxation-funded health care model, which could simultaneously accommodate market structures; its association with Sweden and Denmark made it seem modern and pragmatic.

---

44 Jeremy Laurance, "Bed Blocking the Scandinavian Solution," *The Independent*, 19 April 2002; Patricia Hewitt, "Investment and Reform: Transforming Health and Healthcare," Annual health and social care lecture, 13 December, 2005, transcript, The National Archives, https://webarchive.nationalarchives.gov.uk/ukgwa/20100408103750/http://www.dh.gov.uk/en/MediaCentre/Speeches/Speecheslist/DH_4124484.

45 Giddens, The Third Way and Its Critics (Cambridge: Polity, 2000), 17.

46 Giddens, *The Third Way*, 30–31.

47 Department of Health, *Delivering the NHS Plan: Next Steps on Investment Next Steps on Reform*, April 2002. https://webarchive.nationalarchives.gov.uk/ukgwa/20130107105354/http://www.dh.gov.uk/prod_consum_dh/groups/dh_digitalassets/@dh/@en/@ps/documents/digitalasset/dh_118524.pdf.

This association of market-based health reform with the Nordic countries continued into the late 2000s.[48] Patricia Hewitt, Health Secretary during the third Blair government 2005–2007, approvingly quoted the Social Democratic slogan from the Göran Persson era, "proud, but not satisfied," arguing that this reflected the new natural state of Labour government.[49] Ironically, this slogan was considered unimaginative and complacent in Sweden.[50] However, from the perspective of the Labour government, adopting Nordic political solutions – with reference to well-established social democratic rhetoric about Sweden and Norden – offered a potential means of justifying otherwise controversial policies. By domesticating Swedish marketization policies and subsuming them within British political logics, New Labour had missed the change in public sentiment in Sweden, away from Social Democratic modes of government.

The Nordic countries were thus the "social laboratories" from earlier eras, now considered experiments in the application of market solutions to the problems of "globalised" societies. Of all the Nordic countries, Sweden in particular featured in this rhetoric, despite its relatively late and partial move towards marketization, compared to, say, Norway. Politically, these earlier models had been underwritten by a hegemonic social democracy which could efface the social tensions and antagonisms of Swedish and Nordic societies. In the aftermath of the financial crisis of 1991–92 and the efforts of the Bildt government (in office 1991–94) to contest the meaning of "Swedish" and "Nordic," these signifiers began to acquire new meanings. The weakening of the social democratic hegemony was an opportunity for new articulations of Sweden and Norden to develop, which were more amenable to free-market policy programmes, both domestically and abroad.

Liberal conservative centrism

The adoption of "radical centrism" in the early 2000s by the Swedish Moderate Party therefore makes significant sense. The foundational strategic arguments of Blair's Third Way rested on a calculation that the Conservative Party was the

---

48 Tom Hoctor, "Beveridge or Bismarck? Choosing the Nordic Model in British Healthcare Policy 1997–c.2015," in *Making and Circulation of the Nordic Model*, ed. Haldor Byrkjeflot et al. (London: Routledge, 2021), 209–228.
49 Patricia Hewitt, "Creating a Patient-Led NHS: The Next Steps Forward" (speech), 10 January, 2006, transcript, The National Archives, http://webarchive.nationalarchives.gov.uk/20130107105354/http://www.dh.gov.uk/en/MediaCentre/Speeches/Speecheslist/DH_4126499.
50 Andersson, *The Library and the Workshop*, 150–51.

dominant force in British politics. Any attempt to win office meant accepting the basic small "c" conservatism of the British electorate. For Fredrik Reinfeldt, leader of the Moderate Party 2003–2015, the same basic situation held, but with social democracy the hegemonic political force. Where Blair embraced the individualism and economic policies of the Thatcher era, Reinfeldt focused on labour market exclusion among Sweden's young and migrant populations and focused on jobs,[51] even going so far as to brand the Moderates as "the new worker's party" [det nya arbetarpartiet].[52] This was a sharp contrast from some of the positions Reinfeldt had adopted in the early 1990s, during the era of the Bildt government.[53] The liberal conservative Alliance for Sweden [Alliansen] won the 2006 election on this platform.

David Cameron became leader of the UK Conservative Party in 2005 and quite explicitly imitated Reinfeldt's tack to the centre, adopting much of the same strategic logic as New Labour and the Moderates. This included embracing social justice and ecological issues, in his so-called "hug a hoodie" and "hug a huskie" campaigns, much to the chagrin of social democrats and Conservative Thatcherites.[54] This was also the era of "Compassionate Conservatism," which later became the "Big Society" agenda. Indeed, taking a cue from the Moderates, the Conservatives branded themselves "the worker's party" from 2014 in the lead-up to the 2015 General Election.[55]

As well as the shared political strategies, there were also emergent links between the two parties during this era. In 2008, Fredrik Reinfeldt gave a speech to

---

51 Christine Agius, "Sweden's 2006 Parliamentary Election and after: Contesting or Consolidating the Swedish Model?," *Parliamentary Affairs* 60, no. 4 (2007): 585–600, doi:10.1093/pa/gsm041.

52 "Det nya arbetarpartiet är moderat nyspråk," *Aftonbladet*, 20 July, 2006, https://www.aftonbladet.se/ledare/a/zLAnrw/det-nya-arbetarpartiet-ar-moderat-nysprak; Dimitris Tsarouhas, *Social Democracy in Sweden: The Threat from a Globalized World* (London: Tauris Academic Studies, 2008), 176.

53 Fredrik Reinfeldt, *Det sovande folket*, ed. Christer Söderberg and Per Schlingmann (Stockholm: Rätt Blankett & Trycksaksproduktion AB, 1993).

54 Gaby Hinsliff, "Cameron Softens Crime Image in 'Hug a Hoodie' Call," *The Guardian*, 9 July, 2006, https://www.theguardian.com/politics/2006/jul/09/conservatives.ukcrime; George Jones, "Cameron Turns Blue to Prove Green Credentials," *The Daily Telegraph*, 21 April, 2006, https://www.telegraph.co.uk/news/uknews/1516276/Cameron-turns-blue-to-prove-green-credentials.html; Ruth Lister and Fran Bennett, "The new 'champion of progressive ideals'? Cameron's Conservative Party: poverty, family policy and welfare reform," *Renewal* 18, no. 1/2 (2010): 84–109.

55 James Frayne, "The Conservatives Are Now the True Worker's Party," *The Daily Telegraph*, 15 May, 2015, https://www.telegraph.co.uk/news/politics/conservative/11605411/The-Conservatives-are-now-the-true-workers-party.html.

the London School of Economics (LSE) for which David Cameron was a discussant. This, in particular, made explicit the similarity between the way the two leaders had styled themselves. Reinfeldt set the tone of his speech with a self-deprecating joke: when he was at school, he was taught that Sweden was the only world superpower with just nine million inhabitants.[56] The anecdote though contained a serious kernel since it positioned Reinfeldt to reject the idea of a Swedish model. If there ever were "aspirations of a modelling kind," he claimed, it was not a Swedish but a Scandinavian model, and, in any case, the relevance of model-building had been undermined by the process of globalisation.[57] In other words, the most that could be achieved was regulatory inspiration, rather than any visionary political or social programme.

This represented a significant departure from the rhetoric of the Social Democrats, who had always maintained the opposite, even during the era of the Third Way. Göran Persson memorably urged those interested in Sweden to study "the flight of the bumblebee, rather than the beating of its wings."[58] This idea was taken up by other Swedish social democratic politicians in British political networks, notably Pär Nuder, a former Social Democratic Finance Minister and Katrine Kielos, a journalist and commentator.[59] Moreover, argued Reinfeldt, despite its domestic and international reputation, the high era of the Swedish model – the 1950s to the 1970s – was not a time of success, but a "mad quarter of a century." This shared characteristics with rhetoric used in the 1990s by the Bildt government, but it also staked a claim to a different vision of Sweden as part of a Scandinavian or Nordic model, rather than as a regional leader with a claim to a universalising social democratic discourse. The Moderates could therefore legitimately claim that Sweden was bound by participation in the global economic system and moreover that Sweden's fundamental success should be located in the pre-social democratic era as a consequence of the rule of law, property rights, and so on. Strategically speaking, this also set a tone for Cameron's deployment of the idea of the "Broken Society" later the same year.[60]

---

56 Fredrik Reinfeldt, "The New Swedish Model: A Reform Agenda for Growth and the Environment." Speech at London School of Economics, 26 February 2008. Regeringskansliet, https://www.regeringen.se/49bb53/contentassets/b9cf14e1905b4bc2af652bdfc89e7ae9/tal-2006–2010—fredrik-reinfeldt (London: London School of Economics, 2008).

57 Reinfeldt, The New Swedish Model.

58 Persson quoted in Peter Lindert, "The Welfare State Is the Wrong Target: A Reply to Bergh," *Econ Journal Watch* 3, no. 2 (2006): 237.

59 Pär Nuder, *Saving the Swedish Model* (London: Institute for Public Policy Research, 2012); Katrine Kielos, "Flight of the Swedish Bumblebee," *Renewal* 117, no. 2 (2009): 61–66.

60 David Cameron, "Fixing Our Broken Society" (speech), Glasgow, 2008, Conservative Speeches, https://conservative-speeches.sayit.mysociety.org/speech/599630.

Perhaps the Moderates' most audacious attempt to re-articulate the Nordic countries was in the *Nordic Way* pamphlet, submitted to the World Economic Forum in Davos in 2011.[61] Despite its Nordic focus, the pamphlet was developed by the Swedish government, further developing the idea of a Nordic region, rather than a Swedish model. The principal economic claims made in the report were twofold. Firstly, that financial crises in the Nordic states had created a collectivity of individual responses which focused on budgetary, fiscal, and monetary discipline.[62] In contrast to earlier articulations of the Swedish model as unaffected by global economic conditions, *The Nordic Way* portrayed the Nordic countries as exposed to the "economic cycle," but capable of ameliorating the consequences of busts by way of orthodox financial measures taken in difficult circumstances. The second claim characterised the Nordic countries as open and flexible, hostile to protectionism, with limited regulations, buttressed by strong public welfare systems which socialise the risks of their flexible labour markets.[63]

This echoed the arguments made by Reinfeldt at the LSE in 2008, but it also masked a highly contested understanding of the Nordic model, which was fiercely disputed by the Social Democrats.[64] Despite this, it was remarkably successful in UK political discourse, partly as a result of the growing association of the Nordic states with markets, but also in its attempt to situate a form of "Nordic capitalism" which possessed "fundamental coherence and vitality."[65] This appealed to liberal conservative figures in the UK who had been trying for some time to create coherent policies which satisfied the need for social solidarity as well as allowing intervention from non-governmental actors. Notably, the "Compassionate Conservativism" and "Big Society" agendas were attempts to achieve this, though both were ultimately failures.[66]

The Conservative Universal Credit and Free Schools policies were explicitly modelled on Nordic ideas. Free Schools ideas had been mooted within the Con-

---

61 Klas Eklund, Henrik Berggren, and Lars Trägårdh, *The Nordic Way: Shared Norms for the New Reality* (Davos: World Economic Forum, 2011).
62 Eklund, Berggren, and Trägårdh, *The Nordic Way*, 5–11.
63 Eklund, Berggren, and Trägårdh, *The Nordic Way*, 9–11.
64 Göran Eriksson, "Slaget om Norden," *Svenska Dagbladet*, 9 February 2012, https://www.svd.se/slaget-om-norden.
65 Eklund, Berggren, and Trägårdh, *The Nordic Way*, 22.
66 Tom Hoctor, "Coming to Terms with the Market: Accounts of Neoliberal Failure and Rehabilitation on the British Right," *British Politics* Online First (June 2020) 1–16. doi: 10.1057/s41293–020–00141–9.

servative Party and various affiliated and non-affiliated policy organs since the late 1990s.[67] A particular attraction of the policy was the potential for the involvement of independent for-profit school chains such as *Kunskapsskolan AB*, which had been involved in advocating for private for-profit school ownership in the UK since the New Labour era. The adoption of the policy by the Conservatives and its positioning as a centrist policy could be seen, in a sense, as the culmination of a project aligning Cameron's Conservatives with Reinfeldt's Moderates in the "radical centre." It could be considered the most important rhetorical success of the centre-right version of the Nordic model.

Conclusions

The Nordic model is undoubtedly a key concept in the rhetorics of Nordicness, but the meanings of the model are highly contested. The term became established during the 1980s, at least in English-speaking contexts, when it was used mostly by academics to refer to political systems and welfare policies shaped by the influence of social democracy. The Nordic or Scandinavian model was often synonymous with the Swedish model, based on the electoral dominance of the Swedish Social Democratic Party. The early 1990s was a watershed for the Nordic region and for social democratic parties alike, leading to proclamations of the end of the Nordic model from some quarters. The term did not disappear; rather it has become ever more prevalent in academic and political debates, while at the same time its meanings are ever more contested.

As an analytical term the Nordic model continued to function as an ideal type for comparative analysis. For some, the model could only be referred to in the past tense, as a category which described the social and political structures of previous decades. "It is hard to avoid the conclusion that a very distinct Nordic model of party politics no longer exists," wrote Erik Allardt in 2000, though he assessed the "Nordic model of social and welfare policy" to be weaker but still distinct.[68] For others, this pessimism was unjustified, as analyses of the

---

67 Linda Rönnberg, "Marketization on Export: Representations of the Swedish Free School Model in English Media," *European Educational Research Journal* 14, no. 6 (November 2015): 549–65, doi:10.1177/1474904115610782.

68 Erik Allardt, "A Political Sociology of the Nordic Countries," *European Review* 8, no. 1 (February 2000): 129–141, doi:10.1017/S1062798700004634. Jan-Erik Lane and colleagues wrote in 1993 that, "The Scandinavian model *was* a regulative notion comprising a set of concepts and ideas about what is good government in a wide sense, as well as about the proper way of structuring the public sector, and connecting the public and private lives of the population" [empha-

Nordic political or welfare model revealed that the impact of the changes of the 1990s remained fairly limited, and that many aspects of the Nordic model remained intact.[69] Since 2000, the impression is of a tendency to emphasize the need for a more nuanced picture of the Nordic region, which highlights the differences between the countries and plays down their exceptionalism in comparison with other regions.[70] But as an ideal type, the "Nordic model" continued to function as a starting point for such comparative analyses.[71]

Even as the model was questioned, there was simultaneously a proliferation in the meanings attached to the term: *the* Nordic model became Nordic *models*. In the third and substantially revised edition of his *Scandinavian Politics Today*, published in 2016, David Arter identified no fewer than six Nordic models: the party system, political representation, government and policy-making, welfare, parliamentarianism, and regional co-operation. Arter concluded that any one of these variants of the Nordic model remained "a useful organising concept" for comparative analyses of the region, but he suggested that the last – regional co-operation – was the most convincing.[72] In other words, as "traditional" Nordic models of the welfare state and social democratic politics were questioned, new ones emerged to take their place. Examples include a Nordic model of gen-

sis added]. Jan-Erik Lane et al., "Scandinavian Exceptionalism Reconsidered," *Journal of Theoretical Politics* 5, no. 2 (April 1993): 197, doi:10.1177/0951692893005002003..

69 E. g. David Arter, "Party System Change in Scandinavia since 1970: 'Restricted Change' or 'General Change'?," *West European Politics* 22, no. 3 (1 July 1999): 139–58, doi:10.1080/01402389908425319; Virpi Timonen, *Restructuring the Welfare State: Globalization and Social Policy Reform in Finland and Sweden* (Cheltenham: Edward Elgar, 2003); Torben M. Andersen, "Challenges to the Scandinavian Welfare Model," *European Journal of Political Economy* 20, no. 3 (September 2004): 743–54, doi:10.1016/j.ejpoleco.2004.02.007; Mikko Kautto et al., eds., *Nordic Welfare States in the European Context* (London: Routledge, 2001); Stein Kuhnle, "The Scandinavian Welfare State in the 1990s: Challenged but Viable," *West European Politics* 23, no. 2 (April 2000): 209–228, doi:10.1080/01402380008425373.

70 Kautto, "The Nordic Countries"; Kasper M. Hansen and Karina Kosiara-Pedersen, "Nordic Voters and Party Systems," in *The Routledge Handbook of Scandinavian Politics*, ed. Peter Nedergaard and Anders Wivel (New York: Routledge, 2017), 122; Åsa Bengtsson et al., *The Nordic Voter: Myths of Exceptionalism* (Colchester: ECPR Press, 2014).

71 For an example see: Guðmundur Jónsson, "Iceland and the Nordic Model of Consensus Democracy," *Scandinavian Journal of History* 39, no. 4 (8 August 2014): 510–28, doi:10.1080/03468755.2014.935473.

72 Arter, *Scandinavian Politics Today*, 11–12. Arter also noted that these political models had been defined by Nordic political scientists, not outsiders. See also Johan Strang, "Introduction: The Nordic Model of Transnational Cooperation?" in *Nordic Cooperation: A European Region in Transition*, ed. Johan Strang (London: Routledge, 2016), doi:10.4324/9781315755366–1.

der equality or marriage;[73] Nordic models of peace and diplomacy;[74] a Nordic model of citizenship;[75] and a Nordic model of economic management – the latter frequently concerned with the apparent paradox of strong competitiveness in highly regulated economies.[76]

These changing meanings reflect the way in which the Nordic model became decoupled from its associations with the electoral success of social democratic parties. Put another way, where it might once have been common to refer to the Nordic model *as* social democracy, in the 2010s there were examples of the Nordic model *of* social democracy, among other political understandings of the model.[77] This also implied a temporal shift in the understanding of the roots of the model. The Nordic model was now considered the outcome not exclusively of social democratic policies in the post-war era but of a longer historical tradition. In this tradition, the "Nordic model" could refer to a distinctive political culture rooted in the early modern period, influenced especially by the Lutheran Reformation and its legacies for state organisation.[78] For example, historians Pasi Ihalainen and Karin Sennefelt presented their 2011 study of Scandinavian politics in the late eighteenth-century age of revolution as "an alternative story of an incipient transition towards modernity, a 'Nordic model' in which radical change takes place within an apparent continuity of the established order, without open revolution."[79]

---

73 Lauri Karvonen and Per Selle, *Women in Nordic Politics: Closing the Gap* (Aldershot: Dartmouth, 1995); Kari Melby et al., "The Nordic Model of Marriage," *Women's History Review* 15, no. 4 (September 2006): 651–61, doi:10.1080/09612020500530851.

74 In his introduction to an edited volume on "Nordic Peace," Clive Archer had a section called "Lessons learned," suggesting that a "Nordic model" of peace may be relevant to the EU. Clive Archer, "Introduction," in *The Nordic Peace*, ed. Clive Archer and Pertti Joenniemi (Aldershot: Ashgate, 2003); Martin Marcussen, "Scandinavian Models of Diplomacy," in *The Routledge Handbook of Scandinavian Politics*, ed. Peter Nedergaard and Anders Wivel (New York: Routledge, 2017).

75 Bengtsson et al. *The Nordic Voter.*

76 Sören Blomquist and Karl Moene, "The Nordic Model," in "The Nordic Model," edited by Soren Blomquist and Karl Moene, special issue, *Journal of Public Economics* 127 (1 July 2015): 1–2. doi:10.1016/j.jpubeco.2015.04.007; Darius Ornston, *Good Governance Gone Bad. How Nordic Adaptability Leads to Success* (Ithaca: Cornell University Press, 2018).

77 Nik Brandal, Øivind Bratberg and Dag Einar Thorsen, *The Nordic Model of Social Democracy* (Basingstoke: Palgrave Macmillan, 2013).

78 See, for example, chapter two of Uffe Østergård, *Hvorhen Europa?* (København: Djøf forlag, 2018).

79 Pasi Ihalainen and Karin Sennefelt, "General Introduction," in *Scandinavia in the Age of Revolution: Nordic Political Cultures 1740–1820*, ed. Pasi Ihalainen et al. (Farnham: Ashgate, 2011), 7.

Taken to extremes, this suggested an understanding of the Nordic model as the description of a highly specific regional culture, which was thus not available for emulation elsewhere.[80] The authors of the pamphlet, presented to the World Economic Forum in 2011, referred to the "Nordic way," and explicitly warned readers that they were not describing "a free-floating Nordic model that can be applied to other countries."[81] Rather, Nordic exceptionalism was rooted in cultural specificity that meant it was impossible to export.[82] From the mid-2000s centre-right politicians in Sweden began to assert the idea of Nordic distinctiveness and gradually also to adopt the term Nordic model, based on competitiveness, pragmatism and constant reform.[83] Carl Marklund has suggested that for centre-right politicians in Sweden, references to a *Nordic* model were a means to distance themselves from a Swedish model that was too strongly identified with social democracy.[84] In response, the Swedish Social Democratic Party applied in 2012 to the Swedish Patent and Registration office to claim their ownership of the term "Nordic model," and the Nordic Labour Movement Co-operation Committee (SAMAK) produced its own statement on the Nordic model in 2014.[85] Meanwhile in Scotland, campaigners on the "yes" and "no"

---

80 Nina Witoszek and Atle Midttun, "Sustainable Modernity and the Architecture of the 'Well-Being Society': Interdisciplinary Perspectives," in *Sustainable Modernity: The Nordic Model and Beyond*, ed. Nina Witoszek and Atle Midttun (London: Routledge, 2018), 1–17.

81 Henrik Berggren and Lars Trägårdh, "Social trust and radical individualism: The paradox at the heart of Nordic capitalism," in *The Nordic Way*, 13.

82 The point about the specific cultural context of the Nordic countries was cited by foreign commentators too: see for example Madeleine Bunting, "We may admire the Nordic way, but don't try to import it," *The Guardian*, August 15, 2008. See also Lars Trägårdh, "Swedish Model or Swedish Culture?," *Critical Review* 4, no. 4 (September 1990): 585, doi:10.1080/08913819008459622. Lars Trägårdh, "Statist Individualism: On the Culturality of the Nordic Welfare State," in *The Cultural Construction of Norden*, ed. Øystein Sørensen and Bo Stråth (Oslo: Universitetsforlaget, 1997); Lars Trägårdh, "Mellem liberalism og socialisme: Om det særlige ved den nordiske model," *Kritik* 45, no. 206 (2012).

83 See also Martin Ågerup, "Hvad er den nordiske model egentlig?," *Politiken*, October 15, 2011. Ågerup was director of the independent liberal think tank CEPOS.

84 Carl Marklund, "The Nordic Model on the Global Market of Ideas: The Welfare State as Scandinavia's Best Brand," *Geopolitics* 22, no. 3 (July 2017): 623–39, doi:10.1080/14650045.2016.1251906.

85 SAMAK, *The Sørmarka Declaration: We Build the Nordics*, SAMAK, November 2014, http://www.samak.info/wp-content/uploads/2015/11/Sormarka-declaration_English.pdf. See also, Nordiska ministerrådet, *Den nordiska modellen i en ny tid: Program för Sveriges ordförandeskap i Nordiska ministerrådet 2013*, 2013, http://www.regeringen.se/contentassets/9cec796705ac45aba8c5284eb55aab52/den-nordiska-modellen-i-en-ny-tid--program-for-sveriges-ordforandeskap-i-nordiska-ministerradet-2013. The Social Democratic Party's application for copyright was challenged by the Nordic Council, which argued that "[t]he Nordic model is a general Nordic posses-

sides of the 2014 independence referendum referred to a social democratic Nordic model, echoing earlier references to the Nordic region in the devolution debates of the late 1970s and after.[86]

These domestic struggles over the meaning of the Nordic model were mirrored in the UK, where the term was debated. While for Blair and Giddens, Nordic policies had served as inspiration for a revitalized "New Labour" party as part of a wider European discussion of the "Third Way" in the 1990s, Conservative politicians including David Cameron cited aspects of the Nordic model as inspirational for their own politics, both in opposition and in government from 2010. This is not to imply of course that the model was simply imported. The relationship between the Swedish Moderates and the British Conservatives did not necessitate the articulation of a political or policy programme which resembled the Nordic countries. Just as the Third Way was a highly decentred force with different responses to the central contradictions of social democracy, the same could also be said of liberal-conservative "radical centrism." Whereas Reinfeldt's commitment to a growth agenda was explicitly articulated as a means to achieve full employment – a fundamentally social democratic goal – Cameron's central agenda was less clearly asserted. However, the logic of the Conservatives' austerity policy suggests that in practice the goal was counter inflationary. In other words, despite the formal similarities, it would be a mistake to think that there had been a total re-alignment of goals between the Moderates and the Conservatives. Nonetheless, as with the "middle way" debate of the 1930s, this example shows how recent constructions of the Nordic model have been formed in a complicated interaction between auto- and xenostereotypes.

A model is something that can be learned from and possibly transferred. It is one of the ways in which international comparisons are used to shape the search for new ideas and policies.[87] This points to what Pauli Kettunen has highlighted as the paradox of the Nordic model: the model is threatened by the challenges of

---

sion... and part of the political heritage for the whole of Norden and its inhabitants." "Nordiska Rådet: Vi tänker inte sluta använda 'Nordiska Modellen,'" Nordiska Rådet, accessed November 26, 2020, https://www.norden.org/no/node/4004.

86 On the debates in Scotland see Newby, "In Building a Nation"; Michael Keating and Malcolm Harvey, *Small Nations in a Big World: What Scotland Can Learn* (Edinburgh: Luath Press, 2014); Malcolm Harvey, "A Social Democratic Future? Political and Institutional Hurdles in Scotland," *The Political Quarterly* 86, no. 2 (April 2015): 249–56, doi:10.1111/1467–923X.12155.

87 Pauli Kettunen and Klaus Petersen, "Introduction: Rethinking Welfare State Models" and Pauli Kettunen, "The Transnational Construction of National Challenges: The Ambiguous Nordic Model of Welfare and Competitiveness," in *Beyond Welfare State Models: Transnational Historical Perspectives on Social Policy,* ed. Pauli Kettunen and Klaus Petersen (Cheltenham: Edward Elgar, 2011).

globalization, but it is also a means to respond to those challenges in a competitive international world.[88] During the early part of the 2010s, this could be presented as a conflict between the social democratic interpretation of the Nordic model as something fixed and needing to be defended against external threats, and centre-right claims that the Nordic model was not connected to any fixed ideologies and could therefore serve as inspiration for necessary reforms. References to "threats" were found not only on the political left – expressed, for example, in the trade unions' fears of attempts to undermine collective wage agreements. The right also claimed that the Nordic model was threatened, by multiculturalism and the undermining of common cultural values.[89]

Understandings of the Nordic model have clearly changed over time, but of course they also vary in different contexts. Despite the overtly political meanings that seem to be attached to the Nordic model, the concept is also still widely used in academic research, though its meanings have become fragmented. There is thus inevitably a danger that we are creating the object of our own research, and unpicking the fluctuating meanings of the Nordic model thus requires considerable critical reflexivity on the part of researchers.

---

88 Pauli Kettunen, "The Power of International Comparison: A Perspective on the Making and Challenging of the Nordic Welfare State," in *The Nordic Model of Welfare*, ed. Christiansen et al.; Kettunen, "The Transnational Construction."
89 See for example, Lars Trier Mogensen, "Fogh frelste den nordiske model," *Politiken*, September 5, 2009. Asle Toje of the Norwegian Progress Party praised former Danish prime minister Anders Fogh Rasmussen for "saving" the Nordic model from "cultural radicalism" and multiculturalism.

Johan Strang

The Rhetoric of Nordic Cooperation: From the *Other* Europe to the *Better* Europe?

Introduction

Despite the recent surge in rhetoric of (New) Nordicness, the term "Nordic cooperation" continues to evoke a mixture of feelings among most people in the region. On the one hand, the term refers almost unconditionally positively to the
special kinship associated with the idea of *Norden* as a cultural, linguistic,
and historical community, and as such it involves a strong sense of normative
obligation. On the other hand, "Nordic cooperation" implies a sense of impotence and irrelevance, relating to the primacy of the transatlantic security regime
and the European economic and political frameworks. A similar tension is also
present in scholarship, which tends to build on pre-determined narratives of Nordic cooperation either as a remarkable success in creating a transnational community, or as a series of failures to formalise cooperation in economic or security
policy.[1] This chapter explores the political struggles to define Nordic cooperation
from the 1950s until today. It will show that the tension between obligation and
impotence has been an enduring part in the rhetoric of Nordic cooperation, but
also that the criteria for success and failure, and indeed the meaning of *Norden*
has changed through time.

   The chapter analyses the debates of the annual sessions of the Nordic Council (NC), focusing primarily on periods of formative importance in negotiating the
tasks and limitations of official Nordic cooperation: the first years of the NC after
its establishment in 1952, the (collapsed) plans for a Nordic customs union
around 1960 and again a decade later, the EU debates during the first half of
the 1990s, and the rise of "the Nordic brand" in the new millennium. A key feature at all these junctures was the omnipresence of "Europe" in the background
of the discussions. "Europe," "European cooperation," "the European Economic
Community (EEC)," or, since the late 1980s and 1990s, "European integration"
and "the European Union (EU)," were for a long time all seen as competitors
to Nordic cooperation, legitimising it and pushing it forward. At the same time

---

1 For a recent discussion of this literature see my "Introduction: The Nordic model of transnational cooperation," in *Nordic Cooperation: A European region in transition*, ed. Johan Strang
(London: Routledge, 2016); Anne Elizabeth Stie and Jarle Trondal, eds., "Rediscovering Nordic
cooperation," special issue, *Politics and Governance* 8 (2020).

European integration also constituted a massive gravitational force whose movements had huge repercussions for Nordic cooperation even before Denmark joined the EEC in 1973 and Finland and Sweden joined the EU in 1995.[2]

Following the terminology of Reinhart Koselleck, "Nordic cooperation" and "European integration" can be analysed as "asymmetric counter-concepts."[3] The rhetoric of Nordic cooperation and European integration was never an antithetical juxtaposition of two equally distinguishable units. Instead, Nordic cooperation was defined through an indeterminate other, associated with a number of vague and usually quite negative attributes. "Europe" served as the supranational, utopian, bureaucratic, capitalist, conservative, or elitist other, which was used to portray Nordic cooperation as democratic, pragmatic, progressive, and socially responsible. Yet, it would be misleading to claim that the discussions at the NC were marked by a general anti-European sentiment; on the contrary, the NC attracted internationally oriented MPs, many of whom were decidedly in favour of European cooperation already in the 1950s. The point of the asymmetrical juxtaposition was to negotiate the relationship between the Nordic and the European frameworks, to bolster the idea of *Norden* as a cultural and political community, as well as to legitimise the NC as an institution.

The rhetoric of Nordic cooperation and European integration was also asymmetric in the sense that the one (*Norden*) in most conventional definitions was understood as part of the other (Europe). The relation between *Norden* and Europe was under constant negotiation, but the 1990s represented a major turning point. The Maastricht Treaty and the European Union were debated across the region, initially reigniting the historical opposition between Nordic cooperation and European integration. Eventually, however, *Norden* was absorbed by Europe, not least as Finland and Sweden joined the EU in 1995. In the new millennium, therefore, many of the old narratives of Nordic cooperation had lost their foundation. Gradually, however, a new rhetoric of Nordicness was invented, which relied less on the European other, but also less on notions of transnational cooperation.

---

2 Thorsten Borring Olesen and Johan Strang, "European challenge to Nordic institutional cooperation: past, present and future," in *Nordic cooperation: A European region in transition*, ed. Johan Strang (London: Routledge, 2016), doi:10.4324/9781315755366–2; Bo Stråth, "The Swedish image of Europe as the other," in *Europe and the other and Europe as the other*, ed. Bo Stråth (Wien: PIE Lang, 2010).

3 Reinhart Koselleck, "The historical-political semantics of asymmetric counter-concepts," in *Futures past: on the semantics of historical time*, trans. Keith Tribe (1979; New York: Columbia, 2004), 155–91; see also Kirill Postoutenko and Kay Junge, eds., *Asymmetrical concepts after Reinhart Koselleck: Historical semantics and beyond* (Bielefeld: transcript Verlag, 2011).

This chapter focuses on the development of two related tropes in the rhetoric of Nordic cooperation. The first half of the chapter explores how the idea of Nordic cooperation as a more democratic and "popular" form of international collaboration than European integration emerged during the first decades of the NC, and how this trope was turned into a celebration of the "flexibility" of Nordic cooperation, and of the close, trusting, personal connections between leading Nordic politicians in the integrating Europe of the post-Cold War period. The second half of the chapter analyses the emergence of the idea of Nordic cooperation as evolving primarily around a culturally, linguistically, and historically founded community and describes how the turn towards branding in the new millennia transformed Nordic culture and welfare into examples of European excellence that were used on the global markets. Together, the two parts of the chapter make the argument that there in the new millennium seems to be more use for "the Nordic" as a pre-existing natural quality of the peoples and products of the region, than of *Norden* as a political community of five nations, which is why the recent wave of Nordic rhetoric has so far failed to bolster Nordic cooperation.

Nordic cooperation and the Nordic Council

The history of Nordic cooperation is usually dated back to the bourgeoning trans-Nordic networks among professionals and voluntary associations in the wake of the Scandinavist movement at the end of the 19th century. Of special importance were the Nordic Lawyers' meetings, arranged regularly since 1872 with the aim of harmonising legislation and creating a common Nordic legal culture.[4] The NC, founded in 1952, grew out of the gradual intensification of the political relations between the Nordic countries during the inter-war period, intense debates on Nordic unification during the Second World War, as well as a general push for regional cooperation and alignment in Western Europe in the emerging Cold War setting.[5] The immediate post-war period saw many Nordic initiatives: a

---

4 Ruth Hemstad, *Fra Indian Summer til nordisk vinter: Skandinavisk samarbeid, skandinavisme og unionsoppløsningen* (Oslo: Akademisk publisering, 2008); Pia Letto-Vanamo and Ditlev Tamm, "Cooperation in the field of law," in *Nordic Cooperation: A European region in transition*, ed. Johan Strang (London: Routledge, 2016), doi:10.4324/9781315755366–5.
5 Jan A. Andersson, "1950-talet: tid att så – tid att skörda," in *Norden i sick-sack: Tre spårbyten inom nordiskt samarbete*, ed. Bengt Sundelius and Claes Wiklund (Stockholm: Santérus, 2000); Franz Wendt, *Cooperation in the Nordic Countries: achievements and obstacles* (Stockholm: Nordic Council, 1981), 33–36.

Nordic Culture Commission was founded in 1946 and discussions on a Nordic customs union began in 1947. Following the Prague coup in February 1948, there were also prestigious negotiations on a Scandinavian defence union, which ultimately broke down in January 1949 when Norway (and then Denmark) decided to join NATO.

According to a common interpretation, the NC was founded as a compensation for the failure of the Scandinavian defence union, and precisely like the defence union – and the Scandinavist movement a century before – it was primarily a Danish-Swedish initiative. Hans Hedtoft, the Danish Social Democratic leader and Prime Minister for the periods 1947–50 and 1953–55, served as a political driving force, and the Swedish Conservative MP and lawyer Nils Herlitz drafted the founding documents. It has been speculated that Hedtoft's interest in Nordic cooperation was motivated by an urge to associate his party with the success of the Swedish Social Democrats, and certainly, the Nordic labour movements had already established strong relations before the war.[6] But *Nordism* was undoubtedly a catch-all ideology at the time, with the Nordic Associations attracting high membership figures across the political spectrum in Denmark and Sweden. Among Norwegian conservatives and farmers there was, however, a lingering suspicion that Nordic cooperation was a tool for Danish or Swedish imperialistic ambitions, and a majority of non-socialist MPs voted against the establishment of the NC in the Norwegian parliament. Also, in Iceland the NC was met with some opposition connected both to economic considerations and to their recent independence from Denmark. Restricted by its relation to the Soviet Union, Finland was unable to join until 1955, but the founding documents left a space open for the easternmost Nordic country.[7] Thus, the geographical extension of the NC's definition of *Norden* was undisputed from the start and has largely remained so until today, despite some discussions of Baltic membership in the early 1990s.

---

6 The Joint Committee of the Nordic Social Democratic Labour Movement was founded in 1932 on the basis of cooperation that had taken place since 1886. See e.g. Andersson, "1950-talet"; Pauli Kettunen et al., "The Nordic Model and the rise and fall of Nordic cooperation," in *Nordic Cooperation: A European region in transition*, ed. Johan Strang (London: Routledge, 2016), doi:10.4324/9781315755366–4; Mirja Österberg, "'Norden' as a transnational space in the 1930s: negotiated consensus of 'Nordicness' in the Nordic Committee of the labour movement," in *Labour, unions and politics under the North Star: the Nordic countries, 1700–2000*, ed. Mary Hilson, Silke Neunsinger, and Iben Vyff (New York: Berghahn, 2017).

7 Andersson, "1950-talet"; Peter Stadius, "Hundra år av nordism," in *Meningen med föreningen: Föreningarna Norden 100 år*, ed. Henrik Wilén (Copenhagen: Föreningarna Nordens Förbund, 2019); Svein Olav Hansen, *Vennskap og kjennskap i 100 år: Foreningen Norden 1919–2019* (Oslo: Gyldendal, 2020); Wendt, *Cooperation*, 35–38.

The annual sessions of the NC take place in the parliament building of a Nordic capital on a rotating basis. Eighty-seven delegates chosen among the national members of parliament gather for three to six days of meetings and debates on Nordic issues.[8] The NC has never had legislative power. Its main role is to give recommendations to the five governments, the normative power of which have varied through time. Even though the NC nominally is an organisation for inter-parliamentary cooperation representatives from the governments, including the Prime Ministers, also take part in the NC sessions. This lends the debates a parliamentary character, where delegates hold governments accountable for their activities.[9] This aspect of the NC was strengthened in 1971, when the governments established their own organisation for Nordic cooperation, the Nordic Council of Ministers (NCM), which also has an independent budget (today an annual of €128 million).

Traditionally, the sessions begin with a general debate, which, formally, concerns an annual report on Nordic cooperation put forward by the presidium of the NC, but which in practice turns into a discussion on the state of Nordic cooperation in general and the most pressing issues of the time.[10] To be sure, focusing on the debates at the NC sessions in order to target the rhetoric of Nordic cooperation involves some methodological challenges. There is an obvious risk, not only that the significance of the rhetoric of Nordicness and Nordic cooperation is exaggerated, but also that the phrase "Nordic cooperation" is used differently in the NC sessions to how it is used in the national parliaments or public debates. The material is particularly likely to contain an overrepresentation of sentimental *Nordism*, and the delegates tend to equate "Nordic cooperation" with the NC and NCM, overlooking other venues for interaction between the

---

8 Iceland has 7 seats and the four larger Nordic countries have 20 each. Two of the Finnish and two of the Danish seats have, since 1970, been reserved for representatives from Åland and the Faroe Islands. Since 1984 an additional two Danish seats have been allocated to delegates from Greenland. Due to the small size of the Icelandic parliament, the sessions in Reykjavik usually take place in another location. In addition to the annual sessions, the NC has, since the end of the 1980s, arranged shorter thematic sessions on a semi-regular basis, usually at a venue outside of the capitals.

9 Of the four key features of a parliament listed by Ihalainen, Ilie, and Palonen, the NC fulfils two: deliberation and representation. The other two features, responsibility and sovereignty, are not fulfilled. See Pasi Ihalainen, Cornelia Ilie, and Kari Palonen, "Parliament as a conceptual nexus," in *Parliament and parliamentarism: A comparative history of a European concept*, ed. Pasi Ihalainen, Cornelia Ilie, and Kari Palonen (New York: Berghahn, 2016).

10 There have, of course, been numerous changes to the agenda and choreography of the NC sessions throughout the years, but the first day(s) of the sessions have usually remained reserved for more general discussions.

five countries. With these caveats in mind, there is arguably no better material for exploring the broad variety and complexity of speech acts associated with the term "Nordic cooperation," as the NC sessions confront both political and national variations of this rhetoric with each other.

From democracy to flexibility: Nordic cooperation and its supranational other

Democracy as national sovereignty

One of the most enduring tropes at the Nordic Council has undoubtedly been that of democratic Nordic cooperation and its supranational and federal European other. Clearly, the NC was not established with any supranational ambitions, but in the 1950s, when the aims and purposes of the NC were still under negotiation, there were many animated discussions on Nordic cooperation and national sovereignty. At the very first sessions in Copenhagen in 1953, the issue surfaced in the form of a debate on the legacy of 19th century Scandinavism. Celebrating the establishment of the NC, Hans Hedtoft argued that the Scandinavist movement had an unfortunately poor reputation as it was remembered particularly for its failure to produce a united Scandinavian kingdom or a more formal union. Its main achievement, Hedtoft argued, was in bringing the Scandinavian peoples together and making war between Nordic countries impossible.[11] This idolisation of the Scandinavist movement provoked a response from the leader of the Norwegian Conservative Party, C. J. Hambro, who explained that his opposition towards the establishment of the NC had not been based on any anti-Nordic sentiments, but on a historically conditioned suspicion against Swedish and Danish great power ambitions. "The word union," Hambro explained, "whether it refers to the Kalmar Union or something else, does not ring well in Norwegian ears."[12] This Norwegian criticism forced Hedtoft to clarify

---

11 Hans Hedtoft (Denmark, Social Democrat), *Nordisk råd 1. session*, København 1953 (København: J. H. Schultz, 1953), 94–100. I refer to the debates at the Nordic Council with the name of the speaker (country, party), *Nordisk råd* (Nordic Council), and the city and year of the meeting. The protocols are available in the so called Blue book series, published at various locations and publishers throughout the years 1953–2011, after which they have been made available online at https://www.norden.org/en/information/past-sessions (accessed September 16 2021). All translations from the Nordic languages are mine.

12 C. J. Hambro (Norway, Conservative), *Nordisk råd*, København 1953, 143–144. On the Norwegian relation to the Scandinavist movement, see Hemstad's chapter in this volume.

that in referring to Scandinavism he was not proposing that the NC would lead the way towards a Nordic union. Rather, in carrying the spirit of Scandinavism, the NC had learned the lesson that cooperation requires respect for the distinctive character of each nation: "the aim of the NC is agreement, not unity," Hedtoft concluded.[13]

Caution was undoubtedly called for, not only with regard to the Norwegian sceptics, but also against the background of the recent failure of the defence union and the different foreign policies pursued by the Nordic countries in the Cold War setting. Indeed, foreign policy was excluded from the agenda of the NC from the start, which in itself contributed to the wide agreement that "Nordic cooperation" had to refrain from supranational and federal aspirations. Following Hedtoft's example, a standard argument was that "cooperation" (dk. *samarbejde*, f. *yhteistyö*, isl. *samstarf*, n. *samarbeid*, sv. *samarbete*) required equal and sovereign partners, and that the breakup of the former Danish and Swedish empires and the independence of the five Nordic nations had enabled peaceful coexistence and collaboration in the region.[14] Initially, this was also interpreted as a strength. Comparisons with European initiatives like the Council of Europe (1949), the European Coal and Steel Community (1951), and Benelux cooperation initiatives were common in order to articulate the advantages of the pragmatic and democratic Nordic model of cooperation. The Danish Conservative Ole Bjørn Kraft, for example, argued in 1954, "Whereas the Council of Europe is founded on the idealistic aim of creating a United States of Europe, Nordic cooperation has grown organically out the independence of the five peoples: it is practically oriented and rejects calls for unification based on dogmatic principles or theoretical speculation."[15] Similarly, in the following year, Hedtoft proudly stated that the NC had not wasted time and energy on fruitless discussions between federalists and functionalists. Instead it had proceeded soberly and pragmatically with the issues at hand, and by paying due respect to the sovereignty of the participating nations. This approach, according to Hedtoft, now served as an example for Europe.[16]

---

13 Hans Hedtoft (Denmark, Social Democrat), *Nordisk råd*, København 1953, 167–169.

14 Magnús Jonssón (Iceland, Conservative Independence Party), *Nordisk råd*, København 1953, 79; Tage Erlander (Sweden, Social Democrats), *Nordisk råd*, Stockholm 1955, 43; Bent Røiseland (Norway, Liberal Venstre), *Nordisk råd*, Stockholm 1955, 57.

15 Ole Bjørn Kraft (Denmark, Conservative), *Nordisk råd*, Oslo 1954, 32.

16 Hans Hedtoft (Denmark, Social Democrat), *Nordisk råd*, Stockholm 1955, 38; see also Hedtoft, *Nordisk råd*, Oslo 1954, 19.

The first years of the NC is often celebrated as a "golden epoch" of Nordic cooperation,[17] but they were certainly not seen as such by contemporaries. To be sure, the period produced a passport union (1952–58), a common labour market (1954), and a social security convention (1955), but these agreements were never central to the debates at the NC – they had been initiated already before the establishment of the NC and were largely uncontroversial.[18] Instead, the discussions were marked by the shadow of the failed defence union on the one hand, and by difficult and divisive negotiations on a Nordic trade deal on the other. Whereas the Danish representatives aimed for a full customs union that also included agricultural products, the Swedes and Norwegians feared that their farmers would be outrivalled. Swedish scepticism was mitigated by the prospect of an expanded market for their thriving industry, which in turn only exacerbated the Norwegian concerns.[19] At the NC, the Norwegian sceptics often associated their resistance with a concern for national sovereignty. Jon Leirfall from the Agrarian (Centre) Party, for example, believed that the advocates of the customs union were aiming at turning the NC into a supranational parliament. Leirfall argued that "Danish and Swedish dreams have often proved to be Norwegian nightmares," pointing also to the historically conditioned Norwegian scepticism against the word "union."[20] The Norwegian liberal Arthur Sundt, in turn, stressed that there were limits to how far Norway could go in political integration only fifty years after gaining sovereignty. He also feared that the NC was aiming too high, and that the success of Nordic cooperation in the field of law and social policy should not be scoffed at just because Europe provided tempting examples of economic integration.[21]

Significantly enough, the proponents of the Nordic trade deal did not object to this framing of supranationality as essentially un-Nordic. Instead, they played along with the rhetoric of democratic Nordic cooperation and federalist European integration, trying to convince the Norwegian sceptics that there were no supranational ambitions in the Nordic plans. The Swedish Prime Minister Tage Er-

---

17 See e.g. Sundelius and Wiklund, *Norden i sick-sack*, 18.
18 Wendt, *Cooperation in the Nordic Countries*, 188–89 and 213–21.
19 Juhana Aunesluoma, *Vapaakaupan tiellä: Suomen kauppa- ja integraatiopolitiikka maailmansodasta EU-aikaan* (Helsinki: SKS, 2011), 176–80; Mikael af Malmborg, *Den ståndaktiga nationalstaten: Sverige och den västeuropeiska integrationen 1945–1959* (Lund: Lund University Press, 1994), 338–341; Bo Stråth, *Nordic industry and Nordic economic cooperation* (Stockholm: Almqvist & Wiksell, 1978); Vibeke Sørensen, "Nordic Cooperation: A Social Democratic alternative to Europe," in *Interdependence versus integration: Denmark, Scandinavia and Western Europe 1945–1960* (Odense: Odense University Press, 1995).
20 Jon Leirfall (Norway, Centre Party), *Nordisk råd*, Oslo 1954, 197.
21 Arthur Sundt (Norway, Liberal), *Nordisk råd*, København 1956, 81 and 204–207.

lander, for example, ensured that national sovereignty and democracy remained priorities, and contrasted this with how the Benelux customs union had been pushed through by the countries' respective governments. The Nordic countries had chosen a more democratic path, Erlander argued, involving the parliaments in the discussion, thus building their cooperation on solid ground.[22]

Nordic cooperation and its accelerating other

Intimately connected to these discussions of democracy, sovereignty, federalism, and supranationality were notions of temporality and the speed of development. If the members of the NC in the early 1950s boasted that Nordic cooperation was "ahead" of Europe, things changed with the complex European free trade nego-tiations in the latter half of the decade. Already in 1955, when the so-called Inner Six (Belgium, France, Germany, Italy, Luxembourg and the Netherlands) agreed upon the Messina plan for economic integration, a worry emerged within the NC that Nordic cooperation was being outpaced. "It seems as if the decisiveness is greater in Europe," the chairman of the Swedish liberals Bertil Ohlin com-plained.[23] At this point, however, there was still wide agreement that the slow-ness of Nordic cooperation was a consequence of the lack of supranationality, and as such a price worth paying: it was "characteristic of the Nordic peoples to build slowly but solidly," which would "serve to reduce frictions in the long run."[24] Just a couple of years later, however, when the Treaty of Rome (1957) es-tablished the European Economic Community (EEC), there was already a wide-spread fear that Nordic cooperation was being left behind. While EEC member-ship was still out of the question, a British proposal for a larger European free trade area was welcomed by the Nordic countries.[25] As the 1958 sessions were postponed from the spring to the autumn in anticipation of the EEC's reaction to the British proposal, impatience and self-criticism grew within the NC. Ohlin, for example, feared that the pace and practices of Nordic cooperation had become a handicap rather than an advantage: "Perhaps, making compre-hensive studies and investigations before every decision serves only to amplify the problems."[26] A month after the 1958 sessions, France pulled out of the

---

22 Tage Erlander (Sweden, Social Democrat), *Nordisk råd*, København 1956, 59.
23 Bertil Ohlin (Sweden, Liberal), *Nordisk råd*, København 1956, 41.
24 Rolf Edberg (Sweden, Social Democrat), *Nordisk råd*, København 1956; Finn Moe (Norway, Labour Party), *Nordisk råd*, Stockholm 1955, 54.
25 af Malmborg, *Den ståndaktiga nationalstaten*, 301.
26 Bertil Ohlin (Sweden, Liberal), *Nordisk råd*, Oslo 1958, 187.

FTA negotiations, which left the UK and the Scandinavian countries stranded without a deal with the EEC. As a response, "the outer seven" (the three Scandinavian countries, UK, Switzerland, Austria and Portugal) established the European Free Trade Association (EFTA) in the summer of 1959.[27]

EFTA effectively put an end to the plans for a tightly integrated Nordic customs union and the NC sessions in November 1959 were again held in a gloomy atmosphere, with many speakers bemoaning the fact that the NC had failed with its key initiative.[28] The Prime Ministers, in turn, argued that EFTA was a success as it created a Nordic common market, but admitted that Nordic cooperation had been overrun by European developments. The Danish Prime Minister H.C Hansen, for example, bemoaned the fact that the Nordic tradition of advancing step by step – so successful in forging the social security convention – had proven at odds with the rules of the game on this particular occasion. But he also emphasised that the prolonged process had served its purpose of forging broad Nordic unanimity: even the Norwegian opposition to the Nordic customs union was in favour of EFTA.[29]

A lasting legacy from the prolonged customs union negotiations was undoubtedly the cementation of "Nordic cooperation" as inherently anti-federalist. Indeed, it was even codified as such in the Helsinki Treaty, signed in March 1962. The aim of the treaty was to signal Nordic unity at a point when external forces seemed to pull the region apart: the Soviet Union was, following the Berlin Crisis, increasing its pressure on Finland, while Denmark and Norway were – along with the UK – considering EEC membership.[30] The result was a treaty with vague and non-committing formulations, which was met with disappointment at the

---

27 Thorsten Borring Olesen, "EFTA 1959–1972: an exercise in Nordic cooperation and conflict," in *Regional cooperation and international organizations: The Nordic model in transnational alignment*, ed. Norbert Götz and Heidi Haggrén (London: Routledge, 2009). Finland was unable to join EFTA in 1960 because of Soviet and UK opposition, but after effective lobbying by Finland in the east and Sweden in the west, Finland became an associate member in 1961 (Finn-EFTA-agreement).

28 Bertil Ohlin (Sweden, Liberal), *Nordisk råd*, Stockholm 1959, 42; Karl-August Fagerholm (Finland, Social Democrat), *Nordisk råd*, Stockholm 1959, 46.

29 H. C. Hansen (Denmark, Social Democrat), *Nordisk råd*, Stockholm 1959, 59–60.

30 Johan Vibe, "Norden – et samarbeide nedenfra?," in *Hva skjedde med Norden? Fra selvbevissthet til rådvillhet*, ed. Iver B. Neumann (Oslo: Cappelen, 1992); Claes Wiklund, "1962 års Helsingforsavtal – den första heltäckande nordiska samarbetstraktaten," in *Norden i sick-sack: Tre spårbyten inom nordiskt samarbete*, ed. Bengt Sundelius and Claes Wiklund (Stockholm: Santérus, 2000).

1962 sessions.[31] The Prime Ministers, however, defended it as "an important declaration of intent," and the Finnish Foreign Minister Ahti Karjalainen even argued that the treaty was "a perfect reflection of Nordic cooperation, bringing the countries together despite the differences in foreign policy orientations."[32]

The un-Nordicness of supranational federalism was also a key element in the negotiations for a Nordic economic union around 1970. The ambitious so-called Nordek plan included, among other things, a customs union and a common investment bank.[33] Considerations had, again, to be paid to the different security policies of the Nordic nations, and to the potential Danish –and Norwegian – membership in the EEC. Accordingly, the governments were careful not to propose any limitations of national sovereignty. The rhetoric of Nordic cooperation and European integration served this purpose well. At the 1969 sessions, the Danish Social Democratic leader Jens Otto Krag recognised that Nordek required new institutions, but emphasised that it was important to stick to "the voluntary and consensual form of Nordic cooperation" and "to avoid majority decision-making procedures like in the EEC."[34] The Norwegian Centre Party Prime Minister, Per Borten, similarly emphasised that Nordic cooperation had to stay true to its "democratic ideals."[35] Nordek would undoubtedly have been a rather strange construction: a comprehensive economic union without supranational institutions. It was, however, the only path available, on the one hand because of the different security policies pursued by the Nordic countries, and on the other hand because Nordic cooperation was defined as inherently anti-federal.

If references to Europe, during the late 1950s and early 1960s, served the purpose of rallying Nordic cooperation in order to keep pace with European developments, the Nordek negotiations were even more strongly marked by the asymmetry between Nordic cooperation and European integration: it was clear that the former had to adapt to the pace of the latter. The Danish government

---

31 Gunnar Helén (Sweden, Liberal), *Nordisk råd*, Helsingfors 1962, 59–60; Kjell Bondevik (Norway, Christian People's Party), *Nordisk råd*, Helsingfors 1962, 77.
32 Tage Erlander (Sweden, Social Democrat), *Nordisk råd*, Helsingfors 1962, 81; Einar Gerhardsen (Norway, Labour), *Nordisk råd*, Helsingfors 1962, 70; Ahti Karjalainen (Finland, Agrarian), *Nordisk råd*, Helsingfors 1962, 197.
33 See Jan Hecker-Stampehl, ed., *Between Nordic ideology, economic interests and political reality: New perspectives on Nordek* (Helsinki: Finnish Society of Letters, 2009); Lasse Sonne, *NORDEK – A plan for increased Nordic economic cooperation and integration* (Helsinki: Finnish Society of Letters, 2007).
34 Jens Otto Krag (Denmark, Social Democrat), *Nordisk råd*, Stockholm 1969, 65.
35 Per Borten (Norway, Centre Party) *Nordisk råd*, Stockholm 1969, 100.

launched the Nordek plan when De Gaulle had vetoed British and Danish membership in the EEC for a second time in 1967: there was a temporary European standstill, which the Nordic countries sought to utilise. The Danish Social Democratic leader Jens Otto Krag urged the Nordic leaders forward arguing that the experience a decade ago had proven that it was dangerous to wait, and the Swedish liberal leader Bertil Ohlin stated that he wished the NC could lock the Prime Ministers in an Arctic hotel to forge the deal.[36]

The reasons for the failure of Nordek have been subject to much discussion, but a key factor was the Danish-Finnish disagreement on the relation between Nordic cooperation and Europe. As pointed out by Danish historian Thorsten Borring Olesen, the normative appeal of Nordic cooperation was that it could be – and often was – used as way for the Nordic countries to influence and direct each other.[37] During the Nordek debates, Krag tried to pull his neighbours closer to the EEC, claiming that "the Nordic union is a desirable and perhaps even necessary step towards something larger: Europe," while the Finnish Prime Minister Mauno Koivisto, out of considerations of Finland's special relations to the Soviet Union, tried to keep the whole of *Norden* outside of the EEC by insisting on the "intrinsic value" of Nordek.[38] These different views came to a head when it gradually became clear that Denmark intended to follow the UK into the EEC, which ultimately provoked Finland to withdraw from the project, causing its collapse.[39]

Flexible cooperation within Europe

The Single European Act in 1986 and the Maastricht Treaty in 1992, which transformed the European community into the European Union (EU), provoked an intense debate on the future of Nordic cooperation. By this time the rhetoric of Nordic cooperation, as something that was unique, pragmatic, and democratic, had

---

36 Jens Otto Krag (Denmark, Social Democrat), *Nordisk råd*, Stockholm 1969, 64; Bertil Ohlin (Sweden, Liberal), *Nordisk råd*, Stockholm 1969, 82.

37 See Olesen and Strang, "European challenge," 32; Thorsten Borring Olesen and Poul Villaume, *Dansk udenrigspolitisk historie V: I blokopdelningens tegn* (Copenhagen: Gyldendal, 2006), 545–51.

38 Jens Otto Krag (Denmark, Social Democrat), *Nordisk råd*, Stockholm 1969, 66; Mauno Koivisto (Finland, Social Democrat), *Nordisk råd*, Stockholm 1969, 102; Koivisto, *Nordisk råd*, Reykjavik 1970, 85.

39 See e. g. Aunesluoma, *Vapaakaupan tiellä*, 231–39; Hecker-Stampehl, *Between Nordic ideology*, 13–17.

become part of the liturgy at the annual NC sessions. In 1989, in typical fashion, the Swedish Prime Minister Ingvar Carlsson applauded how Nordic cooperation brought together not only the governments, but also the peoples in *Norden*, that it was voluntary in character and respected the sovereignty of the nations.[40] An increasing number of delegates, however, started to challenge this rhetoric of Nordic exceptionality, arguing that Nordic cooperation had to adapt to the pace of an accelerating European integration. At the 1988 NC sessions, the Danish Prime Minister Poul Schlüter warned his Nordic colleagues that "the European train" was on the move, and that the rediscovered dynamism in the EC was something that could not be ignored by the NC.[41] Most vocal was the Swedish conservative leader Carl Bildt, who, from 1987 to 1994, relished presenting temporalized arguments that urged the Nordic countries to get involved in European integration. He argued that "when history is accelerating in Europe, the clock must not stand still in *Norden*," warning also that "in stagnating, the NC was risking what it had accomplished."[42] Doing so, Bildt alluded to established notions of the slowness and impotence of Nordic cooperation, as well as to its asymmetrical and reactive relation to European integration. Indeed, one of Bildt's leading themes was to call for a shift towards thinking in terms of *"Norden within Europe"* rather than *"Norden or Europe."*[43]

In the escalating EC/EU debates it was particularly the opponents of Nordic EU membership who were most eager to sustain the rhetoric of Nordic cooperation as a democratic alternative to the federal European other.[44] Criticising the transfer of sovereignty from the national legislatures to Brussels and the "democratic deficit" of the EU apparatus, they celebrated Nordic cooperation as a more democratic model of international cooperation. Olof Johansson, the leader of the Swedish Centre Party, for example, argued that Nordic cooperation was unique in being *mellanfolkligt* ("inter-popular," meaning transnational or international at a non-elite level) in the true sense of the word, and claimed, in

---

40 Ingvar Carlsson (Sweden, Social Democrat), *Nordisk råd*, Stockholm 1989, 88; Páll Péturson (Iceland, Progressive), *Nordisk råd*, København 1991, 54.
41 Poul Schlüter (Denmark, Conservative), *Nordisk råd*, Oslo 1988, 132.
42 Carl Bildt (Sweden, Conservative), *Nordisk råd*, Stockholm 1989, 69; *Nordisk råd*, Mariehamn 1989, 34; *Nordisk råd*, Reykjavik 1990, 95–96.
43 Carl Bildt (Sweden, Conservative), *Nordisk råd*, Helsingfors 1987, 76; *Nordisk råd*, Helsingfors 1992, 62; *Nordisk råd*, København 1991, 57. See also Carl Bildt, *Hallänning, svensk, europé* (Stockholm: Bonniers, 1991).
44 Carsten Schymik, "European Antifederalists," in *Northern Europe and the future of the EU: Nordeuropa und die Zukunft der EU*, ed. Helge Høibraaten and Jochen Hille (Berlin: Intersentia, 2011).

1991, that Nordic cooperation could serve as a model for countries in Eastern Europe who, in recently having regained their independence, were hardly keen on new supranational constraints.[45]

On the pro-European side, which included the governments, it became a key task to frame not only European integration, but also supranationality and federalism in a more positive light. The standard argument was that in binding the European nations together, supranational European integration had been crucial in creating peace in Europe. Some, like the Norwegian Foreign Minister Thorvald Stoltenberg, also claimed that "binding cooperation" actually was in the interest of small states like the Nordic ones. With the creation of the EU, France and Germany were no longer able to pursue their foreign policies without taking smaller European nations into account.[46] Supranationalism and binding international cooperation were also presented as inevitable parts of post-Cold War globalisation. Most explicit was, again, the Swedish Prime Minister Carl Bildt, who, notably tired of the sovereignty debate, claimed that "[t]here is no place for Robinson Crusoe politics in the modern world." He argued that if Crusoe had been sovereign on his deserted island, he was certainly very happy to share some of it when Friday came along.[47]

Significantly enough, the governments reserved their propensity for binding and supranational cooperation for the European framework. When it came to Nordic cooperation, they continued to emphasise the right of every nation to pursue its own interests. The Norwegian Prime Minister Gro Harlem Brundtland, for example, argued that while Finland, Norway, and Sweden would pursue the EU negotiations separately, the governments would constantly keep each other informed using the unique informal networks that exist between the Nordic countries. According to Brundtland, Nordic cooperation had not been created through formal decisions or treaties; rather, its defining feature and special strength was the multitude of informal networks that existed between politicians, bureaucrats, unions, and businesses in the different countries, and the cultural and historical affinity based on shared values.[48] In this way, the governments gradually redeployed the rhetoric of Nordic cooperation and its supranational European other: the non-binding and democratic character of Nordic cooperation evolved into an argument about a pre-existing affinity between the Nordic governments, and the flexibility and efficiency of their informal relations. If the previous argu-

---

45 Olof Johansson (Sweden, Centre Party), *Nordisk råd*, Mariehamn 1989, 54; *Nordisk råd*, Mariehamn 1991, 88; Marianne Samuelsson (Sweden, Green Party), *Nordisk råd*, Mariehamn 1989, 53.
46 Thorvald Stoltenberg (Norway, Labour Party), *Nordisk råd*, Århus 1992, 52.
47 Carl Bildt (Sweden, Conservative), *Nordisk råd*, Stockholm 1994, 77.
48 Gro Harlem Brundtland (Norway, Labour Party), *Nordisk råd*, Århus 1992, 39 & 44.

ment had been that the Nordic countries *could not unite* because of their different security or economic interests, the argument now was that the Nordic countries *did not need to unite* because they shared so many networks and values.

This gradual redescription of Nordic cooperation coincided with a series of reforms which increased the role of the prime ministers and decreased the funding of the NCM.[49] Critics were swift to notice that the celebration of the unique informal networks were used to cushion or even conceal a dismantling of Nordic institutional cooperation. As president of the Nordic Council in 1994, the Swedish Social Democrat Sten Andersson expressed his concerns that Prime Ministers were blocking the NC and the parliamentarians' ability to influence decision-making and that Nordic cooperation was developing a democratic deficit like the EU.[50] The Swedish Prime Minister Carl Bildt responded that while the governments were improving formal institutions, unique informal networks were efficient and something that the Nordic countries should be proud of.[51]

Informality and flexibility replaced democracy and sovereignty as the main characteristic of Nordic cooperation. In 1995, the new Swedish Prime Minister Ingvar Carlsson proudly stated that Nordic cooperation was part of his everyday routine: "Among the Nordic Prime Ministers, we phone each other when we need to, in order to check our positions – it is fast and easy."[52] At this point, the rhetoric of informal Nordic cooperation was used particularly against the idea of formalising Nordic cooperation on EU matters. One of the most determined voices was the Finnish Prime Minister Paavo Lipponen, who repeatedly testified to the intimate informal relations between the three Nordic EU members while vehemently rejecting the idea of creating a "Nordic block."[53] In his federal vision of the EU, there were no place for permanent alliances. Aiming at taking Finland to "the core of the EU," Lipponen was also reluctant to associate with Denmark and Sweden, whose governments still struggled with significant domestic scepticism against particularly the Economic and Monetary Union.[54]

---

49 Olesen and Strang, "European challenge," 35–36; Bjørn Otto Sverdrup, "Europeisering som de-institusjonalisering – nordisk politisk samarbeid i endring," in *Europa i Norden: Europeisering av nordisk samarbeid*, ed. Johan P. Olsen and Bjørn Otto Sverdrup (Oslo: Tano Aschehoug, 1998).

50 Sten Andersson (Sweden, Social Democrat), *Nordisk råd*, Stockholm 1994, 56–57.

51 Carl Bildt (Sweden, Conservative), *Nordisk råd*, Stockholm 1994, 72–73.

52 Ingvar Carlsson (Sweden, Social Democrat), *Nordisk råd*, Reykjavik 1995, 63.

53 Paavo Lipponen (Finland, Social Democrat), *Nordisk råd*, København 1996, 49; *Nordisk råd*, Stockholm 1999, 51; *Nordisk råd*, Reykjavik 2000, 49.

54 Richard Brander, *Finland och Sverige i EU: tio år av medlemskap* (Helsingfors: Schildts 2004), 65–75; Tapio Raunio and Teija Tiilikainen, *Finland in the European Union* (London: Frank Cass, 2003), 150.

As the majority of the Nordic countries were members of the EU, the rhetoric of Nordic cooperation and its supranational and federal European other became a way of expressing the special informal bonds between the Nordic countries within a larger European framework. Clearly, it was an attempt to make a virtue of necessity. In a more cynical interpretation, however, it was also a way of reducing Nordic cooperation to a matter of informal contacts and relations in the shadow of European integration, and of legitimising or even disguising budgetary cuts in the NCM. The rhetoric of the unique democratic, pragmatic, and informal Nordic cooperation served as a handy narrative *against* strengthening Nordic institutional cooperation. It provided the governments with an opportunity to frame themselves as pro-Nordic while at the same time refusing to commit themselves to more formalised cooperation.

In the new millennia, there was a somewhat surprising return of the Scandinavist dream of a formalised Nordic union, associated primarily with the Swedish historian Gunnar Wetterberg and his 2010 yearbook of the Nordic Council calling for a *United Nordic Federation*.[55] Despite receiving quite a lot of public attention across the region, the politicians at the NC politely ignored Wetterberg's proposal as a valuable source of inspiration.[56] The former Norwegian foreign minister Thorvald Stoltenberg's report with 13 proposals for strengthening Nordic security and defence cooperation made a more significant impact on the debates.[57] Some observers have claimed that the circle became complete, as the discussion had returned to the same theme that had started Nordic political cooperation in the wake of the Second World War. It was an opportunity to make good for the failure of the defence union in 1948.[58] It is, however, important to emphasise that the Stoltenberg report did not propose any supranational elements, that it did not address the divisive NATO question, and that it was celebrated for its pragmatism and flexibility.[59] Indeed, as the Nordic countries in the

---

55 Originally proposed in an opinion article in *Dagens Nyheter* in 2009, the NC promptly asked Wetterberg to develop the idea in book form. Gunnar Wetterberg, *The United Nordic Federation* (Copenhagen: Nordic Council, 2010).

56 Asta Ragnheidur Johannesdottir (Iceland, Social Democrat), *Nordisk råd*, Reykjavik 2010, 36; Bente Dahl (Denmark, Social Liberal), *Nordisk råd*, Reykjavik 2010, 50).

57 Thorvald Stoltenberg, *Nordic cooperation on foreign and security policy* (Oslo: Norwegian Government Security and Service Organisation (G.S.S.O.), 2009), https://www.regjeringen.no/ globalassets/upload/ud/vedlegg/nordicreport.pdf.

58 Bengt Sundelius and Claes Wiklund, "Quo vadis? Tretton insikter om Norden," in *Norden sett inifrån: Det fjärde spårbytet*, ed. Bengt Sundelius and Claes Wiklund (Stockholm: Santérus, 2017), 312.

59 At the NC, see e.g. Espen Barth Eide, *Nordisk råd*, Helsingfors 2012, (https://www.norden. org/en/event/64th-session-2012) speech 142.

wake of the Stoltenberg report have strengthened their foreign and security policy cooperation, the rhetoric of the successful informal Nordic cooperation prevails, while proposals for a more formalised framework for foreign and security policy cooperation has fallen on deaf ears.[60]

From distinctiveness to distinction: Nordic cooperation and its conservative and capitalist other

The Nordic cultural community

Closely related to the notion of Nordic cooperation as a particularly democratic and "popular" form of transnational cooperation, is the idea of *Norden* as a unique community of shared languages, cultures, and values.[61] This has also been a central trope in the rhetoric at the Nordic Council, serving as a legitimation of the NC itself, and as part of the motivations for various cooperation initiatives. The first sessions of the NC in 1953 were, understandably, marked by much sentimental rhetoric of Nordic kinship and unity. According to Hans Hedtoft, for example, the NC was "the latest shoot on the tree whose roots run deep in the Nordic peoples."[62] Comparisons to Europe were common, and a standard argument was that if "Europe" had succeeded in forging cooperation schemes and trade deals, the Nordic countries should also be able to do so given the exceptional cultural ties between the countries. Launching the Nordek initiative in 1968, for example, the Danish Liberal Prime Minister Hilmar Baunsgaard argued that the affinity between the Nordic peoples had "the potential for developing into something more concrete," while his foreign minister Poul Hartling claimed

---

60 There have been repeated proposals to include foreign and security policy in the institutional framework of the NCM, and in 2014 Thorvald Stoltenberg himself suggested the establishment of a Nordic defence commission. Thorvald Stoltenberg, *Nordisk råd*, Stockholm 2014, speech number 292, https://www.norden.org/en/node/18902.

61 See e. g. Iver B. Neumann, "Tre Innfallsvinkler til Norden: Kulturfelleskap, oppdemming for stormaktspolitikk, regionbygging," in *Hva skjedde med Norden*, ed. Iver B. Neumann (Oslo: Cappelen, 1992).

62 Hans Hedtoft (Denmark, Social Democrat), *Nordisk råd*, København 1953, 95 and 101; Vilhelm Buhl (Denmark, Social Democrat), *Nordisk råd*, København 1953, 78; Nils Herlitz (Sweden, Conservative), *Nordisk råd*, København 1953, 86.

that the region, by virtue of the special kinship between its peoples, had "outstanding pre-conditions for economic integration."[63]

More common, however, than using culture and identity as a lever for deeper integration was to refer to the cultural and linguistic community as a way to strengthen the rhetoric when Nordic cooperation had experienced a backlash.[64] In the wake of the collapsed customs union negotiations, the Norwegian Christian Democrat Erling Wikborg argued that in language and culture there was more that tied the Nordic countries together than there was pulling them apart, while the Danish Conservative Ole Bjørn Kraft bemoaned the Nordic failures in defence policy and trade, but urged the NC to take its third chance in the field of culture.[65] When the Nordek deal broke down in 1970 and Denmark was moving towards the EEC, the Danish Social Democratic Prime Minister Jens Otto Krag called upon the NC to strengthen its focus on areas that remained outside the Rome Treaty, most notably the field of culture.[66] His Finnish colleague from the Centre Party, Ahti Karjalainen, even claimed that "Finland has always seen culture as one of the most important fields of Nordic cooperation."[67] Indeed, it was often those who, for various reasons, had toppled Nordic integration schemes who felt obliged to praise Nordic cultural unity and the rhetoric was also often backed up financially by initiatives and investments to further cooperation in the field of culture and education. After the collapse of the customs union the NC established the Literature Prize in 1962 and a Nordic Culture Fund in 1966. Similarly, the breakdown of the Nordek negotiations led to a new culture treaty in 1971 and a significant rise in funding for the Nordic Culture Fund.[68]

---

63 Hilmar Baunsgaard (Denmark, Social Liberal), *Nordisk råd*, Oslo 1968, 62; Poul Hartling (Denmark, Liberals), *Nordisk råd*, Oslo 1968, 87.

64 Nils Andrén, "Det officiella kultursamarbetet i Norden," *Den Jyske Historiker* 69 – 70 (1994): 213 – 27; Anna Kharkina, *From Kinship to Global Brand: The discourse on culture in Nordic cooperation after World War II* (Stockholm: Acta Universitatis Stockholmiensis, 2013); Bengt Sundelius, *Managing Transnationalism in Northern Europe* (Boulder: Westview Press, 1978), 88.

65 Erling Wikborg (Norway, Christian People's Party), *Nordisk råd*, København 1961, 54. Ole Bjørn Kraft (Denmark, Conservative), *Nordisk råd*, Stockholm 1964, 64.

66 Jens Otto Krag (Denmark, Social Democrat), *Nordisk råd*, København 1971, 60 – 61.

67 Ahti Karjalainen (Finland, Centre Party), *Nordisk råd*, København 1971, 82.

68 Kharkina, *From Kinship to Global Brand*, 57–70; Anne-Marie Mai, "Dreams and realities: The Nordic Council Literature Prize as a symbol for the construction of Nordic cultural cooperation," in *Nordic Cooperation: A European region in transition*, ed. Johan Strang (London: Routledge, 2016), doi:10.4324/9781315755366 – 6.

Of course, from today's horizon it would perhaps be easy to argue that the aim of the rhetoric of cultural unity and Nordic cultural cooperation was to create a culturally (and even racially) homogenous *Norden*. In some structural sense, this might be the case, but it is important to remember that in the 1960s and 70s, cultural policy was not primarily associated with national conservatism; rather, it formed a key part of the toolbox of progressive Social Democrats who wanted to counter marketisation and make culture available for larger sections of society.[69] It was seen as a pivotal vehicle for democratising society and building the welfare state, and in this sense, Nordic cooperation in culture was not merely a compensation for failures in other areas, but part of a progressive programme for modernising society.

In fact, the use of culture as a rhetorical scapegoat was more pertinent in connection with the reforms of the NC/NCM structure after Finland and Sweden joined the EU in 1995. For example, although Carl Bildt had warned in 1990 that the NC would be "reduced to a forum of cultural manifestations" if it refused to take European integration seriously, he claimed that the common cultural identity was the very core of Nordic unity when he was Prime Minister in 1994.[70] In his opening speech at the 1995 sessions, the Danish Prime Minister Poul Nyrup Rasmussen emphasised the importance, at this critical juncture, of strengthening the Nordic community and its shared values and cultures.[71] Naturally, concerns were raised that the governments were using cultural cooperation in order to compensate for, or even conceal, the cuts in other sectors of the Nordic budget.[72] However, as the future of the NC/NCM structure was cast in doubt, there was no opposition against singling out culture as a key focus area of Nordic cooperation. In a period of Europeanisation, cultural cooperation re-emerged as a tool for legitimising Nordic cooperation in general and the NC/NCM apparatus in particular. It provided the governments with an alibi against accusations of not taking Nordic cooperation seriously.

The explicit othering of Europe – or other regions – was rare in this rhetoric of Nordic cultural unity and cooperation. However, the compensatory logic of investing in culture in the wake of failures in trade arguably contributed to a self-propelling narrative according to which Nordic cooperation was *primarily* about

---

69 Peter Duelund, ed., *The Nordic Cultural Model* (Copenhagen: Nordic Cultural Institute, 2003); see e.g. Kulturrådet, *Ny kulturpolitik: nuläge och förslag* (Stockholm: Allmänna förlaget, 1972), 66.

70 Carl Bildt (Sweden, Conservative), *Nordisk råd*, Reykjavik 1990, 96; *Nordisk råd*, Stockholm 1994, 73.

71 Poul Nyrup Rasmussen (Denmark, Social Democrat), *Nordisk råd*, Reykjavik 1995, 37–38.

72 Tora Aasland Houg (Norway, Socialist), *Nordisk råd*, Århus 1992, 83.

culture and identity, while European integration was *primarily* a matter of trade and economy. Indeed, it has often been claimed that the Nordics have approached European integration mainly as a matter of trade and economy, while remaining rather reserved about European identity building projects.[73]

Nordic cooperation and the welfare state

The European other was more pertinent in the discussions on the Nordic welfare state. The idea that the Nordic countries share social and welfare political ambitions had been a central part of the rhetoric of Nordic distinctiveness, since, perhaps, the 1930s. This rhetoric had often been encouraged by foreign interest and modelled on foreign examples.[74] At the Nordic Council, Nordic welfare exceptionalism was construed particularly by othering European conservatism and capitalism, which, as shown by Swedish historians Bo Stråth and Lars Trägårdh, formed central tropes in Swedish anti-EEC rhetoric from the 1960s onwards.[75] At the NC, this rhetoric was most pronounced among delegates from the left wing, who already in the 1960s and 70s described the EEC as an "unholy Roman Empire" dominated by capitalistic interests threatening the solidaristic Nordic wel-

73 Caroline Howard Grøn, Peter Nedergaard, and Anders Wivel, "Mr. Svensson Goes to Brussels: Concluding on the Nordic Countries and the European Union," in *The Nordic Countries and the European Union*, ed. Caroline Howard Grøn, Peter Nedergaard, and Anders Wivel (London: Routledge, 2015); Mary Hilson, *The Nordic Model: Scandinavia since 1945* (London: Reaktion Books, 2008), 134–44.

74 Nils Edling, *The Changing Meanings of the Welfare State: Histories of a key concept in the Nordic countries* (New York: Berghahn, 2019); Pauli Kettunen, "The transnational construction of national challenges: the ambiguous Nordic model of welfare and competitiveness," in *Beyond welfare state models: transnational perspectives on social policy*, ed. Pauli Kettunen and Klaus Petersen (Cheltenham: Edward Elgar, 2011); Klaus Petersen, "National, Nordic and trans-Nordic: transnational perspectives on the history of the Nordic welfare states," in *Beyond welfare state models: transnational perspectives on social policy*, ed. Pauli Kettunen and Klaus Petersen (Cheltenham: Edward Elgar, 2011); Klaus Petersen & Carl Marklund, "Return to sender: American images of the Nordic welfare states and Nordic welfare state branding," *European Journal of Scandinavian Studies* 43 (2013): 245–57, doi:10.1515/ejss-2013–0016.

75 Bo Stråth, "Poverty, Neutrality and welfare: Three key concepts in the modern foundation of the myth of Sweden," in *Myth and memory in the construction of community: Historical patterns in Europe and beyond*, ed., Bo Stråth (Wien: PIE Lang, 2000); Bo Stråth, "The Swedish image", 374–75; Lars Trägårdh, "Sweden and the EU: welfare state nationalism and the spectre of 'Europe'" in *European integration and national identity: The challenge of the Nordic states*, ed. Lene Hansen and Ole Wæver (London: Routledge, 2002).

fare states.[76] It would, however, be incorrect to reduce the idea of Nordic welfare exceptionalism to a left-wing construction. Liberals like Bertil Ohlin were also wary of sharing social policy ambitions with continental Europe, while the Norwegian Conservative leader Kåre Willoch, in the wake of the Nordek breakdown, argued that *Norden* was a natural region for cooperation because of "the natural fellowship of the Nordic countries, based upon common culture and traditions, and somewhat similar visions for developing our welfare societies."[77] The Nordic welfare state served as a legitimation of Nordic cooperation across the political spectre.

In social policy discourse, the asymmetrical comparisons to Europe were often temporalised, but contrary to the discussions on economic integration, welfare was a field where the Nordics considered themselves as more progressive than their European others, at least until the turning point of the 1990s. This pertained both to the idea of the Nordic social systems as more advanced than the European ones, and to the achievements of Nordic cooperation in this area – for example, the social security convention of 1955. Even pro-Europeans like the Danish Liberal Prime Minister Hilmar Baunsgaard used temporalised rhetoric to claim that the Nordic countries by virtue of their "achievements in social welfare, democracy and freedom" had much to offer Europe.[78]

There were, however, also internal Nordic dynamics to this temporalised rhetoric. As shown by welfare state historians Pauli Kettunen, Klaus Petersen, and others, Nordic cooperation served as an arena for sharing best practices, and it was not unusual that the countries competed to claim the most advanced social legislation.[79] Being ahead – usually the privilege of Sweden – was to a significant degree a matter of having the power of determining the "Nordic" solution to a particular problem. In a Nordic latecomer like Finland, by contrast, the rhetoric of Nordicness signified, in the words of Pauli Kettunen, "a future code and normative standard of Finnish society."[80] At a time when social policy

---

76 Einar Olgeirsson (Iceland, Socialist), *Nordisk råd*, Helsingfors 1962, 97–98; C.H. Hermansson (Sweden, Socialist), *Nordisk råd*, København 1971, 100; Aksel Larsen (Denmark, Socialist), *Nordisk råd*, København 1971, 149.

77 Bertil Ohlin (Sweden, Liberal), *Nordisk råd*, Helsingfors 1957, 101; Kåre Willoch (Norway, Conservative), *Nordisk råd*, Helsingfors 1972, 95.

78 Hilmar Baunsgaard (Denmark, Social Liberal), *Nordisk råd*, Reykjavik 1970, 76.

79 Kettunen et al. "The Nordic Model"; Petersen, "National, Nordic and trans-Nordic."

80 Pauli Kettunen et al., "The Nordic Model", 77–78; Pauli Kettunen, "The Nordic Welfare State in Finland," *Scandinavian Journal of History* 26, no. 3 (2001): 234, doi:10.1080/034687501750303864; see also Stefan Nygård and Johan Strang, "Conceptual Universalization and the Role of the Peripheries," *Contributions to the History of Concepts* 12, no. 1 (1 June 2017): 55–75, doi:10.3167/choc.2017.120105.

modernisation was thought of as a linear and almost deterministic development, "the Nordic" became synonymous to "the most advanced" and even "the future".

Curiously, however, the rhetoric of Nordic cooperation could also have a conservative function. A pertinent example was the discussions on the Swedish marriage law reforms at the NC in the early 1970s which aimed at strengthening the position of wives, making it easier for couples to divorce each other, and improving the legal position of unmarried couples. This provoked conservatives at the NC to mobilise the rhetoric of Nordic cooperation against the proposed reform, claiming that Sweden was abandoning a century-long tradition of Nordic legal harmonisation. According to the Norwegian Conservative Berte Rognerud, for example, the Swedish reform represented not only a radical break with western traditions and conceptions of marriage. It was also a violation of the Helsinki Treaty, as Sweden intended to transform its legislation without paying due respect to the situation in other Nordic countries.[81] Carl Lidbom, the legal advisor in Olof Palme's Social Democratic cabinet, responded that as a result of Danish EEC membership "harmonisation was no longer a realistic ambition for Nordic cooperation," but he also expressed fears that the calls for harmonisation were slowing down the development of the welfare state.[82] Prime Minister Palme made the point even more forcefully, arguing that "Nordic cooperation must never become a conservative hindrance for a country to move forward along the path of progress."[83] Among legal scholars, the debates on the Swedish marriage law are often referred to as a turning point in the history of Nordic legal cooperation: the point at which Sweden single-handedly abandoned the aim of Nordic legal harmonisation.[84] It is more accurate, however, to view it as a clash between two different understandings of Nordic cooperation: a *progressive* one according to which Nordic cooperation was a forum where the laggards could learn from the more advanced, and a *deliberative* one where Nordic cooperation was a forum for negotiating common solutions. In temporal terms, the question was whether the Nordic countries would synchronise around the most advanced or around an average speed of development.[85]

---

81 Berte Rognerud (Norway, Conservative), *Nordisk råd*, Oslo 1973, 125–126.
82 Carl Lidbom (Sweden, Social Democrat), *Nordisk råd*, Oslo 1973, 80–83.
83 Olof Palme (Sweden, Social Democrat), *Nordisk råd*, Oslo 1973, 122.
84 Letto-Vanamo and Tamm, "Cooperation in the field of law," 104–105; Kjell Åke Modéer, "Comparative critical legal studies: US and the Nordic countries – a review article," *Retfærd* 37 (2014): 128.
85 Helge Jordheim and Einar Wigen, "Conceptual Synchronisation: From Progress to Crisis," *Millennium: Journal of International Studies* 46, no. 3 (June 2018): 421–39, https://doi.org/10.1177/0305829818774781.

The welfare state was in the 1960s and 70s seen as both a product of Nordic cooperation and as somethig that legitimised it, but it was not until the 1990s that "the Nordic welfare state" became a key concept at the NC sessions – conspicuously at a time when it no longer self-evidently represented the future.[86] The end of the Cold War pulled the rug from under the rhetoric of the Nordic middle way between socialism and capitalism, and the economic recession in Finland and Sweden raised serious questions about the viability of a large public sector and comprehensive social services. Moreover, the acceleration of European integration and the ensuing EU debates across the region challenged the relationship between *Norden* and its asymmetrical European other.

At the NC sessions it was, again, particularly the left-wing members who saw European integration as a threat to both Nordic cooperation and the Nordic welfare state. They claimed that the EU was a neoliberal design that played into the hands of big corporations, capital, and business, and argued that the Conservatives were using the EU as a tool for dismantling the Nordic welfare state.[87] Some, like the Norwegian socialist Kjellbjørg Lunde, even tried to mobilise intensified Nordic cooperation as a pro-welfare state alternative to the EU.[88] For the Social Democrats European integration was a divisive issue. However, a popular argument, especially among Swedish Social Democrats, was that Nordic cooperation could become a vehicle for exporting the welfare state to Europe – that Europe could become more Nordic, at least as much as *Norden* became more European.[89] The Finnish Social Democrat Erkki Tuomioja, in turn, was less buoyant and referred ironically to "the admirable self-confidence by which Ingvar Carlsson has professed the aim of realising Margaret Thatcher's nightmare of a wel-

---

86 Pauli Kettunen, "The conceptual history of the welfare state in Finland," in *The changing meanings of the welfare state: Histories of a key concept in the Nordic countries*, ed. Nils Edling (New York: Berghahn, 2019); Bo Stråth, "Den nordiska modellen. Historisk bakgrund och hur talet om en nordisk modell uppstod," *Nordisk tidskrift för vetenskap, konst och industri* (1993), 55–61. Moreover, as pointed out elsewhere in this volume, the 1990s was also when the "Nordic welfare state" was canonised in academic discourse through the Danish social scientist Gøsta Esping-Andersen's book *Three Worlds of Welfare Capitalism* (Cambridge: Polity Press, 1990). **87** Lars Werner (Sweden, Socialist), *Nordisk råd*, Oslo 1988, 148; Claes Andersson (Finland, Socialist), *Nordisk råd*, Mariehamn 1989, 35–36. **88** Kjellbjørg Lunde (Norway, Socialist), *Nordisk råd*, Oslo 1993, 73. The Finnish Centre Party politician and devoted EU opponent Paavo Väyrynen also proposed a Nordic community as an alternative to the EU. Pertti Joenniemi, "Finland in the new Europe: A Herderian or Hegelian concept," in *European integration and national identity: The challenge of the Nordic states*, ed. Lene Hansen and Ole Wæver (London: Routledge, 2002), 206. **89** Mats Hällström (Sweden, Social Democrat), *Nordisk råd*, København 1991, 100; Ingvar Carlsson (Sweden, Social Democrat), *Nordisk råd*, Stockholm 1994, 66.

fare Europe."[90] Conservatives across the region were overwhelmingly in favour of European integration, which also translated into a somewhat ambivalent attitude towards the legacy of the (Social Democratic) Nordic welfare state. The Danish Prime Minister Poul Schlüter, for example, argued that Nordic EC membership could have something important to offer Europe, "in their societal model, even if it has some deficiencies."[91] Most explicit in their anti-Nordic rhetoric were libertarians in the Danish and Norwegian Progressive Parties, who saw themselves as representatives of a liberal wave sweeping across Europe that eventually would emancipate also the Nordic countries from socialist authoritarianism. The Norwegian Progressive Party chairman Carl I. Hagen professed in 1991 that "The epoch of strong states, high taxes and bureaucracy is over," calling also for the NC to be shut down, as it was a Cold War construction that had overplayed its role.[92] The fate of the Nordic welfare state and Nordic cooperation were intimately related to each other in these early 1990s discussions on European integration.

The New Nordic brand

The EC/EU debates of the early 1990s were clearly a turning point in the rhetoric of Nordic cooperation. It was the first time that doubts over, and even criticism of, the idea of *Norden* as a distinct region were heard at the NC. As the asymmetrical opposition to European integration dissolved, there was a growing confusion as to the meaning and purpose of Nordic cooperation. The professed anti-*Nordists*, however, remained few, and the rhetoric of Nordic kinship continued to figure in celebratory speeches at the NC, but the discussions were undoubted-

---

90 Erkki Tuomioja (Finland, Social Democrat), *Nordisk råd*, Mariehamn 1991, 93.

91 Kimmo Sasi (Finland, Conservative), *Nordisk råd*, Mariehamn 1989, 74–75; Poul Schlüter (Denmark, Conservative), *Nordisk råd*, Reykjavik 1990, 6.

92 Carl I. Hagen (Norway, Progressive), *Nordisk råd*, Reykjavik 1990, 89; *Nordisk råd*, København 1991, 62; *Nordisk råd*, Mariehamn 1991, 42; *Nordisk råd*, Oslo 1993, 65; Pia Kjærsgaard (Denmark, Progressive), *Nordisk råd*, København 1991, 147; *Nordisk råd*, Århus 1992, 67; Pål Atle Skjervengen (Norway, Progressive), *Nordisk råd*, Reykjavik 1990, 66. The right-wing populists changed their position on the EU following the Maastricht Treaty 1992 (and their view on the welfare state in the early 2000s). See Ann-Cathrine Jungar and Anders Ravik Jupskås, "Populist Radical Right Parties in the Nordic Region: A New and Distinct Party Family?," *Scandinavian Political Studies* 37, no. 3 (September 2014): 215–38, doi:10.1111/1467–9477.12024; Jens Rydgren, "Explaining the Emergence of Radical Right-Wing Populist Parties: The Case of Denmark," *West European Politics* 27, no. 3 (May 2005): 474–502, doi:10.1080/0140238042000228103.

ly marked by a sense of marginalisation of "the Nordic." It did not take long, however, before culture and welfare returned as key features of the debates at the NC, but as a significantly transformed rhetoric that relied little on the European other, and even less on Nordic cooperation. Instead, "the Nordic" was reinvented as a global brand, as a trademark to be used on global markets.

According to Swedish historian Anna Kharkina, the 2005 report *Norden – en global vinderregion* (Norden – a global winner region) was particularly significant in introducing the concept of branding to the NC/NCM apparatus. Commissioned by the NCM and produced by the Danish think tank *Mandag Morgen*, the report painted a picture of globalisation as simultaneously a threat and an opportunity for the Nordic countries.[93] Threatened by intensified global competition, the success of the Nordic countries in different international rankings, such as the *World Competitiveness Index*, was a source for optimism. According to the report, the region shared a number of culturally embedded values that formed crucial ingredients in the recipe for a successful innovation economy, and thus *Mandag Morgen* urged the Nordic governments to redefine the aim and purpose of Nordic cooperation towards branding the region on the basis of these distinctive Nordic values and the cultural legacy of the region.[94]

The idea of "*Norden* as a global winner region" captured the imagination of the politicians at the NC, who were eager to capitalise on the improved global reputation of the Nordic countries. In 2006, the NC devoted the Prime Ministers' summit to a discussion of the report. The Norwegian Prime Minister Jens Stoltenberg did raise a warning that the Nordics should not attempt to become global winners at the expense of others.[95] But the general sentiment among the Nordic leaders was that the Nordics had succeeded in balancing a free market with social security, and as such provided an example for others to learn from. The Finnish Prime Minister Matti Vanhanen proudly noted that "the awareness of the Nordic model has increased lately, not only within the region itself. The Nordic brand is spreading around the world. Our success in the international rankings has given the Nordic countries well-deserved attention."[96] The Danish Prime Minister Anders Fogh Rasmussen in turn, praised the Danish model of "flexicur-

---

93 Mandag Morgen, *Norden som global vinderregion: På sporet af den nordiska konkurrencemodel* (Copenhagen: Nordic Council and Nordic Council of Ministers, 2005); Kettunen, "The transnational construction."

94 Mandag Morgen, *Norden som global vinderregion*, 81–84.

95 Jens Stoltenberg (Norway, Labour Party), *Nordisk råd*, København 2006, 58.

96 Matti Vanhanen (Finland, Centre Party), *Nordisk råd*, København 2006, 39.

ity" and called for joint Nordic branding initiatives to strengthen the position of Nordic countries in the global markets.[97]

The Nordic welfare state had throughout the history of the NC been thought of as a model for other countries to learn from, but there was something new in this turn to region branding. The *Mandag Morgen* report can be related to the contestation of the Social Democratic ownership of the welfare state, which had started already in the 1990s both in politics and in research.[98] As the origins of the welfare state were traced further back in history, the welfare state was decoupled from social democracy and became an expression of a common Nordic cultural legacy which every political party could claim to represent – albeit in different ways. The cultural turn played into the hands of the xenophobic right, for whom the welfare state was threatened by globalisation and immigration, but also the Conservatives claimed to represent the Nordic model in a series of political campaigns that framed them as "the true labour parties" and "the new welfare parties."[99] Even the Social Democrats embraced the cultural turn proclaiming the values of the welfare state as the natural values of the Nordic nations: they were Nordic values – "*nordiska värderingar.*" Intended as a move to monopolise the welfare state, the redescription of the welfare state from politics to culture served the contrary purpose of stretching the concept, making it available for a broader variety of political actors. Indeed, as pointed out by the Swedish political historian Jenny Andersson, the appeal to national values and unity was a way of silencing conflicts around change.[100]

Crucially, however, the cultural turn and the rhetoric of "Nordic values" also disconnected the welfare state from Nordic *cooperation*, putting the emphasis on Nordicness alone. The Danish historian Mads Mordhorst, for example, has argued that nation branding transformed the idea of the nation from a social construct to an ontological object with an essence. Branding was a nationalism for

---

97 Anders Fogh Rasmussen (Denmark, Liberal), *Nordisk råd*, Reykjavik 2005, 2; *Nordisk råd*, København 2006, 74.

98 Lønning, Ojala, Stavad, NC 2005, 31–40; Peter Baldwin, *The Politics of Social Solidarity: Class Bases of the European Welfare State, 1875–1975* (Cambridge: Cambridge University Press, 1990), doi:10.1017/CBO9780511586378; Øystein Sørensen & Bo Stråth, ed., *The Cultural Construction of Norden*, (Oslo: Scandinavian University Press), 1997.

99 See the individual chapters in Nils Edling, ed., *The changing meanings of the welfare state: histories of a key concept in the Nordic countries* (New York: Berghahn, 2019); Carl Marklund, "The Nordic Model on the Global Market of Ideas: The Welfare State as Scandinavia's Best Brand," *Geopolitics* 22, no. 3 (July 2017): 623–39, doi:10.1080/14650045.2016.1251906. See also Hilson and Hoctor in this volume.

100 Jenny Andersson, *The Library and the Workshop: Social Democracy and Capitalism in the Knowledge Age*, (Stanford: Stanford University Press, 2010), 43–61.

the new competition state, bringing together the call for economic competitiveness and the quest for cultural belonging in a period of neoliberal globalisation.[101] As such, the nation became less an internal concern of *creating* a common horizon of meaning and values, and more an external strategy for *promoting* the interest of the nation on the global market. The rhetoric of Nordicness served this purpose well as it built a bridge between the competitive and modern Nordic model and the primordial Nordic culture and values on which it allegedly was based. Nordic cooperation was no longer part of the narrative.[102]

Something similar also happened to the role of culture in Nordic cooperation. If cultural cooperation previously had served identity building purposes, strengthening connections across the region, "the Nordic" was now turned into an attribute or quality of the cultural products of the region. The task of the NC/NCM framework was no longer to promote dialogue or interaction between cultural institutions or independent cultural actors in the different Nordic countries, but to take successful initiatives from the creative industries and promote them on the global markets. The turn towards branding redefined the purpose of the NCM, who compensated for its marginalisation as a political forum by accentuating its role as an advertising agency. In the years that followed the *Mandag Morgen* report the NCM streamlined its institutions and redirected funds to grant schemes and a series of region branding projects, like the New Nordic Food programme analysed by Lily Kelting in this volume.[103] The rhetoric of Nordic cooperation and European integration was replaced by a rhetoric of "New Nordicness," where not only the asymmetrical European other, but also the ambition of forging a transnational Nordic community, had lost currency.

By way of paradox, however, this essentialisation of "the Nordic" did not entail a return of "the European other." As suggested by British IR scholar Christopher Browning, the idea of something distinctively Nordic was, since the end of the Cold War, undermined by a melding of Nordic and European norms and val-

101 Peter Duelund, "Nordic Cultural Policies: A Critical View," *International Journal of Cultural Policy* 14, no. 1 (February 2008): 18–19, doi:10.1080/10286630701856468; Mads Mordhorst, "Nation branding and nationalism," in *Nationalism and the Economy: Explorations into a Neglected Relationship*, ed. Stefan Berger and Thomas Fetzer (Budapest: Central European University Press, 2019).
102 Kettunen et al, "The Nordic Model and the rise and fall of Nordic cooperation."
103 Duelund, "Nordic cultural policies"; Kharkina, *From kinship to global brand*; Mathias Danbolt, "New Nordic Exceptionalism: Jeuno JE Kim and Ewa Einhorn's *The United Nations of Norden* and Other Realist Utopias," *Journal of Aesthetics & Culture* 8, no. 1 (January 2016): doi:10.3402/jac.v8.30902; Kharkina, *From Kinship to Global Brand*, 113–162.

ues.[104] Indeed, when Matti Vanhanen in 2006 praised the global success of the Nordic model, he also emphasised that "Europe and *Norden* share a similar attitude towards the soft sectors, to social security and sustainable development."[105] Defined less in terms of social democracy and more through global competitiveness and international rankings, the Nordic model was transformed from an alternative to a superior implementation of a common European theme. When the Nordic ceased to signify "the *other* Europe," it was reinvented as "the *better* Europe."[106]

Conclusions

This chapter has revisited the debates on the purpose and nature of Nordic cooperation at the Nordic Council, not to revise the traditional narratives of Nordic cooperation, but with the aim of exploring how these narratives were created in the first place. Strategic security concerns and economic interests undoubtedly pulled the Nordic countries apart, making more binding forms of cooperation, let alone a formalised supranational Nordic federation, impossible. In the wake of failures in security and trade, cooperation was directed towards the fields of culture and welfare, which gradually became defining features of Nordic cooperation itself. More often than not, this rhetoric of Nordic cooperation was based on an asymmetrical juxtaposition to European integration. Nordic cooperation was framed as democratic and "popular," anchored in shared cultural legacies and a common social political vision, in contrast to the supranational, conservative, and trade-focused European integration.

The rhetoric of Nordic cooperation was never static, it was constantly adjusting to a mutating relationship to Europe. Particularly when, in the 1990s, the opposition between *Norden* and Europe was dissolved, the traditional narratives of Nordic cooperation had to be redescribed. The democratic and popular character of Nordic cooperation was turned into a matter of flexibility, anchored in deep

---

104 Christopher S. Browning, 'Branding Nordicity: Models, Identity and the Decline of Exceptionalism', *Cooperation and Conflict* 42, no. 1 (March 2007): 27–51, doi:10.1177/0010836707073475.
105 Matti Vanhanen (Finland, Centre Party), *Nordisk råd*, København 2006, 39–40. See also e.g. Inge Lønning (Norway, Conservative), *Nordisk råd*, Reykjavik 2005, 18–19.
106 On the notion of the Nordic region and Nordic cooperation as "the other Europe," see for example, Barry Turner and Gunilla Nordquist, *The Other European Community: Integration and Cooperation in Northern Europe* (Houndmills: Palgrave, 1982); or more recently, Caroline Howard Grøn, Peter Nedergaard, and Anders Wivel, eds., *The Nordic Countries and the European Union: Still the Other European Community?* (London: Routledge, 2015).

and trusting personal relations between leading politicians in the region, while Nordic cultural and welfare exceptionalism were reinvented as key aspects of a "New Nordic brand" to be promoted in international arenas. Both developments point to a redeployment of "the Nordic" from a transnational community that the NC/NCM was *creating*, to a pre-existing quality and an attribute that the NC/NCM would help Nordic actors to *utilise*. As such, it is not a surprise that the rhetoric of (New) Nordicness has not served to encourage Nordic cooperation.

Today, there seems to be more use for the Nordic brand than there is for the Nordic community. The purpose of this chapter is not to present a nostalgic call for a return to the past. In an age of Europeanisation and globalisation, it was arguably quite reasonable that the NC and NCM turned outwards, focusing on branding the region at a global level. The rhetoric of "the (New) Nordic" served as a way for the NC and NCM to legitimise themselves in a period when the interest in political cooperation on a Nordic level was diminishing. It becomes problematic only when branding replaces cooperation, because the first can hardly survive without the other. There a danger that the rhetoric of Nordicness loses its rhetorical force without the complex practices of comparing and contrasting the countries with each other. As such, the NC and NCM might not need a European other, but they certainly need to acknowledge their fundamental role in construing "the Nordic" through Nordic cooperation.

Pirjo Markkola

Nordic Gender Equality: Between Administrative Cooperation and Global Branding

The presentation of the Nordic countries as world leaders in gender equality

The Nordic countries are commonly renowned for their comprehensive welfare states, a high level of social services and a dual-earner family model. They also hold top positions in international rankings of welfare policies, social security, and gender equality, among others.[1] One such ranking is the World Economic Forum's annual Gender Gap Report, introduced in 2006. The aim of the report is to reveal role models in economic gender equality as well as to provide information in support of the Forum's initiatives to close the economic gender gap globally.[2] Based on four criteria – opportunities for economic participation, educational attainment, health and survival, and political empowerment – the ranking indicates aspects of equal opportunities between men and women and the ways in which resources, scarce or ample, are divided between them. So, the rankings measure only gender-based disparities. Nevertheless, as Saadia Zahidi wrote in Huffington Post in 2013, the Nordic countries stick out:

> Although no country in the world has yet achieved gender equality, the Nordic countries consistently stand out in the World Economic Forum's annual Global Gender Gap Report,

1 Johan Strang, "Introduction: The Nordic model of transnational cooperation," in *Nordic Cooperation: A European region in transition*, ed. Johan Strang (London: Routledge, 2016), 1–27, doi:10.4324/9781315755366–1; Johanna Kantola, "Persistent paradoxes, turbulent times. Gender equality policies in the Nordics in the 2010s," in *The Nordic Economic, Social and Political Model. Challenges in the 21ˢᵗ Century*, ed. Anu Koivunen, Jari Ojala, and Janne Holmén (London: Routledge, 2021), 212.
2 Klaus Schwab, "Preface," In *The Global Gender Gap Report 2009*, ed. Ricardo Hausmann et al. (Geneva: World Economic Forum, 2009), v; For the reports, see, *World Economic Forum*, accessed 17 September, 2020 https://www.weforum.org/projects/closing-the-gender-gap-gender-parity-task-forces.

which measures how well countries are doing at removing the obstacles that hold women back.[3]

According to the 2014 report, for example, "[n]o country in the world has fully closed the gender gap, but all five of the Nordic countries have closed more than 80% of it."[4] The Nordic countries held all five top positions. They were referred to as "role models in terms of their ability to achieve gender parity."[5] In 2020, the ranking appeared quite similar. The top was still occupied by the Nordic countries; however, Denmark was only fourteenth, a position to which it had dropped in 2017.[6] Of course, the rankings are problematic, and their results are always partial. More importantly, changes in the rankings indicate that gender equality is a process and that the gender gap, as measured by one inquiry, can also widen. In terms of gender equality, countries are in constant motion.

The Nordic countries are clearly presented as world leaders in gender equality. However, any historian or social scientist interested in gender issues could point out a long list of failures and shortcomings in Nordic gender equality policies and gender relations, whether national or regional. According to several critical assessments since the 1970s and 1980s, attempts to reach gender equality constantly encounter both structural and ideological obstacles based on various factors in education, the labour market, family relations, and general attitudes.[7] This dilemma, where the Nordic countries are presented as world leaders on the

---

3 Saadia Zahidi, "What Makes the Nordic Countries Gender Equality Winners?" *Huffington Post*, 24 October 2013, https://www.huffpost.com/entry/what-makes-the-nordic-cou_b_4159555#:~:text=All%20Nordic%20countries%20reached%2099,to%20primary%20and%20secondary%20education.
4 World Economic Forum, *The Global Gender Gap Report 2014* (Geneva: World Economic Forum, 2014), 7.
5 World Economic Forum, *Global Gender Gap 2014*, 37.
6 World Economic Forum, *Global Gender Gap Report 2017* (Geneva: World Economic Forum, 2017), 8; World Economic Forum, *Global Gender Gap Report 2020* (Geneva: World Economic Forum, 2020), 9.
7 Elina Haavio-Mannila, "The Position of Women," in *Nordic Democracy*, ed. Erik Allardt et al (Copenhagen: Det danske selskab, 1981); Elina Haavio-Mannila et al., *Unfinished democracy: women in Nordic politics* (Oxford: Pergamon Press, 1985); Marja Keränen, *Finnish 'undemocracy': Essays on gender and politics* (Helsinki: Finnish Political Science Association, 1990); Nordic Council of Ministers, *Kön och våld – Gender & Violence: Ett nordiskt forskningsprogram 2000– 2004 slutrapport. A Nordic Research Programme 2000–2004 Final Report* (Copenhagen: Nordic Council of Ministers, 2005), 7. Among the more current studies, see Johanna Kantola, Kevät Nousiainen, and Milja Saari, eds., *Tasa-arvo toisin nähtynä. Oikeuden ja politiikan näkökulmia tasa-arvoon ja yhdenvertaisuuteen*, (Helsinki: Gaudeamus, 2012); Kantola, "Persistent paradoxes."

one hand and filled with problems on the other, is intriguing. What makes seemingly successful Nordic gender equality policies so complicated?

In this chapter, I am interested in the ways in which understandings of equality between women and men were rhetorically presented and formed a transnational *Nordic* gender equality policy, which was shared and confirmed by several agreements and action plans. The current assessment of the Nordic countries as leaders in gender equality presupposes not only a historical change in the concept of equality but also a historical process of conceptualizing gender equality as specifically Nordic. To understand how "Nordicness" in the field of gender equality was established, I will give an overview of the Nordic cooperation on gender equality, initiated in the early 1970s, and explore how certain gender equality policies were gradually named Nordic. This chapter argues that the 1990s were a turning point in the Nordic cooperation on gender equality. Since the 1990s, naming and even branding gender equality as Nordic gained ground among the Nordic gender equality agencies. The Nordic-Baltic cooperation, in particular, served to establish a platform for the rhetoric of Nordicness in the field of gender equality. Moreover, the European Union challenged the Nordic gender equality officials to sharpen their conceptions. This chapter explores how policies became "Nordic," how the concept of "Nordic" was used, and how the Nordic countries came to be presented as world leaders in gender equality.

The main sources consist of documents produced by Nordic gender equality agencies. The Nordic Council of Ministers, founded in 1971, was the main body to coordinate Nordic cooperation on equal rights. Its publications include action plans for Nordic cooperation and various project reports and programmes since the 1970s. The concept of "gender equality" is used as an analytical concept, my tool to study Nordic cooperation in policy and politics. At the same time, my intention is to be historically sensitive to the changing conceptualizations of "gender equality" (S. *jämställdhet*, N. *likestilling*, DK. *ligestilling*, I. *jafnrétti*, F. *tasa-arvo*). Until the turn of the 21st century, *jämställdhet* and its Nordic synonyms were often translated as equal opportunities in English language publications. Equal opportunities referred to the same rights, responsibilities, and possibilities for women and men; moreover, women and men were mainly understood as binary categories. Later timelines and histories summarizing the early years of Nordic cooperation often use the concept "gender equality,"[8] but it

---

8 E.g. Nordic Council of Ministers, *Together for Gender Equality – a stronger Nordic Region. Nordic co-operation programme on gender equality 2015–2018* (Copenhagen: Nordic Council of Ministers, 2015).

was not the concept used by contemporaries. As the Finnish political scientist Anne Maria Holli has argued, "gender equality" as a linguistic construction is always a context-bound concept. Other scholars have also stressed the importance of studying "gender equality" as a historical concept, as its content not only varies according to time and place but also can have differing meanings in the same historical context.[9] Therefore, a historically sensitive reading of concepts is needed. When it comes to "Nordic gender equality," the rhetorical aspects of Nordicness further underline the need to be historically specific.

Equal rights become Nordic in the 1970s

There is a long tradition of Scandinavian and Nordic cooperation since the 19th century, that can be tracked through the meetings, conferences, and comparative projects of professionals and civil society organisations. Academic scholars and civil servants formed Nordic networks and launched Nordic journals and other publications. Lawyers started inter-Nordic meetings in 1872 and other professions followed the same pattern. Institutionalised Nordic cooperation in the fields of social policy and child welfare were established after the First World War. In the 1920s, following the inter-Nordic cooperation of lawyers and activists in the women's movement, there were national reforms in family law. By 1929, relatively similar marriage laws were passed in all the Nordic countries.[10]

Social policy experts, politicians, and civil servants played a major role in Nordic cooperation, and their work together lead to a shared interest in gender issues as well. The Nordic scholars Thorsten Borring Olesen and Johan Strang

---

9 Anne Maria Holli, "Kriittisiä näkökulmia tasa-arvon tutkimukseen," in *Tasa-arvo toisin nähtynä. Oikeuden ja politiikan näkökulmia tasa-arvoon ja yhdenvertaisuuteen*, ed. Johanna Kantola, Kevät Nousiainen, and Milja Saari (Helsinki: Gaudeamus, 2012), 74; On historical context, see Kari Melby, Anna-Birte Ravn, and Christina Carlsson Wetterberg, eds., "A Nordic model of gender equality? Introduction," in *Gender equality and welfare politics in Scandinavia. The limits of political ambition?* (Bristol: Policy Press, 2008), 18–20.

10 Strang, "Introduction," 6–8; Kari Melby et al., *Inte ett ord om kärlek. Äktenskap och politik i Norden ca 1850–1930* (Göteborg & Stockholm: Makadam förlag, 2006); Klaus Petersen, "Constructing Nordic welfare? Nordic Social Political Cooperation 1919–1955," in *The Nordic Model of Welfare. A Historical Reappraisal*, ed. Niels Finn Christiansen et al. (Copenhagen: Museum Tusculanum Press, 2006), 70–71; Kari Melby et al., "What is Nordic in the Nordic gender model?" in *Beyond Welfare State Models: Transnational Historical Perspectives on Social Policy*, ed. Pauli Kettunen and Klaus Petersen (Cheltenham & Northampton MA: Edward Elgar, 2011), 150–51; Astri Andresen et al., *Barnen och välfärdspolitiken. Nordiska barndomar 1900–2000* (Stockholm: Dialogos Förlag, 2011).

state that official Nordic cooperation "contributed to a Nordification of political discourse and to the promotion of inter-Nordic exchange of ideas among governments, parliamentarians and civil servants."[11] Simultaneously, new popular movements, especially second-wave feminism in the 1960s and 1970s, had an impact on the Nordic arena. Moreover, international organisations and transnational movements highlighting human rights and the rights of women were often used as a point of reference in the Nordic countries. The 1945 Charter of the United Nations and the 1948 Universal Declaration of Human Rights provided not only international inspiration but also more compelling incentives for Nordic gender equality policies. As historian Kristine Kjærsgaard shows, the Danish participation in the UN conferences on women in 1975, 1980, and 1985 served in various ways the promotion of national gender equality policies in the 1970s and 1980s.[12]

Nordic cooperation on equality between men and women became institutionalised in the 1970s. The Nordic Council of Ministers (hereafter Council of Ministers) was the main agency to coordinate Nordic cooperation on equal rights. This has been pointed out by the Danish historian Bente Rosenbeck who argues that

> over a number of years, the Nordic Council of Ministers has prioritized equal rights, sponsoring a committee for equal rights issues made up of council officials as well as setting up the post of official equal rights consultant, a position later renamed equal rights advisory officer.[13]

In 1974, the Council of Ministers decided that the Nordic governments should nominate representatives to liaise with the other governments on equality be-

---

11 Thorsten Borring Olesen and Johan Strang, "European challenge to Nordic institutional co-operation: Past, present and future," in *Nordic Cooperation: The European region in transition*, ed. Johan Strang (London: Routledge, 2016), 29, doi:10.4324_9781315755366–2.

12 Nordic Council of Ministers, *Women and Men in the Nordic Countries: Facts on Equal Opportunities 1988* (Copenhagen: Nordic Council of Ministers, 1988), 6; Helvi Sipilä, "Yhdistyneitten Kansakuntien toiminta sukupuolten tasa-arvon edistämiseksi," in *Toisenlainen tasa-arvo*, ed. Sirkka Sinkkonen and Eila Ollikainen (Kuopio: Kustannuskiila Oy, 1982), 13–20; Kristine Kjærsgaard, "International Arenas and Domestic Institution Formation: The Impact of the UN Women's Conferences in Denmark, 1975–1985," *Nordic Journal of Human Rights* 36 (2018): 271–86; Heidi Kurvinen and Arja Turunen, "Toinen aalto uudelleen tarkasteltuna. Yhdistys 9:n rooli suomalaisen feminismin historiassa," *Sukupuolentutkimus* 3/2018, 21–34.

13 Bente Rosenbeck, "Nordic women's studies and gender research," in *Is there a Nordic Feminism? Nordic feminist thought on culture and society*, ed. Drude von der Fehr, Anna G. Jónasdóttir, and Bente Rosenbeck (London: UCL Press, 1998), 354.

tween women and men. The following year, when the UN women's decade on equality, development, and peace commenced, the Council of Ministers established a Nordic contact group on equal rights. In 1978, it published the first *Nordic Equality Bulletin* and presented a proposal to establish a Committee of Senior Officials for Equality. Since then, the Council of Ministers has regularly approved and confirmed an action plan for Nordic cooperation on equality between women and men. The Committee assumed responsibility for Nordic cooperation on equality in 1980, and an advisor with responsibility for equal rights was appointed to the Council of Ministers' secretariat in 1981.[14] During the following years these decisions defined the administrative structures of the inter-Nordic work for equality.

Policies to promote gender equality were thus institutionalized from above, which continued and extended the national equality policies that were often called "state feminism," a concept coined by the Norwegian political scientist Helga Maria Hernes in 1987 to describe the ties between the welfare state and feminism. According to Hernes, the Nordic welfare states were not necessarily woman friendly, but they had capacity to develop into woman-friendly societies. The political scientists Dorothy McBride and Amy Mazur define state feminism as consisting of "the actions by women's policy agencies to include women's movement demands and actors into the state to produce feminist outcomes in either policy processes or societal impact or both."[15] In the Nordic countries, state feminism materialized on both a national and transnational, Nordic level. Moreover, one crucial aspect of state feminism has consisted of the focus on knowledge production, as the historian Eirinn Larsen has indicated in her study of the political process that led to the establishment of the Norwegian Secretariat for Feminist Research in 1977.[16] In the Nordic debates, state feminism has been criticized by feminist scholars, but it has also been used as a relatively neutral concept to describe gender policies in the Nordic welfare states.

---

14 Nordic Council of Ministers, *Together for Gender Equality – a stronger Nordic Region: Nordic co-operation programme on gender equality 2015–2018* (Copenhagen: Nordic Council of Ministers, 2015), 26–27.
15 Helga Maria Hernes, *Welfare State and Woman Power: Essays in State Feminism* (Oslo: Norwegian University Press, 1987); Amy Mazur and Dorothy McBride, "State Feminism," in *Politics, Gender and Concepts: Theory and Methodology*, ed. Gary Goertz and Amy Mazur (Cambridge: Cambridge University Press, 2008), 244–69; Dorothy McBride and Amy Mazur, *The Politics of State Feminism: Innovation in Comparative Research* (Philadelphia: Temple University Press, 2010).
16 Eirinn Larsen, "State feminism revisited as knowledge history: The case of Norway," in *Histories of Knowledge in Postwar Scandinavia. Actors, Arenas, and Aspirations*, ed. Johan Östling, Niklas Olsen, and David Larsson Heidenblad (London: Routledge, 2020).

The Nordic contact group, since 1978 the Nordic Committee of Senior Officials for Equality, took immediate action to arrange seminars and meetings between politicians, civil servants, researchers, and activists in the Nordic countries. In 1976, the first joint seminar *Equality between Men and Women in Family and Work* was arranged in Sweden. Another seminar, this time in Finland, discussed legal guarantees of equality between women and men in the Nordic region. The themes of these meetings suggest that, from the very beginning, family, work, and legislation were central elements in the debate on Nordic equality between women and men. Most publications and seminar programmes did not, however, name these aspects "Nordic" or define the Nordic characteristics of equality. An explicitly Nordic gender equality was not on the agenda. Instead, the adjective "Nordic" was regularly used as a descriptor for region, or cooperation. Nordic cooperation took place in the Nordic region, but the other rhetoric of Nordicness was not very powerful at this time.

The several projects launched by the Committee of Senior Officials for Equality reveal other interesting aspects of contemporary concepts of equality. In general, the concept of equality (*jämlikhet*) became central in the language of Nordic social policy in the 1970s, as Nils Edling, Jørn Henrik Petersen, and Klaus Petersen have concluded. The language of equality was promoted not only by Social Democrats and the trade unions but also by feminists who introduced equality between women and men (*jämställdhet*) to the social policy language.[17] Among the first projects on the inter-Nordic level were the 1977 project on paternal leave, the 1977 project about mass media and equality, and the 1978 project on marriage and livelihood in the Nordic region. Projects on social planning and types of housing, the gender-segregated labour market, and the impact of new technology on equality in the workplace also belonged to the first initiatives.[18] All these topics were typical social issues of the 1970s. The topics of the projects also indicate that key areas of equal opportunities and equality between women and men dealt with families, parenthood, and the labour market.

---

17 Nils Edling, Jørn Henrik Petersen, and Klaus Petersen, "Social policy language in Denmark and Sweden," in *Analysing social policy concepts and language: Comparative and transnational perspectives*, ed. Daniel Béland and Klaus Petersen (Bristol: Policy Press, 2014), 24.
18 Nordic Council of Ministers, *Women and Men 1988*, 6; Nordic Council of Ministers, *Together for Gender Equality*, 26.

Introduction of Nordic programmes

A more systematic way of promoting equality between women and men on the Nordic level consisted of specific programmes and action plans, while the practice of launching projects continued. As the Presidency of the Council of Ministers rotated among the member countries, each country in turn had a mandate to prioritise themes and topics in gender equality. In 1982, the first Nordic programme on equality between women and men, approved by the Council of Ministers for Equal Opportunity, was launched. During the period of the first programme, there were projects on violence in relationships and women in Nordic politics. One achievement during this period was a 1986 Nordic report *The Divided Labour Market* which showed that the labour market continued to be a key arena in the Nordic struggle for equality.[19] The priority is evident in the slogan "from women's pay to equal pay."

Some new aspects of gender equality were added by the projects "Men and gender equality" and "Muslim immigrant women," both created in 1987. These projects are the first indication that gender equality was to be understood as intersectional; it was not only the position of women that was at stake but also class, ethnicity, religion, and other categories. However, the binary categories of women and men continued to dominate debates on gender equality. In 1988, a statistical publication on women and men in the Nordic countries defined the two Swedish concepts of equality as *jämställdhet* and *jämlikhet*. Equality as *jämställdhet* referred to equality between women and men. It meant that women and men were to have the same rights, responsibilities, and possibilities with regard to employment that would provide them with economic independence, childcare, housework, politics, and trade unions, among others. Equality as *jämlikhet* was defined as a wider concept. It was based on the premise that all people were equal regardless of their sex, ethnicity, religion, and social background, and so on. Equality between women and men (*jämställdhet*) was stated to be not only one of the most important aspects of equality as *jämlikhet* but to be applicable to everyone, women and men. In the 1994 publication, *Women and Men in the Nordic Countries*, the translation of *jämställdhet* was "equal opportunities."[20] This translation suggests that the contemporary understanding of Nordic cooperation in gender equality emphasized formal equality.

---

19 Nordic Council of Ministers, *The Divided Labour Market* (Copenhagen: Nordic Council of Ministers, 1986).

20 Nordic Council of Ministers, *Women and Men 1988*, 6; Nordic Council of Ministers, *Women and Men in the Nordic Countries. Facts and Figures 1994* (Copenhagen: Nordic Council of Minis-

A dualistic understanding of equality was more broadly reflected in the Nordic legislation on gender equality. Legislation to promote equality between women and men was passed in the Nordic countries from the 1970s: in Iceland in 1976, in Denmark in 1976 and 1978, in Norway in 1979, Sweden in 1980, and Finland in 1986. All these laws focused on equality between women and men. Other forms of discrimination, on the basis of age, language, religion, ethnic origin, disability, and sexual orientation, were later covered by Non-Discrimination Acts.[21] On the one hand, the Equality Acts forbade gender-based discrimination and on the other hand, it demanded measures to promote equality between women and men. When it came to positive measures, there were some differences between each country's acts. The Swedish act, for example, obliged employers to promote equality whereas the Norwegian and the Finnish acts obliged public authorities. These Nordic principles of equality legislation emphasised structural changes, promoted equality in the labour market, and were tied to the welfare state.[22]

In 1987, the Council of Ministers approved a new Nordic programme for equal opportunities 1989–1993. The second programme period focused on the role of women in economic development. Another prioritized theme dealt with the opportunities for women and men to combine family and work. According to the senior advisor Carita Peltonen, "the focus was on women's participation in political decision-making, education, equal pay, the situation of immigrant women and on how women can combine their family life with their working life."[23] Here, again, we can note two themes in the Nordic cooperation for equal rights: women's position in the labour market, and tensions between work and family in the daily life of both women and men. The Nordic equality policy was intended to push women into the labour market and men into parenting and care.

---

ters, 1994), 12. On difficulties to translate the Swedish (and Finnish) concepts, see also Nousiainen, "Käsitteellisiä välineitä tasa-arvon käsittelyyn," 32.

21 Sinikka Mustakallio, *Tulokseksi tasa-arvo. Kokemuksia valtionhallinnon tasa-arvotyöstä Pohjoismaissa* (Helsinki: Valtion painatuskeskus, 1993), 29; On problems of non-discrimination in Finland, see Anne Maria Holli and Johanna Kantola, "State feminism Finnish style: Strong policies clash with implementation problems," in *Changing state feminism*, ed. Joyce Outshoorn and Johanna Kantola (Houndmills: Palgrave Macmillan, 2007), 94–95.

22 Mustakallio, *Tulokseksi tasa-arvo*, 29; Kantola, "Persistent paradoxes," 214–15.

23 Peltonen presents this as the first five-year programme, but it was preceded by the 1982 programme. Carita Peltonen, "Nordic men – Cooperation on Gender Equality," in *Possibilities and Challenges? Men's Reconciliation of Work and Family Life – Conference Report*, ed. Jouni Varanka and Maria Forslund (Copenhagen: Nordic Council of Ministers, 2006), 126.

International cooperation to promote the position of women, together with the fact that Nordic statisticians share a long tradition in Nordic cooperation, was reflected in gender-related projects. In advance of the 1985 UN Conference on Women, the central statistical bureaus of the Nordic countries initiated a joint project to publish statistics on equality between women and men in the Nordic countries. The first booklet, presented in the UN Nairobi conference in 1985, can be seen as a turning point in the rhetoric of Nordicness and the Nordic framing of issues related to gender equality.[24] After the Nairobi conference, the Nordic Committee of Senior Officials for Equality proposed to the Nordic chief statisticians that a Nordic contact group on statistics of equal opportunities should be established and that an updated version of statistics should be published for the forthcoming regional conference. The regional conference to follow up the Nairobi decisions was arranged in Oslo in 1988 in conjunction with the Women's Forum, in which the Nordic work on equal opportunities was one of the main topics. The first results of the cooperation between the Nordic statisticians and equality officials came out as a publication offering "current information on the differences and similarities in women's and men's situations in the Nordic countries, in the form of tables, diagrams, and textual analysis."[25]

The role assumed by the national statistical bureaus gave Nordic cooperation on gender equality a statistical, fact-based character, in which Nordic (in) equality became a measurable phenomenon. The aim of compiling these statistics was to reveal shortcomings and failures in the achievement of equality, rather than to measure equality itself. Moreover, the scholarly field of women's studies was promoted by Nordic institutional cooperation and state feminism. For example, there was a direct link between the 1988 Women's Forum and the appointment of a Nordic coordinator for women's studies. The coordinator, affiliated with Åbo Akademi University in Finland in 1991–1995, was also involved in the Nordic action programme for equal rights.[26] Knowledge production, not only in the form of policy programmes and the provision of statistical facts to decision-makers, but also through support for women's studies became crucial ways for the Council of Ministers' equality officials to promote equality in the

24 Nordic Council of Ministers, *Facts and Figures about Women and Men in the Nordic Countries. Kvinnor och män i Norden* 1985 (Copenhagen: Nordic Council of Ministers, 1985).
25 Nordic Council of Ministers, *Women and Men 1988*, 3.
26 Christina Österberg and Birgitta Hedman, *Women and Men in the Nordic Countries: Facts on equal opportunities yesterday, today and tomorrow 1994* (Copenhagen: Nordic Council of Ministers, 1994); Nordic Council of Ministers, *Nordic Gender Equality in Figures* (Copenhagen: Nordic Council of Ministers, 2015); Rosenbeck, "Nordic women's studies," 351; Larsen, "State feminism," 160–63.

Nordic countries. The Council of Ministers funded research on politics and the labour market. A 1980s project *Unfinished democracy*, sponsored by the Council of Ministers, studied Nordic women in political decision-making.[27] The project led also to a handbook in women's representation. It was authored by the Danish feminist and political scientist Drude Dahlerup and published in five Nordic languages. Another book based on interviews with female politicians was also issued. Moreover, Dahlerup contributed to the Council of Ministers' work for gender equality by coordinating a Nordic-wide project entitled *BRYT* – which means "break down" – on breaking down sex segregation in the labour market.[28]

Until the mid-1990s, the Nordic publications on equal rights tended to emphasize shortcomings and failures in equal opportunities for women and men. For example, *Women and Men in the Nordic Countries* (1994), as well as a booklet presenting excerpts from it, motivated this kind of knowledge production. The publications listed the following reasons for the urgent need for basic statistics on the position of women and men in Nordic societies: "1) to raise consciousness, persuade policymakers, and promote change; 2) to stimulate ideas for change; 3) to provide an unbiased basis for policies and measures; and 4) to monitor and evaluate policies and actions taken."[29] A firm belief in the need for gender-based knowledge production and gender statistics was made explicit in the publication series of the Council of Ministers.

The Nordic publications presenting basic statistics on equality between women and men pointed at several problems that were also analysed by contemporary studies on women and gender. When it came to political decision-making, Nordic facts and figures revealed male dominance at all levels, supporting the notions of what feminist scholars termed "unfinished democracy" or "undemocracy."[30] Feminist scholars in the Nordic countries analysed women's and men's paid and unpaid labour in the 1980s and early 1990s, and noted how "women and men work the same amount, but women do more unpaid work, men more paid work." Intensive Nordic research on the labour market was also echoed by statistical publications which noted that men had higher incomes than

---

27 Haavio-Mannila, *Unfinished Democracy*.

28 Drude Dahlerup, *Vi har ventet længe nok: Håndbog i kvinderepræsentation* (Copenhagen: Nordic Council of Ministers, 1988). In Icelandic 1988, Norwegian 1989, Swedish 1989, and Finnish 1990; Drude Dahlerup, ed., *Blomster & Spark. Samtaler med kvindelige politikere i Norden* (Copenhagen: Nordic Council of Ministers, 1985).

29 Numbering added by PM. Nordic Council of Ministers, *Women and Men 1994*, 19; Österberg & Hedman, *Women and Men 1994*, 5; Nordic Council of Ministers, *Women and Men 1988*, 18.

30 Haavio-Mannila, *Unfinished democracy*; Keränen, *Finnish "undemocracy."*

women and that women tended to reach the basic pension only.[31] Nordic gender equality was not presented as an international model to be followed by the rest of the world. On the contrary, it was full of shortcomings and a work in progress.

Gender equality goes European and global as Nordic

In the 1990s, the concept of gender became more widely adopted in Nordic equality policies. The 1995 World Conference on Women in Beijing, in particular, introduced new concepts and policies, such as gender mainstreaming.[32] The Nordic equality bodies were quick to adopt new concepts that also were familiar from the expanding field of gender studies. Simultaneously, a growing interest in regional and European cooperation intensified with the expansion of the European Union. Finland and Sweden joined the EU in 1995, Denmark had been a member state since 1973, and Norway and Iceland chose to not join. In line with many other policy fields, a dialogue between European and Nordic policies to promote gender equality was found necessary. The EU also posed several challenges for Nordic cooperation on gender equality.[33] In the Nordic countries, legislation on equality was mainly based on promoting equality between women and men in the labour market, while anti-discrimination legislation, emphasised by the EU, was less developed. Many Nordic gender equality agencies were worried about the negative impact of the EU on their progressive gender equality policies; at the same time, they anticipated that, as new member countries, Sweden and Finland would strengthen the EU's gender equality policies.[34] These ambiv-

---

31 Nordic Council of Ministers, *Women and Men 1994*, For gender studies, see, for example, Marja-Liisa Anttalainen, *Rapport om den könsuppdelade arbetsmarknaden* (Oslo: Nordic Council of Ministers, 1984); Hernes, *Welfare State and Woman Power*; Arnlaug Leira, *Welfare States and Working Mothers: The Scandinavian Experience* (Cambridge: Cambridge University Press, 1992); Liisa Rantalaiho and Tuula Heiskanen, eds., *Gendered Practices of Working Life* (London: Macmillan, 1997).
32 Marjaana Jauhola and Johanna Kantola, "Globaali sukupuolipolitiikka Suomessa," in *Sukupuolikysymys*, ed. Marita Husso and Risto Heiskala (Helsinki: Gaudeamus, 2016), 223; Raija Julkunen, "Sukupuoli valtiollisen politiikan kohteena," in *Sukupuolikysymys*, ed. Husso and Heiskala, 251.
33 Olesen & Strang, "European challenge," 32–36; Johanna Kantola and Kevät Nousiainen, "Euroopan unionin tasa-arvopolitiikka: Velvoittavaa lainsäädäntöä ja pehmeää sääntelyä," in Kantola, Nousiainen, and Saari, eds., *Tasa-arvo toisin nähtynä*.
34 Holli & Kantola, "State feminism Finnish style"; Jauhola & Kantola, "Globaali sukupuolipolitiikka Suomessa," 219–20.

alent expectations obviously urged the Nordic gender equality agencies to clarify their message on the "Nordicness" of gender equality.

The new Nordic programme on gender equality for the period 1995–2000 aimed to influence "European and international developments in gender equality."[35] This goal was also made explicit in the 1994 publication on gender statistics which, for the first time, highlighted a united Nordic approach and a common Nordic platform in gender equality.[36] Among the more concrete aims in the 1995–2000 programme were the following: equal access for women and men to political and economic decision-making, economic equality and equal influence, an equal labour market, and improved opportunities for both women and men to reconcile parenthood and careers. In 1998, the Finnish gender equality activist and former Gender Equality Ombudsman Tuulikki Petäjäniemi interpreted these goals as a Nordic decision to become international leaders regarding men and gender equality.[37] Moreover, as Ylva Waldemarson has stressed, the Nordic Council and the Nordic Council of Ministers tended to strengthen the international visibility of the Nordic countries by using the rhetoric of Nordic identity partially based on the Nordic model of gender equality.[38] Work towards gender equality in the Nordic countries was transforming into the "Nordicness" of gender equality.

The "Nordic" gender equality policies were to assign men and masculinities a crucial role. In 1997, an action plan for men and gender equality was approved. A Nordic coordinator position for men's studies was founded by the Council of Ministers, and its host organisation became the Nordic Institute for Women's Studies and Gender Research (NIKK), founded in 1995 and located in Oslo.[39] Critical studies on men and masculinities appeared simultaneously in other parts of the world, and the European Union was also funding projects on men and gender equality. Nevertheless, the men's studies coordinator Øystein Gullvår Holter

---

35 Nordic Council of Ministers, *Together for Gender Equality*, 25; Ylva Waldemarson, "Gender equality the Nordic way: The Nordic Council's and Nordic Council of Ministers' cooperation with the Baltic States and Northwest Russia in the political field of gender equality 1999–2010," in *Gender equality on a Grand Tour: Politics and institutions – the Nordic Council, Sweden, Lithuania and Russia*, ed. Eva Blomberg et al (Leiden: Brill, 2017), 34.

36 Nordic Council of Ministers, *Women and Men 1994*, 4.

37 Tuulikki Petäjäniemi, "Naisten ja miesten tasa-arvo – yhteinen etu," in Jarmo Tarkki and Tuulikki Petäjäniemi, *Tasa-arvo: Saavutuksia ja haasteita* [Equality: Achievements and challenges] (Jyväskylä: Atena Kustannus, 1998), 18.

38 Waldemarson, "Gender equality the Nordic way," 38.

39 Nordic Council of Ministers, *Together for Gender Equality*, 24; Rosenbeck, "Nordic women's studies," 350–51.

stated in 2003: "the connection between the policy level and welfare development is in many ways unique to the Nordic region, along with a large proportion of women in the labour force, a high level of women in politics, and a general emphasis on gender-equal status and opportunities. This region is a bit of a social laboratory regarding gender."[40] The idea of a specific Nordic gender equality gradually developed as the Nordic equality policies were exposed to the European Union and other contacts beyond the Nordic region.

The dissolution of the Soviet Union in 1991 led to a changing situation in the Baltic region. The newly independent Baltic states Estonia, Latvia, and Lithuania posed new challenges not only to Nordic equality policies but to official Nordic cooperation more broadly. In 1991, the Council of Ministers had established information offices in the Baltic capitals and Baltic politicians were invited to the meeting of the Nordic Council, a cooperative body of the Nordic parliaments.[41] In 1995 the Council of Ministers decided to survey the prospects for cooperation between the Nordic countries and the Baltic states. This initiative led to a publication which strongly recommended Nordic-Baltic cooperation and a joint forum to be organised as soon as possible. The Baltic counterparts motivated the need for immediate action with reference to the ongoing rapid changes in the Baltic states. Consequently, the first Nordic-Baltic meeting of ministers for gender equality was arranged in Oslo in 1997. The meeting approved the first programme for Nordic-Baltic cooperation on gender equality from 1998 to 2000.[42]

Governmental cooperation became a crucial part of the Nordic-Baltic cooperation programmes. In the beginning, the Nordic counterparts presented Nordic gender equality activities to the Baltic counterparts and national policy instruments were established in the Baltic states. Joint seminars in which the Nordic Gender Equality Ombudsmen introduced the Nordic gender equality legislation were one way to establish cooperation – and to export the "Nordicness" of gender equality. Differing policies within the Nordic region were less relevant in the common attempts to construct a coherent image of the Nordic gender equality

---

40 Øystein Gullvåg Holter, *Can men do it? Men and gender equality – the Nordic experience* (Copenhagen: The Nordic Council of Ministers, 2003), 7–8; Nordic Council of Ministers, *Miehet ja tasa-arvo – toimintaohjelma ja taustamuistio* (Copenhagen: Nordic Council of Ministers, 1997.)
41 Olesen & Strang, "European challenge to Nordic institutional cooperation," 34; Anna Kharkina, *From Kinship to Global Brand: The Discourse on Culture in Nordic Cooperation after World War II* (Stockholm: Acta Universitatis Stockholmiensis, 2013), 85–86.
42 Nordic Council of Ministers, *Nordic Baltic co-operation on gender equality 1998–2003* (Copenhagen: Nordic Council of Ministers, 2004), http://norden.diva-portal.org/smash/record.jsf?pid=diva2%3 A701499&dswid=-6425. Nordic Council of Ministers, *Together for Gender Equality*, 23–24; Waldemarson, "Gender equality the Nordic way," 44–45.

policies. Moreover, as Anna Kharkina has pointed out, the values and contents of cooperation were often determined by the Nordic side of the partnership. She states that cultural cooperation, in particular, aimed at promoting "Nordic values." Those values consisted not only of democracy, the welfare state, and environmental policy but also of gender equality.[43]

In terms of gender equality, the Nordic-Baltic cooperation resulted in a joint campaign against the trafficking in women in the Nordic and Baltic countries. This campaign was commonly seen as an outcome of shared values. Governmental gender equality institutions were also established in all Baltic states but attempts to promote the Nordic understanding of gender equality in the Baltic legislation or to introduce top-down quotas and gender mainstreaming turned out to be less successful. The American scholar Denise M. Horn, who has compared the US and the Nordic gender projects in Estonia, concludes that the Nordic discourse of gender equality did not translate very well to the Estonian reality.[44] Nevertheless, Nordic cooperation with their eastern neighbours extended to Northwest Russia and Poland. The changing power constellations in Northern Europe intensified efforts to present the Nordic gender equality policy as a model and to share the established Nordic experiences of cooperation in gender policies.

When it came to inter-Nordic issues, men and masculinities remained on the agenda of "Nordic" gender equality initiatives. The gender equality programme for 2001–2005 prioritized the themes of "Men and gender equality," as well as "Violence against women."[45] During this programme period, the Council of Ministers' working group on men and gender equality promoted research on men's reconciliation of work and family life. In 2005, the final conference in Helsinki targeted fatherhood. The Finnish Minister of Social Affairs and Health, Tuula Haatainen, referred to the special role of the Nordic people in the following manner: "I find it important that we Nordic people raise on the agenda the gender equality aspect, which has been traditionally important to us. In the Nordic

---

43 Nordic Council of Ministers, *Nordic Baltic co-operation 1998–2003*; Kharkina, *From Kinship to Global Brand*, 80–82, 93, 100.

44 Nordic Council of Ministers, *Nordic-Baltic Campaign Against Trafficking in Women: Final Report 2002* (Copenhagen: Nordic Council of Ministers, 2004); Nordic Council of Ministers, *Nordic Baltic co-operation 1998–2003*; Nordic Council of Ministers, *Nordic-Baltic co-operation on gender equality 2004–2006* (Copenhagen: Nordic Council of Ministers, 2004), http://urn.kb.se/resolve? urn=urn:nbn:se:norden:org:diva-2103; Denise M. Horn, "Setting the agenda: US and Nordic gender policies in the Estonian transition to democracy," *International Feminist Journal of Politics* 10, no. 1 (March 2008): 70–71, doi:10.1080/14616740701747675.

45 The third priority, and a new one, was the integration of a gender perspective into Nordic state budgets. Nordic Council of Ministers, *Together for Gender Equality*, 24.

countries women's status in society has in many respects long been different from the gender and family patterns prevalent elsewhere in Europe."[46] She explained that the starting point in the Nordic countries was equal opportunities for men and women in the labour market and equal rights and responsibilities within the family. This dual approach was presented not only as something that differed from the rest of the world but also as something that was inherent in Nordic culture. However, despite the strong discursive emphasis on fatherhood in the Nordic countries, men's share of parental leave remained rather small. Only Iceland, formerly a latecomer, had managed to attract fathers to take parental leave to a remarkable extent.[47] When it came to social benefits, the idea of Nordic fatherhood was stronger in rhetoric than in practice.

However, in the same conference the Finnish senior advisor Carita Peltonen from the Council of Ministers indicated the shared traditions and mutual benefits of the Nordic cooperation on gender equality. Moreover, she stressed that "[t]he Nordic focus on men and gender equality is unique in an international context and provides a good example of the advantages and necessity of involving all groups in gender equality work."[48] It was now quite common to indicate these unique features of Nordic gender equality policies. A similar emphasis was expressed in the final report of a Nordic research programme on Gender and violence in 2005. The report stated that "the common tradition of welfare and gender equality policies within the Nordic countries constitutes a unique point of departure for research."[49] The report also assumed that the Nordic perspective would be important both in the European Union and in the international research community.

Active participation in the global arena became part of the Nordic gender equality policies and supported Nordic branding. Among these branding measures, a good number of Nordic fringe events or side events on equality issues were arranged in conjunction with the annual meeting of the UN Commission on the Status of Women. Starting in 2005, the Nordic themes in New York

46 Tuula Haatainen, "Opening speech," in *Possibilities and Challenges? Men's Reconciliation of Work and Family Life – Conference Report*, ed. Jouni Varanka and Maria Forslund (Copenhagen: Nordic Council of Ministers, 2006), 11.
47 In 2003, men's share of total days of parental leave was 27.6 percent in Iceland, 18.3 percent in Sweden, 8.6 percent in Norway, 5.3 percent in Finland, and 5.1 percent in Denmark. Frida Rós Valdimarsdóttir, "Nordic Experiences on Parental Leave and its impact on Gender Equality," in *Possibilities and Challenges? Men's Reconciliation of Work and Family Life – Conference Report*, ed. Jouni Varanka and Maria Forslund (Copenhagen: Nordic Council of Ministers, 2006), 73.
48 Carita Peltonen, "Nordic men – cooperation on gender equality," 125.
49 Nordic Council of Ministers, *Gender and Violence: A Nordic Research Programme 2000– 2004 – Final report* (Copenhagen: Nordic Council of Ministers, 2005), 16.

were gender and youth, women's participation in politics and management (2006), the new Nordic role of the father (2007), combating men's violence against women (2008), gender equality and climate change (2009), and results and challenges in relation to Beijing+15 (2010, 2011). In 2012 a panel of Nordic ministers discussed equality between women and men as "the Nordic way," a concept that had been launched in 2010.[50] A small booklet published by the Council of Ministers clearly revealed that gender equality had become a brand: "Nordic co-operation has been striving to improve gender equality for more than 30 years. The aim is to make policies of gender equality in the Region the best in the world and a model for other countries."[51] This message was brought to the UN fringe events and other international arenas. All former attempts by state feminists and equality officials to reveal and combat the problems of inequality were utilized as a strength and turned into a narrative of great progress in gender equality.

The official Nordic cooperation on gender equality celebrated its 40th anniversary in 2014 in a changing context. The old issues of women's participation in the labour market, men's right to be caregivers, and the reconciliation of work and family did not disappear, but the long-lasting focus on heteronormative family patterns and monocultural Nordic countries in the Nordic discourses expanded to include intersectional approaches in which diversity had a stronger role. In the gender equality programme, that ran from 2006 to 2010, it had been underlined that a systematic minority perspective must be incorporated in all initiatives for gender equality, and new intersectional aspects were promoted. However, the equal rights of lesbian, gay, bisexual, trans, and intersex (LGBTI) people were recognized very late. It was not until September 2019 that the Nordic programme on gender equality was supplemented with a programme on equal rights and opportunities for LGBTI people.[52] Moreover, on the global level the focus was on more traditional aspects of equality between women and men.

50 Nordic Council of Ministers, *Together for gender equality*, 19 – 23; Nordic Council of Ministers, *The Nordic cooperation programme on gender equality 2005* (Copenhagen: Nordic Council of Ministers, 2005), 4, 9; Nordic Council of Ministers, *Gender equality – the Nordic Way* (Copenhagen: Nordic Council of Ministers, 2010).
51 Nordic Council of Ministers, *Gender Equality – the Nordic Way*, 4; Also, Waldemarson, "Gender equality the Nordic way," 37 – 38.
52 Nordic Council of Ministers, *Together for gender equality*, 23; Nordic Council of Ministers, *Focus on gender – working toward an equal society: Nordic gender equality co-operation programme 2006 – 2010* (Copenhagen: Nordic Council of Ministers, 2006), 13; Nordic Council of Ministers, *Supplement to Nordic co-operation programme on gender equality 2019 – 2022: Equal rights, treatment and opportunities for LGBTI people in the Nordic region* (Copenhagen: Nordic Council of Ministers, 2020), 4.

The Nordic tradition of gender mainstreaming, however, incorporated other issues, such as sustainable societies. Climate change and sustainability were made Nordic gender issues in the global context as well as in the local arena.

Conclusions

The Nordic cooperation on equality between women and men was introduced in the early 1970s simultaneously with the introduction of national policies to promote equal rights for women and men. The early years of Nordic cooperation witnessed many events, projects, and publications in which the particulars of equal rights were defined. Women's participation in the labour market was one of the key issues, and the reconciliation of work and family was made into a shared Nordic equality issue. Interestingly, there seemed to be little interest in naming these efforts Nordic. The adjective Nordic was mainly used to qualify cooperation and to name the geographical region where this cooperation took place. In the inter-Nordic dialogue, it seemed to be less relevant to name equality policies Nordic. As the Nordic cooperation turned towards international arenas, the need to define the contents of their cooperation as Nordic became obvious. The UN Nairobi conference in 1985 was one of those external impulses that led to some more explicit expressions of the Nordic. Moreover, the concept of gender was introduced in the equality discourse in the 1990s. This impulse came from the 1995 conference in Beijing.

The collapse of the Soviet Union and the new cooperation with the Baltic states was one of the turning points in which Nordic gender equality was made into a product for export. As the product needed to be named and qualified, the rhetoric of Nordicness served as the marketing. Nordic Equality Ombudsmen were the new ambassadors of gender equality. I see a clear turning point in the early 1990s, in contrast to previous assumptions that the Nordic countries had aimed to persuade other governments to "do gender equality the Nordic way"[53] since the 1970s. The first decades of the Nordic cooperation on equal opportunities between women and men focused on pointing out problems, compiling statistics on the lack of equality, and seeking improvements within the Nordic countries. However, I agree with the previous conclusions that the cooperation with the Baltic states and Northwest Russia really aimed at promoting gender equality the Nordic way, i.e. taking "Nordic" gender equal-

---

53 Waldemarson, "Gender equality the Nordic way," 20.

ity abroad.[54] Since the 1990s, the Nordic model of gender equality was consciously constructed as a model, and the rhetoric of Nordicness served to promote that model.

Another explicit turning point strengthening Nordicness can be dated to the mid-1990s when Finland and Sweden joined the European Union. Now it became important to compare the Nordic gender equality with the European conception of equality. The Nordic gender equality was based on the values of the welfare state, women's labour market participation, men's family responsibilities, and the possibilities for women and men to combine working life and family. The European traditions of anti-discrimination legislation and bans on discrimination were less central in Nordic gender equality. Gender equality was a concept referring to power relations between women and men whereas non-discrimination referred to other forms of equality, encompassing age, health, ethnic origin, sexuality, religion, and other bases of discrimination. When the Nordic legislators adjusted to the European standards, Finland passed a separate Non-Discrimination Act and made amendments to the Equality Act whereas Sweden and Norway chose to integrate legislation on gender equality and non-discrimination. Moreover, since 2006, the mergers of Equality Ombudsmen and Discrimination Ombudsmen or their offices have taken place in most of the Nordic countries. The integration of the rights of the LGBTI people into the "Nordic" gender equality remains tardy, however.[55]

Despite the fact that the Nordic countries have been obliged to adjust to European standards in equality legislation, gender equality has become a hallmark of the Nordic societies, often used in various contexts. The UN fringe events, in particular, provided opportunities to market the "Nordic way" globally. The Nordic Council of Ministers does not hesitate to publish brochures in which the leading position of the Nordic countries in the field of gender equality is emphasised, or to organise events on the Nordic model of gender equality. Over forty years of cooperation on equality between women and men, and equal opportunities resulted in a construction of the Nordic gender equality as a brand with some "unique" characteristics. The Nordic cooperation contributed to a discursive construction of Nordicness. The working mother and the woman in the labour market became a characteristic representation of a Nordic woman. The Nordic cooperation has also shifted the focus towards men and masculinities and made the caring man a crucial discursive construction of a Nordic man. In the rhetoric of

---

54 Horn, "Setting the agenda," 61; Waldemarson, "Gender equality the Nordic way," 21.
55 Waldemarson, "Gender equality the Nordic way," 36; Nordic Information on Gender (NIKK), accessed 20 October, 2020, https://nikk.no/en/home/.

Nordicness, the Nordic father, in particular, became one of the finest outcomes of the Nordic gender equality.

Tero Erkkilä
Transparency and Nordic Openness in Finland: Ideational Shift, Invented Tradition, and Anders Chydenius

Introduction

Information access laws have spread rapidly since the 1990s primarily as part of the global drive for good governance, and also due to national political context and conflicts.[1] Transparency has become one of the key concepts of contemporary politics.[2] It is a new term in the political language of the Anglo-American world and beyond, and there are, in addition, liberal market notions bound up with the term that have made their way into national political contexts. This is perhaps most apparent in developing countries that are dependent on foreign direct investment and development aid.[3] But countries with a significant institutional history of openness, such as the Nordic countries, are also exposed to the new connotations of transparency.[4]

International policy discourses often tend to take nationalistic forms.[5] While an analysis of all national variants of the debate in the Nordic countries is beyond the scope of this chapter, the Finnish discourse on Nordic openness is one example of this. It constructs a nationalistic, collective positioning of

---

1 Daniel Berliner, "The Political Origins of Transparency," *The Journal of Politics* 76, no. 02 (April 2014): 479–91, doi:10.1017/S0022381613001412; Christopher Hood, "Transparency in Historical Perspective," in *Transparency: The Key to Better Governance?*, ed. David Heald and Christopher C. Hood (Oxford: Oxford University Press, 2006), 3–23.
2 Todd Sanders and Harry G. West, "Power Revealed and Concealed in the New World Order," in *Transparency and Conspiracy: Ethnographies of Suspicion in the New World Order*, ed. Todd Sanders and Harry G. West (Durham: Duke University Press, 2003).
3 Abraham Azubuike, "Accessibility of Government Information as a Determinant of Inward Foreign Direct Investment in Africa," in *Best Practices in Government Information: A Global Perspective*, ed. Irina Lynden and Jane Wu (München: K.G. Saur, 2008), 243; Jeannine E. Relly and Meghna Sabharwal, "Perceptions of Transparency of Government Policymaking: A Cross-National Study," *Government Information Quarterly* 26, no. 1 (2009): 148–57, doi:10.1016/j.giq.2008.04.002.
4 Erkkilä, *Government Transparency: Impacts and Unintended Consequences* (Houndmills: Palgrave Macmillan, 2012).
5 Vivien A. Schmidt, *The Futures of European Capitalism* (Oxford: Oxford University Press, 2002), 211.

Finns as members of an open Nordic society at the top of global economic competition. This chapter analyses the historical tradition of institutional openness in Finland. I will argue that there is an increasing awareness of this tradition, apparent in policy discourse on "Nordic openness," which portrays openness and access to government information as distinctive characteristics of Finland.[6] While openness is usually linked with the consensual tradition of governing typical for the Nordic countries,[7] awareness of this globally distinctive tradition also results from reflexivity over institutional history that is seen to provide advantage in global economic competition.[8] Global rankings and indicators that measure the performance of states in regard to good governance associate transparency with economic competitiveness. The Nordic countries have fared well in these rankings.

The public sphere has been a central element in studies of nation building, and has been used to explain the contextual differences of collective identities, nationhood, and nationalism.[9] In a world where convergence is seen to occur via grand processes such as "modernisation" and "globalisation," there are still differing national trajectories in political and economic institutions, concerning citizen rights and freedoms, as well as "us vs. them" narratives of nationhood. The public sphere has been theorised as both a structure or as a discursive space.[10] The latter position marks an opening for a genealogical conceptual analysis of the "public," an approach which is also adopted in this text. This approach makes concepts such as "publicity," "openness," and "transparency" instrumental in defining the institutional boundaries of the public sphere.[11] As a

---

6 Tero Erkkilä, *Government Transparency: Impacts and Unintended Consequences.*

7 Pekka Kettunen and Markku Kiviniemi, "Policy-Making in Finland: Consensus and Change," in *The Work of Policy – an International Survey,* ed. Hal Colebatch (New York: Lexington Books, 2006), 147–60; Johanna Rainio-Niemi, "Small State Cultures of Consensus: State Traditions and Consensus-Seeking in the Neo-Corporatist and Neutral Policies in Post-1945 Austria and Finland" (Dissertation, Department of Social Science History, University of Helsinki, 2008).

8 Douglass C. North, *Institutions, Institutional Change and Economic Performance* (Cambridge: Cambridge University Press, 1990).

9 Klaus Eder, "The Public Sphere," *Theory, Culture & Society* 23, no. 2–3 (2006): 607–11, doi:10.1177/0263276406062705; Shmuel Eisenstadt and Wolfgang Schluchter, "Introduction: Paths to Early Modernities – A Comparative View," in *Public Spheres and Collective Identities,* ed. Shmuel N. Eisenstadt, Wolfgang Schluchter, and Bjorn Wittrock (New Brunswick: Transaction Publishers, 2001).

10 Eder, "The Public Sphere"; Myra Marx Ferree et al., "Four Models of the Public Sphere in Modern Democracies," *Theory and Society* 31, no. 3 (June 2002): 289–24.

11 Cf. Margaret R. Somers, "What's Political or Cultural about Political Culture and the Public Sphere? Toward an Historical Sociology of Concept Formation," *Sociological Theory* 13, no. 2

social structure, the public sphere is itself a subject of an institutionalisation process, where structural, institutional, and cultural factors meet.[12]

Sweden became the first country to adopt a law granting access to government information in 1766. Publicity in state affairs was debated elsewhere in eighteenth-century Europe, where accounts of failed attempts at breaking absolutist secrecy tend to follow a narrative of how Enlightenment ideas on free speech and freedom of the press battled the "mystery of the state" in vain.[13] There are general features in the adoption – and non-adoption – of access laws in the 20th century,[14] but the country-specific studies stress historical explanations owing mainly to local conditions.[15]

(1995): 113–44; Margaret R. Somers, "Let Them Eat Social Capital: Socializing the Market versus Marketizing the Social," *Thesis Eleven* 81, no. 1 (2005): 5–19, doi:10.1177/0725513605051611.

12 Eder, "The Public Sphere"; Eisenstadt and Schluchter, "Introduction: Paths to Early Modernities – A Comparative View," 17–18; Margaret R. Somers, "Citizenship and the Place of the Public Sphere: Law, Community, and Political Culture in the Transition to Democracy," *American Sociological Review* 58, no. 5 (1993): 587–620.

13 Richard van Dülmen, *Die Gesellschaft Der Aufklärer: Zur Bürgerlichen Emanzipation Und Aufklärerischen Kultur in Deutschland.* (Frankfurt am Main: Fischer Taschenbuch Verlag, 1986); Joris van Eijnatten, "Between Practice and Principle: Dutch Ideas on Censorship and Press Freedom, 1579–1795," *Redescriptions: Yearbook of Political Thought and Conceptual History* 8 (2004): 85–113; Andreas Gestrich, *Absolutismus Und Öffentlichkeit: Politische Kommunikation in Deutschland Zu Beginn Des 18. Jahrhunderts* (Göttingen: Vandenhoeck & Ruprecht, 1994); Tim Knudsen, *Offentlighed i Det Offentlige. Om Historiens Magt* (Aarhus: Aarhus Universitetsforlag, 2003); Timo Konstari, *Asiakirjajulkisuudesta Hallinnossa. Tutkimus Yleisten Asiakirjain Julkisuudesta Hallinnon Kontrollivälineenä* (Helsinki: Suomalainen lakimiesyhdistys, 1977); Wolfgang Martens, *Die Botschaft Der Tugend: Die Aufklärung Im Spiegel Der Deutschen Moralischen Wochenschriften* (Stuttgart: Metzler, 1971); Andreas Würgler, "Conspiracy and Denunciation: A Local Affair and Its European Publics (Bern, 1749)," in *Cultures of Communication from Reformation to Enlightenment: Constructing Publics in the Early Modern German Lands*, ed. James Van Horn Melton (Aldershot: Ashgate Pub Ltd, 2002), 119–131.

14 Colin J. Bennett, "Understanding Ripple Effects: The Cross-National Adoption of Policy Instruments for Bureaucratic Accountability," *Governance* 10, no. 3 (1997): 213–33, doi:10.1111/0952–1895.401997040.

15 John Durham Peters, *Courting the Abyss: Free Speech and the Liberal Tradition*, 1st ed. (Chicago: University of Chicago Press, 2005); Tore Grønlie and Anne-Hilde Nagel, "Administrative History in Norway," *Jahrbuch Für Europäische Verwaltungsgeschichte* 10 (1998): 307–32; Isabelle Häner, *Öffentlichkeit Und Verwaltung* (Zürich: Schulthess Polygraphisher Verlag, 1990); Knudsen, *Offentlighed i Det Offentlige: Om Historiens Magt*; Konstari, *Asiakirjajulkisuudesta Hallinnossa: Tutkimus Yleisten Asiakirjain Julkisuudesta Hallinnon Kontrollivälineenä*; Barry Owen, "France," in *Comparative Public Administration*, ed. J. A. Chandler (London: Routledge, 2000), 200; K. G. Robertson, *Public Secrets: A Study in the Development of Government Secrecy* (New York: St. Martin's Press, 1982); Susan Rose-Ackerman, *From Elections to Democracy: Building Accountable Government in Hungary and Poland* (New York: Cambridge University Press, 2005); Spence,

There has been a distinctive historical trajectory in the Nordic countries,[16] where access to government documents is a constitutional principle of governance, namely the "principle of publicity" (Swedish: "offentlighetsprincipen," Finnish: "julkisuusperiaate"). In Finland, the principle of publicity gained legal status in an access law adopted in 1951.[17] Acknowledged as a constitutional right, the principle of publicity declares all government documents to be public unless otherwise indicated: "[D]ocuments and recordings in the possession of the public authorities are public, unless their publication has for compelling reasons been specifically restricted by an Act."[18] The principle is conceptually broader than mere public access to official documents, as it is often seen to cover openness of government activities and public access to court rooms and decision-making venues.

The issue of institutional openness was debated in Denmark on various occasions from the mid-1800s onwards. For example, the freedom of the press was debated in the early 1770s leading to a short era of liberalisation, but this freedom did not acquire a similar kind of institutional status as in Sweden and did not lead to the breaking of administrative secrecy.[19] In Norway, then part of Denmark, efforts to break absolutist secrecy had a similar fate. The issue of institutional openness was debated on several occasions from the mid-1800s onwards, but it was not until 1970 that Denmark and Norway gained access legislation. In Norway, this was part of a larger process towards the democratisation of public administration.[20]

"Italy," in Comparative Public Administration, ed. J. A. Chandler, 1st ed. (London: Routledge, 2000), 126–47; A. P. Tant, British Government: The Triumph of Elitism: A Study of the British Political Tradition and Its Major Challenges (Aldershot: Dartmouth, 1993); Richard C. Thurlow, The Secret State: British Internal Security in the Twentieth Century (Oxford: Blackwell, 1994).

16 Carol Harlow, "Global Administrative Law: The Quest for Principles and Values," The European Journal of International Law 17, no. 1 (2006): 193.

17 Finland as a former part of Sweden had a Swedish administrative model that mostly remained intact over the period of Russian rule, 1809–1917. Konstari, Asiakirjajulkisuudesta Hallinnossa: Tutkimus Yleisten Asiakirjain Julkisuudesta Hallinnon Kontrollivälineenä; Seppo Tiihonen, Herruus: Ruotsi ja Venäjä (Helsinki: Hallintohistoriakomitea, 1994), 6.

18 Finnish Const. 731/1999, 12 §.

19 Knudsen, Offentlighed i Det Offentlige: Om Historiens Magt, 69–82.

20 Einar Høgetveit, Hvor Hemmelig? Offentlighetsprinsippet i Norge Og USA, Særlig Med Henblikk På Militærpolitiske Spørsmål. (Oslo: Pax Forlag, 1981), 70; Grønlie and Nagel, "Administrative History in Norway," 308, 329.

The issue of access to government information became topical in 18th-century Sweden amid a transition from absolutist to liberal-bourgeois rule.[21] Jürgen Habermas's work on the structural transformations of the public sphere has been used to explain the institutional developments that made government information public in Sweden.[22] Yet the anti-religious emphasis of this narrative is misinformed in this context, for the clergy was responsible for spreading the ideas of the Enlightenment, as well as demanding information on state affairs.[23]

Indeed, it was the Ostrobothnian clergyman and representative in the Swedish Diet Anders Chydenius who is often credited with initiating the legislation in 1766. Chydenius was active in social issues and published widely.[24] He has been seen as one of the forefathers of state theoretical thinking in Finland[25] and there is now increasing interest in his work. But often works on older historical periods tell us more about the time in which we live than the time we study. I will show how Anders Chydenius's persona became drawn into the debates on Nordic openness and why he has become such an appealing figure at this time.

---

21 Knudsen, *Offentlighed i Det Offentlige: Om Historiens Magt*, 63; Konstari, *Asiakirjajulkisuudesta Hallinnossa: Tutkimus Yleisten Asiakirjain Julkisuudesta Hallinnon Kontrollivälineenä;* Perry Anderson, *Lineages of the Absolutist State* (London: Verso, 1993), 190–91; Tiihonen, *Herruus: Ruotsi ja Venäjä*, 57.

22 Cf. Jürgen Habermas, *The Structural Transformation of the Public Sphere: An Inquiry into a Category of Bourgeois Society* (London: Polity Press, 1989); Knudsen, *Offentlighed i Det Offentlige: Om Historiens Magt*, 63; Konstari, *Asiakirjajulkisuudesta Hallinnossa: Tutkimus Yleisten Asiakirjain Julkisuudesta Hallinnon Kontrollivälineenä*.

23 There are also other historical cases, often disregarded in the analysis of the "historical publics," where religion and science provided both topics and forums for public debates. Marc Forster, "Debating the Meaning of Pilgrimage: Maria Steinbach 1733," in *Cultures of Communication from Reformation to Enlightenment: Constructing Publics in the Early Modern German Lands*, ed. James Van Horn Melton (Aldershot: Ashgate Pub Ltd, 2002); Robert von Friedeburg, "The Public of Confessional Identity: Territorial Church and Church Discipline in 18th-Century Hesse," in *Cultures of Communication from Reformation to Enlightenment: Constructing Publics in the Early Modern German Lands*, ed. James Van Horn Melton (Aldershot: Ashgate Pub Ltd, 2002), 93–103; David Zaret, "Religion, Science, and Printing in the Public Spheres in Seventeenth-Century England," in *Habermas and the Public Sphere*, ed. Craig Calhoun (Cambridge: The MIT Press, 1992).

24 Jyrki Käkönen, "Anders Chydenius Ja 1700-Luvun Suomalainen Valtio-Opillinen Ajattelu," in *Valtio Ja Yhteiskunta. Tutkielmia Suomalaisen Valtiollisen Ajattelun Ja Valtio-Opin Historiasta.*, ed. Jaakko Nousiainen and Dag Anckar (Juva: Werner Söderström, 1983), 42–43; Juha Manninen, "Anders Chydenius and the Origins of World's First Freedom of Information Act," in *The World's First Freedom of Information Act. Anders Chydenius' Legacy Today*, ed. Anders Chydenius Foundation (Kokkola: Anders Chydenius Foundation, 2006), 18–53.

25 Käkönen, "Anders Chydenius Ja 1700-Luvun Suomalainen Valtio-Opillinen Ajattelu."

The term "transparent," originally of Latin origin (Latin: *transpārēnt-em*, French: *transparent*), has optical connotations, referring to the way light or images travel through material, allowing one to see objects on the other side. The term "transparent" has come into the English language through French and has attained remarkable international attention in recent debates on power and society.[26] In contemporary political vocabulary, transparency usually has connotations of openness and clarity in political and administrative processes. But it is increasingly also regarded as an economic virtue,[27] owing to paradigm shifts in information economics that largely embody the efficiency-laden virtues of good governance.[28]

The notion of the virtuous circle is often used when referring to economic competitiveness resulting from tightly interlinked institutional developments.[29] The OECD and the World Bank have promoted openness and access to government information as part of their policies on good governance since the mid-1990s.[30] There are also global rankings and indicators measuring the state of transparency in nation states. These policy instruments have been effective in formulating policy prescriptions on transparency that now link the issue to economic competitiveness. In Finland, institutional openness is seen as an advantage in global economic competition. Here the accounts of Nordic openness serve as an invented tradition that helps to address future challenges related to economic globalisation.[31] As I will show in the analysis, institutional openness is now seen as an element of "virtuous circles," where several institutional and contextual factors reinforce each other to grant some nations economic advantage over others.

---

26 Hood, "Transparency in Historical Perspective."

27 Erkkilä, *Government Transparency: Impacts and Unintended Consequences.*

28 Wolfgang Drechsler, "Governance, Good Governance, and Government: The Case for Estonian Administrative Capacity," *TRAMES*, no. 4 (2004): 388–96; Joseph Stiglitz, "Information and the Change in the Paradigm in Economics," *American Economic Review*, 92, no. 3 (2002): 460–501; Joseph Stiglitz, "Is There a Post-Washington Consensus Consensus?," in *The Washington Consensus Reconsidered: Towards a New Global Governance*, ed. Serra and Joseph Stiglitz (Oxford: Oxford University Press, 2008), 41–56.

29 Geoffrey Garrett, "Global Markets and National Politics: Collision Course or Virtuous Circle?," *International Organization*, 52, no. 4 (1998): 787–824.

30 OECD, *Open Government: Fostering Dialogue with Civil Society* (Paris: OECD, 2003); Catherine Weaver and Christian Peratsakis, "Engineering Policy Norm Implementation: The World Bank's Transparency Transformation," in *Implementation and World Politics: How International Norms Change Practice*, ed. Alexander Betts and Phil Orchard (Oxford: Oxford University Press, 2014), 179–94.

31 Erkkilä, *Government Transparency: Impacts and Unintended Consequences*; Hobsbawm, "Introduction: Inventing Traditions."

Kettunen has referred to this discourse of national competitiveness as a "coercive circle" that diminishes the sphere of politics and democracy.[32] Erkkilä and Piironen assess similar potentials in global country rankings, using the Weberian term "iron cage." They argue that by quantifying the criteria of "good governance" the governance indicators have the potential to limit the sphere of politics and ethics.[33] Ironically, the policy of "virtuous circles" has long been seen as a normative standard for the Nordic countries,[34] emphasising the values of efficiency, solidarity, and equality, and binding together economics, politics, and ethics.[35] This normative ideal was based on the perception that economic growth, widening democracy and increased equality were mutually reinforcing, rather than working in opposite directions. The Nordic countries grew to depend largely on exports, which was balanced with planning, the welfare state, and labour market policies, premised on the broad inclusion of actors.[36] These institutional practices also hinge on the Nordic openness of governing and access to government information.

Though openness is at present discussed as a tradition of Nordic governing, there is an apparent conceptual reframing of institutional practices in Finland. There is a distinctive institutional trajectory towards openness and access to government information in the Nordic countries, linked to democracy and political accountability. However, current awareness of this tradition is linked to a global drive for transparency where access to government information is seen as an attribute of economic competitiveness. This also concerns the historical roots of institutional openness that is now seen to bring a competitive advantage to Finland. While access to government information has traditionally been discussed under the concept of *publicity*, belonging to the semantic field of democracy,

---

32 Kettunen, *Globalisaatio ja Kansallinen Me: Kansallisen Katseen Historiallinen Kritiikki*, 12.
33 Tero Erkkilä and Ossi Piironen, "Politics and Numbers: The Iron Cage of Governance Indices," in *Ethics and Integrity of Public Administration: Concepts and Cases*, ed. Raymond W. Cox III (Armonk: ME Sharpe, 2009), 125–45; cf. Max Weber, *Economy and Society*, vols. 1 and 2, (Berkeley: University of California Press, 1978).
34 Kettunen, *Globalisaatio ja Kansallinen Me: Kansallisen Katseen Historiallinen Kritiikki*, 142–45; Pauli Kettunen, "The Society of Virtuous Circles," in *Models, Modernity and the Myrdals.*, ed. Hanna Eskola and Pauli Kettunen, Renvall Institute Publications 8 (Helsinki: Helsinki University, 1997).
35 Pauli Kettunen, "The Nordic Model and the Making of the Competitive 'Us,'" in *The Global Economy, National States and the Regulation of Labour.*, ed. Paul Edwards and Tony Elger (London: Mansell Publishing, 1999), 123; Paula Tiihonen, "Good Governance and Corruption in Finland," in *The History of Corruption in Central Government*, ed. Seppo Tiihonen (Amsterdam: IOS Press, 2003), 99–118.
36 Kettunen, "The Nordic Model and the Making of the Competitive 'Us,'" 129.

there has been a shift towards notions of *openness* and *transparency*, carrying connotations of trust and economy. These ideational shifts come about with the help of an invented tradition[37] that now also includes a historical reading of Anders Chydenius, who is often regarded as the father of the world's first information access law, passed in Sweden in 1766.

Analysing these changes in Finland, I will show how the discourse on Nordic openness emerged in the mid-1990s during a critical juncture for Finnish governance, due to economic crisis, intensifying economic globalisation, and Finland's accession to the EU. In explaining the rise of the policy discourse of Nordic openness and its communicative and coordinative forms, I will build on the work of Pauli Kettunen, Martin Marcussen, and Vivien Schmidt.[38] In assessing the conceptual shifts and the political use of concepts, I refer to the work of Reinhart Koselleck and Quentin Skinner.[39]

I will first analyse the conceptual changes in governance discourse, using government platforms and selected publications of the Economic Council of Finland as my sources. I will then explore the communicative aspects of the policy discourse and the construction of a collective memory of Nordic openness in Finland in the historical accounts of the mid-2000s, when openness was also a theme for the Finnish EU Presidency (2006). I conclude that the "virtues" of good governance that are circulating internationally are now seen to have historical reference points in Finnish policy discourse, portraying Anders Chydenius as the forebear of openness in Finland. Yet, the cognitive aspects of this discourse point to political innovation and reassessments of institutional openness as an element of economic competitiveness.

---

37 Eric Hobsbawm, "Introduction: Inventing Traditions," in *The Invention of Tradition*, ed. Eric Hobsbawm and Terence Ranger (Cambridge: Cambridge University Press, 1987), 1–14.

38 Pauli Kettunen, *Globalisaatio ja Kansallinen Me: Kansallisen Katseen Historiallinen Kritiikki* (Tampere: Vastapaino, 2008); Martin Marcussen, *Ideas and Elites: The Social Construction of Economic and Monetary Union* (Aalborg: Aalborg University Press, 2000); Schmidt, *The Futures of European Capitalism*; Vivien A. Schmidt, "Discursive Institutionalism: The Explanatory Power of Ideas and Discourse," *Annual Review of Political Science* 11, no. 1 (2008): 303–26, doi:10.1146/annurev.polisci.11.060606.135342.

39 Reinhart Koselleck, *Futures Past: On the Semantics of Historical Time* (New York: Columbia University Press, 2004); Quentin Skinner, "Meaning and Understanding in the History of Ideas," *History and Theory* 8, no. 1 (1969): 3–53; Quentin Skinner, "Language and Political Change," in *Political Innovation and Conceptual Change*, ed. Terence Ball, James Farr, and Russell L. Hanson (Cambridge: Cambridge University Press, 1989), 6–23.

Nordic Openness in Finland: Conceptual Change and Political Innovation

The invented tradition and discourse of Nordic openness carries nationalistic connotations depicting Finland as a particularly open Nordic society and a league table winner in the global rankings. These rankings have been a source of national pride in Finland, constructing an image of a particularly open and successful nation. The construction of a notion of a competitive "us"[40] becomes effective through "subjectification," where actors acquire patterns of identities linked to proposed actions to maintain "our national competitiveness".[41] Below, I show how the economic understanding of openness and access to government information have been acknowledged in government platforms in Finland, visible also in the conceptual shift from "publicity" to "openness and transparency." This shift is also visible in the documents of the Economic Council of the Finnish Government. To use Schmidt's words,[42] these documents represent the "coordinative discourse" on Nordic openness, whereby the cognitive aspects of the policy prescriptions on transparency are communicated and shared among the policy actors. In order to legitimate the changes, the "communicative discourse" of Nordic openness evokes an invented tradition[43] that accommodates and legitimizes the changes at hand.

Conceptual Shifts in Government Platforms: Publicity, Openness, Transparency

The shifts in the rhetoric of governing, i.e. arguments for its justification, are not only a reflection of the institutional state of affairs but also carry the potential for institutional change. These shifts can be seen to represent changes in the perceived responsibilities and goals of government. In institutional theory, an "ideational life-cycle" is often seen as consisting of periods of consensus, interrupted by an external shock or ideational uncertainty, during which change is possible or necessary.[44] Once the ideational and normative consensus is again sought,

---

40 Kettunen, *Globalisaatio ja Kansallinen Me: Kansallisen Katseen Historiallinen Kritiikki.*
41 Tero Erkkilä and Ossi Piironen, *Rankings and Global Knowledge Governance: Higher Education, Innovation and Competitiveness* (New York, NY: Palgrave Macmillan, 2018).
42 Schmidt, "Discursive Institutionalism."
43 Hobsbawm, "Introduction: Inventing Traditions."
44 Cf. Marcussen, *Ideas and Elites: The Social Construction of Economic and Monetary Union.*

that is as ideas become embedded or institutionalised,[45] another stable period follows. Scholars have identified institutional change as an outcome of ideational and ideological change, also entailing political conflict.[46] Here ideational change largely rests on shifts in political rhetoric and narratives.[47]

The discourse of "Nordic openness," a perception of Nordic institutional tradition that separates Finland from other nations, emerged in the 1990s, coinciding with the end of the Cold War, Finnish membership of the EU and financial crisis. This juncture allowed new institutional practices and ideas to be introduced into the Finnish model of governing.[48] In Reinhart Koselleck's *Begriffsgeschichte*, such a critical juncture is termed *Sattlezeit* – a period of crisis during which new concepts emerge and old ones are critically altered.[49] According to Koselleck, conceptual change occurs when the gap between our experiences (*Erfahrungsraum*) and future expectations (*Erwartungshorizont*) grows too large.[50] It is here that the vocabulary tends to change, as actors need to re-conceptualise the new environment. Looking at the political concepts used in Finnish government platforms since the 1917, neither "publicity" nor "openness," let alone "transparency," have traditionally been part of the political vocabulary, but instead started to appear in the 1990s. This new discourse makes references to past traditions, such as the "principle of publicity."

Internationally, the adoption of information access laws has usually been preceded by a political debate on the topic, often crucial for the adoption.[51] The term "publicity" did not appear in the Finnish government platforms at the time of adoption of the Act on the Publicity of Government Documents in 1951. There were hardly any references to "publicity" or "openness" before the 1990s, when the notion of "openness" started to appear in the government platforms of Prime Ministers Harri Holkeri (1987–1991), Esko Aho (1991–1995), Paavo Lipponen (1995–1999, 1999–2003), Anneli Jäätteenmäki (2003), Matti

---

45 Margaret R. Somers and Fred Block, "From Poverty to Perversity: Ideas, Markets, and Institutions over 200 Years of Welfare Debate," *American Sociological Review* 70, no. 2 (2005): 260–87.

46 Guy B. Peters, Jon Pierre, and Desmond S. King, "The Politics of Path Dependency: Political Conflict in Historical Institutionalism," *The Journal of Politics* 67, no. 04 (2005): 1275–1300, doi:10.1111/j.1468–2508.2005.00360.x; Schmidt, *The Futures of European Capitalism*.

47 Schmidt, "Discursive Institutionalism"; Somers and Block, "From Poverty to Perversity," 280.

48 Cf. Marcussen, *Ideas and Elites: The Social Construction of Economic and Monetary Union*; Peters, Pierre, and King, "The Politics of Path Dependency."

49 Koselleck, *Futures Past*; Melvin Richter, *The History of Political and Social Concepts: A Critical Introduction* (Oxford: Oxford University Press, 1995), 17.

50 Koselleck, *Futures Past*, 256.

51 Bennett, "Understanding Ripple Effects."

Vanhanen (2003–2007, 2007–2010), Mari Kiviniemi (2010–2011), Jyrki Katainen (2011–2014), Alexander Stubb (2014–2015), Juha Sipilä (2015–2019), Antti Rinne (2019) and Sanna Marin (2019-).[52] At the turn of the 1990s, there was an apparent confusion between the concepts of "public" and "open" – the former referred to the public sector and government and the latter was understood in economic terms, as referring to "open," unregulated, sectors. The vocabulary then shifted, as "openness" gained democratic connotations such as "openness of governance." The economic connotations were associated with a new term, "transparency," which also introduced the idea that the government was responsible to the market.

In the government platform of Prime Minister Harri Holkeri (published in April 1987) there were no references made to "openness" with regard to responsible rule, but a reference was made to "open labour markets." Similarly, the platform of Prime Minister Esko Aho (1991) contained references to "openness" in the context of economy. The government platform of Paavo Lipponen (1995), titled "The government of employment and joint responsibility," mentioned functioning labour markets and labour market agreements as the keys to success. The "open" labour market deliberations became an element of national competitiveness.[53]

The democratic connotations of openness first started to appear systematically in 1995 in the context of European governance (Finland joined the EU in 1995). The first Lipponen government stated that Finland would "enhance the openness of the decision-making of the European Union," which became a legitimizing argument for Finnish accession to the Union. Openness remained a topic in Finnish EU politics in the platform of the second government of Paavo Lipponen (April 1999). The platform stated that the government would act so that the EU's decision-making and administration would be developed according to the principles of "openness," "responsibility," and "efficiency." At the same time, there were references to openness in relation to global economics and electoral funding. Transparency, a newcomer to the Finnish political vocabulary, appeared for the first time as "transparency" of pricing and financing in domestic politics.

At the same time, the institutional practices were in turmoil, as the relevant legislation was being updated and several policies were adopted.[54] This led to the adoption of the Act on the Openness of Government Activities (1999), the Personal Data Act (1999), and the Administrative Procedure Act (2004). Indeed, the

---

52 The Finnish government platforms are all available online. Finnish Government, accessed 3 September, 2021, https://valtioneuvosto.fi/tietoa/historiaa/hallitusohjelmat.

53 Cf. Kettunen, "The Nordic Model and the Making of the Competitive 'Us.'"

54 Erkkilä, *Government Transparency: Impacts and Unintended Consequences.*

legislation used up until this time was from 1951 and was even drafted before the Second World War (in 1939). Given the changes due to digitalisation of public administration alone, it is noteworthy that the revision took this long, particularly in a country that now identifies with openness so prominently.

The government platforms published in the 2000s continued the agenda, where the openness of decision making in the EU was a priority. While openness still received some mentions in the context of open markets, the economic connotations were mostly found under "transparency." The government platform of Antti Rinne (2019), taken over in turn by Sanna Marin and titled "Inclusive and Competent Finland," also aimed to enhance collaboration with other Nordic countries that arguably "share similar values concerning democracy, openness and welfare state."

To conclude, over the years the references to open government have emerged in the government platforms. "Openness" was first used as an antonym of "public" and started to obtain market connotations in the late 1980s. It was later displaced by the term "transparency," a newcomer to Finnish political vocabulary that now predominantly carries references to the market economy. The government discourse shifted from the semantic field of democracy towards the market. In government rhetoric, openness appeared as a state tradition that was also promoted in the EU, which appeared as the secretive "other" of the open Nordic countries such as Finland.

Transparency and Economic Understanding of Openness

The two debates around openness and transparency – the Finnish exceptional openness in the EU context (Nordic openness) and the economic potential of transparency – meet in a nationalistic discourse. The Finnish concern over the secretiveness of the EU in the mid-1990s initiated a narrative of openness as a Nordic tradition in Finnish governing, separating "us" from "them." National competitiveness, which openness and transparency are increasingly seen as enhancing, is also debated under the same logic of inclusion and exclusion: "our" competitive edge over "the others." The coupling of efficiency and economic performance with openness is a novel and not so readily apparent idea. In fact, in the past, mainstream economics assumed that open systems were less efficient than closed ones.[55] This conceptual change in government vocabulary points to

---

55 Mark Skousen, "The Perseverance of Paul Samuelson's Economics," *Journal of Economic Perspectives* 11, no. 2 (1997): 137–52.

political innovation due to a paradigm change in economics,[56] where the ideas of market efficiency increasingly build on transparency.

The emergence of new political concepts also entails political innovation and shifts in belief systems.[57] Here the study of conceptual change and the historical analysis of institutions converge in their aim to reveal how social beliefs are formed and institutionalised.[58] Conceptual change therefore gives an insight into why and how certain policy problems arise, how they are constructed, and how these problems can be arguably solved. Political concepts are means for governing and sudden referencing to a policy concept is an indication of active "politicking," making the issue politically "playable."[59]

In the early 2000s, institutional economics was a rising topic in economic policy-making,[60] featuring also prominently in the reports of the Economic Council of the Finnish Government at that time.[61] In these texts, the open market and the availability of information are seen as mutually reinforcing and the role of the state is perceived as enabling market activities. In the past, reference to the Nordic model had provided an argument for synchronisation with other Nordic countries and Sweden in particular.[62] However, the debate on Nordic openness, despite its explicit referencing of "Nordicness," now marked the synchronization of Finnish institutional practices with transnational institutional models of transparency stemming from international organisations such as the

---

56 Stiglitz, "Information and the Change in the Paradigm in Economics."

57 James Farr, "Understanding Conceptual Change Politically," in *Political Innovation and Conceptual Change*, ed. Terence Ball, James Farr, and Russell L. Hanson (Cambridge: Cambridge University Press, 1989), 25; Skinner, "Language and Political Change," 20.

58 Bo Rothstein and Sven Steinmo, ed., *Restructuring the Welfare State: Political Institutions and Policy Change* (New York: Palgrave Macmillan, 2002), 16.

59 Kari Palonen, "Four Times of Politics: Policy, Polity, Politicking, and Politicization," *Alternatives* 28, no. 2 (2003): 55; Skinner, "Meaning and Understanding in the History of Ideas."

60 Torben Iversen, "The Dynamics of Welfare State Expansion: Trade Openness, De-Industrialisation and Partisan Politics," in *The New Politics of the Welfare State*, by Paul Pierson (Oxford: Oxford University Press, 2001), 45–79; Ugo Pagano, "Economics of Institutions and the Institutions of Economics," in *Transforming Economics: Perspectives on the Critical Realist Project*, ed. Paul Lewis (London: Routledge, 2004), 252–67; Dani Rodrik, "Why Do More Open Economies Have Bigger Governments?" *The Journal of Political Economy* 106, no. 5 (1998): 997–1032.

61 Valtioneuvoston kanslia, "Euroopan Rakenteelliset Jäykkyydet," Valtioneuvoston kanslian julkaisusarja (Helsinki: Valtioneuvoston kanslia, 2002); Valtioneuvoston kanslia, "Osaava, Avautuva ja Uudistuva Suomi. Suomi Maailmantaloudessa –Selvityksen Loppuraportti," Valtioneuvoston kanslian julkaisusarja (Helsinki: Valtioneuvoston kanslia, 2004).

62 Pauli Kettunen, "The Nordic Welfare State in Finland," *Scandinavian Journal of History* 26, no. 3 (September 1, 2001): 225–47, doi:10.1080/034687501750303864.

World Bank and the OECD.[63] This also entailed a shift in the self-understanding and narrative of Finland's place in the world.

During the Cold War Finland was seen as a gateway between East and West and references to "Nordic" democracy and society were used to highlight the fact that Finland was not part of the Eastern Bloc.[64] The current references to Nordic openness indicate a repositioning, where Finland is portrayed as a member of a Nordic bloc within the EU but is also depicted as a leader in globalisation. The Nordic model is now closely linked to a discourse on national competitiveness and to a related pattern of identity, the competitive "us."[65] The global indicators have ranked Nordic countries high in competitiveness, democracy, and good governance, which are also linked to institutional traditions in education, gender equality, and welfare.

One of the institutional characteristics that stands out in global comparisons is the history of openness and access to government information. Transparency International's *Corruption Perception Index* (published in 1995) has ranked Finland and the other Nordic countries consistently within the top ten of least corrupt countries. While this ranking does not measure transparency but corruption – specifically bribery – it has been a source of great national pride in Finland that it is now arguably one of the most "open" and least corrupt countries in the world. Transparency is also implied in the World Economic Forum's *Global Competitiveness Index* (published in its current form since 2004) that focuses on the institutional determinants of national economic performance. The Nordic countries, Finland included, again rank well.

In 2006 the World Economic Forum found that the Nordic countries were among the most competitive in the world, due to virtuous circles of transparency and openness. Its chief economist and director of the Global Competitiveness Programme Augusto Lopez-Claros, stated in 2006:

> In many ways the [Nordic countries] have entered virtuous circles where various factors reinforce each other to make them among the most competitive economies in the world. [...] These are also countries that have public institutions that are characterised by an exceptionally high level of transparency and openness and this has contributed to improve business confidence.[66]

---

63 Erkkilä, *Government Transparency: Impacts and Unintended Consequences.*
64 Kettunen, "The Nordic Welfare State in Finland," 234.
65 Kettunen, "The Nordic Model and the Making of the Competitive 'Us.'"
66 Augusto Lopez-Claros, *The Global Competitiveness Report 2005–2006:* Video Interviews, Augusto Lopez-Claros, http://www.weforum.org/en/initiatives/gcp/GCR20052006VideoInterviews/index.htm.

Together with the Finnish success in the OECD's PISA ranking, which depicted Finnish primary education as a global leader and a model for others to follow, these indicators have further contributed to the discourse of Nordic openness that builds on an imaginary of global competitiveness and is used to construct the notion of the competitive "us."[67] Indeed, one of the mechanisms through which global indicators become effective is "subjectification," where actors acquire patterns of identities linked to proposed action to maintain competitiveness.[68] While the storyline is not always clear, there is a shared understanding of the positive qualities of openness and transparency that carry the promise of a governance system that is at the same time democratic and efficient. Effectively, transparency becomes a "third term"[69] which allows the bypassing of dichotomies such as democracy/efficiency, public/private, market/hierarchy (bureaucracy); instead of either-or, it promises both.

The Open and Direct Finn: Anders Chydenius and Global Economy

During the 2000s, the perception of "openness" as a Finnish historical trait grew. The positive portrayal of Finland in the governance indices provided social scientific proof for the narrative adopted earlier. This narrative also offered Finland a new self-image, bearing connotations of progress and modernity, which also lent credibility to Finnish attempts to export and promote institutional openness elsewhere. In 2006, Finland named a "transparent and effective Union" as its objective for its EU presidency, highlighted also in the transparent logo of the presidency. The theme was based on Finnish identity of being "open" and "direct" as well as "progressive."[70] Here we again see the dialectic between democracy (open) and efficiency (direct).

In Finnish political architecture the issue of transparency had become topical earlier in the construction of the Finnish Parliament supplementary building, completed in May 2004. Even though the proposal that won the bid for the construction project did not go particularly far in utilising glass materials, the vast majority of the proposals submitted in 1999 proposed that glass was a

67 Kettunen, *Globalisaatio ja Kansallinen Me. Kansallisen Katseen Historiallinen Kritiikki.*
68 Erkkilä and Piironen, *Rankings and Global Knowledge Governance.*
69 Bob Jessop, "The Rise of Governance and the Risks of Failure: The Case of Economic Development'," *International Social Science Journal* 155 (1998): 29–45.
70 Finnish EU Precidency 2006, [http://www.eu2006.fi/].

symbol of the "principle of publicity."[71] While transparent architecture in political buildings was in fashion at the time,[72] the metaphor of transparency[73] is now linked with a historical tradition of openness in Finland.

The narrative of openness has even entered historical inquiry. This is most obvious in the historical accounts of Anders Chydenius, who together with his peer Peter Forsskål has attracted international interest.[74] Behind Chydenius's ideas on freedom of print and the right of acquiring information on state matters was his opposition to the mercantilist tradition in eighteenth-century Sweden, embodied in Stockholm's trade privileges over peripheries. In Finland, historians have drawn attention to the "Finnish" roots of this eighteenth-century thinker, but at the same time used Chydenius to highlight the Swedish lineages of the Finnish state, sharing a legal and administrative tradition.[75] The historical accounts of Chydenius and his "Nordic" legacy hence stress Finland's history as part of Sweden, but at the same time portray Finland as a periphery, and a nation to come, struggling against Stockholm.

---

71 Eduskunta, "Lisärakennuksen arkkitehtuurikilpailu" (Eduskunta, 1999).

72 Deborah Ascher Barnstone, *The Transparent State: Architecture and Politics in Postwar Germany* (New York: Routledge, 2005); Nigel Whiteley, "Intensity of Scrutiny and a Good Eyeful: Architecture and Transparency," *Journal of Architectural Education* 56, no. 4 (2003): 8–16, doi:10.1162/104648803321672915.

73 William Whyte, "How Do Buildings Mean? Some Issues of Interpretation in the History of Architecture," *History and Theory* 45, no. 2 (2006): 153–177, doi:10.1111/j.1468–2303.2006.00355.x.

74 John M. Ackerman and Irma E. Sandoval-Ballesteros, "The Global Explosion of Freedom of Information Laws," *Administrative Law Review* 58, no. 1 (2006): 85–130; Hood, "Transparency in Historical Perspective.," 8; Stephen Lamble, "Freedom of Information, a Finnish Clergyman's Gift to Democracy," *Freedom of Information Review 97*, no. February 2002 (2002): 2–8; Ulla Carlsson and David Goldberg, ed., *The Legacy of Peter Forsskål: 250 Years of Freedom of Expression* (Gothenburg: Nordicom, University of Gothenburg, 2017), https://www.nordicom.gu.se/sv/system/tdf/publikationer-hela-pdf/the_legacy_of_peter_forsskal._250_years_of_freedom_of_expression.pdf?file=1&type=node&id=38645&force=0.

75 Jyrki Käkönen, "Anders Chydenius ja 1700-Luvun Suomalainen Valtio-Opillinen Ajattelu," in *Valtio Ja Yhteiskunta: Tutkielmia Suomalaisen Valtiollisen Ajattelun ja Valtio-Opin Historiasta*, ed. Jaakko Nousiainen and Dag Anckar (Juva: Werner Söderström, 1983), 46–49; Manninen, "Anders Chydenius and the Origins of World's First Freedom of Information Act"; Ilkka Patoluoto, "Hyödyllinen Luomakunta: Hyötyajattelun Maailmankuvalliset Perusteet 1700-Luvun Ruotsin Valtakunnassa," in *Hyöty, Sivistys, Kansakunta: Suomalaista Aatehistoriaa*, ed. Juha Manninen and Ilkka Patoluoto (Oulu: Kustannusosakeyhtiö Pohjoinen, 1986); Virrankoski, *Anders Chydenius: Demokraattinen Poliitikko Valistuksen Vuosisadalta*.

In his writings Chydenius portrays the "free state" or "free nation" not as an enemy of libertarian freedoms, but rather as their keeper.[76] When describing the state, he uses metaphors such as a "ship," "body," or "clock," which describe the state as an intact entity, in need of "steering" and "well-performing" components.[77] Chydenius argued for a widening of political inclusion, for which information on state matters was a necessity. The state was to inform its citizens about its successes and misfortunes alike so that they would know the "truth." It was in the search for truth that Chydenius saw the rationality of governance based on the "free state."[78] The truth was to be sought by an exchange of ideas and opinions and Chydenius encouraged his readers to engage in public debates.[79] These debates he saw as ideally taking place through writing. The results of this "competition of pens" were to be spread across the nation through the new printing technique.[80]

A symbolic figure in Finland, his face on the old 1000 Finn Mark note, Chydenius is often seen as a father of Finnish state theoretical thinking,[81] a Nordic Adam Smith or an interpreter of Montesquieu.[82] Even though Anders Chydenius himself regarded his work for the liberalising of print as his major achievement,[83] it took future generations some 240 years to take an interest in this. Since the early 2000s, Chydenius has appeared in the speeches and public appearances of Finnish politicians.[84] Chydenius's ideas are now seen as a Finnish "export product."[85] Swedish politicians have also made claims for this thinker, but it turns out that his legacy is less known in Sweden than in Finland. In

---

76 Anders Chydenius, "Den nationala vinsten," in *Politiska skrifter af Anders Chydenius* (Helsinki: G. W. Edlunds förlag, 1880), 31.
77 Chydenius, 31.
78 Chydenius, 31.
79 Chydenius, *Valitut Kirjoitukset* (Porvoo: Werner Söderström, 1929), 170.
80 Chydenius, "Den nationala vinsten," 31.
81 Käkönen, "Anders Chydenius ja 1700-Luvun Suomalainen Valtio-Opillinen Ajattelu."
82 Kimmo Sarje, "Anders Chydenius – Montesquieun Ihailija," *Politiikka* 4 (1979): 297–304.
83 Chydenius, *Valitut Kirjoitukset*, 434–37.
84 Tuija Brax, "Julkisuusperiaatteen Haasteet." (Tietämisen vapauden päivän seminaari, Puhe tietämisen vapauden päivän seminaarissa, November 30, 2007), http://www.om.fi/Etusivu/Ajankohtaista/Ministerinpuheita/Puhearkisto/Puheet2007Brax/1196159328843; Tarja Halonen, *Puhe Anders Chydeniuksen juhlavuoden pääjuhlassa Kokkolassa 1.3.2003*, Anders Chydenius Säätiö, 2005) (speech at the main celebration of the Anders Chydenius Jubilee Year); Jacob Söderman, "Salailusta on Tullut Maan Tapa," *Helsingin Sanomat*, November 19, 2006, https://www.hs.fi/sunnuntai/art-2000004441307.html; Jacob Söderman, "On Transparency" (presentation, IIAS conference, Monterrey, Mexico, July 16, 2006).
85 Manninen, "Anders Chydenius and the Origins of World's First Freedom of Information Act," 16.

2009, a Finnish delegation delivered a portrait of Chydenius to Anders Borg, the Swedish Minister of Finance, who wanted to have Chydenius on the wall of his office, because no picture of Chydenius could be found in Sweden.[86] This shows how Chydenius has been reinvented for political use.

In Chydenius's home region of Ostrobothnia, the issue of accessing state information had arisen in the tar export trade, as revenues were channelled to the ruling elite in Stockholm rather than to local tradesmen. Anders Chydenius wanted accurate information on the sales that the mercantilist rule of Stockholm was making at the expense of the local tar producers and also the uprooting of corruption was seen to play a role.[87] Ostrobothnia, on the west coast of modern-day Finland, was the biggest manufacturer of tar and Sweden's wealthiest region, but it lacked the rights to export tar independently. This now provides an analogy for contemporary globalization,[88] just as the rise of printing technology in the eighteenth century is a fitting metaphor for the current issues of digitalisation and the internet. The ideas of Chydenius are seen as relevant in the contemporary context, especially when analysing the global transformations in trade and democracy, where openness and transparency are coupled with ideas of low corruption, rule of law, democracy, and competitiveness.

Chydenius and his ideas have great metaphoric value, making him appear as a forbear of the contemporary problem of joining global trade and democracy. His historical legacy can with good reason be described as "multipurpose."[89] The different readings of Chydenius have also sparked debates on his political use.[90] Chydenius is either a Finn battling against the Swedes[91] or a Swedish-Finn,[92] a construct used in Finnish history when referring to Finland under

---

86 Kalle Koponen, "Talouspappi Chydenius Pääsi Valtiovarainministerin Seinälle Ruotsissa," *Helsingin Sanomat*, 9 January, 2009.

87 Juha Manninen, "Anders Chydenius and the Origins of World's First Freedom of Information Act," in *The World's First Freedom of Information Act: Anders Chydenius' Legacy Today*, ed. Anders Chydenius Foundation (Kokkola: Anders Chydenius Foundation, 2006), 18–53; Pentti Virrankoski, *Anders Chydenius: Demokraattinen Poliitikko Valistuksen Vuosisadalta* (Juva: Werner Söderström, 1986), 109.

88 Halonen, *Puhe Anders Chydeniuksen juhlavuoden pääjuhlassa Kokkolassa 1.3.2003*

89 Pauli Kettunen, "Yhteiskunta Ohjattavana ja Ohjaajana – Historiallinen Näkökulma: Monikäyttöinen Chydenius," Anders Chydenius foundation, accessed 3 September, 2021, http://www.chydenius.net.

90 Henrikki Heikka, "Kokkolan Kirkkoherra Parantaa Terroristit," *Kosmopolis* 34, no. 1 (2004): 63–68; Jyrki Käkönen, "Henrikki Heikka Chydeniuksesta, Terrorismin Parantamisesta ja Vapaakaupasta," *Kosmopolis* 34, no. 1 (2004): 111–14.

91 Heikka, "Chydeniuksesta, Vapaasta Kaupasta ja Terrorismista"; Käkönen, "Henrikki Heikka Chydeniuksesta, Terrorismin Parantamisesta ja Vapaakaupasta."

92 Brax, "Julkisuusperiaatteen Haasteet"; Söderman, "Salailusta on Tullut Maan Tapa."

Swedish rule. In his time, Chydenius regarded himself as a Swede.[93] He did talk about the prosperity of "Finns" under the Swedish King, but his understanding of this was mostly regional, limited to Ostrobothnia and Åbo.[94]

There is a tendency for historical references to political theorists to often become mixed with contemporary political concepts and arguments. These theorists become part of a political debate or ideological grouping that they, in their time, would never have recognised.[95] Because of his influence on liberalising print, which also came to result in the abolition of absolutist secrecy, Chydenius is now portrayed as the father of the "Freedom of Information Act"[96] or the "right to know," both concepts of Anglo-American origin. Chydenius is also seen as a forbear of "free trade" or the abolition of "trade barriers."[97] The "principle of publicity" becomes translated into the "principle of transparency" and the high ranking of the Nordic countries in the Transparency International's Corruption Perception Index is seen as a legacy of Chydenius.[98] The principle of publicity has become a Finnish invention that has spread as far as Nokia and the sauna.[99] A recent English translation of Ander Chydenius's texts carries the title "Anticipating the Wealth of Nations," linking Chydenius to Adam Smith.[100] However, Skinner highlights the importance of understanding ideas in their context, and argues that such anticipations are mostly unwarranted in conceptual history.[101]

Chydenius stands as a historical reference point in a time when the relations of centre and periphery were being rethought. A vigorous opponent to mercantilism, Chydenius easily gets drawn into debates where notions of (neo) mercantilist and (neo) liberalist viewpoints meet. Even the Finnish narratives and im-

---

93 Chydenius, *Valitut Kirjoitukset*, 426.

94 Juha Manninen, *Valistus ja Kansallinen Identiteetti: Aatehistoriallinen Tutkimus 1700-Luvun Pohjolasta* (Helsinki: Suomalaisen Kirjallisuuden Seura, 2000), 43; compare Manninen, "Anders Chydenius and the Origins of World's First Freedom of Information Act"; Jouko Nurmiainen, "Particular Interests and the Common Good in Swedish Mid-18th-Century Diet Politics: The 'Finnish' Perspective," *Scandinavian Journal of History* 32, no. 4 (2007): 388–404, doi:10.1080/03468750701659350.

95 Skinner, "Meaning and Understanding in the History of Ideas."

96 Manninen, "Anders Chydenius and the Origins of World's First Freedom of Information Act."

97 Heikka, "Chydeniuksesta, Vapaasta Kaupasta ja Terrorismista."

98 Söderman, "On Transparency."

99 Manninen, "Anders Chydenius and the Origins of World's First Freedom of Information Act," 17.

100 Anders Chydenius, *Anticipating the Wealth of Nations: The Selected Works of Anders Chydenius, 1729–1803*, ed. Maren Jonasson and Pertti Hyttinen (London: Routledge, 2011).

101 Skinner, "Meaning and Understanding in the History of Ideas."

ages carrying a collective memory of openness contain a dialectic between democracy (open) and efficiency (direct). Though the storyline is not always fully explicit, there are references to global markets and globalisation and the role of information in organising them.

However, the present concerns of globalisation were beyond the reach of this eighteenth-century thinker. The references to Chydenius and his work are part of the politically motivated uses of the normatively appealing concepts of openness and transparency.[102] The narrative of Chydenius and other references to history become part of the "communicative discourse" of Nordic openness,[103] which now also accommodates the new ideas on transparency that have become internationally diffused. Leaping over history, Chydenius has become the embodiment of the "open and direct Finn": Nordic, educated, incorruptible, and engaged in trade.

Conclusions

To sum up, the policy discourse on openness has resonated particularly well with the Finnish institutional context, where the legislation on accessing government information and the principle of publicity has existed for a long time (see Table 1). Since the mid-1990s the discourse of Nordic openness has appeared in Finnish government platforms and bills, in policy documents and strategies, in public speeches of politicians, and in narratives told by civil servants.[104] It is also found in governance indices and their interpretations, contemporary historical analyses, and even in architecture and design of political relevance. The cognitive aspects of this new policy discourse tap into the social scientific perceptions of governance, and institutional and information economics. The normative, legitimating discourse of Nordic openness extends to Finnish national history, inventing a tradition of Nordic governing. The notion of "Nordic" openness is convenient here, as it portrays Finns as members of a particularly open society as opposed to other nationalities, but at the same time also references the fact that Finland was a part of Sweden prior to 1809, highlighting and co-opting the Swedish institutional practices that exist in Finland and that are now drawing global attention. Furthermore, this (Nordic) discourse also bypasses the era of Russian rule in Finland (1809–1917), characterised by censorship.

---

102 Skinner, "Language and Political Change."
103 Schmidt, "Discursive Institutionalism."
104 See also Erkkilä, *Government Transparency: Impacts and Unintended Consequences.*

Table 1. Ideational dimensions of the discourse on openness and their representations in Finland[105]

	Form	Ideational core	Representations
Cognitive	legislative reform, policy on public sector information, administrative ethics reform, initiatives of public hearings, accountability reform, better regulation programme	new social scientific perceptions of governance, institutional and information economics	government platforms, government bills, policy documents, strategies, public speeches, public programmes, numbers (indices, rankings), narratives of civil servants, contemporary historical analysis, political architecture and design
Normative	Nordic openness, the open and direct Finn	Openness as a Nordic tradition of Finnish governing	

The shifting belief systems among policy actors carry new cognitive aspects but this is largely hidden in the normatively appealing talk on openness as a tradition. Because institutional openness has a long history as a virtue of the Enlightenment, the Nordic welfare state, and liberalism, the new connotations seem to find an ideational root in the above philosophies. In the era when the Finnish welfare state was built, the exchange of information and negotiations between various groups were an underlying and unspoken norm of governing.[106] Amid economic globalisation, "openness," "public sector information," and "transparency" become political and economic concerns that are actively governed. History is therefore not only a marker for institutional continuity but also carries a potential for institutional change.

Though the above developments in political rhetoric are seemingly independent of institutional affairs, they converge in the rationalities and mechanisms of change. The shift in the political rhetoric and concepts of governing not only reflects institutional change but also propels it. In terms of accountability, the shift in conceptualisation reframes the mechanism of government control. This also points to new external demands and audiences to whom civil servants bear responsibilities. Somewhat paradoxically, the sudden awareness of a democratic trajectory marks an opening for its reframing in economic terms.

Consequently, the openness of government activities has become part of a new political imaginary of national competitiveness. There is a perceivable reassessment of the responsibilities of the government, marking a new ideational

---

105 After Schmidt, *The Futures of European Capitalism*, 214.
106 Kettunen, "The Nordic Model and the Making of the Competitive 'Us.'"

cycle: Finnish governments now increasingly bear responsibilities towards market actors through openness and transparency.[107] Though the democratic connotations of openness would intuitively imply greater government responsibility towards citizens, the emergence of this discourse coincides with mounting demands for Finland's competitiveness in an open economy.

Comparing the relevant policy documents with the public speeches of politicians, one can identify cognitive and normative aspects in the discourse of openness that are in dissonance, though economic aspects are also slowly entering the normative talk on openness. There is an apparent construction of the collective memory of openness as a Nordic tradition of Finnish governing. This is part of Finland's new European identity. The historical aspects are also prominently present in the coordinative discourse shared by policy actors. The discourse on Nordic openness is a local variant of the global discourse on transparency. While references to institutional history allow it to contain a nationalistically appealing normative message, the cognitive aspects of this discourse are increasingly linked to global economic competitiveness. This invented tradition now also concerns Anders Chydenius, who has become the embodiment of the "open and direct" Finn.

---

107 Cf. Marcussen, *Ideas and Elites: The Social Construction of Economic and Monetary Union.*

Lily Kelting

New Nordic Cuisine: Performing Primitive Origins of Nordic Food

> "With Noma, our aim was to change food in Denmark.... [It was] a rhetorical instrument, just another one in my toolkit ... to redefine Nordic food."
> —Claus Meyer

2011: Rene Redzepi is a small man in a big tent. He wears jeans, rubber wading boots laced over his knees, and a T-Shirt reading "MAD foodcamp." His moppy brown bangs are pushed to the side and he wears a flesh-colored, over-ear mic. Based on the huge, resounding round of applause, cheers, and shouts, one unfamiliar might think Redzepi is not a chef, but a rock star. 2011 marked a high point for Noma, Rene Redzepi's two-Michelin-star restaurant in Copenhagen, Denmark: Noma was named the best restaurant in the world for the second year running, and Redzepi found himself as much celebrity as chef. Founded in 2003 by gastronomic entrepreneur Claus Meyer, Noma is not just a restaurant. In 2008, Meyer and Redzepi added a research wing to the restaurant, the Nordic Food Lab, where chefs and scientists tinker with culinary experiments that may end up on the menu. And in this first Mad symposium in 2011, Redzepi turned his culinary praxis into a marketable, shareable worldwide conversation about how we should eat.

Noma is so media saturated that the origin story of the restaurant that Redzepi told at MAD foodcamp is already something like a mythos in the contemporary food world. Redzepi grew up between Copenhagen and his father's native Macedonia. In industrialized Copenhagen, "people ate fast food and microwave food. I don't have any good food memories from my Danish childhood."[1] Writing about the New Nordic movement in their article "From Label to Practice: The Process of Creating New Nordic Cuisine," Haldor Byrkjeflot, Jesper Strandgaard Pedersen, and Silviya Svejenova assert that Nordic food was an "empty label," which was transformed into a robust set of cultural practices by Redzepi, Meyer, Magnus Nilsson, and other gastro-entrepreneurs, chefs, high-level government supporters, scientists, media disseminators, and foodies from around 2002 to the present.[2] New Nordic food is a cultural construction, a confluence

1 Andreja Lajh, "Rene Redzepi on His Origins," *Haut De Gamme*, November 10, 2015, https://hautdegamme.net/2015/11/10/rene-redzepi-on-his-origins/.
2 Haldor Byrkjeflot, Jesper Strandgaard Pedersen, and Silviya Svejenova, "From Label to Practice: The Process of Creating New Nordic Cuisine," *Journal of Culinary Science & Technology* 11,

of social, economic, political and cultural factors relating to the production and consumption of Nordic food. New Nordic Food is powerful branding and a media phenomenon; it is chefs, food-thinkers, and the media that write about them; it is a Nordic Counsel of Ministers initiative funded at over 2 million DKK.[3] New Nordic Food is also, according to the restaurateur who coined the phrase, a "rhetoric."[4]

I focus not on the creation—or, indeed, death[5]—of New Nordic Food as a matter of narrative teleology. Instead, this chapter attends to resonances between these two vibrating strings of label and practice. In other words, I use methodologies of discourse analysis and conceptual history to demonstrate how, by whom, and why the ambivalent label of "New Nordic" is applied.[6] "New Nordic food" is one of the earliest applications of the label "New Nordic," if not the first itself. The concept of the "New Nordic" emerged in the early 2000s either directly from or alongside a movement to revitalize the identity of the Nordic culinary industry.[7] Governmental bodies seized on the concept as soon as it appeared—formalizing "New Nordic Food" with a 2004 pan-Nordic manifesto of values and well-funded programs to put those values onto Nordic plates.

New Nordic food is thus a highly successful rhetorical application of the concept of "the Nordic" and a very powerful international brand. But what does this brand actually signify? The "New Nordic" brings to mind a range of associations, often contradictory. New Nordic food is pure and simple, but it is also innovative and artistic. It can be applied to singular chefs—Rene Redzepi, for one—or to the governmental programs of the Nordic Council of Ministers using local food traditions in the Nordic countries as external-facing gastrodiplomacy to promote

---

no. 1 (March 2013): 36–55, doi:10.1080/15428052.2013.754296. This article also contains a helpful appendix of bibliographical references on New Nordic Cuisine, for those looking to explore this fairly vast media scape.

3 Jonatan Leer, "The Rise and Fall of the New Nordic Cuisine," *Journal of Aesthetics & Culture* 8, no. 1 (January 1, 2016), doi:10.3402/jac.v8.33494..

4 In Byrkjeflot, Pedersen, and Svejenova, "From Label to Practice," 43.

5 Leer, "Rise and Fall."

6 As distinct, for example, from sociological methodologies assessing actual practices of cooking and eating in the Nordic region.

7 Matthias Danbolt writes, in his survey of Nordic exceptionalism and New Nordic rhetorics, "The use of 'New Nordic' as a novel brand emerged in particular from the discussions around the so-called New Nordic Food-movement in the early 2000s." In an introduction to a cluster of articles about the aesthetics of the New Nordic, Danish art historian Mette Sandbye notes: "Suddenly, in the early 2000s, a new term started to be prevalent: 'The New Nordic.'" It mainly appeared in relation to food, as 'New Nordic Food.'"

ideas of Nordic exceptionalism abroad.[8] The New Nordic gestures toward its own contemporaneity while also looking to the past and future. And lastly, the New Nordic need have little to do with Northern Europe at all. New Nordic Food can be a smørrebrød in Claus Meyer's Nordic Food Hall in New York City or chapulines (grasshopper) tacos served at a Noma pop-up in Mexico. "New Nordic" can, indeed, be a line of herbal supplements with "Scandinavian values" promising increased vitality and ingredient purity to consumers from Copenhagen to China.[9]

This chapter charts these various rhetorics of New Nordic Food in order to survey who calls what "Nordic" and to what end. I orient the rhetorical work done by these many players along two axes—time and place. "Time and Place" is not only the subtitle of the first Noma cookbook, it is also a phrase which occurs everywhere in the rhetorics of the New Nordic Food movement. In short, I conclude that the New Nordic's mingling of ancient techniques – hunting and gathering – with utopian rhetoric creates a kind of full circle, an ideological loophole, in which a return to eating lichen and ants is both a fantasy of the paleolithic and a model for gastronomy's future. In transporting Nordisk Mad (Nordic food: no-ma) to Japan, Mexico, New York, and other markets, local and the global are not at odds but intermingled: creating, paradoxically, a new rhetorical definition of terroir divorced from specific ecologies. Ultimately, I argue that the intentional ambiguity of the label "New Nordic" in terms of time and place gives its culinary applications staying power on the international scene while performatively and rhetorically obscuring other dynamics at play in terms of race, gender, and class.

---

8 Nordic Council of Ministers, "Nordic Food Diplomacy," *Nordic Food Diplomacy*, accessed 1 January 2019, http://www.nfd.nynordiskmad.org.

9 This is not to suggest that New Nordic food can be anything and everything. One obvious point of contrast in terms of the international circulation of Nordic Food is IKEA. IKEA, whose food division has an annual turnover of over $2 billion, seems to represent everything which the New Nordic Cuisine does not: IKEA's menu is mass culture, budget friendly, kid friendly, widely popular, and geographically accessible around the world. But these two Nordic Food juggernauts are indeed not as separate as their reputations suggest. Claus Meyer, for example, is doing sustainability consulting with IKEA to veganize at least half of the chain's menu by 2025. This supports my thesis that the New Nordic Cuisine is not simply a set of recipes, chefs, or restaurants but ideological rhetoric with extremely far-reaching political and cultural effects.

What is New Nordic Food?

Writing about "new Southern" food in the United States, scholar Marcie Cohen Ferris writes that, "the challenge of food studies remains food itself."[10] To define a food movement requires collating many fleeting experiences of cooking and eating, from home kitchens to government nutrition protocols, involving social actors from celebrity chefs to food critics to eaters to academics. As such, this research has the same methodological constraints as all food studies scholarship: an unstable and ephemeral source material. As such, my perspective brings together rhetorical discourse analysis with a more specific focus on the performative, agential use of speech acts by specific social actors. I focus on cookbooks, interviews, media, and other print materials to assess "what we talk about when we talk about New Nordic Food."

There has accumulated, over the past ten years, a small body of academic research on the New Nordic Food movement from those affiliated with culinary institutions (Noma "staff-anthropologist" Mark Emil Hermansen) to cultural studies academics (Jonathan Leer). Let me very humbly here outline my own interventions—first, as a performance studies scholar, to attune to the sensory experiences and embodied knowledge immanent to writing about a cuisine, descriptions which I often miss in sociological or anthropological analysis. Jonathan Leer writes that New Nordic Food has been largely uncriticized by media, which also makes scholarly analysis difficult; there is seemingly no outside to food media hype. Here, I attempt to write from that outside position, reading this mediascape against the grain. The other day, as I sat writing this essay, a student from Bangalore popped into my office and immediately asked about the stack of New Nordic cookbooks on my desk: "Do you know what Rene Redzepi is doing at that restaurant Noma in Copenhagen? It's like everything they serve is an artwork!" What seemed at first a great challenge, writing this chapter from India, is in some senses also a great boon—from an outside vantage, the tension is clear between food, that deeply ephemeral and personal sensory experience, and its social meanings, which traverse the whole world through various media.

As the chapters in this volume demonstrate, the definition of "Nordic" is not nearly straightforward; "Nordicness" stretches far beyond the geopolitical region. More concretely, my analysis here centres around key figures and institutions of the movement as they circulate both within and outside Nordic countries: Noma, its chef Rene Redzepi and creator Claus Meyer, chef Magnus

---

10 Marcie Cohen Ferris, *The Edible South: The Power of Food and the Making of an American Region* (Chapel Hill: University of North Carolina Press, 2014), 2.

Nilsson and his restaurant Fäviken, which opened in 2008 in remote Jämtland. By focusing on the most famous and vocal proponents of New Nordic food, and by centring further around discourses which originate in Denmark and Sweden, I do not mean to reproduce discourses which recentre all conceptions of the Nordic around the region's most powerful and wealthy nations. Instead, I hope to underscore the centrality of these celebrity chefs and these two nations in the international representation of Nordic food.

While the "new Nordic" cuisine is certainly the product of elite circles in major cities,[11] the pan-Nordic and inclusive rhetorics of New Nordic food have carried the label to every corner of the region. The initiatives developed by the Nordic Council of Ministers around the label underscores that "New Nordic Food" rhetorics are explicitly pan-regional. Their first collective initiative, the New Nordic Cuisine Manifesto, carefully included signatories from across the Nordic nations including Iceland, Greenland, and the Faroe Islands, for example. Perhaps there is something about the ecological focus of New Nordic Food which resists both national boundaries as well as even regional ones.[12] Rene Redzepi explained in a 2017 interview with Anthony Bourdain: "We need to better understand what the hell does it mean to actually be a cook in the north. Are you a local or not a local? People consider [Noma] to be a local restaurant but the menu right now has ingredients that come from 1000 kilometres away, which is nothing local. The reality is that Denmark has more in common with Germany than with Finland or Norway, especially when it comes to food."[13]

I stress the gap between the discourse of "New Nordic Food" and what people are actually cooking and eating in Nordic countries in order to highlight power relations at play. The "New Nordic" as a food media sensation is an elite movement that originates in urban fine dining with visible and mobile celebrity chefs as its face. As a result, these rhetorics are not neutral but can actually *elide* other conceptions of Nordic food, especially with regard to indige-

---

11 With the obvious counterexample of very remote gastrotourist destinations, like Fäviken. Mark Emil Hermansen writes about the way in which Noma consolidates Nordic identity for its "natives"; I wonder rather whether those natives might be an international cadre of elite diners, journalists, and fellow food industry people rather than the people of Copenhagen (cf. Leer, "Rise and Fall").
12 Although even this move towards regionalism over nationalism is unevenly distributed across the Nordic nations. Cf. Nicklas Neuman and Jonatan Leer, "Nordic Cuisine but National Identities: 'New Nordic Cuisine' and the gastronationalist projects of Denmark and Sweden," *Anthropology of food*, no. 13 (July 19, 2018), doi:10.4000/aof.8723.
13 Rene Redzepi, "Rene Redzepi on the new Noma," *Parts Unknown*, 13 April 2017, accessed 26 December 2018, https://explorepartsunknown.com/copenhagen/rene-redzepi-on-the-new-noma/

nous chefs, vegetarians, immigrant foodways, and so on. After a panel in Berlin on Nordic food and cultural diplomacy, I began to ask a woman from the Swedish embassy about the impact of New Nordic food in Germany, she furrowed her brows and shrugged. She mentioned that the local grocery has started carrying metal tubes of Kalles Kaviar, is that what I meant? No. What I am writing about here is not – or not primarily – the material networks through which Nordic foods circulate but the way that rhetorics surrounding the New Nordic food move promiscuously from Copenhagen to the hallways of a university in India.

Indeed, the label "New Nordic" is sometimes so powerful that its own key practitioners reject affiliation with the movement. Fäviken chef and cookbook author Magnus Nilsson,[14] for example, originally rejected the comparison with Redzepi and label New Nordic. In his encyclopaedic 2015 documentation of home cooking across the Nordic countries, *The Nordic Cook Book*, Nilsson writes, "I don't consider myself to be Nordic; I am, in fact, Swedish or possibly Jämtlandian."[15] One of Noma's most notable "graduates," Christian Puglisi, writes, "I do not feel that I'm a part of the New Nordic movement, as I don't adhere to a dogma of using only ingredients from Denmark or the surrounding Nordic region. I am an individual, and [Copenhagen restaurant] Relæ is a unique restaurant with its own identity."[16] Thus, I emphasize that this analysis must remain on the level of rhetorics rather than a sociological investigation of Nordic food which might catalogue actual modes of Nordic eating (or indeed trace Scandiphilia across other nations like the UK).

But to suggest that New Nordic Food is primarily a cultural force is not to diminish its material effects. The cultural is never "merely" cultural. Indeed, much of the rhetoric of Nordic exceptionalism in the 2000s and 2010s – from *hygge* mania to more policy-oriented conversations around democratic socialism, maternity leave, and education policy – are bulwarked by the success of the New Nordic Food movement.[17]

---

14 Magnus Nilsson, *Fäviken* (London: Phaidon Press, 2015).

15 Magnus Nilsson, *The Nordic Cook Book* (London: Phaidon Press, 2015), 11.

16 Christian Puglisi, *Relæ: A book of ideas*, (Berkeley: Ten Speed Press 2014), 32–34.

17 That is, "NCoM [Nordic Council of Ministers]'s numerous strategy plans and branding initiatives for the NNF over the last decade has not only been central in making New Nordic Cuisine into a celebrated trademark internationally, it has also turned the "New Nordic" into a brand that has aided the promotion of contemporary art, architecture, design, performing arts, films, TV shows, and other realms of cultural production from the Nordic region internationally" in Mathias Danbolt, "New Nordic Exceptionalism: Jeuno JE Kim and Ewa Einhorn's *The United Nations of Norden* and Other Realist Utopias," *Journal of Aesthetics & Culture* 8, no. 1 (January 2016): 10, doi:10.3402/jac.v8.30902.

TIME

"The New Nordic primitives"

Despite being some of the most expensive and desirable commodities available in the early twenty-first century, the dishes at Copenhagen restaurant Noma are not ostentatiously lavish, nor scientifically adventurous, but instead show a kind of stereotypical Danish restraint. Indeed, rather than into a gastronomic future of olive spheres and scented air, the plates at Noma gesture ever backwards. Redzepi's most famous dishes hearken back to a primitive, prehistoric, or pre-European past. Take, for example, "langoustines and sea flavours," served on a slab of rock – as are many of Noma's dishes. The sole langoustine tail is cooked for 32 seconds in a pan. The "sea flavours," of course, take more time to develop – the rock itself is dotted with a kind of mayonnaise-like emulsion of oyster flesh and juice, strewn with rye breadcrumbs and dulse dust. The impression given by such plating is that the lobster has simply been found like this – not manipulated in any way – and that the dish is somehow timeless. In the Noma cookbook, photographs of dishes are interspersed with photographs of the raw ingredients, such that an image of a razor clam nestled in seaweed rubs up against a photo of the plated restaurant version, "razor clam with parsley, horseradish, mussel juice" which involves freezing juiced horseradish into a light tumble of snow.[18]

On the other hand, these dishes are intensely of the moment. One word frequently used to describe New Nordic dishes is a "snapshot" – "a snapshot of the seasons," as chef Esben Holmboe Bang describes the menu at his three-Michelin-starred restaurant Maaemo in Oslo.[19] Less – or perhaps more? – poetically, Redzepi writes of a dish of mackerel and a broth from the first peas of the early summer: "It was almost like being bitch-slapped by the season."[20] Indeed, the "new Noma," reopened in March 2018, does not follow a typical fine dining progression from vegetables to meat to sweets; each menu is based instead on "three different seasons, and there will be a period of microseasons within each of them."[21] These are not "spring, summer, winter and fall" but are defined in deep relation to the Danish landscape: "when the oceans are ice-cold," "the

---

18 Rene Redzepi, *Noma: Time and Place* (London: Phaidon Press, 2010).
19 Esben Holmboe Bang, "Culinary journeys". *CNN Travel TV*, 2016. https://www.youtube.com/watch?v=rwUj2PY5_HM.
20 Rene Redzepi, *A Work in Progress: A Journal* (London: Phaidon Press 2013), 91.
21 Redzepi, "Rene Redzepi on the New Noma."

green season" and "the game season, when the leaves begin to fall."[22] Thus, time in New Nordic Cuisine is both intensely of the moment, hearkens to a primitive past, and gestures toward the future of food. It is this non-linear, wild time that gives the cuisine its rhetorical force.

The Nordic Kitchen Manifesto, signed in 2004 by twelve chefs from Sweden, Norway, Denmark, Finland, Iceland, Greenland, and the Faroe Islands, demonstrates the ways in which these aesthetic choices become codified as ethical imperatives. The first three items in the manifesto all suggest that the rhetorics of intense seasonality and locality are not merely accidental but hallmarks of the New Nordic Food movement. They declare that they intend, "1) to express the purity, freshness, simplicity and ethics we wish to associate to our region; 2) to reflect the changes of the seasons in the meal we make; 3) to base our cooking on ingredients and produce whose characteristics are particularly in our climates, landscapes."[23] Thus, embedded in the very creation of "New Nordic" food discourse is idea that food must be seasonal and local so that it can represent Nordic values of purity, freshness, simplicity, and ethics. In this sense, the New Nordic Food Movement is connected to other terms that associate "The Nordic" with a kind of atemporal wilderness – for example "nordic" is used as a label for walking with poles, cross-country skiing, or generally being out in nature (*Friluftsliv* in Scandinavian). [24]

As such, the New Nordic becomes lastingly associated with a kind of primitive, ahistorical time which makes it difficult to trace the contours of this rhetoric and the power mechanics of its functioning. It is not only the plating, but also culinary techniques which stand liminally between "the raw and the cooked" – such as smoking and pickling – which again associate the rhetoric of new Nordic food with the rhetorics of prehistoricity and primitivity.[25] Fäviken serves a beef heart tartare, as well as marrow scooped from a cow shinbone, sawed in half tableside in the small dining room. Eating ants or lichen has be-

---

22 Pete Wells, "The New Noma: FAQ," 24 April 2018, https://www.nytimes.com/2018/04/24/dining/noma-restaurant-copenhagen.html

23 Nordic Council of Ministers, "The New Nordic Food Manifesto," *Nordic Co-operation*, accessed May 30, 2021, https://www.norden.org/en/information/new-nordic-food-manifesto.

24 Indeed "Friluftsliv" is poised to be the latest hot Scandinavian "lifestyle trend" – the new "hygge" – as North America and Europe look for strategies to cope with Covid-19 restrictions in the wintertime. See also Aronssen and Graden, eds., *Performing Nordic Heritage* (Surrey: Ashgate, 2013).

25 A distinction central to mid-century anthropology's concept of societies, as in Claude Lévi-Strauss, *The Raw and the Cooked: Introduction to a Science of Mythology* (New York: Harper Colophon Books, 1975) or Mary Douglas, *Purity and Danger: An Analysis of Concept of Pollution and Taboo*, Routledge Classics (London: Routledge, 2005).

come so associated with Noma's avant-garde kitchens as to become a punchline. Esben Holmboe Bang's restaurant Maaemo, to take a different example, comes from an Old Norse word that means "all things that are living," directly combining the "New Nordic food" ethos of expanding the definition of the edible with invocations of Old Norse language and culture.

This temporal play between the unmediated deep past and the extreme present creates the wonder at the heart of Noma's mission. Indeed, such tensions have run throughout discourses of "the Nordic" throughout the 20th century. Historians Carl Marklund and Peter Stadius note that "inter-war Scandinavia was portrayed as capable of somehow combining the past with the future, the old with the new."[26] The Nordic region, then, has long stood for both the progressive and modern as well as the primitive and natural—the region is and has been defined precisely by this friction.

"How the Vikings Conquered Dinner"[27]

This kind of "cave man cooking" is not, of course, neutral.[28] In promoting these primitive visions of the Nordic located in a kind of fantasy past, the New Nordic only continues a long tradition of romanticizing the Nordic Middle Ages.[29] Here I turn to one such rhetoric as a case study: Viking masculinities. In a spread in the popular American glossy food magazine *Bon Appetit*, Magnus Nilsson stands wrapped in furs, a thick blonde beard falling into the grey folds of the fur pelt, his blonde hair falling past his shoulders. He is set against the red wood walls of his restaurant, Fäviken, in northern Sweden. The photograph is from 2011, but it could be an illustration from *Asterix*, where Asterix and Obelix

---

26 Carl Marklund and Peter Stadius, "Acceptance and Conformity," *Culture Unbound* 2 (2010): 609 – 34

27 Brett, Martin, "How the Vikings Conquered Dinner," *GQ*, July 29, 2014, https://www.gq.com/ story/best-nordic-scandinavian-restaurants-noma.

28 It is probably no coincidence that the rarified primitivism of the New Nordic Food movement boomed in the same period (2005 – 2015) as the more widespread paleo food craze, with its focus on "manly" steaks and functional fitness. See Linda Lapiņa and Jonatan Leer, "Carnivorous Heterotopias: Gender, Nostalgia and Hipsterness in the Copenhagen Meat Scene," *NORMA* 11, no. 2 (April 2, 2016): 89 – 109, doi:10.1080/18902138.2016.1184479.

29 See: Julian D. Richards, *The Vikings: A Very Short Introduction*, Very Short Introductions (Oxford: Oxford University Press, 2005); Kevin J. Harty, *The Vikings on Film: Essays on Depictions of the Nordic Middle Ages* (Jefferson: McFarland, 2014); Elisabeth I. Ward, "Viking Pop Culture on Display: The Case of the Horned Helmets," *Material Culture Review* 54, vol. 1 (Autumn 2001): 6 – 20.

meet their marauding neighbour to the North, the horned-helmeted Olaf.[30] Nilsson has gotten a lot of press for his work at Fäviken, and journalists draw the link again and again that Nilsson is "the head of the class of the Nordic Primitives."[31] *GQ* sends a fine-dining reporter across Scandinavia to report on "how the Vikings conquered dinner."[32] Food critic Allen Jenkins paints the scene for *The Guardian:* "We head upstairs past an ancient wolfskin coat to the restaurant... [the] dining room is punctuated with a curtain of cod roe; air-dried pieces of pig hang from the ceiling, giant jars of dried mushrooms and flowers line the side tables."[33] *Smithsonian Magazine* writer Rachel Nuwer opens her review of the restaurant with Nilsson clapping his "bear-paw-sized hands"; her first course at the restaurant is accompanied by a glass of mead—"just like the Vikings used to drink," according to sommelier Robert Andersson.[34]

The rhetorical linkages between masculine Vikings, Nordic primitivism, and New Nordic food are manifold. The frontispiece of Redzepi's first cookbook, *NOMA: Time and Place*, shows a greyscale map of the Nordic region, countries textured with pine and leaves. The caption reads "Rene's voyages"—dotted lines span from Copenhagen to the Faroe Islands, to Iceland, to Greenland, looping back. It looks, more than anything, like a map of the Viking Leif Eriksson's voyages. A map like this – starting from Copenhagen and looping towards Greenland – also hints at the history of intra-Nordic colonialism elided within New Nordic Food's rhetoric, particularly the pan-regional, co-operational, and celebratory vision offered by programs funded by the Nordic Council of Ministers.

The association of New Nordic food with stereotypes of Viking/colonial male heroic pasts serves to elide other modes in which we might talk about Nordic food. We might instead discuss home baking done by women in Nordic countries. We might critique the near total absence of women chefs from this powerful New Nordic Food rhetoric. Redzepi might seem an odd figure to centre these critiques around, as the son of an Macedonian immigrant, a slight, brown-haired

---

30 E.g. in Stefan Fjeldmark et al,, *Asterix et les Vikings [Asterix and the Vikings]* (Montreal: Alliance Atlantis Vivafilm, 2006), DVD.

31 Adam Sachs, "Fäviken Rising," *Bon Appetit*, 15 August 2011, https://www.bonappetit.com/test-kitchen/cooking-tips/article/f-viken-rising

32 Brett Martin, "How the Vikings Conquered Dinner."

33 Allen Jenkins, "Magnus Nilsson: the Rising Star of Nordic Cooking," *The Guardian*, 22 January, 2012, https://www.theguardian.com/lifeandstyle/2012/jan/22/magnus-nilsson-faviken-sweden-chef.

34 Rachel Nuwer, "Deep in the Swedish Wilderness, Discovering One of the World's Greatest Restaurants," *Smithsonian Magazine*, 21 August, 2013, https://www.smithsonianmag.com/travel/deep-in-the-swedish-wilderness-discovering-one-of-the-worlds-greatest-restaurants-818172.

fellow. Still, the Nordic variation of the shouty, hyper-masculine celebrity chef trope has the same effect: it creates a hostile and exclusive kitchen culture. Redzepi has written and spoken extensively about his anger problems: "Mr. Redzepi admits he is not entirely a reformed man. He uses the C-word (and it is not "cook") in the first paragraph of his article and asks whether there is "still room for guys like me" in the industry."[35] "Guys like me" – underdogs, Vikings, kitchen warriors – dominate the rhetoric of New Nordic Food and foreclose the inclusion of other modes of cooking and eating, those associated with *women*, for example, within the "New Nordic" brand.

As food media becomes big business – and celebrity chefs are not just famous chefs but widely known celebrities – the uncritical valorization of masculinity creates rhetorics which continue to haunt the material conditions of the contemporary kitchen. In the heyday of Noma's position as "the best restaurant in the world," Rene Redzepi appeared on the cover of Time Magazine alongside chefs David Chang and Alex Atala with the caption "Gods of Food" emblazoned across their serious faces.[36] The "Gods of Food" issue featured not a single woman chef. The response given by editor Howard Chua-Eoan after the issue faced backlash was that women chefs lacked the "reach and influence" of men like Redzepi – alluding to the rhetorics of masculinity straight from the previous millennium, and the "reach and influence" of "Rene's voyages" across the Northern Atlantic.[37]

A different example might be Elaine Asp, chef at the restaurant Haavi i Glen in the tiny village of Glen, one of 51 Sami villages in Sweden. Asp is famous for her gampasuele: reindeer blood pancakes. It would be easy to market such a dish as "metal" within the rhetoric of guitar-shredding, testosterone-fuelled kitchen culture. Her restaurant, like Fäviken, is nestled in a small town of fourteen residents, requiring a kind of pilgrimage to visit. But no one is calling Asp one of the "New Nordic primitives," she is neither a chef-saint nor a burly, "bearpawed" Viking. Her cuisine, rather, stems from indigenous Sami practices of cooking and eating each part of the reindeer, of foraging as a result of following herds, and living lightly off the land.

---

35 Andrew Hill, "Too Many Angry Cooks Spoil the Business Broth," *Financial Times*, August 24, 2015, https://www.ft.com/content/0d81ad46 – 4722 – 11e5-b3b2 – 1672f710807b.

36 "The Gods of Food," editorial, *Time*, November 18, 2013, http://content.time.com/time/magazine/article/0,9171,2156845,00.html.

37 Hillary Dixler Canavan, "Time Editor Howard Chua-Eoan Explains Why No Female Chefs Are 'Gods of Food,'" *Eater*, November 7, 2013, https://www.eater.com/2013/11/7/6334005/time-gods-of-food-controversy-howard-chua-eoan-women-chefs.

How new is the New Nordic?

Paradoxically, while both New Nordic culinary aesthetics and the movement's media coverage refer to the past, it is also a utopian project. This future orientation likely gives the movement its thrust and sticking power as a cultural force. In 2013, chef and author Alice Waters wrote of Redzepi in the Wall Street Journal: "Rene Redzepi is focused on the future in the biggest way possible."[38] This utopianism is even evident from a management perspective, for example the authors of this market food trend report state: "Unlike contemporary culinary trends in other European regions, e. g., the Mediterranean, the value proposition of the NNC is not primarily driven by a wish to revive local traditions. Rather the NNC is a futuristic quest."[39] Between the MAD symposium founded by Redzepi and the experimental culinary work done at the Nordic Food Lab, one gets the sense that those mad geniuses in Copenhagen are not only serving ants in order to create an avant-garde culinary experience – they are serving ants to save the world.

And they're not wrong. Certain directions of the New Nordic movement might not only be a punchline but also provide more sustainable and ethical foodways across the world – for example, by questioning the limits of the edible in a food-insecure and overpopulated world. By changing aesthetics around foraging, bug eating, and the deliciousness of wild things, Noma may in fact be actively participating in a better future – and not just rhetorically.

The multiplicity of temporal perspectives is striking here, combining an exoticized past, microseasonality, and the far future. Perhaps the runaway success of the New Nordic Food movement lies in its performative frisson, its "never for the first time"-ness. Jeff Gordiner writes for the New York Times: "Paradoxically, the *New* Nordic movement strives to carry diners way back to a more ancient realm of flavour. Even when looking forward, it summons a sort of Norse gastronomic mythology centered on twigs, berries, roots, weeds, bark, hay, grass, kelp, fish, soil and barrel-fermented funk."[40]

---

38 Howie Kahn, "Noma's Rene Redzepi Never Stops Experimenting," *The Wall Street Journal*, 5 November, 2013, https://www.wsj.com/articles/nomas-rene-redzepi-never-stops-experimenting-1415237540.
39 Tino Bech-Larsen, Trine Mørk, and Sussanne Kolle, "New Nordic Cuisine: Is There Another Back to the Future? – An Informed Viewpoint on NNC Value Drivers and Market Scenarios," *Trends in Food Science & Technology* 50 (April 1, 2016): 249, doi:10.1016/j.tifs.2016.01.020.
40 Jeff Gordinier, "A Nordic Quest in New York," *The New York Times*, February 18, 2014, Food, https://www.nytimes.com/2014/02/19/dining/a-nordic-quest-in-new-york.html.

Food reporter Julia Moskin writes: "It is sometimes called 'new Nordic,' although [Redzepi] and some other chefs from the region prefer the broader label 'authentic cuisine.' It is earthy and refined, *ancient and modern*, both playful and deeply serious. Instead of the new (techniques, stabilizers, ingredients), it emphasizes the old (drying, smoking, pickling, curing, smoking) with a larger goal of returning balance to the earth itself [italics mine]."[41] While Moskin creates a tension between the twin labels of progressive "New Nordic" and past-oriented "authentic cuisine," I argue that these two rhetorics of Nordic food are two sides of the same coin. The coexistence of mythical pasts, the present, and the bold future orientation of the New Nordic is indeed the movement's very signature. As Redzepi concludes in his 2013 *A Work in Progress: A Journal:* "When past and present merge, something new happens."[42]

PLACE

Nordic Terroir: Rooted in Place

Just as the "New" in "New Nordic Food" encompasses both the movement's futurity as well as primitive pasts, "Nordic" has a similar wide-ranging rhetorical function. Nordic ecology is on the one hand essential to the authenticity of New Nordic Food. And on the other, the global strength of New Nordic Food rhetorics demand that the idea of the "Nordic" slips away, even from its own regional borders. Danish-Icelandic artist Olafur Eliasson writes in the preface to *Noma: Time and Place:*

> When we look at the plate, we should really also see the greater ecosystem. Finding out where the food comes from and where it goes to – maybe this knowledge can be made into a kind of flavour enhancer. It matters whether the potatoes come from New Zealand or the Lammefjord area of Denmark, and I can see great potential in not dividing knowledge and flavour (just as in art, you should not separate form and content).[43]

Eliasson's exhortation that the dish should reflect the ecosystem encapsulates a key strand in the movement. The pages of the cookbook that follow show sweep-

---

41 Julia Moskin, "New Nordic Cuisine Draws Disciples," *The New York Times*, August 24, 2011, Food, https://www.nytimes.com/2011/08/24/dining/new-nordic-cuisine-draws-disciples.html.
42 Redzepi, *A Work in Progress: A Journal*, 119.
43 Redzepi, *Noma: Time and Place*, 9.

ing coastlines, dense forests, and local shell fishermen in their orange hip waders. We can be nowhere but north.

It is no surprise – given that the book *Noma*, the restaurant Noma, and the New Nordic Cuisine manifesto are all the brainchild of Claus Meyer – to see an insistence on place throughout. After all, the principles associated with New Nordic Cuisine (purity, freshness, simplicity and ethics) are tied not only to seasonality but to "our climates, landscapes, and waters."[44] This insistence on place is one of the key defining factors of the New Nordic. But perhaps this emphasis on "place" in fact simply recapitulates one of the key concepts in gastronomy – that all food is connected to the land. The importance of terroir in southern Europe led to the creation of AOC and DOP labels in the 1930s, certifying as "authentic" only wines, cheeses, or other foods from distinct agricultural regions. By the twenty-first century, ideas about terroir had fallen out of popular discourse with the rise of globalization. So to hear Eliasson riff that "knowledge is a kind of flavour enhancer" feels suddenly new; one might credit Redzepi, Meyer, and other chefs of the New Nordic movement, with bringing back the concept of terroir to popular discourse, where it has spread like wildfire.[45] Eliasson is, of course, right: miso made in Copenhagen will taste different from miso made in Aarhus will taste different from miso made in a coastal town outside Tokyo. Different microbes float in on the breeze. Knowledge of these differences – the kind of knowledge generated by the Nordic Food Lab – *does* make these foods more delicious. Just ask the diners eating the results of their research into fermentation, ageing, and the limits of the edible next door at Noma. This, too, is terroir.

Despite its global power and inclusive sweep, at the heart of the rhetoric of the New Nordic food is indeed a specific landscape, a terroir, and food systems, which are inextricable from the cold waters and extreme seasons of the Nordic region. Noma in particular is famous for its exclusive use of ingredients native to the region. No black pepper and no lemons mean that acidity and bite come instead from ants' stress hormones or funky ferments. Because each flavour must be coaxed out of a limited palate of ingredients native to the Nordic region, many dishes become a kind of portrait of the landscapes from which the ingredients come. In his *Journal*, Redzepi describes the thought process behind his dish of hare with bitter greens and walnuts – "Torsten was the first to

---

44 Nordic Council of Ministers, "The New Nordic Food Manifesto,"
45 Indeed the Google Books Ngram review provides the data: appearances of "terroir" in English-language books increase exponentially after about 2004, as do appearances of the associated terms "slow food," "food miles," "farm to table" and "eating local." The graphs of these usages are nearly identical to a search for "Rene Redzepi."

pick up the hare carcass. 'What do you think its last meal was?' I asked, 'Do you think we should try to stuff it back in?'"[46] This melding of food with a natural environment shook the food world in the early 2000s, especially in comparison to French gastronomy which has so dominated elite fine dining before this Nordic ascendency. Food editor Joshua David Stein writes in his review of Noma, "the wood infuses into the broth, creating a very special flavour that you somehow recognize – it's almost as if you're walking through a forest and smelling the forest. It sounds crazy. You're recognizing it, you're eating it."[47]

Terroir's people

The Nordic Food Lab brought on a staff anthropologist, Mark Emil Hermansen, who wrote an essay called: "Cultivating Terroir," in which he chews through the cultural work done by the chefs at Noma in creating a sense of place.[48] Similarly to the way that New Nordic dishes are described as moments frozen in time, "snapshots of the season," Hermansen uses the language of anthropology to theorize ways that the food at Noma provides a portrait of Nordic terroir. Hermansen cites reviews of the restaurant which pick up this theme:

> At different times he [Redzepi] discovered how an ingredient should taste, its links to time and place: a Swedish truffle, birch-tree sap, a Danish mushroom, succulent seaweed, the potential of hazelnut and elderflower and nasturtium... "We cook the way we cook because this is what we found," Redzepi said. He's a chef for a shrinking planet, the man who found a terroir beneath the permafrost.[49]

Such descriptions are everywhere in media appraisal of New Nordic restaurants because they are the very cornerstone of the New Nordic philosophy: that food should taste like where it comes from and that where it comes from should be very close at hand.

Ecological terroir, however, is not the whole truth. Food scholar Amy Trubek writes in her book on terroir, *The Taste of Place*, "Terroir and goût du terroir are categories for framing and explaining people's relationship to the land, be it sen-

---

46 Rezepi, *A Work in Progress: A Journal*, 150.

47 Joshua David Stein, "Sleep Noma." *Tasting Table*, 26 July 2016, https://www.tastingtable.com/dine/national/noma-restaurant-copenhagen-rene-redzepi-joshua-david-stein.

48 In Mark Emil Hermansen, "Creating Terroir – An Anthropological Perspective on New Nordic Cuisine as an Expression of Nordic Identity," *Anthropology of Food* S7 (22 December 2012).

49 Hermansen, "Creating Terroir."

sual, practical, or habitual. This connection is considered essential, as timeless as the earth itself."[50] But, of course, it is *not* essential but highly rather socially and culturally created: "ultimately the cultural domain, the foodview, creates the goût du terroir."[51] Hermansen, too, concludes that New Nordic terroir is not only a culinary connection between food and the land but also a cultural site of identity formation. He even notes that New Nordic food is a site of "banal" nationalism for Nordics usually averse to overt nationalistic displays. Hermansen concludes,

The idea of a Nordic folk when exposed to the modern world of globalization, migration and electronic mediation exists to allow for a production of locality in everyday discourse; but rather than basing its idea of itself on the perceived historical ties that make out claims to blood or land, "native" bodies are reproduced via a continued production of locality – "this is who we are." This allows for a way to view the New Nordic Cuisine as a sort of postnational movement, especially because it reproduces a Nordic imagined community based on the (re)creation of a Nordic cuisine that takes its meaning from the production of locality, in the form of the Nordic terroir.

In essence, I understand Hermansen to argue for the hyper-local, wild, "taste of the North" New Nordic Food as a site for identity formation for Nordic people. Rather than construct a folk out of blood or soil, a race of Nordic People are tied to, if not the land in a autochthonic sense, then the distinct foods of that land, tastes from childhood. But these two rhetorics are, of course, intertwined.[52] Hermansen's claims for Noma's *folkishness* might inoculate against charges of elitism, they do seem to echo other contemporary populist rhetorics which connect the "folk" to the land. Charlotte Higgins' essay in the Guardian, "The Hygge Conspiracy," connects the explosive interest in all things *hygge* with growing anti-immigrant sentiments in the U.K. before Brexit.[53] Ulla Holm, adding together the emphasis on purity, fear of "contamination by outsiders," and even brown shirts of the front of house staff,[54] puts a finer point on it in her op-ed in the Danish newspaper, *Politiken:* "Noma is fascism."[55]

---

50 Amy Trubek, *The Taste of Place: A Cultural Journey into Terroir* (Berkeley: University of California Press, 2008),18.
51 Trubek, *Taste of Place*, 20.
52 See Merle Weßel's chapter in this volume.
53 Charlotte Higgins, "The Hygge Conspiracy," *The Guardian*, November 22, 2016, http://www.theguardian.com/lifeandstyle/2016/nov/22/hygge-conspiracy-denmark-cosiness-trend.
54 On this point Holm is (I assume) being ironic.
55 Ulla Holm, "Noma er fascisme i avantgardistiske klæ'r," *Politiken*, May 8, 2011, https://politiken.dk/debat/kroniken/art5509397/Noma-er-fascisme-i-avantgardistiske-kl%C3%A6r.

I did not go foraging with Rene Redzepi

Eating wild foods became so entangled with the New Nordic brand that one writer wrote an article for online food magazine Eater titled, "The Era of the 'I Foraged With René Redzepi' Piece."[56] The article rounds up media contributions to the "I foraged with Rene Redzepi" genre of food criticism. There are many. What started as pragmatics soon became the chefs' aesthetics. Aesthetics so remarkable that the media all over the world reported about the ants, the lichen, the leaf broth, and how good it all somehow tasted. Smoking, fermenting, pickling, and storing the summer's bounty for the winter may indeed have originated as uniquely Northern strategies for coping with seasonal extremes, but for the last fifteen years, they have been packaged as rhetorics. The most recent addition to this genre is the *Noma Guide to Fermentation*, published by Phaidon in late 2018.

It becomes more complicated when these hyperlocal technologies, such as foraging, proliferate as freely as digital hype pieces, cookbooks, and recipes. After one "I went foraging with Rene Redzepi piece" detailed the author and Redzepi's adventures foraging for wild mushrooms in London's Hampstead Heath, amateur foragers began to overrun the park. Park authorities warned: "If one in a thousand [park visitors] decided to pick funghi, that would be 8,000 foraging trips a year. We are on a point where, if it carries on, we could see serious species loss on Hampstead Heath, particularly with the funghi."[57]

In 2017, Redzepi again attempted to spread the love of wild food beyond the elite restaurant kitchen and to the populace by founding a foraging platform and phone app, Vild Mad. Though it is designed for use in Denmark, the app FAQ notes that "We hope that our program will inspire other wild food models around the world."[58] This ability of a restaurant to engage professional foragers to reinscribe a taste for forgotten local foods, to resignify weeds as fine products, is indeed a new turn in the fine dining landscape and a clarion call in a world with increasingly precarious food systems. The power of rhetoric, though, shows the ways in which a desire for wild food can escalate, spread, and proliferate far beyond the localities in which these foods grow. There is, then, a real tension be-

---

56 Paula Forbes, "The Era of the 'I Foraged With René Redzepi Piece,'" *Eater*, May 3, 2011, https://www.eater.com/2011/5/3/6683095/the-era-of-the-i-foraged-with-rene-redzepi-piece.

57 "Noma Head Chef Accused of Illegal Mushroom Picking," editorial, *The Telegraph*, 23 November 2010, https://www.telegraph.co.uk/foodanddrink/8154563/Noma-head-chef-accused-of-illegal-mushroom-picking.html.

58 "VILD MAD – Frequently Asked Questions," *Vild Mad*, accessed May 30, 2021, https://vild-mad.dk/application/files/5815/0227/5901/FAQ_US.pdf.

tween Noma's philosophy of the local and the technologized global infoscape in which it operates and spreads its brand.

Nordic food deterritorialized

But the spread of the New Nordic outside the North is not only digital. I have spent 2018 writing this essay and eating "Nordic" food all over the world, often wondering what exactly, ties the dishes before me to the terroir or "food-view" of the Nordic region. New York, NY: I stop in the open Art Deco Vanderbilt Hall at restaurateur Claus Meyer's Great Northern Food Hall. I pay four dollars for a croissant for "research": I'm not in the mood for a brussels sprouts and bacon *smørrebrød* and don't want to shell out for a poached egg and cheddar cheese "grain bowl" –supposedly an ode to Danish *grød* but right on time for America's low-carb, West-Coast inspired "bowl" craze. The croissant is not "Nordic" in any way I can recognize. Minneapolis, Minnesota: I have a cocktail with aquavit, carrot juice, and dill at a "New Nordic" restaurant. It is bitterly cold outside, and my Swedish-American friend and I are seated across from a blazing fire, sharing a pleasant pheasant terrine with pickled persimmons, cornichons, and some kind of quince mostarda.

Berlin: Olafur Eliasson's younger sister, Victoria Eliasdottir, is opening a "New Nordic" restaurant in Berlin. The first thing they place on the table alongside thick slices of light rye bread is a combination of bacon fat and brown butter. I am surprised because I was offered the very same spread with biscuits at Husk, in Charleston, South Carolina, another restaurant deeply committed to the local foodways of the American South. What makes this particular spread "Nordic"? Did the butter come from Icelandic cows? The fat from Danish pigs? Is there something about the seasonality, the sustainability, the innovation of these dishes that made them clearly New Nordic? I couldn't say.

A fourth example: Tulum, Mexico. The core Noma restaurant team helicopters in and prepares what sounds like, frankly, the greatest meal of all time – or "the meal of the decade" as Tom Sietsema described it.[59] And yet this final example most clearly encapsulates the problem of the highly local New Nordic

---

59 Tom Sietsema, "A World-Class Chef Built a $600 Pop-up in the Mexican Jungle. It Might Be "the Meal of the Decade,'" *Washington Post*, April 25, 2017, Food, https://www.washingtonpost.-com/lifestyle/food/a-world-class-chef-built-a-600-pop-up-in-the-mexican-jungle-it-might-be-the-meal-of-the-decade/2017/04/25/e3b75244–284e-11e7-a616-d7c8a68c1a66_story.html.

food as a global phenomenon. Critic Pete Wells writes in an exceptional essay on Noma Mexico, "What I find hard to run through my critical algorithms, though, is the idea of a meal devoted to local traditions and ingredients that is being prepared and consumed mostly by people from somewhere else."[60] Tulum is a place, but it is also a kind of no-place, a resort town. Half the residents live in moderate to extreme poverty.[61] This spectacular menu is designed to be eaten by global food intelligentsia, not local people. Nor was celebrating indigenous Mexican culinary knowledge an explicit part of Redzepi's project. Wells asks: "can a restaurant really be of its place if it doesn't bend and sway to the breezes of local tastes and local demands?... I'd rather review a restaurant that has its roots in the ground."[62]

This is the key question: when New Nordic food is so deeply associated with terroir, with "I went foraging with Rene Redzepi"—what happens when you go to Mexico? How do you translate these relationships with foragers and fishermen while also popping into countries with radically different food traditions like Mexico and Japan? How is this then *nordisk mad*, which gives Noma its name? What is then being exported? The possibility of a Noma Mexico highlights the power of New Nordic as a rhetoric, that it can be so completely estranged from even its own core tenets of time and place. Noma is not just a restaurant or mode of cooking – it is an enormously powerful brand, maybe even a cult of personality. "New Nordic" stands for and commercializes a hyper-specific ethos of microseasonality and extreme locovorism while obscuring the fact that the very existence of Noma Mexico requires performative and fluid definitions of time and space. To be New Nordic is to be local, but that "local" can be anywhere from Sydney to Tokyo to Tulum. As Jonathan Leer quips regarding Meyer's New York Nordic Food Hall: "if you can make it (Nordic) there, you can make it (Nordic) anywhere."[63]

The New Nordic movement associated itself so strongly with the very concept of localness itself that the above-mentioned concepts of "purity," "freshness," and "primitiveness" *themselves* become Nordic concepts. As Ryan Miller of New York's Momofuku Ssam puts it: "It's not like I learned about some new Danish cheese and came back and put it on my menu.... I learned to respect organization and education and making food in the most natural way possi-

---

60 Pete Wells, "Why I'm Not Reviewing Noma Mexico," *The New York Times*, 23 May 2017, https://www.nytimes.com/2017/05/23/dining/noma-tulum-pete-wells-mexico-rene-redzepi.html.
61 Pete Wells, "Why I'm Not Reviewing Noma Mexico."
62 Pete Wells, "Why I'm Not Reviewing Noma Mexico."
63 Leer, "Rise and Fall."

ble."[64] This idea of "the natural," it seems, is what "Nordic" signifies in "New Nordic Food": which is, of course, a cultural construction. "Nordic" does not signify Norway, Sweden, Denmark, Iceland, Finland, or Greenland but instead a portable series of rhetorics, in which terroir is on the one hand central and on the other has little to do with any specific terrain, culture, or history. The New Nordic has come to stand in for an anytime and anyplace while gesturing toward a Northern right here and right now. Writer Hank Shaw reiterates in *The Atlantic:* "The lesson Redzepi is teaching us is to make beautiful food that is only possible where you are right now – in the moment, and in the place."[65]

Conclusions

I have a confession to make. I have never eaten at Noma. It is, quite frankly, far too expensive.[66] It is strange, to spend so long writing an essay about a restaurant with so few seats – where, as Pete Wells notes, most of the diners were likely paid to be there, and where most of the diners likely flew to Copenhagen just to eat there. I have written about the ways in which "New Nordic Food" rhetorics manipulate and multiply time and place with exclusionary effects with regards to gender. But class exclusion is the real engine behind New Nordic discourse. To return to the "labels and practices" framework offered by Haldor Byrkjeflot, Jesper Strandgaard Pedersen, and Silviya Svejenova, class is where the rhetorical labels and material practices of the New Nordic Cuisine diverge. The rhetorics of New Nordic Food associate "the Nordic" with "nature" rather than any specific environment, with "the past and future" rather than any specific history; New Nordic Food rhetorics deterritorialize terroir itself and rhetorics of New Nordic Food gesture at once the deep past and the utopian future as chefs and writers strive to balance on the knife-edge of the season. But these rhetorics – as commercially viable and media-saturating as they are – cannot account for the sensory, embodied practices of the New Nordic cuisine. Indeed, perhaps so many people talk about Noma precisely *because* very few can afford to experience it for themselves. "New Nordic" food is expensive food. It generates as much meaning as it does because it is a commodity; it generates as much discourse as it does because to have an opinion about Rene Redzepi is a form of cultural

---

64 Moskin, "New Nordic Food Draws Disciples."
65 Hank Shaw, "Cook Like a Super-Locavore With Lessons From 'Noma,'" *The Atlantic*, March 23, 2011, https://www.theatlantic.com/health/archive/2011/03/cook-like-a-super-locavore-with-lessons-from-noma/72898/.
66 At the time of writing, dinner costs €550, including wine.

capital. Like Pete Wells, I wonder about the ethics of paying so much to eat something so extravagantly self-effacing. I wonder whether I am not simply jealous.

This is the other great paradox of Noma, that, as Wells writes, "as an aesthetic project, it is also about questioning received hierarchies of value."[67] Redzepi famously gave his dishwasher since 2003, Ali Sonko, a ten percent share in the restaurant (Redzepi himself owns twenty percent). Yet the optics of the white Noma team wearing matching shirts with Sonko's face on it when celebrating an award in London – Sonko emigrated from The Gambia – read to me as woefully naive. But still, the best aspects of New Nordic food have trickled down from Noma's 46 tables to the rest of us, namely, an expanded and curious definition of the delicious. New Nordic chefs and the governmental bodies that support them are explicitly interested in advocacy – from the Nordic Food Lab's research on and celebration of entomological proteins, to the Mad Symposium's knowledge sharing, to the foraging app Vild Mad's outreach to school children in the hopes of popularizing foraged foods. The Nordic Council of Ministers intends these social developments to have not only regional but global reach. Will a more accessible utopianism become as essential to the movement as seasonality and terroir?

---

67 Wells, "The New Noma: FAQ."

Jakob Stougaard-Nielsen

Nordic Noir: Branding Nordicness as British Boreal Nostalgia

In the first decades of the twenty-first century, Nordic crime fiction has become a local and a global obsession, constituting a sub-genre of crime fiction in its own right.[1] With a stock of glum detectives, cold, desolate landscapes and a penchant for social critique, crime novels and television series from the Nordic countries form a recognisable international brand, which is used in the marketing and export of not only the crime stories themselves, but also consumer goods, tourist destinations, Nordic lifestyles, and social values.

This chapter explores how the reading and consumption of Nordic crime fiction in the 2010s, particularly in the UK, became enmeshed in a much wider and pervasive rhetoric of Nordicness made recognisable under the brand name of Nordic noir. I am going to argue that when Nordic crime fiction travels abroad, it is consumed as a globalised cultural good, desirable for its blend of transnational generic forms and its exotic local anchoring. A utopian Nordicness or *borealism* – a term to be discussed later in this chapter – may best describe the allure of what is associated with Nordic noir in its British reception. Here, all things Nordic have come to represent an imagined, desirable topography[2] bestowed with stereotypical Nordic traits, sampling everything from social values to well-designed consumer products, which can be accessed *en bloc* through the consumption of crime fiction.

One suggestive example of how Nordic crime fiction has been used in the branding of non-Nordic consumer products is a British television commercial used in a marketing campaign for the petrol company Esso. The company's creative agency produced a commercial in the style of a Scandinavian crime drama, complete with a minimalist, gloomy set and actors speaking in Danish with English subtitles.[3] In the commercial, a witness, who turns out to be an Esso engi-

---

1 See Kerstin Bergman, *Swedish Crime Fiction: The Making of Nordic Noir* (Milan: Mimesis, 2014), 173; Barry Forshaw, *Death in a Cold Climate: A Guide to Scandinavian Crime Fiction* (Houndmills: Palgrave Macmillan, 2012); and Jakob Stougaard-Nielsen, *Scandinavian Crime Fiction* (London: Bloomsbury, 2017).
2 I am using the term "topography" (literally, "place writing") to designate the confluence of real, physical places and their complex and changing discursive, affective, or rhetorical figurations. See J. Hillis Miller, *Topographies* (Stanford: Stanford University Press, 1995), 3–4.
3 Esso, "Esso – Fuel Engineer," 1 September, 2017, YouTube video, 1:00, https://youtu.be/g9caGx-RkTc. In the UK, subtitled foreign television programmes were a rarity, until the screen-

neer with a remarkable eye for detail, helps the Danish detectives solve a case with Scandinavian-style meticulousness. It is implied that "Esso is renowned for having meticulous attention to detail in everything it does – including developing fuel formulations that are designed on a molecular level to help improve engine performance."[4] The connection between Nordic noir and a new fuel system is far-fetched, to say the least. Why did Esso choose to use Danish television drama as a vehicle for its branding, especially since there is no shortage of homegrown television drama or British detectives obsessed with forensic detail? The commercial suggests not only how iconic subtitled Nordic crime drama has become in the UK over the past decade; more importantly, it points to an implicit set of images that have become popularly associated with a contemporary rhetoric of Nordicness.[5]

The Esso commercial was meant to reach a segment of British middle-class consumers, readers, and television viewers, which, I argue, is no longer looking for confirmation of their own identities and social aspirations exclusively within the Anglophone sphere. To these viewers the affective engagement with Nordicness has become synonymous with wider aspirational cosmopolitan desires. However, the cosmopolitan consumption of Nordic noir and a concomitant desire for Nordicness is a complex phenomenon to locate, as it is stimulated partly by Nordic self-presentations and a receiving culture's analogous use of the Nordic to express its own local desires and concerns. While Esso could have drawn from a locally sourced list of perfectionist detectives, the Nordicness of subtitled quality television drama allows the advertiser to target an audience who wants to participate in current, legitimate consumer behaviour. The Nordic noir brand-

---

ing of Nordic television dramas on BBC FOUR from 2009 onwards. The experience of reading subtitles on the screen became a marker for the fascination with – and exotic foreignness of – Nordic noir drama series (see Jakob Stougaard-Nielsen, "Nordic Noir in the UK: The Allure of Accessible Difference," *Journal of Aesthetics & Culture* 8, no. 1 (January 2016): 32704, doi:10.3402/jac.v8.32704.

4 John Wood, "New Synergy Supreme + Unleaded launched," *Forecourt Trader Online*, 1 September, 2017, https://forecourttrader.co.uk/news/new-synergy-supreme-unleaded-launched/640519.article.

5 In a UK context, it is significant that even though the original language spoken by the actors in the commercial is Danish, the associated cultural background, as understood by viewers, is of a general Nordic character. Furthermore, the choice of the term "images" in this paragraph is informed, as my analyses and argument in this chapter generally, by the theory of image studies or imagology, associated with the work of Joep Leerssen. See, for instance, Joep Leerssen, "Here follows A summary of imagological theory," *Imagologica: Dedicated to the critical study of national stoeretypes*, n.d., para 6, accessed 1 May, 2021, https://imagologica.eu/theoreticalsummary.

ing also allows the company to draw on a set of positive values associated with the Nordic region (e.g. that it is egalitarian, socially just, functionalist, rational, healthy, and harmonious), which have become re-actualised and re-articulated through the popularisation of Nordic crime fiction, the "mystery" of Nordic happiness, NOMA's locally foraged Nordic food and the Danish hygge-craze.[6]

In the following, I shall discuss how the publishing, marketing, and reception of Nordic crime fiction in the UK, along with television documentaries and a recent deluge of articles and popular books on life, hygge, and happiness in the Nordic countries, present the region neatly packaged to the extent that all recognisable elements – history, art, culture, food, and consumer trends – appear mutually dependent, causal and, importantly, essentially local or regional. Viewed through contemporary popular cultural discourses in the UK, Nordic social realities are portrayed as attractive and authentic destinations that provide what might have been lost at home, but also as destinations that have already been prepared for a "tourist gaze."[7] As such, this chapter will argue that the rhetoric of Nordicness, around the international success of Nordic crime fiction at home and abroad, poses both a challenge and an opportunity for re-assessing what the rhetoric of Nordicness may signify in the twenty-first century.

From Nordic Crime Fiction to Nordic Noir

The story about the international success of Nordic crime fiction is by now well known.[8] The details of the genre's success in the Anglophone world, leading to the widespread adoption of the term Nordic noir, are worthwhile summarising nevertheless as they demonstrate the genre's unique impact and formation within a complex contemporary media situation, in a changing commercial and transnational field.

---

6 See Lily Kelting's chapter in this volume.

7 John Urry, *The Tourist Gaze: Leisure and Travel in Contemporary Societies* (London: Sage Publications, 1990).

8 Susan Bassnett, "Detective Fiction in Translation: Shifting Patterns of Reception," in *Crime Fiction as World Literature*, ed. Louise Nilsson, David Damrosch, and Theo D'haen (London: Bloomsbury, 2017), 149; Barry Forshaw, *Nordic Noir: The Pocket Essential Guide to Scandinavian Crime Fiction, Film and TV* (Harpenden: Pocket Essentials, 2013); Wendy Lesser, *Scandinavian Noir: In Pursuit of a Mystery* (New York: Farrar, Straus and Giroux, 2020); Andrew Nestingen and Paula Arvas, "Introduction: Contemporary Scandinavian Crime Fiction," in *Scandinavian Crime Fiction*, ed. Andrew Nestingen and Paula Arvas (Cardiff: University of Wales Press, 2011); Stougaard-Nielsen, *Scandinavian*; and Steven Peacock, *Swedish Crime Fiction: Novel, Film, Television* (Manchester: Manchester University Press, 2014).

It started with the global publishing phenomenon of Stieg Larsson's Millennium trilogy.[9] In Sweden, the trilogy was well received and praised for its blending of social indignation with a thrilling plot. Originally published by Sweden's oldest independent publishing house, Norstedts, the Trilogy's international rise to fame was initiated when published in French by the independent publisher Actes Sud. When subsequently published in English in 2008 by yet another independent publisher, Quercus, it was, against all odds, set on its way to becoming "the biggest publishing phenomenon of the 21st century," according to British journalist and author Mark Lawson.[10] Indeed, as David Geherin reminds us, Larsson's *The Girl Who Played with Fire* became "the first translated novel in 25 years to top the coveted *New York Times* best seller list."[11] While the Anglophone publishing markets have been notoriously impenetrable to foreign language fiction,[12] several Nordic crime series have subsequently been translated into English and dozens more languages, and authors such as the Swedes Arne Dahl, Camilla Läckberg and Liza Marklund, the Norwegian Jo Nesbø and the Dane Jussi Adler-Olsen have sold millions of copies of their crime novels outside of the Nordic region.[13]

The success of Scandinavian crime fiction, particularly in the UK, has given birth to expressions such as "Scandimania," "the Nordic invasion," and "the Swedish crime fiction miracle,"[14] a rhetoric suggesting how rare it is for literatures from smaller language areas to make an impact on the UK and US markets.[15] Curiously, while the Nordic countries have generally been perceived as small, peripheral, or semi-peripheral nations on the northern fringe of the European cultural and linguistic centres, the Nordic countries punch well above their

---

9 Larsson, Stieg, *The Girl with the Dragon Tattoo* (2005; New York: Alfred A. Knopf, 2008); Larsson, Stieg, *The Girl Who Played with Fire* (2006; New York: Alfred A. Knopf, 2009); Larsson, Stieg, *The Girl Who Kicked the Hornets' Nest* (2007; New York: Alfred A. Knopf, 2009).
10 Mark Lawson, "Crime's grand tour: European detective fiction," *The Guardian*, 26 October, 2012, https://www.theguardian.com/books/2012/oct/26/crimes-grand-tour-european-detective-fiction.
11 David Geherin, *The Dragon Tattoo and its Long Tale: The New Wave of European Crime Fiction in America* (London: McFarland, 2012), Kindle.
12 See Rajendra Chitnis et al., eds., *Translating the Literatures of Small European Languages* (Liverpool: Liverpool University Press, 2020).
13 See Nestingen and Arvas, "Introduction," and Forshaw, *Death*.
14 Johan Svedjedal, "Svensk skönlitteratur i världsperspektiv," in *Läsarnas Marknad, marknadens läsare: En forskningsantologi utarbetad för Litteraturutredningen*, ed. Ulla Carlsson and Jenny Johannisson (Göteborg: Nordicom, 2012), 209.
15 See Chitnis, *Translating*.

weight when it comes to international publishing. Monitoring the language spread of bestsellers on several European markets between 2008 and 2014, Miha Kovač and Rüdiger Wischenbart have found that the impact of Nordic authors on translations and sales is striking, establishing a cohort very similar to authors writing in English:

> The readers' rush for Nordic crime is the tip of a giant iceberg that has grown over several decades ... After Stieg Larsson's success, a new dynamics led to an explosion of translations, with new incoming authors to include Liza Marklund, Camilla Läckberg, Jens Lapidus, Lars Kepler, Jo Nesbø, Arnaldur Indriðason, Yrsa Sigurðardóttir and many others. Their reach was further broadened by international acclaim for Scandinavian TV series of the same genre, such as The Killing, The Bridge, The Protectors, Unit One and Mamon.[16]

Significantly, Kovač and Wischenbart suggest that the international publishing success of Nordic crime fiction is closely tied to regional (Nordic) synergies and cross-mediality: the success of Larsson's novels (adapted for both a Swedish and an English-language film); the success of authors from across the Nordic region and the coincident successes of Swedish television adaptations; and original Danish television drama followed by serials from the rest of the region. In fact, in 2008, the same year that Larsson's first instalment of the Millennium trilogy was published in English translation, the UK public broadcaster BBC witnessed the first signs of a dramatic shift in the popularity of subtitled foreign television drama, beginning with the Swedish series based on Henning Mankell's Wallander novels. This subtitled series aired on the niche channel BBC FOUR alongside BBC's own English language adaptation of the Wallander novels, filmed in and around Ystad with British actors including Kenneth Branagh. The British adaptation aired on the main channel BBC ONE to great acclaim and with a much larger audience – 5–6 million viewers – than the 150,000 who regularly viewed the original Swedish adaptation – a reach that still constituted a relative success for BBC FOUR.[17]

Subtitled foreign drama had been a rarity in the UK, and literary translations have consistently represented an insignificant share of the total publishing mar-

---

16 Miha Kovač and Rüdiger Wischenbart, "Diversity Report 2016: Trends and references in literary translations across Europe," *Verein für kulturelle transfers*, accessed 13 September 2018, www.culturaltransfers.org, 27.
17 Andrea Esser, "Form, Platform and the Formation of Transnational Audiences: A Case Study of How Danish TV Drama Series Captured Television Viewers in the United Kingdom," *Critical Studies in Television: The International Journal of Television Studies* 12, no. 4 (December 2017): 419–20, doi:10.1177/1749602017729649.

ket, lingering at around 4 percent.[18] The BBC's subsequent venture into purchasing the rights to the twenty-episode Danish original crime series *Forbrydelsen* (2007–12; *The Killing* 2011–12) became a game changer, and it was followed by several successful Nordic productions and co-productions such as *Borgen* (2010–13; UK 2012–13) and *Broen/Bron* (2011–2018; *The Bridge* 2012–18).[19] While outperforming previous attempts to screen subtitled television series, these Nordic series still reached a relatively small share of around one million viewers. However, *Forbrydelsen* made Nordic series a "cult hit" in the British press, it fuelled the burgeoning consumption of "box sets" – *Forbrydelsen* sold 300,000 units in the UK – and helped consolidate the brand BBC FOUR as a platform "offering an ambitious range of innovative, high quality output that is intellectually and culturally enriching."[20] Judging by sales and viewer numbers, Larsson's Millennium trilogy and BBC's *Wallander* had much wider public appeal. However, the relative niche phenomenon of original Nordic television drama imbued the genre with a status only afforded high-end consumer products, prestigious cultural experiences, and the rise of what has been called "complex TV."[21]

The international success of Scandinavian crime fiction and television drama around 2008–9 was to some extent accidental. The trajectory of Larsson's Millennium Trilogy from a national and regional bestseller to a global phenomenon three years after its original publication was made possible by smaller independent publishers abroad. The simultaneous English language adaptation of Mankell's Wallander series by the BBC, and the attempt by BBC to reinvigorate their niche channel through the Swedish Wallander series, led to the acquisition of the Danish drama series *Forbrydelsen*, which was inexpensive at the time. While popular and well received in Denmark, the success of *Forbrydelsen* as a cultural trendsetter in a central, international television market such as the UK's was unpredictable and unprecedented.[22] However, together these Scandina-

---

18 See Chitnis, *Translating.*

19 See Linda Badley, Andrew Nestingen, and Jaakko Seppälä, eds., *Nordic Noir, Adaptation, Appropriation* (Cham: Palgrave, 2020), and Esser, "Form."

20 Esser, "Form," 418. See Jakob Stougaard-Nielsen, "Revisiting the Crime Scene: Intermedial Translation, Adaptation, and Novelization of The Killing," in *Nordic Noir, Adaptation, Appropriation*, ed. Linda Badley, Andrew Nestingen, and Jaakko Seppälä (Cham: Palgrave, 2020).

21 Jason Mittell, *Complex TV: The Poetics of Contemporary Television Storytelling* (New York: New York University Press, 2015).

22 According to Pia Majbritt Jensen, after *Forbrydelsen*, Danish audio-visual drama series experienced an "unprecedented global boom in exports." Pia Majbritt Jensen, "Global Impact of Danish Drama Series: A Peripheral, Non-commercial Creative Counter-flow," *Kosmorama* 263 (2016), https://www.kosmorama.org/en/kosmorama/artikler/global-impact-danish-drama-series-pe-

vian "accidents" drew attention from publishers, broadcasters, media, and critics who began to look for common denominators – a secret Nordic formula behind the success of their crime dramas – and the next Stieg Larsson.

The earliest instances of the use of the term "Nordic noir," which became the reference for this formula, may have been in a *Wall Street Journal* article in early 2010 and by the Nordic Noir Crime Fiction Book Club established by the Department of Scandinavian Studies at University College London, which started its activities in the Spring of the same year.[23] Subsequent "agents" that propelled the consolidation of the term in the public imagination and contributed to the growth of its symbolic capital, at least in the UK, include: the BBC documentary *Nordic Noir: The Story of Scandinavian Crime Fiction* (December 2010); reviews and blogs hosted by *The Guardian*; the distributor of television drama and films Arrow Films, who adopted the brand name Nordic Noir for their Scandinavian TV dramas and established the Nordicana festival in London in 2013; and Barry Forshaw's survey of the genre in his book *Death in a Cold Climate* (2012).[24]

Moreover, actors such as publishers and media corporations within the Nordic region soon capitalised on and helped promote the brand of national and Nordic crime fiction. Karl Berglund has convincingly demonstrated, for instance, that particularly the rise of literary agents in Sweden, who rely heavily on the sale of translation rights, coincided with and helped propel the international

---

ripheral-non-commercial-creative-counter. On the transnational dissemination and remaking of Nordic television drama, see Badley, *Nordic Noir*; Pei-Sze Chow, Anne Marit Waade, and Robert A. Saunders, "Geopolitical Television Drama Within and Beyond the Nordic Region," *Nordicom Review* 41, no. s1 (1 September 2020): 11–27, doi:10.2478/nor-2020–0013; and Stougaard-Nielsen, *Revisiting*.

23 Ove Solum, "What is it about Nordic Noir?," in *Perspectives on the Nordic*, ed. Jakob Lothe and Bente Larsen (Oslo: Novus Press, 2016), 115–18; Gunhild Agger, "Nordic Noir – Location, Identity and Emotion," in *Emotions in Contemporary TV Series*, ed. Alberto N. García (Houndmills: Palgrave, 2016), 138.

24 For the sake of full disclosure, it should be mentioned that I was the founder of the Nordic Noir Book Club. See "The History of the 'original' Nordic Noir Book Club in London," *Nordic Noir Book Club*, accessed 8 September 2021, https://scancrime.wordpress.com/events. I was also interviewed for the BBC documentary and Forshaw's *Death in a Cold Climate*, and wrote a short history of Scandinavian crime fiction for Arrow Films, which they used as an inlay for box sets. My colleagues and I, in the UCL Department of Scandinavian Studies, have frequently been interviewed for articles in *The Guardian* and have collaborated with the newspaper on creating additional content for their coverage of Nordic television drama and cultures. This exemplifies the extent to which invested agents have been centrally involved in the promotion and, not least, contextualisation of Nordic noir in the UK.

success of Swedish crime writers in the 2000s.[25] Therefore, the rise of what has become known as the transnational Nordic noir brand came to exemplify what Claire Squires has called a "cultural shift" in publishing, towards a marketing-led publishing culture with its "growing professionalization and business-based practice of publishing."[26] Following this cultural shift, the circulation of literature and other media started to take place in more fluid, mutually fertilising, and open networks driven by commercial interests and audience expectations and desires.

The somewhat coincidental cross-media success of Nordic crime fiction together with its wider matrix of related brands, demonstrates, as argued elsewhere, that "literature does not travel solo and nor does it travel light; it is carried and accompanied by films, television series, translators, publishers, state subsidies, and all manner of lifestyle goods."[27] This prompts us to consider Nordic noir a complex, ever evolving transnational brand. As suggested in a handbook entry on "Nordic Noir," the concept is "associated with a region (Scandinavia), with a mood (gloomy and bleak), with a look (dark and grim), and with strong characters and a compelling narrative."[28] However, "confusingly" it is also "associated with disparate, bleak dramas set in particular locations outside the Nordic region ... such as Wales, Italy, France, Mexico, and the United States."[29]

As a brand, Nordic noir has become thoroughly mobile, loosening its ties to "actual" Nordic topographies, writers, languages, and cultures. The British television drama *Fortitude* (written by Simon Donald, 2015) is an example of how late Nordic noir has transformed the "Nordic" from its "authentic" locations into a set of loose references to previous series (the leading role is played by Sofie Gråbøl known from *Forbrydelsen*), Nordic names and words in an otherwise Anglophone and multicultural location ("Politi" on the crest of police uniforms) and geographical references to the Arctic and the Northern lights. This continuing internationalisation of Nordic crime fiction points to the fact that it

---

25 Karl Berglund, "With a Global Market in Mind: Agents, Authors, and the Dissemination of Contemporary Swedish Crime Fiction," in *Crime Fiction as World Literature*, ed. Louise Nilsson, David Damrosch, and Theo D'haen (London: Bloomsbury, 2017).

26 Claire Squires, *Marketing Literature: The Making of Contemporary Writing in Britain* (Houndmills: Palgrave, 2009), 35.

27 C. Claire Thomson and Jakob Stougaard-Nielsen, "A faithful, attentive, tireless following: Cultural Mobility, Crime Fiction and Television Drama," in *Danish Literature as World Literature*, ed. Dan Ringgaard and Mads Rosendahl Thomsen (London: Bloomsbury, 2017), 237.

28 Annette Hill and Susan Turnbull, "Nordic Noir," *Oxford Research Encyclopedia of Criminology*, 26 April, 2017, doi.org/10.1093/acrefore/9780190264079.013.294.

29 Hill and Turnbull, "Nordic Noir," para. 1.

only became a recognisable genre or brand as novels and television series became widely translated, subtitled, and adapted into foreign languages and markets.[30] Nordic crime fiction is only really "Nordic" when viewed or read from abroad – when published, marketed, and sold in bookshops, book fairs or at broadcasting trade fairs, where the branding of national or regional peculiarities is essential for attracting the attention of potential funders, publishers, agents, and book buyers in a crowded, globalised field.[31]

As a popular and bestselling genre, crime fiction has always operated in the more commercialised end of the publishing spectrum. In their introduction to the anthology, *Perspectives on the Nordic*, Jakob Lothe and Bente Larsen write that a productive "reciprocity" between various perspectives on the Nordic across genres and media is "often marginalized and suspended by the noise of the culture industry that in the name of commercialism turns 'the Nordic' into a cliché, thus making it into a kind of commercial brand."[32] According to the authors, Nordic noir is "one of the most important elements of the commercial branding of the Nordic region."[33] It is also a cliché "prompted by a number of Nordic television series that became hugely popular in many countries."[34]

We need to consider whether it is possible to identify perspectives on the Nordic across genres and media without accounting for the "noise of the culture industry" and its attendant commercialism. As a commercial brand, Nordic noir tends to smooth over the local and national particularities of the region – differences that seem particularly important to the peoples living within the Nordic region. Kim Toft Hansen and Anne Marit Waade are aware of this tension between the somewhat empty brand value of the term and the potentially productive, "reciprocal," access it offers to the "use value" of Nordic locations: "Basically, 'Nordic Noir' sounds slightly more sexy and appealing than 'Scandinavian crime fiction,' or the abbreviated 'Scandi-crime'. It is infused with brand value."[35] However, since "Nordic Noir refers to the place of origin

---

30 Though the novelty of Nordic crime fiction on international markets has worn off, Nordic crime novels continue to be translated in disproportionate numbers considering the size of the home markets. Writers outside of the Nordic region continue to write "Nordic Noir" crime novels set in the Nordic region, and Nordic television series continue to find viewers abroad and are adapted and appropriated for early-2020s foreign markets.
31 Jakob Stougaard-Nielsen, "Nordic noir in the UK."
32 Jakob Lothe and Bente Larsen, ed. *Perspectives on the Nordic* (Oslo: Novus Press, 2016), 10.
33 Lothe and Larsen, *Perspectives*, 19.
34 Lothe and Larsen, *Perspectives*, 11.
35 Kim Toft Hansen and Anne Marit Waade, *Locating Nordic Noir: From Beck to The Bridge* (London: Palgrave, 2017), 8.

or the narrative diegetic space" it is also congruent with "crime fiction as a world brand," which makes it "hardly surprising that narratives taking place locally are used locally to brand places. Altogether, places, themes, and characters are closely tied in crime fiction – and this clearly applies to Nordic Noir as well."[36]

Their approach in *Locating Nordic Noir* is not to ask what Nordic noir is, as one would have done in a traditional genre study, but instead to inquire "Where is Nordic Noir?" They thereby emphasise, on the one hand, the centrality of authentic topographies and "local colour" in the narratives themselves,[37] and on the other, how real and imagined locations are shaped in the reciprocal branding and consumption across invested interest groups, agents, and nations. Examples of place branding are particularly evident in television drama where local and regional interest groups, such as municipalities and local film funds, find an opportunity to put their location "on the map" by promoting and enabling access to relevant locations. Subsequently, such "fictionalised" actual locations can be used by tourism agencies as desirable destinations. The well-known case of Ystad's promotion of "Wallanderland" is one notable early example of Nordic noir place branding.[38]

While the specific Nordic locations together with their national languages may appear to erode with the profusely transnational brand of Nordic noir, several studies have argued for the centrality of the genre's perceived Nordicness. In his detailed genealogy of the term in the international press, Ove Solum argues that "crime fiction has become the most important area for cultural export and the unprecedented international appeal of Nordic Noir, in tandem with a growing international interest in what in short can be described as Scandinavianness, has been utilized to promote the 'Nordic' and Nordic culture."[39] With reference to the London-based Nordicana fair mentioned earlier, which co-promoted Nordic-noir television drama by inviting Nordic actors, and showcasing Nordic travel destinations and food items, Solum points out that popular genres have become instrumental in the branding of the Nordic region by foregrounding both actual and imagined "Nordic" places and locations. Such place-branding used by an external actor to sell television box sets has in turn prompted the tourism industry in the Nordic countries to embrace the phenomenon for its own purposes. "Nordic Noir," Solum concludes, "is not only expanding as a

---

36 Toft Hansen and Waade, *Locating*, 9.

37 Toft Hansen and Waade, *Locating*, 10.

38 See Anne Marit Waade, *Wallanderland: Medieturisme og Skandinavisk TV-krimi* (Aalborg: Aalborg Universitetsforlag, 2013).

39 Solum, "What is it," 122.

genre beyond the Nordic countries; it has also become a phenomenon that far exceeds the group of texts that constitutes the genre."[40]

It is, in other words, impossible to understand the rise of Nordic noir without considering the wider commercial interests and agents involved in and gaining from the making and branding of the phenomenon: from writers, publishers, literary agents, translators, and production companies to television distributors, media outlets, educational, cultural, and tourism institutions both in and outside the Nordic region. What is, perhaps, most salient about the Nordic noir brand from a UK perspective is the fact that the vast range of literary and audio-visual texts it subsumes, located variously within and beyond the Nordic region, are made to participate in a rhetoric of Nordicness that attaches certain persistent values to images and discursive constructions of the "North."

Branding Borealism

Louise Nilsson has noted the importance of accounting for the marketing and media discourses in reception countries to understanding the success and impact of Nordic noir. She suggests that "[i]n the case of Nordic Noir, ... the marketing and media discourse visually merged a local literature with crime fiction's global discursive field and its mediascape by successfully connecting to a cosmopolitan imaginary of the north."[41] Reviewers in Anglophone newspapers, according to Nilsson, construct a discursive image of the Nordic region through repeated use of figures such as coldness, ice, and morose detectives. This rhetoric of Nordicness has been used profusely in the marketing of Nordic noir abroad (as demonstrated by Agnes Broomé's study of "Nordic" book-cover designs), and Nilsson suggests that the foreign appeal of Nordic noir may partly rest "on a longstanding culturally forged idea of the north."[42]

A suggestive term for such a deeply rooted rhetoric of Nordicness at the heart of the recent "Scandimania" in the UK is "borealism."[43] Sylvain Briens's invalu-

---

40 Solum, "What is it," 123.

41 Louise Nilsson, "Mediating the North in Crime Fiction," *Journal of World Literature* 1, no. 4 (2016): 542, doi:10.1163/24056480 – 00104007.

42 Agnes Broomé, "Swedish literature on the British market 1998 – 2013: A systemic approach" (PhD diss., University College London, 2014); Nilsson, "Mediating", 546.

43 Sylvain Briens, "Boréalisme: Pour un atlas sensible du Nord," *Études Germaniques* 2 (2018): 151– 76; Kristinn Schram, "Banking on Borealism: Eating, Smelling, and Performing the North," in *Iceland and Images of the North*, ed. Sumarliði Ísleifsson, in collaboration with Daniel Chartier (Québec: Presses de l'Université du Québec, 2011).

able discussion of the term corresponds to a "reciprocal perspective" on the Nordic or the North and brings out the significance of topography and the reciprocal rhetoric of Nordicness, which I see as central to the phenomenon of Nordic noir. Briens argues that borealism involves an external view that perceives the North as a homogeneous whole and foregrounds topographical and climatic aspects that are also central to the Nordic noir brand. The etymological root of the word, "Boreas," refers to the Ancient Greek God of the North wind, and has cultural roots in a "North-South schematization of temperamental oppositions"[44] – the North as cool, frugal, cerebral, morally inclined and the South as warm, sensual, opulent and immoral. According to Joep Leerssen, this has been "one of the more long-standing matrices imposed on the imaginary of Europe's cultural landscape": "In the European imagination, the image of Scandinavia and the Nordic countries has been deeply influenced by this master-polarity. Climate is associatively correlated with landscape, with human habitation patterns, with social and political organization, and in turn rationalized by reference to the inhabitants' purported 'character.'"[45]

As a brand, Nordic noir is deeply enmeshed in a borealist discourse, a term around which we find a congregation of multi-directional desires and affective responses. Nordic crime fiction became an "accidental" trigger for a new borealism in the UK fuelled by various sources: the coincidental international success of Stieg Larsson and Nordic television drama produced by an increasingly internationalised, commercialised, and intermedial market for cultural products; and the global infatuation with the Nordic welfare state as an (utopian) model for creating just, egalitarian, and, not least, happy societies in the wake of the global financial crisis (2007–8). Nordic noir came into being as a product of these converging generic, affective, topographical, medial, and boreal perspectives or rhetorics. In the following section of this chapter, examples from the media, television documentaries, nation branding, popular ethnography, and lifestyle journalism will be discussed as exemplifying the borealist and multidirectional perspectives on the Nordic that have followed the "Scandimania" initiated by the success of Nordic noir in the UK.

---

44 Joep Leerssen, "Forword." in *Images of the North: Histories, Identities, Ideas*, ed. Sverrir Jakobsson (Amsterdam: Rodopi, 2009), 16.
45 Leerssen, "Forword," 16.

Inspector Norse

One of the first examples of journalistic treatments of the Nordic crime phenomenon in the Anglophone world, the 2010 article "Inspector Norse" published in *The Economist*, captures in its title a key fascination with the Nordic as both recognisable and somewhat exotic, and, importantly, conforming to deeply rooted figurations of the Nordic. The title refers to the British crime television series *Inspector Morse.*[46] By replacing Morse with Norse, it references an external homogeneous understanding of the inherent Nordicness of the new crime wave, while recalling a deep-seated cultural memory and British stereotype of invading (Norse) Vikings.

The article presents a more current image of the Nordic countries as orderly, crime free, and with enviable well-functioning welfare states that seem to contradict the image presented in crime novels: "The neat streets of Oslo are not a natural setting for crime fiction." This paradox leads to the question: why have Nordic detective novels become so successful? Some shared characteristics are emphasised. Apart from the always gloomy, melancholic detectives, the article points to a particular Nordic style of crime writing characterised by simple and plain writing devoid of metaphor. This attractive style of crime writing is complemented with the lure of the Nordic setting, which links imagined landscapes of the "cold, desolate north" with a dystopian view of the fate of the Nordic welfare societies: "The countries that the Nordic detectives call home are prosperous and organised ... But the protection offered by a cradle-to-grave welfare system hides a dark underside."[47]

This figure of a Nordic "dark side" would become central to the image of Nordic noir, and it was repeated in another early article on the phenomenon, Ian MacDougall's review of Stieg Larsson's trilogy "The Man Who Blew Up the Welfare State." While Swedish crime fiction, according to MacDougall, "owes its greatest debt to its British forebear, whose plots it cheerfully rips off ... the Swedish model distinguishes itself by infusing these plots with a social and political consciousness."[48] He summarises Larsson's main themes as "the failure of the welfare state to do right by its people and the failure of men to do right by women" – a theme that was more obviously foregrounded in the Swedish title of

46 *Inspector Morse*, ITV, 1987–2000.

47 "Inspector Norse: Why Are Nordic Detective Novels So Successful?" *The Economist*, 11 March, 2010, accessed 1 May, 2021, http://www.economist.com/node/15660846.

48 Ian MacDougall, "The Man Who Blew Up the Welfare State," *n+1 Magazine*, 27 February, 2010, https://nplusonemag.com/online-only/book-review/man-who-blew-up-welfare-state.

the first novel in the Trilogy, *Män som hatar kvinnor*, which translates as *Men Who Hate Women*. The novels' critical depiction of the welfare state's "well-polished façade" and "welfare-state comforts", hiding widespread moral and political corruption, exemplify a now widely accepted view of Nordic crime fiction as depicting "the comprehensive failure of the world's most comprehensive welfare system", as it is poignantly formulated by MacDougall.

Larsson's deceptively realist and socio-critical style (devoid of metaphor), MacDougall suggests, allows us to imagine (from abroad) that all is not right in Sweden, an orderly, rather boring place hiding a dark underbelly. Of course, the setting of violent crime stories involving misogynist Nazi serial killers and a corrupt police state in locations commonly perceived to be peaceful, democratic, egalitarian and just is an enticing premise – one that perhaps counter-intuitively highlights a Nordic exceptionalism instead of succeeding in "blowing it up". However, to some readers like MacDougall the realism effects of Nordic crime writing present a stark critique of the utopian socialist paradise in the North, much in the same way the British journalist Roland Huntford's notorious *The New Totalitarians* (1971) critiqued the moral and psychological demise of the social-democratic welfare state.[49]

Perhaps in a dual effort to exploit the global popularity of Larsson's Swedish crime novels for nation-branding purposes and to counteract the possible misconception that Larsson was necessarily drawing an accurate picture of Sweden, the Swedish Institute (SI) produced the report *Sweden beyond the Millennium and Stieg Larsson*.[50] The Institute, which has since the 1940s worked to produce and promote a Swedish national image abroad[51] – explains that they had noticed, when reviewers abroad wrote about Larsson's Millennium trilogy, they often went into greater details about Sweden as well: "The Millennium trilogy is in some ways a dramatization of 21st century Swedish society."[52] The report, therefore, tries to understand this "new" perspective on Sweden offered by the books and attempts to respond to and participate in the branding of Sweden, including the significance of the welfare state.

That nation branding and tourism are central aspects of the report is evident from its abundant illustrations of Swedish locations, landscape images, and

---

49 Roland Huntford, *The New Totalitarians* (London: Allen Lane, 1971).

50 The Swedish Institute, *Sweden beyond the Millennium and Stieg Larsson* (Stockholm: Swedish Institute, 2012), https://issuu.com/swedish_institute/docs/sweden_beyond_the_millennium.

51 Nikolas Glover, "Imaging Community: Sweden in "Cultural Propaganda" Then and Now," *Scandinavian Journal of History* 34, no. 3 (23 September 2009): 246–63, doi:10.1080/03468750903134707.

52 The Swedish Institute, *Sweden beyond the Millennium*, 34.

even the northern lights, some of which have little relevance for the books themselves. Through its report, the SI participates self-consciously in a jostling for control over the image of Sweden "beyond the Millennium," since "it is a known fact that cultural expressions such as film and literature can have an effect on people's impression of a place, for example a country."[53]

The SI walks a fine line between accepting the brand value of Larsson's bleak view of the modern Swedish welfare state – arguing that Larsson's portrait of Sweden makes the country appear less utopian and less dull ("the notion of Sweden as a conflict-free model nation is shattered"), which has been great for tourism – and attempting to control the brand by explaining that the Sweden of the books is not what you would find if you visited from abroad.[54] SI reminds us that the books also portray a modern, industrious nation with proud democratic traditions, where, for instance, a journalist has the right to speak out against the state. Through suggestive illustrations, Sweden is promoted as a country rich in majestic, markedly Nordic landscapes and a well-functioning state.

Apart from demonstrating the to-and-fro branding of Nordicness taking place between internal and external agents, the branding of Sweden through crime fiction – in consort with a host of other cases where local tourism boards use famous crime stories to brand their cities, towns, and regions across Scandinavia – risks participating in the maintenance of an un-reflexive boreal branding and the construction of essentialist national or regional identities, what David Pitcher has called, "a corporate model of Nordic ethnicity." According to his study of consumer practices and ethnicity in the contemporary UK:

> The repeated connection between landscape and aesthetics produces a highly consistent portrait of a Nordic temperament. Psychological dispositions and ethical, social and spiritual values are shown to be the simultaneous product of a place and the ideas and practices it generates. This corporate model of Nordic ethnicity is, I want to suggest, precisely what has given Nordic style such a strong purchase in a contemporary British context.[55]

Importantly, this "corporate model" is not exclusively produced by internal agents such as tourism boards or by the crime stories themselves but become "incorporated" in the transnational exchange of boreal imagery and Nordic imaginings with markets, consumers, reviewers, readers, and viewers outside of the Nordic region.[56]

---

53 The Swedish Institute, *Sweden beyond the Millennium*, 5.
54 The Swedish Institute, *Sweden beyond the Millennium*, 34–5.
55 David Pitcher, *Consuming Race* (London: Routledge, 2014), 66.
56 See the similar case and argument in Kelting's chapter on "New Nordic Cuisine" in the present volume.

Cracking the Norse Code: From Boreal Utopianism to Scandimania

As implied in the reviews and report discussed above there is a particularly striking, some might say troubling, element to the contemporary British fascination with Nordic culture – an infatuation, Pitcher identifies as, "a romanticized reading of the politics of Nordic social liberalism and social democracy as produced out of the same 'natural' combination of climate, geography and culture."[57] Nowhere is this eighteenth-century climate theory and borealist perspective on the Nordic more explicitly and self-consciously stated than in Andrew Graham-Dixon's three-part BBC documentary *Art of Scandinavia*.[58]

In his introduction to the series, it becomes clear that a running theme throughout the series will be an exploration of what the national and regional art of Scandinavia may tell us about the "Scandinavian mind" and how it has been shaped by its "northern" locations and landscapes. While it is clear that the presenter is well aware that a "climate theory" of national or regional belonging has been discredited and proven dangerous fodder for ethno-essentialist ideologies, it is similarly clear that his encounter with the Nordic landscape per excellence – the sublime Norwegian fjords – leaves him unable to understand Nordic art, culture, and societies as anything but the products of their topographies. He finds himself perpetually in an "exotic" North where the "forbidding beauty" of the landscapes and their "remoteness" from an unspecified cultural centre – the South, likely London – impress themselves as self-evidently "so far north" that the landscapes themselves must present the key to unlocking the Scandinavian mind:

> Scandinavia. The Nordic lands. So far north, they've often been simply left off the map of world civilisations. Art, literature, philosophy – these belonged to the lands of the south. Of sunshine, warmth, the light of reason. To the north lay the shadow lands, the lands of perpetual midnight and darkness. But that's not the whole story.... The art of Scandinavia reflects their stormy history, played out in landscapes of forbidding beauty. Nature's been the great enemy, but it's also been the great inspiration. Not just for painting and poetry, but for architecture and design. Inspired by the frozen forms of ice, or dark forests of pine. You could say the Scandinavian mind itself has been shaped by nature, like a landscape formed by a glacier. Despite their remoteness, the Nordic peoples have managed to fashion one of

---

57 Pitcher, *Consuming*.
58 *Art of Scandinavia*, presented by Andrew Graham-Dixon, BBC 4, 2016, 4,https://www.bbc.co.uk/programmes/b0745j6 m.

the most remarkable civilisations. And the art of Scandinavia shares many of the characteristics of the Scandinavian landscape – hardness, sharpness, clarity. I think the north has also given it some of its most distinctive moral and psychological characteristics. Pride – tempered by a sense of living at the margins – anxiety, loneliness, melancholy. And blowing through it all, like a cold, piercing wind, an absolute determination to endure, come what may.[59]

This "rhetoric of Nordicness" makes generous use of borealist imagery (coldness, ice, dark, frozen, glaciers, remoteness). Graham-Dixon links the features of an imagined, homogeneous, and perpetual climate with unchanging and distinctive "moral and psychological characteristics" of the Scandinavian nations and the region (Norden). Nordicness, therefore, begins with landscapes and a climate that have inevitably been impressed on the Nordic peoples. Their art reveals national and regional, moral and psychological characteristics, and leads us to understand why it is the Nordic countries have become "remarkable civilizations" – the much admired, successful welfare societies of the twentieth and twenty-first centuries.

Guided by representatives of the Nordic noir craze such as the Danish actor Søren Malling, famous in Britain as Jan Meyer from the first season of *Forbrydelsen*, and the Swedish crime-writing team behind the pseudonym Lars Kepler, Graham-Dixon goes in search for Danish "happiness" and the "underbelly of the Modern Swedish welfare state."[60] Although persuaded that "Nordic noir dredges up ugly truth"[61] about the Swedish welfare state, and being told to take the train out of Stockholm to the suburbs if he wants to experience the shadows of the welfare state in situ, he:

> can't find the Badlands described by the social critics of modern Sweden. Nothing truly Noir, for sure. In fact, if I had to name a city that exemplifies failing social services, a crumbling transport infrastructure and yawning chasms of wealth, I'd pick London any day over Stockholm. And on even the most remote station, the Swedish underground still does really beautiful benches.[62]

Art of Scandinavia begins with the nations' topographies, their national-romantic, anxious landscape paintings and ends with a perception of the art of Scandinavia as always, in one way or the other, engaged in national self-presenta-

---

59 *Art of Scandinavia*, episode 1, "Dark Night of the Soul," directed by Ian Leese, presented by Andrew Graham-Dixon, aired 14 March, 2016, on BBC 4, https://www.bbc.co.uk/programmes/b073mp87.
60 *Art of Scandinavia*, episode 1, "Dark Night of the Soul."
61 *Art of Scandinavia*, episode 1, "Dark Night of the Soul."
62 *Art of Scandinavia*, episode 1, "Dark Night of the Soul."

tions, as borne out of a "Scandinavian mind" and how this mind eventually shaped the Nordic model of welfare. This perception illustrates the curse of small nationhood: cultural expressions are reduced to homogeneous national characteristics in comparison with the cultural centre – while local diversity, temporal discontinuities, contradictions or cosmopolitan traits are unacknowledged.

It is, of course, easy to dismiss such causal simplifications regarding topography, art, and identity. While the documentary does suggest a notable cosmopolitan British interest in the Nordic countries, it is an interest less preoccupied with understanding the foreign not merely as different but also diverse and potentially cosmopolitan. However, the rhetoric of Nordicness may ultimately have not much to do with the Nordic region itself. One could view Graham-Dixon's borealism as less interested in Scandinavian art and its local uses and more preoccupied with how these Nordic national arts can be used to critically assess current social conditions and national discourses in Britain. It is not a simple British nostalgic longing for a utopian welfare society, the Nordic region is imagined as a grouping of "authentic" and "rooted" societies that have been able to respond critically and creatively to the social transformations brought on by neoliberalism and globalisation. This rhetoric of Nordicness in the UK, I would argue, represents an internal British attempt to come to terms with the nation's own inability to present a unified, "corporate ethnic," national narrative. Such a narrative would stretch from the landscapes of Turner and Wordsworth to a harmonious, homogeneous, and thoroughly content twenty-first century nation, without having to consider contemporary British dislocations, the disharmonies of historical imperialism, social inequalities, and the ravages of a thoroughly neoliberal welfare state.

British borealism is a complex multi-focal "ethnography of looking at the North" where images and narratives produced in and of the Nordic allow for the sharing of certain "affective topographies" – "the kind of affect that binds people to places or that imbues a place with desire."[63] In the contemporary use of the "Nordic" in the UK, these are commonly linked to perceptions of what makes a good society. The Nordic does not represent a distant, exotic, topographic other employed to bolster a sense of British superiority. On the contrary, Nordicness represents a utopian ideal of a more "tidy," "cleaner and neater" Britain. An example of this was expressed in a piece of tongue-in-cheek travel journalism recounting a tour of Scandinavia in 2018:

---

63 Lila Ellen Gray, *Fado Resounding: Affective Politics and Urban Life* (Durham and London: Duke University Press, 2013), 137.

The British relationship with Scandinavia is not complex. We are in awe. They are better-governed, better-dressed, better-looking and write better crime novels. Of course, we can always claim a bit of shared ancestry. Many of the quiet Danish villages I had passed through on the train to Hirtshals had names that would fit seamlessly into the Lincolnshire or Yorkshire Wolds. In fact this rolling rural landscape dotted with woodland is not dissimilar, though cleaner and neater. As I'd gazed out that train window, I'd wondered: what if the Vikings had persisted a little longer with their civilising ventures into Britain, would London have the unhurried cool of Copenhagen, could Essex be tidy, and might there be no need for Luton at all?"[64]

This alternative boreal British past realised in a tidy, ordered contemporary Scandinavia suggests a widespread, but also paradoxical type of nostalgia: a borealist nostalgia expressed in a longing for the north as a home that was never realised; a transnational nostalgia for the simplicity of a time now long gone both in the Nordic region and in the UK. Such a "welfare nostalgia" for a culturally appropriated Nordic past was perhaps best exhibited in the set design for the BBC Wallander series. The home of Wallander and the police station in Ystad were consciously styled in the fashion of 1950s Scandinavian design, using functionalist welfare aesthetics to give them the air of a coolly rational, socially engineered society – which Mankell described as disintegrating in Wallander's Sweden of the early 1990s.

According to the production designer, she "wanted to symbolize the Swedish utopia of the 1950s and 1960s by choosing Scandinavian interior design and architecture from this period."[65] Some Nordic scholars have noted the exotification of Sweden or the "banal nationalism" presented in the British Wallander adaptation. Ingrid Stigsdotter remarks that "the ubiquity of classic wooden desks, lampshades and decorative furnishing ... stand out as being at once a little too stylish and a little too old-fashioned to be quite real."[66] In her view, this translation or adaptation sees Sweden predominantly through a touristic lens. However, the nostalgic Swedish utopia encoded in the location and the set of

64 Kevin Rushby, "King of Denmark: How to Create Hygge in a Cabin by the Sea," *The Guardian*, 5 August, 2018, https://www.theguardian.com/travel/2018/aug/05/denmark-beach-seaside-scandinavia-holiday-cabin.

65 Quoted in Anne Marit Waade, "Crime Scenes: Conceptualizing Ystad as Location in the Swedish and the British Wallander TV Crime Series," *Northern Lights: Film & Media Studies Yearbook* 9, no. 1 (28 July 2011): 20, doi:10.1386/nl.9.9_1.

66 Ingrid Stigsdotter, "Crime Scene Skåne: Guilty Landscapes and Cracks in the Functionalist Façade in Sidetracked, Firewall and One Step Behind," in *Regional Aesthetics: Locating Swedish Media*, ed. Erik Hedling, Olof Hedling, and Mats Jönsson (Stockholm: Mediehistoriskt Arkiv, 2010), 254.

the Wallander series may also point to the way in which nostalgic borealism functions as a significant affective topography in contemporary Britain.

Therefore, this particular example of converging national and transnational nostalgia demonstrates an important point raised by Toft Hansen and Waade concerning what they call "Norientalism": "Norientalism may thus be both an image held by the reader of Nordic fiction, but there is also a good chance that the international spatial image, whether brightly romantic or melancholically ambivalent, is motivated by the self-image portrayed in written fiction."[67] Just as Nordic crime fiction can be seen to exhibit nostalgia for the utopian ideals of a bygone golden age of the welfare state (as in Mankell's Wallander novels), so the infatuation with the Nordic in the UK may be understood as a transnational nostalgia for a place and a time that never belonged to the British – an affective topography exhibiting a borealist nostalgic longing for the north as a home that never was.[68]

This would also partly explain why the Nordic noir craze has petered out into an obsession with Nordic lifestyles, wellness, and popular Nordic buzzwords such as Swedish *lagom*, Danish *hygge*, and Norwegian *friluftsliv*. A deluge of lifestyle television programmes and books have appeared in the UK portraying the Nordic countries individually and together as mostly utopian societies, as a desirable yet unattainable nostalgic "elsewhere." A pertinent example is Hugh Fearnley-Whittingstall's food, travel, and lifestyle series *Scandimania*.[69] (Channel 4, 2014). His tour of Scandinavia presents a veritable "nation-crush", a "scandimania" for Nordic wellness, institutionalised egalitarianism, a dedication to sustainability, a strong sense of community and quality of life. Fearnley-Whittingstall's narrated introduction is a further example of the converging interests in "all things Nordic" where landscape, food, society and crime fiction make up a seemingly un-breakable or untranslatable "Norse code", which he will, nevertheless, attempt to "crack" to reveal why these nations, and not Britain, are among the happiest in the world:

> There's a lot of talk about Scandinavia at the moment. Their food is setting the gastronomic world on fire. Nordic noir dramas have us glued to our screens. And Sweden, Norway and Denmark are officially three of the happiest countries in the world. I want to find out why. Is it their connection to nature and their breath-taking landscapes? Their spirit of coopera-

---

67 Toft Hansen and Waade, *Locating*, 111.
68 See Stougaard-Nielsen, *Scandinavian*, 115–21.
69 *Scandimania*, presented by Hugh Fearnley-Whittingstall, aired 2014, on Channel 4, https://distribution.channel4.com/programme/scandimania.

tion? And does the famed dark side of Scandinavia really exist? To crack the Norse code, I'm about to immerse myself in Scandimania.[70]

The potential for branding consumer goods, arising from this popularised boreal view of the Nordic region as seen from the UK, was not lost on Carlsberg, which in 2017 started a marketing campaign, which included a television commercial that aired on Channel 4 in the UK with the slogan "brewed in the UK the Danish way."[71] The commercial is rendered in nostalgic autumnal colours and light and features the internationally renowned Danish actor Mads Mikkelsen riding an old-fashioned bicycle through Copenhagen's cobbled streets, past national landmarks and a "hyggelig" forest picnic, finally to arrive at the Carlsberg brewery. Throughout the commercial, Mikkelsen philosophises about the secret to Danish happiness: "Could it be that we find joy in nature? Could it be that we keep life and work in perfect balance? Is it that we make time for hygge, feeling all fuzzy and snuggly together?"[72]

The commercial suggests that British consumers now have the opportunity to follow "the Danish way" by drinking the rebranded Carlsberg Export, a brand of beer brewed in the UK and commonly associated with low-brow consumption and poor quality. The commercial taps into the British import of "hygge" – a craze which erupted in 2016 with more than a handful of books published in the UK on the phenomenon, most notably Meik Wiking's *The Little Book of Hygge.*[73] Wiking's hygge book, which sold more copies than most Nordic crime novels in the UK, is clearly written for a general British audience, as he attempts to explain how "hygge" makes the Danes happy through references to statistics, his own experiences, and "shared" Danish values and traditions. In his presentation of Danish lifestyles and customs, "hygge" conforms to a borealist matrix of values such as simplicity, modesty, casualness, and familiarity. Anti-consumerism, being in nature, playing board games instead of watching television and surrounding oneself with hand-crafted rustic furnishings is "hyggeligt" and,

---

70 *Scandimania*, episode 1, "Sweden," presented by Hugh Fearnley-Whittingstall, aired 2 February, 2014, on Channel 4, https://distribution.channel4.com/programme/scandimania.

71 See Ellen Kythor, "Stereotypes in and of Scandinavia," in *Introduction to Nordic Cultures*, ed. Annika Lindskog and Jakob Stougaard-Nielsen (London: UCL Press, 2020), 219–20.

72 See Carlsberg, "Carlsberg – The Danish Way 60"," 26 April, 2017, YouTube video, 1:00, https://www.youtube.com/watch?v=1v8n7lL-frA&ab_channel=CarlsbergUK.

73 See Alison Flood, "Hygge – the Danish art of living cosily – on its way to UK bookshops," *The Guardian*, 11 June, 2016, https://www.theguardian.com/books/2016/jun/11/hygge-the-danish-art-of-living-cosily-on-its-way-to-uk-bookshops.

he realises towards the end, "hygge" is essentially nostalgic: "I was tripping on nostalgia."[74]

Conclusion

The few cases I have selected – out of a plethora of similar ones – demonstrate the assertion previously quoted by the Swedish Institute that "cultural expressions such as film and literature can [indeed] have an effect on people's impression of a place." However, the origin and effect of the Nordic noir brand within and outside of the Nordic region is by no means monodirectional. In a transnational, cross-medial, and commercialised culture industry, the circulation of national and regional images, stereotypes, and values is thoroughly fluid and dialogic, constantly responding to and sharing affective topographies, which reflect deep-seated historical matrices of geographical polarities.

Genres – and crime fiction in particular – have the power "to shape topographies of affect," to bind people to certain places that hold deep historical and rhetorical values, and reflect current desires for lost opportunities.[75] A transnational genre such as Nordic noir suggests that such desirable places and public feelings need not coincide with one's own location. A segment of British readers, viewers, and consumers has been remarkably receptive to the Nordic noir brand, to the dark nostalgic tales of a "lost welfare paradise," and to stories about losing what once was firmly rooted – and Nordic content providers and agents have responded in kind by preparing and elaborating on the Nordic brand for an external gaze and consumer. Out of this sharing of narratives, self-presentations, and external imaginings, a new rhetoric of Nordicness has evolved that I suggest we name borealist nostalgia – a reciprocal longing for a North that was never one's own.

---

74 Meik Wiking, *The Little Book of Hygge* (London: Penguin, 2016), 281.
75 Gray, *Fado*, 137.

Bibliography

Ackerman, John M., and Irma E. Sandoval-Ballesteros. "The Global Explosion of Freedom of Information Laws." *Administrative Law Review* 58, no. 1 (2006): 85–130.

Adler-Nissen, Rebecca, and Ulrik P Gad. "Introduction: Postimperial Sovereignty Games in the Nordic Region." *Cooperation and Conflict* 49, no. 1 (1 March 2014): 3–32. doi:10.1177/0010836713514148.

Ågerup, Martin. "Hvad er den nordiske model egentlig?" *Politiken*, 15 October 2011.

Agius, C. "Sweden's 2006 Parliamentary Election and After: Contesting or Consolidating the Swedish Model?" *Parliamentary Affairs* 60, no. 4 (12 May 2007): 585–600. doi:10.1093/pa/gsm041.

Aimer, Peter. "The Strategy of Gradualism and the Swedish Wage-Earner Funds." *West European Politics* 8, no. 3 (July 1985): 43–55. doi:10.1080/01402388508424540.

Akintug, Hasan. "The Åland Islands Meet European Integration: Politics of History and the EU Referendums on Åland." MA diss., University of Helsinki, 2020. https://helda.helsinki.fi/handle/10138/318984.

Alexander, Charles C. "Prophet of American Racism: Madison Grant and the Nordic Myth." *Phylon (1960–)* 23, no. 1 (1962): 73–90. doi:10.2307/274146.

Allardt, Erik. "A Political Sociology of the Nordic Countries." *European Review* 8, no. 1 (February 2000): 129–41. doi:10.1017/S1062798700004634.

— ed. *Nordic Democracy: Ideas, Issues and Institutions in Politics, Economy, Education, Social and Cultural Affairs of Denmark, Finland, Iceland, Norway, and Sweden.* Copenhagen: Det Danske Selskab, 1981.

Allen, Julie K. *Icons of Danish Modernity: Georg Brandes and Asta Nielsen.* Seattle, Wash.: University of Washington, 2012.

Allerfeldt, Kristofer. "'And We Got Here First': Albert Johnson, National Origins and Self-Interest in the Immigration Debate of the 1920s." *Journal of Contemporary History* 45, no. 1 (January 2010): 7–26. doi:10.1177/0022009409348019.

Andersen, Torben M. "Challenges to the Scandinavian Welfare Model." *European Journal of Political Economy* 20, no. 3 (September 2004): 743–54. doi:10.1016/j.ejpoleco.2004.02.007.

Anderson, Perry. *Lineages of the Absolutist State.* London: Verso, 1993.

Anderson, Perry. "Mr Crosland's Dreamland." *New Left Review* 1, no. 7 (1961).

Andersson, Jan A. "1950-talet, tid att så – tid att skörda." In *Norden i sicksack: tre spårbyten inom nordiskt samarbete*, edited by Bengt Sundelius and Karin Söder. Stockholm: Santérus, 2000.

Andersson, Jenny. "Drivkrafterna bakom nyliberaliseringen kom från många olika hall." *Respons*, January 2020. http://tidskriftenrespons.se/artikel/drivkrafterna-bakom-nyliberaliseringen-kom-fran-manga-olika-hall/.

— "Nordic Nostalgia and Nordic Light: The Swedish Model as Utopia 1930–2007." *Scandinavian Journal of History* 34, no. 3 (23 September 2009): 229–45. doi:10.1080/03468750903134699.

— *The Library and the Workshop: Social Democracy and Capitalism in the Knowledge Age.* Stanford: Stanford University Press, 2010.

Andersson, Jenny, and Mary Hilson. "Images of Sweden and the Nordic Countries." *Scandinavian Journal of History* 34, no. 3 (23 September 2009): 219–28. doi:10.1080/03468750903134681.

Andrén, Nils. "Det officiella kultursamarbetet i Norden." *Den Jyske Historiker* 69–70 (1994): 213–27.

—— *Government and Politics in the Nordic Countries: Denmark, Finland, Iceland, Norway and Sweden*. Stockholm: Almqvist & Wiksell, 1964.

—— "Nordiska kulturkommissionen lägger grunden." In *Norden i sicksack: tre spårbyten inom nordiskt samarbete*, edited by Bengt Sundelius and Karin Söder. Stockholm: Santérus, 2000.

Andersen, Astri, Ólöf Garðarsdóttir, Monika Janfelt, Cecilia Lindgren, Pirjo Markkola, and Ingrid Söderlind. *Barnen och välfärdspolitiken: Nordiska barndomar 1900–2000*. Stockholm: Institutet för Framtidsstudier, Dialogos förlag, 2011.

Angell, Svein Ivar, and Mads Mordhorst. "National Reputation Management and the Competition State: The Cases of Denmark and Norway." *Journal of Cultural Economy* 8, no. 2 (4 March 2015): 184–201. doi:10.1080/17530350.2014.885459.

Anholt, Simon. *Competitive Identity: The New Brand Management for Nations, Cities and Regions*. London: Palgrave Macmillan UK, 2007. doi:10.1057/9780230627727.

Anttalainen, Marja-Liisa. *Rapport om den könsuppdelade arbetsmarknaden*. Oslo: Nordic Council of Ministers, 1984.

Archer, Clive. "Introduction." In *The Nordic Peace*, edited by Clive Archer and Pertti Joenniemi. Aldershot: Ashgate, 2003.

—— "Nordic Co-operation: A Model for the British Isles." In *The Nordic Model: Studies in Public Policy Innovation*, edited by Clive Archer and Stephen Maxwell. Farnborough: Gower, 1980.

Archer, Clive, and Stephen Maxwell, ed. *The Nordic Model: Studies in Public Policy Innovation*. Farnborough: Gower, 1980.

Arla Foods. 'JÖRÐ Oat Drink | Fresh & Organic'. Accessed 13 December 2020. https://jord plantbased.com/en-gb/oat-drink/.

Árnason, Jóhann Páll, and Björn Wittrock, ed. *Nordic Paths to Modernity*. New York: Berghahn Books, 2012.

Arnlaug, Leira. *Welfare States and Working Mothers: The Scandinavian Experience*. Cambridge: Cambridge University Press, 1992.

Aronsson, Peter, and Lizette Graden, eds. *Performing Nordic Heritage: Everyday Practices and Institutional Culture*. Farnham: Ashgate, 2013.

Arter, David. "Party System Change in Scandinavia since 1970: 'Restricted Change' or 'General Change'?" *West European Politics* 22, no. 3 (1 July 1999): 139–58. doi:10.1080/01402389908425319.

—— *Scandinavian Politics Today*. Manchester: Manchester University Press, 1999.

Asp, Elaine. "Seasonal Chef." Visit Sweden. Accessed 3 January, 2019. https://visitsweden. com/seasonal-chef/.

Aunesluoma, Juhana. *Vapaakaupan tiellä: Suomen kauppa- ja integraatiopolitiikka maailmansodista EU-aikaan*. Helsinki: Suomalasien Kirjallisuuden Seura, 2011.

Aurell, Brontë, Anna Jacobsen, and Lucy Panes. *Nørth: How to Live Scandinavian*. London: Aurum Press, 2017.

Aylott, Nicholas. "A Nordic Model of Democracy? Political Representation in Northern
    Europe." In *Models of Democracy in Nordic and Baltic Europe*, edited by Nicholas Aylott.
—— *Models of Democracy in Nordic and Baltic Europe: Political Institutions and Discourse.*
    Farnham: Ashgate, 2014.
Azubuike, Abraham. "Accessibility of Government Informationas a Determinant of Inward
    Foreign Direct Investment in Africa." In *Best Practices in Government Information: A
    Global Perspective*, edited by Irina Lynden and Jane Wu. München: K.G. Saur, 2008.
Badley, Linda, Andrew Nestingen, and Jakko Seppälä, eds. *Nordic Noir, Adaptation,
    Appropriation.* London: Palgrave Macmillan, 2020. doi:10.1997/978-3-030-38658-0.
Baldwin, Peter. *The Politics of Social Solidarity: Class Bases of the European Welfare State,
    1875–1975.* Cambridge: Cambridge University Press, 1990.
    doi:10.1017/CBO9780511586378.
Bang, Esben Holmboe, interviewee. *Culinary Journeys.* "Part 1: Norway's only
    three-Michelin-starred chef." Aired June 16, 2016, on CNN Travel TV. YouTube video,
    6:39. https://www.youtube.com/watch?v=rwUj2PY5_HM.
Barnes, Michael P. "Linguistic Variety in the Nordics." Nordics.info. 21 February, 2019.
    https://nordics.info/show/artikel/linguistic-variety-in-the-nordic-region/.
Bassnett, Susan. "Detective Fiction in Translation: Shifting Patterns of Reception." In *Crime
    Fiction as World Literature*, edited by Louise Nilsson, David Dramrosch, and Theo
    D'haen, 143–56. London: Bloomsbury, 2017.
Baur, Erwin, Eugen Fischer, and Fritz Lenz. *Menschliche Erblichkeitslehre und Rassenhygiene.*
    München: J.F. Lehmann, 1931.
Bech-Larsen, Tino, Trine Mørk, and Susanne Kolle. "New Nordic Cuisine: Is There Another
    Back to the Future? – An Informed Viewpoint on NNC Value Drivers and Market
    Scenarios." *Trends in Food Science & Technology* 50 (1 April 2016): 249–53.
    doi:10.1016/j.tifs.2016.01.020.
Becker-Christensen, Henrik. *Skandinaviske drømme og politiske realiteter: Den politiske
    skandinavisme i Danmark 1830–1850.* Aarhus: Arusia, 1981.
Bendixsen, Synnove, Mary Bente Bringslid, and Halvard Vike, eds. *Egalitarianism in
    Scandinavia: Historical and Contemporary Perspectives.* London: Palgrave Macmillan,
    2018. doi:10.1007/978-3-319-59791-1.
Bengtsson, Åsa, Kasper M. Hansen, Olafur Hardarson, Hanne Marthe Narud, and Henrik
    Oscarsson. *The Nordic Voter: Myths of Exceptionalism.* Colchester: ECPR Press, 2014.
Bennett, Colin J. "Understanding Ripple Effects: The Cross-National Adoption of Policy
    Instruments for Bureaucratic Accountability." *Governance* 10, no. 3 (1997): 213–33.
    doi:10.1111/0952–1895.401997040.
Berggren, Henrik, and Lars Trägårdh. "Social Trust and Radical Individualism: The Paradox at
    the Heart of Nordic Capitalism." In *The Nordic Way: Shared Norms for the New Reality*,
    Davos: World Economic Forum, 2011.
Berglund, Karl. "With a Global Market in Mind: Agents, Authors and the Dissemination of
    Contemporary Swedish Crime Fiction." In *Crime Fiction as World Literature*, edited by
    Louise Nilsson, David Dramrosch, and Theo D'haen, 77–89. London: Bloomsbury, 2017.
Bergman, Kerstin. *Swedish Crime Fiction: The Making of Nordic Noir.* Milan: Mimesis, 2014.
Berliner, Daniel. "The Political Origins of Transparency." *The Journal of Politics* 76, no. 2
    (April 2014): 479–91. doi:10.1017/S0022381613001412.
Bildt, Carl. *Hallänning, svensk, europé.* Stockholm: Bonnier, 1991.

Birkenes, Magnus Breder, Lars G. Johansen, Arne Martinus Lindstad, and Johannes Ostad. "From Digital Library to N-Grams: NB N-Gram." In *Proceedings of the 20th Nordic Conference of Computational Linguistics*, 293–95. Linköping: Linköping University Electronic Press, 2015.

Björkman, Maria. *Den anfrätta stammen: Nils von Hofsten, eugeniken och steriliseringarna 1909–1963*. Lund: Arkiv förlag, 2011.

Björkman, Maria, and Sven Widmalm. "Selling Eugenics: The Case of Sweden." *Notes and Records of the Royal Society* 64, no. 4 (20 December 2010): 379–400. doi:10.1098/rsnr.2010.0009.

Björkqvist, Jeanette. "Både Finland och Norge öppnar för att hjälpa." *Svenska Dagbladet*, 12 December, 2020. https://www.svd.se/finland-redo-att-hjalpa-sverige-med-coronavard.

Blair, Tony. "Leader's Speech," Blackpool, 1996. British Political Speech. http://www.britishpoliticalspeech.org/speech-archive.htm?speech=202.

Blomquist, Sören, and Karl Moene. "The Nordic Model." In "The Nordic Model," edited by Soren Blomquist and Karl Moene. Special issue, *Journal of Public Economics* 127 (1 July 2015): 1–2. doi:10.1016/j.jpubeco.2015.04.007.

Bodensten, Erik. "Scandinavia Magna: En alternativ nordisk statsbildning 1743." In *Norden Historiker: Vänbok till Harald Gustafsson*, edited by Erik Bodensten, Kajsa Brilkman, David Larsson Heidenblad and Hanne Sanders, 61–75. Lund: Historiska Institutionen, Lunds Universitet, 2018.

Borring Olesen, Thorsten. "Brødrefolk, men ikke våpenbrødre – Diskussionerne om et skandinavisk forsvarsforbund 1948–49." *Den Jyske Historiker* 69–70 (1994).

—— "EFTA 1959–1972: An Exercise in Nordic Cooperation and Conflict." In *Regional Cooperation and International Organizations: The Nordic Model in Transnational Alignment*, edited by Norbert Götz and Heidi Haggrén. London: Routledge, 2009.

Brandal, Nik, Bratberg Øivind, and Dag Einar Thorsen. *The Nordic Model of Social Democracy*. Basingstoke: Palgrave Macmillan, 2013.

Brander, Richard. *Finland och Sverige i EU: Tio år av medlemskap*. Helsingfors: Schildts, 2004.

Brax, Tuija. "Julkisuusperiaatteen haasteet." Presented at the Tietämisen vapauden päivän seminaari, 30 November 2007. http://www.om.fi/Etusivu/Ajankohtaista/Minister inpuheita/Puhearkisto/Puheet2007Brax/1196159328843.

Brett, Martin. "How the Vikings Conquered Dinner." GQ, July 29, 2014. https://www.gq.com/story/best-nordic-scandinavian-restaurants-noma.

Briens, Sylvain. "Boréalisme: Pour un atlas sensible du nord." *Études Germaniques* 2 (2018): 151–76.

Broberg, Gunnar. "Scandinavia: An Introduction." In *Eugenics and the Welfare State: Norway, Sweden, Denmark, and Finland*, edited by Gunnar Broberg and Nils Roll-Hansen, 1–8. East Lansing: Michigan State University Press, 2005.

Broberg, Gunnar, and Mattias Tydén. "Eugenics in Sweden: Efficient Care." In *Eugenics and the Welfare State: Norway, Sweden, Denmark, and Finland*, edited by Gunnar Broberg and Nils Roll-Hansen, 77–150. East Lansing: Michigan State University Press, 2005.

Brommesson, Douglas. "Introduction to Special Section: From Nordic Exceptionalism to a Third Order Priority – Variations of 'Nordicness' in Foreign and Security Policy." *Global Affairs* 4, no. 4–5 (20 October 2018): 355–62. doi:10.1080/23340460.2018.1533385.

Broomé, Agnes. "Swedish Literature on the British Market 1998–2013: A Systemic Approach." PhD diss., University College London, 2014.

Browning, Christopher S. "Branding Nordicity: Models, Identity and the Decline of Exceptionalism." *Cooperation and Conflict* 42, no. 1 (March 2007): 27–51. doi:10.1177/0010836707073475.

Burgers, Johannes Hendrikus. "Max Nordau, Madison Grant, and Racialized Theories of Ideology." *Journal of the History of Ideas* 72, no. 1 (2011): 119–40.

Byrkjeflot, Haldor, Jesper Strandgaard Pedersen, and Silviya Svejenova. "From Label to Practice: The Process of Creating New Nordic Cuisine." *Journal of Culinary Science & Technology* 11, no. 1 (March 2013): 36–55. doi:10.1080/15428052.2013.754296.

Byrkjeflot, Haldor, Lars Mjøset, Mads Mordhorst and Klaus Petersen, eds. The Making and Circulation of Nordic Models, Ideals and Images (London: Routledge, 2021) doi:10.4324/9781003156925.

Callaghan, John. "Old Social Democracy, New Social Movements and Social Democratic Programmatic Renewal, 1968–2000." In *Transitions in Social Democracy: Cultural and Ideological Problems of the Golden Age*, edited by John Callaghan and Ilaria Favretto, 177–193. Manchester: Manchester University Press, 2006.

Cameron, David. "Fixing Our Broken Society" (speech), Glasgow, 2008. Conservative Speeches. https://conservative-speeches.sayit.mysociety.org/speech/599630.

Canavan, Hillary Dixler. "Time Editor Howard Chua-Eoan Explains Why No Female Chefs Are 'Gods of Food.'" *Eater*, 7 November 2013. https://www.eater.com/2013/11/7/6334005/time-gods-of-food-controversy-howard-chua-eoan-women-chefs.

Carlsson, Ulla, and David Goldberg, eds. *The Legacy of Peter Forsskål: 250 Years of Freedom of Expression*. Gothenburg: Nordicom, University of Gothenburg, 2017.

Casteel, James. "Historicizing the Nation: Transnational Approaches to the Recent European Past." In *Transnational Europe: Promise, Paradox, Limits*, edited by Joan DeBardeleben and Achim Hurrelmann, 153–69. London: Palgrave Macmillan, 2011. doi:10.1057/9780230306370_9.

Charlotte Higgins. "The Hygge Conspiracy." *The Guardian*, 22 November 2016. http://www.theguardian.com/lifeandstyle/2016/nov/22/hygge-conspiracy-denmark-cosiness-trend.

Childs, Marquis. *Sweden – the Middle Way*. New Haven: Yale University Press, 1936.

Chitnis, Rajendra A., Jakob Stougaard-Nielsen, Rhian Atkin, and Zoran Milutinović, eds. *Translating the Literatures of Small European Nations*. Liverpool: Liverpool University Press, 2020.

Chow, Pei-Sze, Anne Marit Waade, and Robert A. Saunders. "Geopolitical Television Drama Within and Beyond the Nordic Region." *Nordicom Review* 41 (1 September 2020): 11–27. doi:10.2478/nor-2020-0013.

Christiansen, Niels Finn et al., eds. *The Nordic Model of Welfare: A Historical Reappraisal*. Copenhagen: Museum Tusculanum Press, 2006.

Christiansen, Niels Finn, and Klaus Petersen. "Preface." *Scandinavian Journal of History* 26, no. 3 (September 2001): 153–56. doi:10.1080/034687501750303828.

Christiansen, Niels Finn, and Pirjo Markkola. "Introduction." In *The Nordic Model of Welfare: A Historical Reappraisal*, edited by Niels Finn Christiansen et al. Copenhagen: Museum Tusculanum Press, 2006.

Chydenius, Anders. *Anticipating the Wealth of Nations: The Selected Works of Anders Chydenius, 1729–1803*. Edited by Maren Jonasson and Pertti Hyttinen. London: Routledge, 2011.

—— "Den nationala vinsten." In *Politiska skrifter af Anders Chydenius*. Helsinki: G. W. Edlunds förlag, 1880.

—— *Valitut Kirjoitukset*. Porvoo: Werner Söderström, 1929.

Clerc, Louis, Nikolas Glover, and Paul Jordan, eds. *Histories of Public Diplomacy and Nation Branding in the Nordic and Baltic Countries: Representing the Periphery*. Leiden: Brill, 2015.

Coon, Carlton Stevens. *The Races of Europe*. New York: The Macmillan Company, 1939.

Craig, David, and James Thomson, eds. *Languages of Politics in Nineteenth-Century Britain*. London: Palgrave Macmillan, 2013.

Crosland, C.A.R. *The Future of Socialism*. London: Jonathan Cape, 1980.

Dahlerup, Drude. *Vi har ventet længe nok. Håndbog i kvinderepræsentation*. Copenhagen: Nordic Council of Ministers, 1988.

Dahlerup, Drude, ed. *Blomster & spark: Samtaler med kvindelige politikere i Norden*. Copenhagen: Nordic Council of Ministers, 1985.

Danbolt, Mathias. "New Nordic Exceptionalism: Jeuno JE Kim and Ewa Einhorn's *The United Nations of Norden* and Other Realist Utopias." *Journal of Aesthetics & Culture* 8, no. 1 (January 2016). doi:10.3402/jac.v8.30902.

Danielson, Eva, and Märta Ramsten. *Du gamla, du friska: Från folkvisa till nationalsång*. Stockholm: Atlantis, 2013.

Department of Health, Delivering the NHS Plan: Next Steps on Investment Next Steps on Reform, April 2002. Available at https://webarchive.nationalarchives.gov.uk/ukgwa/20130107105354/http://www.dh.gov.uk/prod_consum_dh/groups/dh_digitalassets/@dh/@en/@ps/documents/digitalasset/dh_118524.pdf.

"Det nya arbetarpartiet är moderat nyspråk." *Aftonbladet*, 20 July 2006.

Djurberg, Daniel. *Geographie för begynnare*. 6th ed. Örebro: N.M. Lindhs förlag, 1815.

Donald, Simon, dir. *Fortitude*. Sky Atlantic, 2015. www.sky.com/watch/title/series/6bede254–961b-46f0-ba29–320c8660f824/fortitude.

Douglas, Mary. *Purity and Danger: An Analysis of Concept of Pollution and Taboo*. London: Routledge, 2005.

Drechsler, Wolfgang. "Governance, Good Governance, and Government: The Case for Estonian Administrative Capacity." *TRAMES*, no. 4 (2004): 388–96.

Duelund, Peter. "Nordic Cultural Policies: A Critical View." *International Journal of Cultural Policy* 14, no. 1 (February 2008): 7–24. doi:10.1080/10286630701856468.

—— ed. *The Nordic Cultural Model: Nordic Cultural Policy in Transition*. Copenhagen: Nordic Cultural Institute, 2003.

Dülmen, Richard van. *Die Gesellschaft der Aufklärer. Zur bürgerlichen Emanzipation und aufklärerischen Kultur in Deutschland*. Frankfurt am Main: Fischer Taschenbuch Verlag, 1986.

Eder, Klaus. "The Public Sphere." *Theory, Culture & Society* 23, no. 2–3 (2006): 607–11. doi:10.1177/0263276406062705.

Edling, Nils, ed. *The Changing Meanings of the Welfare State: Histories of a Key Concept in the Nordic Countries*. New York: Berghahn Books, 2019.

Edling, Nils, Jørn Henrik Petersen, and Klaus Petersen. "Social Policy Language in Denmark and Sweden." In *Analysing Social Policy Concepts and Language. Comparative and Transnational Perspectives*, edited by Daniel Béland and Klaus Petersen. Bristol: Policy Press, 2014.

Eduskunta. *Lisärakennuksen Arkkitehtuurikilpailu.* Eduskunta, 1999.

Eijnatten, Joris van. "Between Practice and Principle. Dutch Ideas on Censorship and Press Freedom, 1579–1795." *Redescriptions: Yearbook of Political Thought and Conceptual History* 8 (2004): 85–113.

Einhorn, Eric S., and John Logue. *Modern Welfare States: Politics and Policies in Social Democratic Scandinavia.* New York: Praeger, 1989.

Eisenstadt, Shmuel N., and Wolfgang Schluchter. "Introduction: Paths to Early Modernities – A Comparative View." In *Public Spheres and Collective Identities*, edited by Shmuel N. Eisenstadt, Wolfgang Schluchter, and Björn Wittrock. New Brunswick: Transaction Publishers, 2001.

Eklund, Klas, Henrik Berggren, and Lars Trägårdh. *The Nordic Way: Shared Norms for the New Reality.* Davos: World Economic Forum, 2011.

Ekman, Kari Haarder. *Mitt hems gränser vidgades. En studie i den kulturella skandinavismen under 1800-talet.* Göteborg: Makadam förlag, 2010.

Elder, Neil, Alastair H Thomas, and David Arter. *The Consensual Democracies? The Government and Politics of the Scandinavian States.* Oxford: Martin Robertson, 1982.

Emmenegger, Patrick, Jon Kvist, Paul Marx, and Klaus Petersen. "*Three Worlds of Welfare Capitalism*: The Making of a Classic." *Journal of European Social Policy* 25, no. 1 (February 2015): 3–13. doi:10.1177/0958928714556966.

Engman, Max. "Är Finland ett nordiskt land?" *Den Jyske Historiker* 69–70 (1994).

Eriksson, Göran. "Slaget om Norden." *Svenska Dagbladet*, 8 February 2012.

Erkkilä, Tero. *Government Transparency: Impact and Unintended Consequences.* Houndmills: Palgrave Macmillan, 2012.

Erkkilä, Tero, and Ossi Piironen. "Politics and Numbers. The Iron Cage of Governance Indices." In *Ethics and Integrity of Publlic Administration: Concepts and Cases*, edited by Raymond W Cox III, 125–45. Armonk: M.E. Sharpe, 2009.

—— *Rankings and Global Knowledge Governance: Higher Education, Innovation and Competitiveness.* New York: Palgrave Macmillan, 2018.

Esping-Andersen, Gøsta. *The Three Worlds of Welfare Capitalism.* Cambridge: Polity Press, 1990.

Esping-Andersen, Gøsta, and Walter Korpi. "From Poor Relief to Institutional Welfare States: The Development of Scandinavian Social Policy." In *The Scandinavian Model: Welfare States and Welfare Research*, edited by Robert Erikson et al.. Armonk: M.E. Sharpe, 1987.

Esser, Andrea. "Form, Platform and the Formation of Transnational Audiences: A Case Study of How Danish TV Drama Series Captured Television Viewers in the United Kingdom." *Critical Studies in Television: The International Journal of Television Studies* 12, no. 4 (December 2017): 411–29. doi:10.1177/1749602017729649.

Farr, James. "Understanding Conceptual Change Politically." In *Political Innovation and Conceptual Change*, edited by Terence Ball, James Farr, and Russell L. Hanson, 24–49. Cambridge: Cambridge University Press, 1989.

Fearnlay-Whittingstall, Hugh. "Scandimania." Channel 4, 2 February 2014. https://youtu.be/nNEOAl8aflw.

Feldborg, Andreas Andersen. *Cursory Remarks on the Mediated Attack on Norway; Comprising Strictures on Madame de Staël Holstein "Appeal to the Nations of Europe"; with Some Historical and Statistical Fragments Relating to Norway*. London: Hamblin & Seyfang, 1813.

Ferris, Marcie Cohen. *The Edible South: The Power of Food and the Making of an American Region*. Chapel Hill: University of North Carolina Press, 2014.

Fitzgerald, F. Scott. *The Great Gatsby*. Cambridge: Cambridge University Press, 1993.

Fjeldmark, Stefan et al., *Astérix et les Vikings [Asterix and the Vikings]*. Montreal: Alliance Atlantis Vivafilm, 2006. DVD.

Flood, Alison. "Hygge – the Danish Art of Living Cosily – On Its Way to UK Bookshops." *The Guardian*, 11 June 2016. https://www.theguardian.com/books/2016/jun/11/hygge-the-danish-art-of-living-cosily-on-its-way-to-uk-bookshops.

Forbes, Paula. "The Era of the 'I Foraged With René Redzepi Piece.'" *Eater*, 3 May, 2011. https://www.eater.com/2011/5/3/6683095/the-era-of-the-i-foraged-with-rene-redzepi-piece.

Forshaw, Barry. *Death in a Cold Climate: A Guide to Scandinavian Crime Fiction*. Houndmills: Palgrave Macmillan, 2012.

—— *Nordic Noir: The Pocket Essential Guide to Scandinavian Crime Fiction, Film and TV*. Harpenden: Pocket Essentials, 2013.

Forster, Marc. "Debating the Meaning of Pilgrimage: Maria Steinbach 1733." In *Cultures of Communication from Reformation to Enlightenment: Constructing Publics in the Early Modern German Lands*, edited by James Van Horn Melton. Aldershot: Ashgate, 2002.

Frayne, James. "The Conservatives Are Now the True Worker's Party." *The Daily Telegraph*, 15 May 2015.

Friedeburg, Robert von. "The Public of Confessional Identity: Territorial Church and Church Discipline in 18th-Century Hesse." In *Cultures of Communication from Reformation o Enlightenment: Constructing Publics in the Early Modern German Lands*, edited by James Van Horn Melton, 93–103. Aldershot: Ashgate, 2002.

Frisch, Hartvig. *Pest over Europa: Bolschevisme – Fascisme – Nazisme*. Copenhagen: Henrik Koppels Forlag, 1933.

Garrett, Geoffrey. "Global Markets and National Politics: Collision Course or Virtuous Circle?" *International Organization* 53, no. 4 (1998): 787–824.

Gasche, Malte. *Der "Germanische Wissenschaftseinsatz" Des "Ahnenerbes" Der SS, 1942–1945: Zwischen Vollendung der "völkischen Gemeinschaft" und dem Streben nach "Erlösung."* Bonn: Verlag Dr. Rudolf Habelt GmbH, 2014.

Geherin, David. *The Dragon Tattoo and Its Long Tail: The New Wave of European Crime Fiction in America*. London: McFarland, 2012.

Van Gerven, Tim. "Scandinavism: Overlapping and Competing Identities in the Nordic World 1770–1919." PhD diss, University of Amsterdam, 2020.

Gestrich, Andreas. *Absolutismus und Öffentlichkeit: Politische Kommunikation in Deutschland zu Beginn des 18. Jahrhunderts*. Göttingen: Vandenhoeck & Ruprecht, 1994.

Giddens, Anthony. *The Third Way and Its Critics*. Cambridge: Polity, 2000.

Glenthøj, Rasmus. *Sønner av de Slagne*. Copenhagen: Gad, 2014.

Glover, Nikolas. "Imaging Community: Sweden in 'Cultural Propaganda' Then and Now." *Scandinavian Journal of History* 34, no. 3 (23 September 2009): 246–63. doi:10.1080/03468750903134707.

Glover, Nikolas, and Andreas Mørkved Hellenes. "A 'Swedish Offensive' at the World's Fairs: Advertising, Social Reformism and the Roots of Swedish Cultural Diplomacy, 1935–1939." *Contemporary European History* 30, no. 2 (May 2021): 284–300. doi:10.1017/S0960777320000533.

Gobineau, Arthur de. *Essai Sur l'inégalité Des Races Humaines.* 3 vols. Hanover: Rumpler, 1853.

Goodman, Peter S., and Erik Augustin Palm. "Pandemic Exposes Holes in Sweden's Generous Social Welfare State." *The New York Times*, 8 October, 2020. https://www.nytimes.com/2020/10/08/business/coronavirus-sweden-social-welfare.html.

Gordinier, Jeff. "A Nordic Quest in New York." *The New York Times*, 18 February, 2014. https://www.nytimes.com/2014/02/19/dining/a-nordic-quest-in-new-york.html.

Götz, Norbert. "*Norden*: Structures That Do Not Make a Region." *European Review of History: Revue Europeenne d'histoire* 10, no. 2 (June 2003): 323–41. doi:10.1080/1350748032000140822.

Götz, Norbert, and Heidi Haggrén, eds. *Regional Cooperation and International Organizations: The Nordic Model in Transnational Alignment.* London: Routledge, 2009.

Grant, Madison. *The Conquest of the Continent.* New York: C. Scribner, 1933.

—— *The Passing of the Great Race or the Racial Basis of European History.* New York: C. Scribner, 1936.

Gray, Lila Ellen. *Fado Resounding: Affective Politics and Urban Life.* Durham and London: Duke University Press, 2013.

Grøn, Caroline, Peter Nedergaard, and Anders Wivel, eds. *The Nordic Countries and the European Union: Still the Other European Community?* London: Routledge, 2015.

Grøn, Caroline, Peter Nedergaard, and Anders Wivel. "Mr. Svensson Goes to Brussels: Concluding on the Nordic Countries and the European Union." In *The Nordic Countries and the European Union*, edited by Caroline Howard Grøn, Peter Nedergaard, and Anders Wivel, 243–57. London: Routledge, 2015.

Grønlie, Tore, and Anna-Hilde Nagel. "Administrative History in Norway." *Jahrbuch Für Europäische Verwaltungsgeschichte* 10 (1998): 307–32.

Gundersen, Bjarne Riiser. *Svenske tilstander: en reise til et fremmed land.* Bergen: Vigmostad & Bjørke, 2019.

Gunhild, Agger. "Nordic Noir – Location, Identity and Emotion." In *Emotions in Contemporary TV Series*, edited by Alberto N. García, 134–52. Houndmills: Palgrave, 2016.

Günter, Hans F.K. *Ritter, Tod und Teufel: Der heldische Gedanke.* Munich: J. F. Lehmann Verlag, 1920.

Guterl, Matthew Pratt. *The Color of Race in America, 1900–1940.* Cambridge, MA: Harvard University Press, 2001.

Haatainen, Tuula. "Opening Speech." In *Possibilities and Challenges? Men's Reconciliation of Work and Family Life – Conference Report*, edited by Jouni Varanka and Maria Forslund, 11–15. Copenhagen: Nordic Council of Ministers, 2006.

Haavio-Mannila, Elina. "The Position of Woman." In *Nordic Democracy*, edited by Erik Allardt et al. Copenhagen: Det Danske Selskab, 1981.

Haavio-Mannila, Elina et al. *Unfinished Democracy: Women in Nordic Politics*. Oxford: Pergamon Press, 1985.

Habermas, Jürgen. *The Structural Transformation of the Public Sphere: An Inquiry into a Category of Bourgeois Society*. London: Polity Press, 1989.

Hagemann, Anine, and Isabel Bramsen. *New Nordic Peace: Nordic Peace and Conflict Resolution Efforts*. TemaNord, 524. Copenhagen: Nordic Council of Ministers, 2019. doi:10.6027/TN2019–524.

Hagerman, Maja. *Käraste Herman: Rasbiologen Herman Lundborgs gåta*. Stockholm: Norstedts, 2015.

Hale, Frederick. "Brave New World in Sweden? Roland Huntford's 'The New Totalitarians.'" *Scandinavian Studies* 78, no. 2 (2006): 167–90.

Hálfdanarson, Guðmundur. "Iceland Perceived: Nordic European or a Colonial Other?" In *The Postcolonial North Atlantic Iceland, Greenland and the Faroe Islands*, edited by Lill-Ann Körber and Ebbe Volquardsen, 39–66. Berlin: Nordeuropa-Institut der Humboldt-Universität, 2014.

Halonen, Tarja. *Puhe Anders Chydeniuksen Juhlavuoden Pääjuhlassa Kokkolassa 1.3.2003*. Anders Chydenius Säätiö, 2005.

Häner, Isabelle. *Öffentlichkeit und Verwaltung*. Zürich: Schulthess Polygraphischer Verlag, 1990.

Hansen, Kasper M., and Karina Kosiara-Pedersen. "Nordic Voters and Party Systems." In *The Routledge Handbook of Scandinavian Politics*, edited by Peter Nedergaard and Anders Wivel. New York: Routledge, 2017.

Hansen, Lene. "Conclusion." In *European Integration and National Identity: The Challenge of the Nordic States*, edited by Lene Hansen and Ole Wæver, 212–25. London: Routledge, 2001.

Hansen, Lene, and Ole Wæver, eds. *European Integration and National Identity: The Challenge of the Nordic States*. London: Routledge, 2001.

Hansen, Svein Olav. *Vennskap og kjennskap i 100 år: Foreningen Norden 1919–2019*. Oslo: Gyldendal, 2020.

Hård af Segerstad, Ulf, Eward Maze, and Nancy Maze. *Scandinavian Design*. Helsinki: Otava, 1961.

Harlow, Carol. "Global Administrative Law: The Quest for Principles and Values." *The European Journal of International Law* 17, no. 1 (2006): 187–214.

Hartog, François. *Regimes of Historicity: Presentism and Experiences of Time*. Translated by Saskia Brown. New York: Columbia University Press, 2015.

Harty, Kevin J. *The Vikings on Film: Essays on Depictions of the Nordic Middle Ages*. Jefferson: McFarland, 2014.

Harvard, Jonas, and Magdalena Hillström. "Media Scandinavism: Media Events and the Historical Legacy of Pan-Scandinavism." In *Communicating the North: Media Structures and Images in the Making of the Nordic Region*, edited by Jonas Harvard and Peter Stadius. Ashgate, 2013.

Harvard, Jonas, and Peter Stadius. "Conclusion: Mediating the Nordic Brand – History Recycled." In *Communicating the North: Media Structures and Images in the Making of the Nordic Region*, edited by Jonas Harvard and Peter Stadius, 319–32. The Nordic Experience. Farnham: Ashgate, 2013.

Harvey, Malcolm. "A Social Democratic Future? Political and Institutional Hurdles in Scotland." *The Political Quarterly* 86, no. 2 (April 2015): 249–56. doi:10.1111/1467–923X.12155.

Hausmann, Ricardo, Laura D'Andrea Tyson, and Saadia Zahidi. *The Global Gender Gap Report 2009.* Geneva: World Economic Forum, 2009.

Hecker-Stampehl, Jan, ed. *Between Nordic Ideology, Economic Interests and Political Reality: New Perspectives on Nordek.* Helsinki: Finnish Society of Science and Letters, 2009.

—— *Vereinigte Staaten des Nordens: Integrationsideen in Nordeuropa im Zweiten Weltkrieg.* München: Oldenbourg, 2011.

Heidar, Knut. "Comparative Perspectives on the Northern Countries." In *Nordic Politics: Comparative Perspectives*, edited by Knut Heidar 262–275. Oslo: Universitetsforlaget, 2004.

Heikel, Cecilia. "Vi använder vår yttrandefrihet för att säga ifrån." Svenska Yle, 28 July 2015. https://svenska.yle.fi/artikel/2015/07/28/vi-anvander-var-yttrandefrihet-att-saga-ifran.

Heikka, Henrikki. "Chydeniuksesta, vapaasta kaupasta ja terrorismista." *Kosmopolis* 34, no. 2 (2004).

—— "Kokkolan kirkkoherra paranaa terroristit." *Kosmopolis* 34, no. 1 (2004): 63–68.

Hellenes, Andreas Mørkved. "Tracing the Nordic Model: French Creations, Swedish Appropriations and Nordic Articulations." In *The Making and Circulation of Nordic Models, Ideals and Images*, edited by Haldor Byrkjeflot et al. 83–101. London: Routledge, 2021. doi:10.4324/9781003156925.

Hemstad, Ruth. "'En skandinavisk nationalitet' som litterært prosjekt: 1840-årenes transnasjonale offentlighet i Norden." In *Nation som kvalitet: 1800-talets litterära offentligheter och folk i Norden*, edited by Anna Bohlin and Elin Stengrundet. Bergen: Alvheim & Eide akademisk forlag, 2021.

—— *Fra Indian Summer til nordisk vinter: skandinavisk samarbeid, skandinavisme og unionsoppløsningen.* Oslo: Akademisk Publisering, 2008.

—— "Fra 'det förenade Scandinavien' til 'Nordens Tvillingrige': Skandinavistisk propaganda før skandinavismen, 1808–1814." In *Skandinavism. en rörelse och en idé under 1800-talet*, edited by Magdalena Hillström and Hanne Sanders. Göteborg: Makadam förlag, 2014.

—— "Geopolitikk og geografibøker for folket: Den Norsk-Svenske unionens besværlige beskrivelser." In *Naturvitenskap i nordisk folkeopplysning 1650–2016*, edited by Merethe Roos and Johan Tønnesson, 101–126. Oslo: Cappelen Damn, 2017.

—— "Literature as Auxiliary Forces: Scandinavianism, Pan-Scandinavian Associations and Transnational Dissemination of Literature." In *The Cultural Politics of Nation-Building in Denmark and Scandinavia 1800–1930*, edited by Sine Krogh, Thor Mednick, and Karina Lykke Grand. Aarhus: Aarhus University Press, 2021.

—— "Madame de Staël and the War of Opinion Regarding the Cession of Norway 1813–1814." *Scandinavica* 54, no. 1 (2015): 100–120.

—— "'Norden' og "Skandinavien": Begrepsbruk i brytningstid." In *Nordens historiker: Vänbok till Harald Gustafsson*, edited by Erik Bodensten et al., 45–60. Lund: Historiska Institutionen, Lunds Universitet, 2018.

—— "Organizational Scandinavianism Abroad: Literature, Sociability and Pan-Scandinavian Associational Life in German-Speaking Europe 1842–1912." In *Mit dem Buch in der Hand: Beiträge zur Deutsch-Skandinavischen Buch- und Bibliotheksgeschichte/A Book in*

Hand. German-Scandinavian Book and Library History, edited by Marie-Theres Federhofer and Sabine Meyer, 159–83. Berlin: Nordeuropa-Institut, 2021.

—— *Propagandakrig: Kampen om Norge i Norden og Europa*. Oslo: Novus forlag, 2014.

—— "Scandinavianism. Mapping the Rise of a New Concept." *Contributions to the History of Concepts* 13, no. 1 (1 June 2018): 1–21. doi:10.3167/choc.2018.130102.

—— "Scandinavianism, Nordic Co-operation and "Nordic Democracy." In *Rhetorics of Nordic Democracy*, edited by Jussi Kurunmäki and Johan Strang, 179–93. Helsinki: Finnish Literature Society, 2010. doi:10.21435/sfh.17.

Hemstad, Ruth, Jes Fabricius Møller, and Dag Thorkildsen, eds. *Skandinavisme: Vision og virkning*. Odense: Syddansk Universitetsforlag, 2018.

Hermansen, Mark Emil. "Creating Terroir – An Anthropological Perspecive on New Nordic Cuisine as an Expression of Nordic Identity." *Anthropology of Food* S7 (December 2012).

Hernes, Helga Maria. *Welfare State and Woman Power: Essays in State Feminism*. Oslo: Norwegian University Press, 1987.

Hewitt, Patricia. "Creating a Patient-Led NHS: The next Steps Forward" (speech). 10 January, 2006, transcript, The National Archives. http://webarchive.nationalarchives.gov.uk/20130107105354/http://www.dh.gov.uk/en/-MediaCentre/Speeches/Speecheslist/DH_4126499.

—— "Investment and Reform: Transforming Health and Healthcare." Annual health and social care lecture, 13 December, 2005, transcript, The National Archives. https://webarchive.nationalarchives.gov.uk/ukgwa/20100408103750/http://www.dh.gov.uk/en/MediaCentre/Speeches/Speecheslist/DH_4124484.

Hill, Andrew. "Too Many Angry Cooks Spoil the Business Broth." *Financial Times*, 24 August 2015. https://www.ft.com/content/0d81ad46-4722-11e5-b3b2-1672f710807b.

Hill, Annette, and Susan Turnbull. "Nordic Noir." In *Oxford Research Encyclopedia of Criminology and Criminal Justice*, by Annette Hill and Susan Turnbull. Oxford: Oxford University Press, 2017. https://doi.org/10.1093/acrefore/9780190264079.013.294.

Hillis Miller, J. *Topographies*. Stanford: Stanford University Press, 1995.

Hilson, Mary. "Consumer Co-operation and Economic Crisis: The 1936 Roosevelt Inquiry on Co-operative Enterprise and the Emergence of the Nordic 'Middle Way.'" *Contemporary European History* 22, no. 2 (May 2013): 181–98. doi:10.1017/S0960777313000040.

—— *The International Co-operative Alliance and the Consumer Co-operative Movement in Northern Europe, c. 1860–1939*. Manchester: Manchester University Press, 2018.

—— *The Nordic Model: Scandinavia since 1945*. London: Reaktion Books, 2008.

Hilson, Mary, and Andrew Newby. "The Nordic Welfare Model in Norway and Scotland." In *Northern Neighbours*, edited by John Bryden, Lesley Riddoch, and Ottar Brox, 211–29. Edinburgh: Edinburgh University Press, 2015. doi:10.3366/edinburgh/9780748696208.003.0010.

Hinsliff, Gaby. "Cameron Softens Crime Image in 'hug a Hoodie' Call." *The Guardian*, 9 July, 2006. http://www.theguardian.com/politics/2006/jul/09/conservatives.ukcrime.

Hobsbawm, Eric. "Introduction: Inventing Traditions." In *The Invention of Tradition*, edited by Eric Hobsbawm and Terence Ranger, 1–14. Cambridge: Cambridge University Press, 1987.

Hoctor, Tom. "Beveridge or Bismarck? Choosing the Nordic Model in British Healthcare Policy 1997–c.2015." In *The Making and Circulation of Nordic Models, Ideals and Images*,

edited by Haldor Byrkjeflot et al. 209–228. London: Routledge, 2021.
doi:10.4324/9781003156925–13

Hoctor, Tom. "Coming to Terms with the Market: Accounts of Neoliberal Failure and Rehabilitation on the British Right." *British Politics* (June 2020). doi: 10.1057/s41293–020–00141–9.

Hoffmann, Tobias and Bröhan-Museum Berlin, eds. *Nordic Design: Die Antwort aufs Bauhaus [Nordic Design: The Response to the Bauhaus].* Stuttgart: Arnoldsche, 2019.

Hofsten, Nils von. *Ärftlighetslära.* Uppsala: P.A. Norstedt & Söner, 1919.

Høgetveit, Einar. *Hvor hemmelig? Offentlighetsprinsippeti Norge og USA, særlig med henblikk på militærpolitiske spørsmål.* Oslo: Pax, 1981.

Höglund, Erik et al., "The Revolution in Scandinavian Design." *Craft Horizons* 18, no. 2 (April 1958). https://digital.craftcouncil.org/digital/collection/p15785coll2/id/4711.

Holli, Anne Maria. "Kriittisiä näkökulmia tasa-arvon tutkimukseen." In *Tasa-arvo toisin nähtynä. Oikeuden ja politiikan näkökulmia tasa-arvoon ja yhdenvertaisuuteen,* edited by Johanna Kantola, Kevät Nousiainen, and Milja Saari, 73–96. Helsinki: Gaudeamus, 2012.

Holm, Sophie. *Diplomatins ideal och praktik: Utländska sändebud i Stockholm 1746–1748.* Helsingfors: Societas Scientiarum Fennica, 2020.

Holm, Ulla. "Noma er fascisme i avantgardistiske klæ'r." *Politiken,* 8 May 2011. https://politiken.dk/debat/kroniken/art5509397/Noma-er-fascisme-i-avantgardistiske-kl%C3%A6r.

Holmberg, Åke. *Skandinavismen i Sverige vid 1800-talets mitt.* Göteborg: Elanders boktrykkeri, 1946.

Holter, Øystein Gullvåg. *Can Men Do It? Men and Gender Equality – the Nordic Experience.* Copenhagen: Nordic Council of Ministers, 2003.

Hood, Christopher C. "Transparency in Historical Perspective." In *Transparency: The Key to Better Governance?,* edited by David Heald and Christopher C. Hood, 3–23. Oxford: Oxford University Press, 2006.

Horn, Denise M. "Setting the Agenda: US and Nordic Gender Policies in The Estonian Transition to Democracy." *International Feminist Journal of Politics* 10, no. 1 (March 2008): 59–77. doi:10.1080/14616740701747675.

—— "Setting the Agenda. US and Nordic Gender Policies in the Estonian Transition to Democracy." *International Feminist Journal of Politics* 10, no. 1 (2008): 59–77.

Huntford, Roland. *The New Totalitarians.* London: Allen Lane, 1971.

Hyde-Price, Adrian. "Epilogue: 'Nordicness' – Theory and Practice." *Global Affairs* 4, no. 4–5 (20 October, 2018): 435–43. doi:10.1080/23340460.2018.1497451.

Ifversen, Jan. "About Key Concepts and How to Study Them." *Contributions to the History of Concepts* 6, no. 1 (15 September 2011). doi:10.3167/choc.2011.060104.

Ihalainen, Pasi, Cornelia Ilie, and Kari Palonen. "Parliament as a Conceptual Nexus." In *Parliaments and Parliamentarism: A Comparative History of a European Concept,* edited by Pasi Ihalainen, Cornelia Ilie, and Kari Palonen. New York: Berghahn, 2016.

—— eds. *Parliaments and Parliamentarism: A Comparative History of a European Concept.* New York: Berghahn Books, 2016.

Ihalainen, Pasi, and Karin Sennefelt. "General Introduction." In *Scandinavia in the Age of Revolution: Nordic Political Cultures 1740–1820,* edited by Pasi Ihalainen, Michael Bregnsbo, and Patrik Winton. Farnham: Ashgate, 2011.

"Inspector Norse: Why Are Nordic Detective Novels So Successful?" *The Economist*, 11 March, 2010. http://www.economist.com/node/15660846.

Ísleifsson, Sumarliði and [with the collaboration of] Daniel Chartier. "Banking on Borealism: Eating, Smelling and Performing the North," 305–28. Québec: Presses de l'Université du Québec, 2011.

Iversen, Torben. "The Dynamics of Welfare State Expansion: Trade Openness, De-Industrialisation and Partisan Politics." In *The New Politics of the Welfare State*, edited by Paul Pierson, 45–79. Oxford: Oxford University Press, 2001.

Jackson, John P., and Nadine M. Weidman. "The Origins of Scientific Racism." *The Journal of Blacks in Higher Education*, no. 50 (2005): 66–79.

Jalava, Marja, and Bo Stråth. "Scandinavia/Norden." In *European Regions and Boundaries: A Conceptual History*, edited by Diana Mishkova and Balázs Trencsényi. New York: Berghahn Books, 2017.

Jalving, Mikael. *Absolut Sverige: En rejse i tavshedens rige*. København: Jyllands-Postens Forlag, 2011.

Janfelt, Monika. *Att leva i den bästa av världar: Föreningarna Nordens syn på Norden 1919–1933*. Stockholm: Carlsson, 2005.

Jauhola, Marjaana, and Johanna Kantola. "Globaali sukupuolipolitiikka Suomessa." In *Sukupuolikysymys*, edited by Marita Husso and Risto Heiskala, 209–30. Helsinki: Gaudeamus, 2016.

Jenkins, Allen. "Magnus Nilsson: The Rising Star of Nordic Cooking," *The Guardian*, 22 January 2012. https://www.theguardian.com/lifeandstyle/2012/jan/22/magnus-nilsson-Fä viken-sweden-chef.

Jensen, Pia Majbritt. "Global Impact of Danish Drama Series: A Peripheral, Non-Commercial Creative Counter-Flow." *Kosmorama* 263 (2016). https://www.kosmorama.org/en/kosmor ama/artikler/global-impact-danish-drama-series-peripheral-non-commercial-creative-coun ter.

Jessop, Bob. "The Rise of Governance and the Risks of Failure." *International Social Science Journal* 155 (1998): 29–45.

Joenniemi, Pertti. "Finland in the New Europe: A Herderian or Hegelian Concept." In *European Integration and National Identity: The Challenge of the Nordic States*, edited by Lene Hansen and Ole Wæver. London: Routledge, 2001.

Johnsen, Lars. "Eldre bøker i den digitale samlingen: Et elektronisk blikk på tekster fra perioden 1650–1850." In *Litterære verdensborgere: Transnasjonale perspektiver på norsk bokhistorie 1519–1850*, edited by Aasta Marie Bjorvand Bjørkøy et al., 190–214. Oslo: National Library of Norway, 2019.

Jones, George. "Cameron Turns Blue to Prove Green Credentials." *The Daily Telegraph*, 21 April, 2006. https://www.telegraph.co.uk/news/uknews/1516276/Cameron-turns-blue-to-prove-green--credentials.html.

Jónsson, Guðmundur. "Iceland and the Nordic Model of Consensus Democracy." *Scandinavian Journal of History* 39, no. 4 (8 August 2014): 510–28. doi:10.1080/03468755.2014.935473.

Jordheim, Helge. "Europe at Different Speeds: Asynchronicities and Multiple Times in European Conceptual History." In *Conceptual History in the European Space*, edited by

Willibald Steinmetz, Michael Freeden, and Javier Fernández Sebastián, 139–74. New York: Berghahn Books, 2017. doi:10.2307/j.ctvw04kcs.9.

Jordheim, Helge, and Einar Wigen. "Conceptual Synchronisation: From Progress to Crisis." *Millennium: Journal of International Studies* 46, no. 3 (June 2018): 421–39. doi:10.1177/0305829818774781.

Julkunen, Raija. "Sukupuoli valtiollisen politiikan kohteena." In *Sukupuolikysymys*, edited by Marita Husso and Risto Heiskala, 231–59. Helsinki: Gaudeamus, 2016.

Jungar, Ann-Cathrine, and Anders Ravik Jupskås. "Populist Radical Right Parties in the Nordic Region: A New and Distinct Party Family?" *Scandinavian Political Studies* 37, no. 3 (September 2014): 215–38. doi:10.1111/1467–9477.12024.

Junge, Kay, and Kirill Postoutenko, eds. *Asymmetrical Concepts After Reinhart Koselleck: Historical Semantics and Beyond*. Bielefeld: transcript Verlag, 2011.

Kahn, Howie. "Noma's René Redzepi Never Stops Experimenting." *Wall Street Journal*, 6 November 2014. https://online.wsj.com/articles/nomas-rene-redzepi-never-stops-ex perimenting-1415237540.

Käkönen, Jyrki. "Anders Chydenius ja 1700-luvun suomalainen valtio-opillinen ajattelu." In *Valtio ja yhteiskunta. Tutkielmia suomalaisen valtiollisen ajattelun ja valtio-opin historiasta*, edited by Jaako Nousiainen and Dag Anckar. Juva: Werner Söderström, 1983.

—— "Henrikki Heikka Chydeniuksesta, Terrorismin parantamisesta ja vapaakaupasta." *Kosmopolis* 34, no. 1 (2004): 111–14.

Kantola, Johanna, and Anne Maria Holli. "State Feminism Finnish Style: Strong Policies Clash with Implementation Problems." In *Changing State Feminism*, edited by Joyce Outshoorn and Johanna Kantola, 82–101. Houndmills: Palgrave Macmillan, 2007.

Kantola, Johanna, and Kevät Nousiainen. "Euroopan Unionin tasa-arvopolitiikka: Velvoittavaa lainsäädäntöä ja pehmeää sääntelyä." In *Tasa-arvo toisin nähtynä: Oikeuden ja politiikan näkökulmia tasa-arvoon ja yhdenvertaisuuteen*, edited by Johanna Kantola, Kevät Nousiainen, and Milja Saari, 121–42. Helsinki: Gaudeamus, 2012.

Kantola, Johanna, Kevät Nousiainen, and Milja Saari. "Johdanto: Tasa-arvosta ja sen lukemisesta toisin." In *Tasa-arvo toisin nähtynä: Oikeuden ja politiikan näkökulmia tasa-arvoon ja yhdenvertaisuuteen*, edited by Johanna Kantola, Kevät Nousiainen, and Milja Saari, 7–27. Helsinki: Gaudeamus, 2012.

Karcher, Nicola. "Schirmorganisation der Nordischen Bewegung: Der Nordische Ring und seine Repräsentanten in Norwegen." *Nordeuropaforum* 1, no. 19 (13 July 2009): 7–36. doi:10.18452/7996.

Karker, Allan. "Den nordiske model." *Den Store Danske*. https://denstoredanske.lex.dk/den_ nordiske_model.

Karvonen, Lauri, and Per Selle. *Women in Nordic Politics: Closing the Gap*. Aldershot: Darthmouth, 1995.

Kautto, Mikko. "The Nordic Countries." In *The Oxford Handbook of the Welfare State*, edited by Francis G. Castles et al. Oxford: Oxford University Press, 2010. doi:10.1093/oxfordhb/9780199579396.003.0040.

Kautto, Mikko et al., eds. *Nordic Welfare States in the European Context*. London: Routledge, 2001.

Kayser Nielsen, Niels. *Bonde, stat og hjem: Nordisk demokrati og nationalisme fra pietismen til 2. verdenskrig*. Aarhus: Aarhus universitetsforlag, 2009.

Keating, Michael and Malcolm Harvey. *Small Nations in a Big World: What Scotland Can Learn.* Edinburgh: Luath Press, 2014.

Keränen, Marja. *Finnish "Undemocracy": Essays on Gender and Politics.* Helsinki: Finnish Political Science Association, 1990.

Kettunen, Pauli. *Globalisaatio ja kansallinen me. Kansallisen katseen historiallinen kritiikki.* Tampere: Vastapaino, 2008.

—— "Review Essay: A Return to the Figure of the Free Nordic Peasant," review of *The Cultural Construction of Norden*, edited by Øystein Sørensen and Bo Stråth. Acta Sociologica 42, no. 3 (July 1, 1999): 259–69. doi:10.1177/000169939904200306.

—— "The Conceptual History of the Welfare State in Finland." In *The Changing Meanings of the Welfare State: Histories of a Key Concept in the Nordic Countries*, edited by Nils Edling, 225–75. New York: Berghahn Books, 2019.

—— "The Nordic Model and the Making of the Competitive 'Us.'" In *The Global Economy, National States and the Regulation of Labour*, edited by Paul Edwards and Tony Elger. London: Mansell Publishing, 1999.

—— "The Nordic Welfare State in Finland." *Scandinavian Journal of History* 26, no. 3 (1 September, 2001): 225–47. doi:10.1080/034687501750303864.

—— "The Power of International Comparison: A Perspective on the Making and Challenging of the Nordic Welfare State." In *The Nordic Model of Welfare: A Historical Reappraisal*, edited by Niels Finn Christiansen et al. Copenhagen: Museum Tusculanum Press, 2006.

—— "The Society of Virtuous Circles." In *Models, Modernity and the Myrdals*, edited by Pauli Kettunen and Hanna Eskola. Renvall Institute Publication 8. Helsinki: Helsinki University, 1997.

—— "The Transnational Construction of National Challenges: The Ambiguous Nordic Model of Welfare and Competitiveness." In *Beyond Welfare State Models: Transnational Historical Perpectives on Social Policy*, edited by Pauli Kettunen and Klaus Petersen. Cheltenham: Edward Elgar Publishing, 2011.

—— "Yhteiskunta ohjattavana ja ohjaajana – Historiallinen näkökulma: Monikäyttöinen Chydenius." Anders Chydenius foundation. http://www.chydenius.net.

Kettunen, Pauli, Urban Lundberg, and Mirja Österberg. "The Nordic Model and the Rise and Fall of Nordic Cooperation." In *Nordic Cooperation: A European Region in Transition*, edited by Johan Strang. London: Routledge, 2016. doi:10.4324/9781315755366.

Kettunen, Pauli, and Klaus Petersen, eds. *Beyond Welfare State Models: Transnational Historical Perspectives on Social Policy.* Cheltenham: Edward Elgar, 2011.

—— "Introduction: Rethinking Welfare State Models." In *Beyond Welfare State Models: Transnational Historical Perpectives on Social Policy*, edited by Pauli Kettunen and Klaus Petersen. Cheltenham: Edward Elgar Publishing, 2011.

Kettunen, Pekka, and Markku Kiviniemi. "Policy-Making in Finland: Consensus and Change." In *The Work of Policy – an International Survey*, edited by Hal Colebatch, 147–60. New York: Lexington Books, 2006.

Kharkina, Anna. *From Kinship to Global Brand: The Discourse on Culture in Nordic Cooperation after World War II.* Stockholm Studies in History 97. Huddinge: Södertörns högskola, 2013.

Kielos, Katrine. "Flight of the Swedish Bumblebee." *Renewal (London, England)* 17, no. 2 (2009): 61–66.

Kjærsgaard, Kristine. "International Arenas and Domestic Institution Formation: The Impact of the UN Women's Conferences in Denmark, 1975–1985." *Nordic Journal of Human Rights* 36 (2018): 271–86.

Kliemann-Geisinger, Henriette. "Mapping the North – Spatial Dimensions and Geographical Concepts of Northern Europe." In *Northbound: Travels, Encounters, and Constructions 1700–1830*, edited by Karen Klitgaard Povlsen, 70–76. Aarhus: Aarhus University Press, 2007.

Knudsen, Tim, ed. *Den nordiske protestantisme og velfrærdsstaten.* Århus: Aarhus universitetsforlag, 2000.

—— *Offentlighed i det offentlige: Om historiens magt.* Aarhus: Aarhus Universitetsforlag, 2003.

Koikkalainen, P. "From Agrarian Republicanism to the Politics of Neutrality: Urho Kekkonen and 'Nordic Democracy' in Finnish Cold War Politics." In *Rhetorics of Nordic Democracy*, edited by Jussi Kurunmäki and Johan Strang. Helsinki: Finnish Literature Society, 2010, doi:10.21435/sfh.17.

Koivunen, Anu, Jari Ojala, and Anh Holmén. "Always in Crisis, Always a Solution?: The Nordic Model as a Political and Scholarly Concept." In *The Nordic Economic, Social and Political Model*, edited by Anu Koivunen, Jari Ojala, and Janne Holmén, 1–19. London: Routledge, 2021. doi:10.4324/9780429026690–1.

Koivunen, Anu, Jari Ojala, and Janne Holmén, eds. *The Nordic Economic, Social and Political Model: Challenges in the 21st Century.* London: Routledge, 2021.

Konstari, Timo. *Asiakirjajulkisuudesta hallinnossa: Tutkimus yleisten asiakirjain julkisuudesta hallinnon kontrollivälineenä.* Helsinki: Suomalainen lakimiesyhdistys, 1977.

Koponen, Kalle. "Talouspappi Chydenius pääsi valtiovarainministerin seinälle Ruotsissa." *Helsingin Sanomat*, 9 January 2009.

Koselleck, Reinhart. "A Response to Comments on Geschichtliche Grundbegriffe." In *The Meaning of Historical Terms and Concepts: New Studies on Begriffsgeschichte*, edited by Hartmut Lehmann and Melvin Richter. Washington, DC: German Historical Institute, 1996.

—— "Einleitung." In *Geschichtliche Grundbegriffe: Historisches Lexikon zur politisch-sozialen Sprache in Deutschland*, edited by Otto Brunner, Werner Conze, and Reinhart Koselleck. Stuttgart: Klett-Cotta, 1972.

—— *Futures Past: On the Semantics of Historical Time.* New York: Columbia University Press, 2004.

—— *Vergangene Zukunft: Zur Semantik geschichtlicher Zeiten.* Frankfurt am Main: Suhrkamp, 1979.

Kovač, Miha, and Rüdiger Wischenbart. "Diversity Report 2016: Trends and References in Literary Translation across Europe." Verein für kulturelle transfers. Accessed 13 September 2018. www.culturaltransfers.org.

Kristjánsdóttir, Ragnheiður. "Facing the Nation – Nordic Communists and Their National Contexts, from the 1920s and into the Cold War." In *Labour, Unions and Politics under the North Star: The Nordic Countries, 1700–2000*, edited by Mary Hilson, Silke Neunsinger, and Iben Vyff, 258–278. New York: Berghahn Books, 2017.

—— "For Equality or Against Foreign Oppression? The Politics of the Left in Iceland Leading up to the Cold War." *Moving the Social* 48 (2012): 11–28. doi:10.13154/mts.48.2012.11–28.

Kuhnle, Stein. Review of *Modern Welfare States*. *The Journal of Politics* 52, no. 3 (1990): 2131854. https://doi.org/10.2307.
—— "The Beginnings of the Nordic Welfare States: Similarities and Differences." *Acta Sociologica* 21 (1978): 9–35.
—— "The Scandinavian Welfare State in the 1990s: Challenged but Viable." *West European Politics* 23, no. 2 (April 2000): 209–228. doi_10.1080/01402380008425373.
Kuldkepp, Mart. "The Scandinavian Connection in Early Estonian Nationalism." *Journal of Baltic Studies* 44, no. 3 (1 September, 2013): 313–38. doi: 10.1080/01629778.2012.744911.
Kulturrådet, *Ny kulturpolitik: Nuläge och förslag*. Stockholm: Allmänna förlaget, 1972.
Kurunmäki, Jussi. "'Nordic Democracy' in 1935: On the Finnish and Swedish Rhetoric of Democracy." In *Rhetorics of Nordic Democracy*, edited by Jussi Kurunmäki and Johan Strang. Helsinki: Finnish Literature Society, 2010. doi:10.21435/sfh.17.
Kurunmäki, Jussi, and Johan Strang, eds. *Rhetorics of Nordic Democracy*. Helsinki: Finnish Literature Society, 2010, doi:10.21435/sfh.17.
Kurvinen, Heidi, and Arja Turunen. "Toinen aalto uudelleen tarkasteltuna. Yhdistys 9:N Rooli Suomalaisen Feminismin Historiassa'. *Sukupuolentutkimus* 3 (2018): 21–34.
Kvinnor och män i Norden: fakta om jämställdheten 1988. Copenhagen: Nordic Council of Ministers, 1988.
Kythor, Ellen. "Stereotypes in and of Scandinavia." In *Introduction to Nordic Cultures*, edited by Annika Lindskog and Jakob Stougaard-Nielsen, 210–24. London: UCL Press, 2020.
Lagerspetz, Mikko. "How Many Nordic Countries?: Possibilities and Limits of Geopolitical Identity Construction." *Cooperation and Conflict* 38, no. 1 (March 2003): 49–61. doi:10.1177/0010836703038001003.
Lajh, Andreja. "Rene Redzepi on His Origins." Haut De Gamme, 10 November 2015. https://hautdegamme.net/2015/11/10/rene-redzepi-on-his-origins/.
Lamble, Stephen. "Freedom of Information, a Finnish Clergyman's Gift to Democracy." *Freedom of Information Review* 97, no. February 2002 (2002): 2–8.
Lane, Jan-Erik et al. "Scandinavian Exceptionalism Reconsidered." *Journal of Theoretical Politics* 5, no. 2 (April 1993): 195–230. doi:10.1177/0951692893005002003.
Lapiņa, Linda, and Jonatan Leer. "Carnivorous Heterotopias: Gender, Nostalgia and Hipsterness in the Copenhagen Meat Scene." *NORMA* 11, no. 2 (2 April 2016): 89–109. doi:10.1080/18902138.2016.1184479.
Larsen, Eirinn. "State Feminism Revisited as Knowledge History: The Case of Norway." In *Histories of Knowledge in Postwar Scandinavia: Actors, Arenas, and Aspirations*, edited by Johan Östling, Niklas Olsen, and David Larsson Heidenblad, 152–70. London: Routledge, 2020.
Larsen, Eirinn, Sigrun Marie Moss, and Inger Skjelsbæk, eds. *Gender Equality and Nation Branding in the Nordic Region*. London: Routledge, 2021.
Laurence, Jeremy. "Bed Blocking the Scandinavian Solution." *The Independent*, 19 April, 2002.
Lawson, Mark. "Crime's Grand Tour: European Detective Fiction." *The Guardian*, 26 October, 2012. https://www.theguardian.com/books/2012/oct/26/crimes-grand-tour-european-detective-fiction.
Leer, Jonatan. "The Rise and Fall of the New Nordic Cuisine." *Journal of Aesthetics & Culture* 8, no. 1 (1 January, 2016): 33494. doi:10.3402/jac.v8.33494.

Leerssen, Joep. "Foreword." In *Images of the North: Histories, Identities, Ideas*, edited by Sverrir Jakobsson, 15–18. Amsterdam: Rodopi, 2009.

—— "A Summary of Imagological Theory." Imagologica: Dedicated to the critical study of national stoeretypes. Accessed 1 May, 2021. https://imagologica.eu/theoreticalsummary.

Leese, Ian, dir. *Art of Scandinavia*, episode 1, "Dark Night of the Soul." Presented by Andrew Graham-Dixon. Aired 14 March, 2016, on BBC 4, https://www.bbc.co.uk/programmes/b073mp87.

Lehti, Marko, and David J. Smith, eds. *Post-Cold War Identity Politics: Northern and Baltic Experiences*. Cass Series – Nationalism and Ethnicity. London: Frank Cass, 2003.

Lenz, Fritz. "Die seelischen Unterschiede der großen Rassen." In *Menschliche Erblichkeitslehre Und Rassenhygiene*, edited by Erwin Baur, Eugen Fischer, and Fritz Lenz, 520–83. Munich: J.F. Lehmann, 1931.

Lesser, Wendy. *Scandinavian Noir: In Pursuit of a Mystery*. New York: Farrar, Straus and Giroux, 2020.

Letto-Vanamo, Pia, and Ditlev Tamm. Co-operation in the Field of Law. In Nordic Cooperation: A European Region in Transition, edited by Johan Strang, 93–107. London: Routledge, 2016. doi:10.4324/9781315755366–5.

Lévi-Strauss, Claude. *Le Cru et Le Cuit*. Mythologiques, vol. 1. Paris: Plon, 1964.

—— *The Raw and the Cooked: Introduction to a Science of Mythology*. New York: Harper Colophon Books, 1975.

Lindert, Peter. "The Welfare State Is the Wrong Target: A Reply to Bergh." *Econ Journal Watch* 3 (1 May, 2006): 236–50.

Lister, Ruth, and Fran Bennett. "The New 'Champion of Progressive Ideals'? Cameron's Conservative Party: Poverty, Family Policy and Welfare Reform." *Renewal: a journal of social democray* 18, no. 1–2 (2010): 84–109.

Logue, John. "Review of *The Consensual Democracies?* by Neil Elder et al.." *Scandinavian Studies* 55, no. 3 (1983).

Lothe, Jakob, and Bente Larsen, eds. *Perspectives on the Nordic*. Oslo: Novus Press, 2016.

Lundborg, Herman. *Rasbiologi och rashygien: Nutida kultur- och rasfrågor i etisk belysning.* Stockholm: P.A.Norstedt, 1922.

—— *Rasfrågor i modern belysning*. Stockholm: P.A. Norstedt, 1919.

—— *Rassenkunde Des schwedischen Volkes*. Jena: Fischer, 1928.

—— *The Racial Characters of the Swedish Nation*. Uppsala: Almquist & Wiksell, 1926.

Lundström, Catrin and Benjamin R. Teitelbaum. "Nordic Whiteness: An Introduction." *Scandinavian Studies* 89, no. 2 (2017). doi:10.5406/scanstud.89.2.0151.

Lutzhöft, Hans-Jürgen. *Der Nordische Gedanke in Deutschland 1920–1940*. Stuttgart: E. Klett, 1971.

MacDougall, Ian "The Man Who Blew Up the Welfare State." *N+1 Magazine*, 27 February, 2010. https://nplusonemag.com/online-only/book-review/man-who-blew-up-welfare-state.

Madame de Staël i. e. A.W. Schlegel. *An Appeal to the Nations of Europe*. Frederikshald: H. Gundersen & H. Larssen, 1833.

Mai, Anne-Marie. "Dreams and Realities: The Nordic Council Literature Prize as a Symbol for the Construction of Nordic Cultural Cooperation." In *Nordic Cooperation: A European Region in Transition*, edited by Johan Strang, 109–130. London: Routledge, 2016. doi:10.4324/9781315755366–6.

Majander, Mikko. *Pohjoismaa vai kansandemokratia? Sosiaalidemokraatit, kommunistit ja Suomen kansainvälinen asema 1944–1951.* Helsinki: Suomalaisen Kirjallisuuden Seura, 2004.

Malmborg, Mikael af. "Den ståndaktiga nationalstaten: Sverige och den västeuropeiska integrationen 1945–1959." PhD diss., Lund University, 1994. https://portal.research.lu.se/portal/sv/publications/den-staandaktiga-nationalstaten–sverige-och-den-vast europeiska-integrationen-19451959(3f616aab-28c0-45ee-b2f0-7c865a86cfae)/export.html.

—— *Neutrality and State-Building in Sweden.* St. Antony's Series. Basingstoke: Palgrave, 2001.

Manninen, Juha. "Anders Chydenius and the Origins of World's First Freedom of Information Act." In *The World's First Freedom of Information Act. Anders Chydenius' Legacy Today,* edited by Anders Chydenius Foundation, 18–53. Kokkola: Anders Chydenius Foundation, 2006.

—— *Valistus ja kansallinen identiteetti: Aatehistoriallinen tutkimus 1700-luvun Pohjolasta.* Helsinki: Suomalaisen Kirjallisuuden Seura, 2000.

Marcussen, Martin. *Ideas and Elites: The Social Construction of Economic and Monetary Union.* Aalborg: Aalborg University Press, 2000.

—— "Scandinavian Models of Diplomacy." In *The Routledge Handbook of Scandinavian Politics,* edited by Peter Nedergaard and Anders Wivel. New York: Routledge, 2017.

Marjanen, Jani. "Nordic Modernities: From Historical Region to Five Exceptions." *International Journal for History, Culture and Modernity* 3, no. 1 (2015): 91–106. doi:10.18352/22130624–00301005.

—— "Transnational Conceptual History, Methodological Nationalism and Europe." In *Conceptual History in the European Space,* edited by Willibald Steinmetz, Michael Freeden, and Javier Fernández Sebastián, 139–74. New York: Berghahn Books, 2017. doi:10.2307/j.ctvw04kcs.9.

—— "Undermining Methodological Nationalism: Histoire Croisée of Concepts as Transnational History." In *Transnational Political Spaces: Agents – Structures – Encounters,* edited by Mathias Albert, Gesa Bluhm, Jochen Walter, Jan Helmig, and Andreas Leutzsch, 2nd ed., 239–63. Frankfurt: Campus Verlag, 2009.

Marklund, Carl. "The Nordic Model on the Global Market of Ideas: The Welfare State as Scandinavia's Best Brand." *Geopolitics* 22, no. 3 (2017): 623–39. doi:10.1080/14650045.2016.1251906.

—— "The Social Laboratory, the Middle Way and the Swedish Model: Three Frames for the Image of Sweden." *Scandinavian Journal of History* 34, no. 3 (2009): 264–85.

Marklund, Carl, and Klaus Petersen. "Return to Sender – American Images of the Nordic Welfare States and Nordic Welfare State Branding." *European Journal of Scandinavian Studies* 43, no. 2 (2013): 245–57. doi:10.1515/ejss-2013–0016.

Marklund, Carl, and Byron Zachary Rom-Jensen. "Vanishing Scandinavian 'Socialism' in the 2020 US Election," 2020. https://nordics.info/show/artikel/scandinavias-vanishing-so cialism-in-the-2020-us-election/.

Marklund, Carl, and Peter Stadius. "Acceptance and Conformity: Merging Modernity with Nationalism in the Stockholm Exhibition in 1930." *Culture Unbound* 2, no. 5 (2010): 609–634. doi:10.3384/cu.2000.1525.10235609.

Marnix, Beyen. "Who Is the Nation and What Does It Do? The Discursive Construction of the Nation in Belgian and Dutch National Histories of the Romantic Period." In *The Historical*

Imagination in Nineteenh-Century Britain and the Low Countries, edited by Hugh Dunthorne and Michael Wintle, 67–85. Leiden: Brill, 2013.

Martens, Wolfgang. *Die Botschaft der Tugend. Die Aufklärung im Spiegel der deutschen moralischen Wochenschriften.* Stuttgart: Metzler, 1971.

Marx Ferree, Myra et al. "Four Models of the Public Sphere in Modern Democracies." *Theory and Society* 31, no. 2 (2002): 289–324.

Mazur, Amy G., and Dorothy McBride. "State Feminism." In *Politics, Gender and Concepts: Theory and Methodology*, edited by Gary Goertz and Amy G. Mazur, 244–69. Cambridge: Cambridge University Press, 2008.

McBride, Dorothy, and Amy G. Mazur. *The Politics of State Feminism: Innovation in Comparative Research.* Philadelphia: Temple University Press, 2010.

Mead, W. R. *An Economic Geography of the Scandinavian States and Finland.* London: University of London Press, 1958.

Mediastream. Royal Library of Denmark. Accessed 4 June 2021. https://www2.statsbiblioteket.dk/mediestream/.

Melby, Kari, Anu Pylkkänen, Bente Rosenbeck, and Christina Carlsson Wetterberg. *Inte ett ord om kärlek: Äktenskap och politik i Norden ca 1850–1930.* Göteborg and Stockholm: Makadam förlag, 2006.

—— "The Nordic Model of Marriage." *Women's History Review* 15, no. 4 (2006): 651–61. doi:10.1080/09612020500530851.

Melby, Kari, Anna-Birte Ravn, and Christina Carlsson Wetterberg. "A Nordic Model of Gender Equality? Introduction." In *Gender Equality and Welfare Politics in Scandinavia: The Limits of Political Ambition?*, edited by Kari Melby, Anna-Birte Ravn, and Christina Carlsson Wetterberg, 1–24. Bristol: Policy Press, 2008.

Melby, Kari, Anna-Birte Ravn, Bente Rosenbeck, and Christina Carlsson Wetterberg. "What Is Nordic in the Nordic Gender Model?" In *Beyond Welfare State Models: Transnational Historical Perspectives on Social Policy*, edited by Pauli Kettunen and Klaus Petersen, 147–69. Cheltenham: Edward Elgar, 2011.

Melvin, Richter. *The History of Political and Social Concepts: A Critical Introduction.* Oxford: Oxford University Press, 1995.

Middell, Matthias, and Lluís Roura i Aulinas, ed. *Transnational Challenges to National History Writing.* Basingstoke: Palgrave Macmillan, 2013.

Mishkova, Diana. *Beyond Balkanism: the Scholarly Politics of Region Making.* London: Routledge, 2018.

Mishkova, Diana, and Balázs Trencsényi. "Conceptualizing Spaces within Europe: The Case of Meso-Regions." In *European Regions and Boundaries: A Conceptual History*, edited by Diana Mishkova and Balázs Trencsényi. New York: Berghahn Books, 2017.

Mishkova, Diana, Balász Trencsényi, and Marja Jalava, eds. *"Regimes of Historicity' in Southeastern and Northern Europe, 1890–1945: Discourses of Identity and Temporality."* Basingstoke: Palgrave Macmillan, 2014. doi:10.1057/9781137362476.

—— ed. *European Regions and Boundaries: A Conceptual History.* New York: Berghahn Books, 2017.

—— "Introduction." In *European Regions and Boundaries: A Conceptual History*, edited by Diana Mishkova and Balázs Trencsényi. New York: Berghahn Books, 2017.

Mittell, Jason. *Complex TV: The Poetics of Contemporary Television Storytelling.* New York: New York University Press, 2015.

Mjøset, Lars. "The Nordic Model Never Existed, But Does It Have a Future?" *Scandinavian Studies* 64, no. 4 (1992): 652–71.

Molbech, Christian. *Lund, Upsala og Stockholm i Sommeren 1842: Nogle Blade af en Dagbog med et Tillæg om "den skandinaviske Enhed."* Copenhagen: Gyldendalske Boghandling, 1844.

Møller, Erik. "Den dynastiske skandinavismens grobunn af grenser, ca. 1845–1870." In *Skandinavismen*, edited by Ruth Hemstad, Jes Fabricius Møller, and Dag Thorkildsen, 257–68 (Odense: Syddansk Universitetsforlag, 2018).

—— *Skandinavisk stræben og svensk politik omkring 1860.* Copenhagen: Gad, 1948.

Møller, Jes Fabricius. "Grundtvig, Danmark og Norden." In *Skandinavismen*, edited by Ruth Hemstad, Jes Fabricius Møller, and Dag Thorkildsen, 99–120. Odense: Syddansk Universitetsforlag, 2018.

Møller, Viggo Sten, ed. *Scandinavian Design: Directory of Arts and Crafts Resources in Denmark, Finland, Norway, Sweden, Copenhagen, 1953.* Copenhagen: Langkjærs Bogtrykkeri, 1953.

Mordhorst, Mads. "Nation Branding and Nationalism." In *Nationalism and the Economy: Exploration into a Neglected Relationship*, edited by Stefan Berger and Thomas Fetzer. Budapest: Central European University Press, 2019.

—— "Nation-Branding og Nationalstaten." *Den Jyske Historiker* 126 (2010): 16–39.

Moskin, Julia. "New Nordic Cuisine Draws Disciples." *The New York Times*, 24 August, 2011. https://www.nytimes.com/2011/08/24/dining/new-nordic-cuisine-draws-disciples.html.

Mouritzen, Hans. "The Nordic Model as a Foreign Policy Instrument: Its Rise and Fall." *Journal of Peace Research* 32, no. 1 (1995): 9–21. doi:10.1177/0022343395032001002.

Musiał, Kazimierz. "Reconstructing Nordic Significance in Europe on the Threshold of the 21st Century." *Scandinavian Journal of History* 34, no. 3 (2009): 286–306. doi:10.1080/03468750903134723.

—— *Roots of the Scandinavian Model: Images of Progress in the Era of Modernisation.* Baden-Baden: Nomos, 2002.

Nairn, Tom. *The Break-up of Britain: Crisis and Neo-Nationalism.* London: Verso, 1981.

Nasjonalbiblioteket [National Library of Norway]. https://www.nb.no/.

Nelson, George R. *Freedom and Welfare: Social Patterns in the Northern Countries of Europe.* The Ministries of Social Affairs of Denmark, Finland, Iceland, Norway, and Sweden, 1953.

Nelson, Robert H. *Lutheranism and the Nordic Spirit of Social Democracy: A Different Protestant Ethic.* Aarhus: Aarhus University Press, 2017. doi:10.2307/j.ctv62hgm7.

Nestingen, Andrew, and Paula Arvas. "Introduction: Contemporary Scandinavian Crime Fiction." In *Scandinavian Crime Fiction*, edited by Andrew Nestingen and Paula Arvas, 1–20. Cardiff: University of Wales Press, 2011.

Neuman, Nicklas, and Jonatan Leer. "Nordic Cuisine but National Identities: 'New Nordic Cuisine' and the Gastronationalist Projects of Denmark and Sweden." *Anthropology of food*, no. 13 (2018). doi:10.4000/aof.8723.

Neumann, Iver B., eds. *Hva skjedde med Norden? Fra selvbevissthet til rådvillhet.* Oslo: Cappelen, 1992.

—— "Tre Innfallsvinkler til Norden: Kulturfelleskap, oppdeming for stormaktspolitikk, regionbygging." In *Hva skjedde med Norden? Fra selvbevissthet til rådvillhet*, edited by Iver B. Neumann. Oslo: Cappelen, 1992.

Newby, Andrew G. "'In Building a Nation Few Better Examples Can Be Found': *Norden* and the Scottish Parliament." *Scandinavian Journal of History* 34, no. 3 (2009): 307–29. doi:10.1080/03468750903134749.

—— "'One Valhalla of the Free': Scandinavia, Britain and Northern Identity in the Mid-Nineteenth Century." In *Communicating the North: Media Structures and Images in the Making of the Nordic Region*, edited by Jonas Harvard and Peter Stadius, 147–69. Farnham: Ashgate, 2013.

Nilsson, Louise. "Mediating the North in Crime Fiction." *Journal of World Literature* 1, no. 4 (2016): 538–54. doi:10.1163/24056480–00104007.

Nilsson, Louise, David Dramrosch, and Theo D'haen. "Introduction: Crime Fiction as World Literature." In *Crime Fiction as World Literature*, edited by Louise Nilsson, David Dramrosch, and Theo D'haen. London: Bloomsbury, 2017.

Nilsson, Magnus. *The Nordic Cook Book*. London: Phaidon Press, 2015.

—— *Fäviken*. London: Phaidon Press, 2015.

"Noma Head Chef Accused of Illegal Mushroom Picking." Editorial. Accessed 30 May, 2021. https://www.telegraph.co.uk/foodanddrink/8154563/Noma-head-chef-accused-of-illegal-mushroom-picking.html.

Nordic Council of Ministers. *Den nordiska modellen i en ny tid – Program för Sveriges ordförandeskap i Nordiska ministerrådet 2013*. Copenhagen: Nordic Council of Ministers, 2012. doi:10.6027/ANP2012–746.

—— *Facts and Figures about Women and Men in the Nordic Countries. Kvinnor och män i Norden 1985*. Copenhagen: Nordic Council of Ministers, 1985.

—— *Focus on Gender – Working toward an Equal Society. Nordic Gender Equality Co-operation Programme 2006–2010*. Copenhagen: Nordic Council of Ministers, 2006.

—— *Gender and Violence. A Nordic Research Programme 2000–2004, Final Report*. Copenhagen: Nordic Council of Ministers, 2005.

—— *Gender Equality – the Nordic Way*. Copenhagen: Nordic Council of Ministers, 2010.

—— *Miehet ja tasa-arvo – Toimintaohjelma ja taustamuistio*. Copenhagen: Nordic Council of Ministers, 1997.

—— "Norden måste lära sig av misstagen under pandemiperioden." Copenhagen: Nordic Council of Ministers. Accessed 22 May, 2021. https://www.norden.org/en/node/50554.

—— *Norden som global vinderregion: På sporet af den nordiske konkurrencemodel*. Copenhagen: Nordic Council and Nordic Council of Ministers, 2005. http://norden.diva-portal.org/smash/get/diva2:701322/FULLTEXT01.pdf.

—— *Nordic Food Diplomacy*. Accessed 1 January, 2019. http://www.nfd.nynordiskmad.org/.

—— *Nordic Gender Equality in Figures 2015*. Copenhagen: Nordic Council of Ministers, 2015.

—— *Nordic-Baltic Campaign Against Trafficking in Women. Final Report 2002*. Copenhagen: Nordic Council of Ministers, 2004.

—— *Nordic-Baltic Co-operation on Gender Equality 1998–2003*. Copenhagen: Nordic Council of Ministers, 2004.

—— Nordic Nordic *Den Nordiska modellen i en ny tid – Program för Sveriges ordförandeskap i Nordiska Ministerrådet 2013*. Copenhagen: Nordic Council of Ministers, 2004. doi:10.6027/ANP2012–746.

—— "Nordiska rådet: Vi tänker inte sluta använda 'Nordiska modellen.'" Copenhagen: Nordic Council of Ministers, 2012. https://www.norden.org/no/node/4004.

—— *The Emergence of a New Nordic Food Culture: Final Report from the Program New Nordic Food II, 2010–2014.* Copenhagen: Nordic Council of Ministers, 2010.
—— *Together for Gender Equality – a Stronger Nordic Region. Nordic Co-operation Programme on Gender Equality 2015–2018.* Copenhagen: Nordic Council of Ministers, 2015.
—— "The New Nordic Food Manifesto," *Nordic Co-operation*, accessed May 30, 2021, https://www.norden.org/en/information/new-nordic-food-manifesto.
—— *Women and Men in the Nordic Countries: Facts and Figures 1994.* Copenhagen: Nordic Council of Ministers, 1994.
—— *Women and Men in the Nordic Countries: Facts on Equal Opportunities Yesterday, Today and Tomorrow 1994.* Copenhagen: Nordic Council of Ministers, 1994.
Nordiska Rådets Session 1953–2014. Stockholm/Copenhagen: Nordiska rådet, 1953–2014. https://www.norden.org/en/information/past-sessions.
Noreen, Erik. "The Nordic Balance: A Security Policy Concept in Theory and Practice." *Cooperation and Conflict* 18, no. 1 (March 1983): 43–56. doi:10.1177/001083678301800104.
North, Douglass C. *Institutions, Institutional Change and Economic Performance.* New York: Cambridge University Press, 1990.
Nousiainen, Kevät. "Käsitteellisiä välineitä tasa-arvon käsittelyyn." In *Tasa-arvo toisin nähtynä: Oikeuden ja politiikan näkökulmia tasa-arvoon ja yhdenvertaisuuteen*, edited by Johanna Kantola, Kevät Nousiainen, and Milja Saari, 31–56. Helsinki: Gaudeamus, 2012.
Nuder, Pär. *Saving the Swedish Model.* London: Insitute for Public Policy Reseach, 2012. https://www.ippr.org/research/publications/saving-the-swedish-model-learning-from-swedens-return-to-full-employment-in-the-late-1990s.
Nurmiainen, Jouko. "Particular Interests and the Common Good in Swedish Mid-18th-Century Diet Politics: The 'Finnish' Perspective." *Scandinavian Journal of History* 32, no. 4 (December 2007): 388–404. doi:10.1080/03468750701659350.
Nuwer, Rachel. "Deep in the Swedish Wilderness, Discovering One of the World's Greatest Restaurants." *Smithsonian Magazine*, 21 August 2013. https://www.smithsonianmag.com/travel/deep-in-the-swedish-wilderness-discovering-one-of-the-worlds-greatest-restaurants-818172/.
Nygård, Stefan. "The Southern Prism of the Northern Breakthrorugh: Georg Brandes and Italy," in *Georg Brandes. Pioneer of Comparative Literature and Global Public Intellectual*, ed. Jens Bjerring-Hansen, Anders Engberg-Pedersen, and Lasse Horne Kjældgaard (Leiden: Brill, forthcoming).
Nygård, Stefan, and Johan Strang. "Conceptual Universalization and the Role of the Peripheries." *Contributions to the History of Concepts* 12, no. 1 (2017): 55–75. doi:10.3167/choc.2017.120105.
—— "Facing Asymmetry: Nordic Intellectuals and Center-Periphery Dynamics in European Cultural Space." *Journal of the History of Ideas* 77, no. 1 (2016): 75–97. doi:10.1353/jhi.2016.0006.
Nygård, Stefan, Johan Strang, and Marja Jalava, ed. *Decentering European Intellectual Space.* European Studies. Leiden: Brill, 2018.
OECD. *Open Government: Fostering Dialogue with Civil Society.* Paris: OECD, 2003.

Ojanen, Hanna, and Tapio Raunio. "The Varying Degrees and Meanings of Nordicness in Finnish Foreign Policy." *Global Affairs* 4, no. 4–5 (2018): 405–418. doi:10.1080/23340460.2018.1533386.

Olesen, Thorsten Borring, and Johan Strang. "European Challenge to Nordic Institutional Cooperation. Past, Present and Future." In *Nordic Cooperation: The European Region in Transition*, edited by Johan Strang, 27–47. London: Routledge, 2016. doi:10.4324/9781315755366–2.

Ørem, Tania. *A Cultural History of the Avant-Garde in the Nordic Countries 1925–1950.* Vol. 1–3. Leiden: Brill, 2012.

Ornston, Darius. *Good Governance Gone Bad: How Nordic Adaptability Leads to Success.* Ithaca: Cornell University Press, 2018.

Ørskov, Frederik Forrai. "In Ideological Transit: German Tourism to Denmark in the 1930s." *Journal of Tourism History* 11, no. 3 (2019): 243–62. doi:10.1080/1755182X.2019.1650127.

Ösgård, Anton. "How Privatization Hobbled Sweden's Response to Coronavirus." Jacobin Magazine, 2020. https://jacobinmag.com/2020/11/sweden-coronavirus-covid-nordic-scandinavia.

Østergaard, Uffe. *Hvorhen Europa?* København: Djøf forlag, 2018.

—— "The Geopolitics of Nordic Identity: From Composite States to Nation States." In *The Cultural Construction of Norden*, edited by Øystein Sørensen and Bo Stråth, 25–71. Oslo: Scandinavian University Press, 1997.

Owen, Barry. "France." In *Comparative Public Administration*, edited by J. A. Chandler, 50–74. London: Routledge, 2000.

Pagano, Ugo. "Economics of Institutions and the Institutions of Economics." In *Transforming Economics: Perspectives on the Critical Realist Project*, edited by Paul Lewis, 252–67. London: Routledge, 2004.

Palonen, Kari. "Four Times of Politics: Policy, Polity, Politicking, and Politicization." *Alternatives* 28, no. 2 (2003): 171–86.

—— *The Politics of Limited Times: The Rhetoric of Temporal Judgment in Parliamentary Democracies.* Baden-Baden: Nomos, 2008.

Partanen, Anu. *The Nordic Theory of Everything: In Search of a Better Life.* New York: Harper Collins, 2016.

Patoluoto, Ilkka. "Hyödyllinen luomakunta: Hyötyajattelun maailmankuvalliset perusteet 1700-luvun Ruotsin valtakunnassa." In *Hyöty, sivistys, kansakunta: Suomalaista aatehistoriaa*, edited by Juha Manninen and Ilkka Patoluoto. Oulu: Kustannusosakeyhtiö Pohjoinen, 1986.

Peacock, Steven. *Swedish Crime Fiction: Novel, Film, Television.* Manchester: Manchester University Press, 2014.

Peltonen, Carita. *Norden och närområdena: Kartläggning av jämställdhetssamarbetet [The Nordic Region and the Adjacent Areas: Map of Equality Co-operation].* Copenhagen: Nordic Council of Ministers, 1996.

—— "Nordic Men – Cooperation on Gender Equality." In *Possibilities and Challenges? Men's Reconciliation of Work and Family Life – Conference Report*, edited by Jouni Varanka and Maria Forslund, 125–30. Copenhagen: Nordic Council of Ministers, 2006.

Petäjäniemi, Tuulikki. "Naisten ja miesten tasa-arvo – yhteinen etu." In *Tasa-arv: Saavutuksia ja haasteita [Equality. Achievements and Challlenges]*, edited by Jarmo Tarkki and Tuulikki Petäjäniemi. Jyväskylä: Atena Kustannus, 1998.

Peters, B. Guy, Jon Pierre, and Desmond S. King. "The Politics of Path Dependency: Political Conflict in Historical Institutionalism." *The Journal of Politics* 67, no. 4 (November 2005): 1275–1300. doi:10.1111/j.1468–2508.2005.00360.x.

Petersen, Klaus. "Constructing Nordic Welfare? Nordic Social Political Cooperation 1919–1955." In *The Nordic Model of Welfare: A Historical Reappraisal*, edited by Niels Finn et al., 67–98. Copenhagen: Museum Tusculanum Press, 2006.

—— "National, Nordic and Trans-Nordic: Transnational Perspectives on the History of the Nordic Welfare State." In *Beyond Welfare State Models*, edited by Klaus Petersen and Pauli Kettunen, 41–64. Cheltenham: Edward Elgar Publishing, 2011. doi:10.4337/9781849809603.00009.

—— "Nordiske værdier: et kritisk reflekterende essay." In *Meningen med föreningen*, edited by Henrik Wilen, 73–83. København: Föreningarna Norden, 2019.

Pitcher, David. *Consuming Race*. London: Routledge, 2014.

Puglisi, Christian F. *Relæ: A Book of Ideas*. Berkeley: Ten Speed Press, 2014.

Qvanten, Emil von. *Fennomani och skandinavism: Om Finnland och dess sednaste utveckling*. Stockholm: Zachrish Haeggerström, 1855.

Rainio-Niemi, Johanna. "Small State Cultures of Consensus: State Traditions and Consensus-Seeking in the Neo-Corporatist and Neutral Policies in Post-1945 Austria and Finland." PhD diss., University of Helsinki, 2008.

Raunio, Tapio, and Teija Tiilikainen. *Finland in the European Union*. London: Frank Cass, 2003.

Redzepi, René. *A Work in Progress: Journal*. London: Phaidon Press, 2013.

—— *Noma: Time and Place*. London: Phaidon Press, 2010.

—— Rene Redzepi, "Rene Redzepi on the new Noma." Parts Unknown, 13 April, 2017, accessed 26 December, 2018. https://explorepartsunknown.com/copenhagen/rene-redzepi-on-the-new-noma.

Reinfeldt, Fredrik. *Det sovande folket*. Edited by Christer Söderberg and Per Schlingmann. Stockholm: Rätt Blankett & Trycksaksproduktion AB, 1993.

—— "The New Swedish Model: A Reform Agenda for Growth and the Environment." Speech at London School of Economics, 26 February 2008. Regeringskansliet, https://www.regeringen.se/informationsmaterial/2014/10/fredrik-reinfeldt-pressmeddela-nden-tal-och-uttalanden-2006–2010/.

Relly, Jeannine E., and Meghna Sabharwal. "Perceptions of Transparency of Government Policymaking: A Cross-National Study." *Government Information Quarterly* 26, no. 1 (January 2009): 148–57. doi:10.1016/j.giq.2008.04.002.

Richards, Julian D. *The Vikings: A Very Short Introduction*. Oxford: Oxford University Press, 2005.

Ripley, William Zebina. *The Races of Europe: A Sociological Study*. New York: D. Appleton and Company, 1899.

Roberston, K. G. *Public Secrets: A Study in the Development of Government Secrecy*. New York: St. Martin's Press, 1982.

Rodrik, Dani. "Why Do More Open Economies Have Bigger Governments?" *The Journal of Political Economy* 106, no. 5 (1998): 997–1032.

Rönnberg, Linda. "Marketization on Export: Representations of the Swedish Free School Model in English Media." *European Educational Research Journal* 14, no. 6 (November 2015): 549–65. doi:10.1177/1474904115610782.

Roosen, Carl B. *Alvorstale i anledning den i Sverig udgivne bog: Geographie eör [Sic] begynnare, Författad as Daniel Djurberg, Rector Scholae.* Frederikshald: H. Gundersen & H. Larssen, 1833.

Rosenbeck, Bente. "Nordic Women's Studies and Gender Research." In *Is There a Nordic Feminism? Nordic Feminist Thought on Culture and Society*, edited by Drude von der Fehr, Anna G. Jónasdóttir, and Bente Rosenbeck, 344–57. London: UCL Press, 1998.

Rothstein, Bo, and Sven Steinmo, eds. *Restructuring the Welfare State: Political Institutions and Policy Change.* New York: Palgrave Macmillan, 2002.

Rushby, Kevin. "King of Denmark: How to Create Hygge in a Cabin by the Sea." *The Guardian*, 5 August, 2018. https://www.theguardian.com/travel/2018/aug/05/denmark-beach-seaside-scandinavia-holiday-cabin.

Rustow, Dankwar A. "Scandinavia: Working Multi-Party Systems." In *Modern Political Parties: Approaches to Comparative Politics*, edited by Sigmund Neumann. Chicago: University of Chicago Press, 1956.

Rydgren, Jens. "Explaining the Emergence of Radical Right-Wing Populist Parties: The Case of Denmark." *West European Politics* 27, no. 3 (May 2004): 474–502. doi:10.1080/0140238042000228103.

Ryner, J. Magnus. "The Nordic Model: Does It Exist? Can It Survive?" *New Political Economy* 12, no. 1 (March 2007): 61–70. doi:10.1080/13563460601068644.

Sachs, Adam. "Fäviken Rising." *Bon Appétit*, 15 August, 2011. https://www.bonappetit.com/test-kitchen/cooking-tips/article/f-viken-rising.

SAMAK. *The Sørmarka Declaration: We Build the Nordics.* SAMAK, November 2014. http://www.samak.info/wp-content/uploads/2015/11/Sormarka-declaration_English.pdf.

Sanders, Todd, and Harry G. West. "Power Revealed and Concealed in the New World Order." In *Transparency and Conspiracy: Ethnographies of Suspicion in the New World Order*, edited by Todd Sanders and Harry G. West. Durham: Duke University Press, 2003.

Sannes, John. *Patrioter, inteligens og skandinaver: Norske reaksjoner på skandinavismen før 1848.* Oslo: Universitetsforlaget, 1959.

Sarah Stephan. "Making Autonomies Matter: Sub-State Actor Accommodation in the Nordic Council and the Nordic Council of Ministers: An Analysis of the Institutional Framework for Accommodating the Faroe Islands, Greenland and Åland within 'Norden.'" *European Diversity and Autonomy Papers EDAP* 3 (2014). http://www.eurac.edu/edap.

Sarje, Kimmo. "Anders Chydenius – Montesquieun Ihailija." *Politiikka* 4 (1979): 297–304.

"Skandinaviska föreningar i utlandet: Se Utlandssvenskar." In *Nordisk Familjebok* 25. 2nd ed. Stockholm, 1917.

Schmidt, Vivien A. "Discursive Institutionalism: The Explanatory Power of Ideas and Discourse." *Annual Review of Political Science* 11, no. 1 (June 2008): 303–326. doi:10.1146/annurev.polisci.11.060606.135342.

—— *The Futures of European Capitalism.* Oxford: Oxford University Press, 2002.

Schwab, Klaus. "Preface." In *The Global Gender Gap Report 2009*, edited by Ricardo Hausmann, Laura D'Andrea Tyson, and Saadia Zahidi. Geneva: World Economic Forum, 2009.

Schymik, Carsten. "European Antifederalists." In *Northern Europe and the Future of the EU: Nordeuropa Und Die Zukunft Der EU*, edited by Helge Høibraaten and Jochen Hille. Berlin: Intersentia, 2011.

Scott, Andrew. "Looking to Sweden in Order to Reconstruct Australia." *Scandinavian Journal of History* 34, no. 3 (2009): 330–52. doi:10.1080/03468750903134756.

—— "Social Democracy in Northern Europe: Its Relevance for Australia." *Australian Review of Public Affairs* 7, no. 1 (2006): 1–17.

Shaw, Hank. "Cook Like a Super-Locavore with Lessons From 'Noma.'" *The Atlantic*, 23 March, 2011. https://www.theatlantic.com/health/archive/2011/03/cook-like-a-super-loca vore-with-lessons-from-noma/72898/.

Sietsema, Tom. "A World-Class Chef Built a $600 Pop-up in the Mexican Jungle. It Might Be "the Meal of the Decade.'" *Washington Post*, 25 April, 2017, Food. https://www.wash ingtonpost.com/lifestyle/food/a-world-class-chef-built-a-600-pop-up-in-the-mexican-jun gle-it-might-be-the-meal-of-the-decade/2017/04/25/e3b75244-284e-11e7-a616-d7c8a68c1a66_story.html.

Silverstolpe, Gustaf Abraham. *Lärobok i svenska historien*. Stockholm: H.A. Nordstöm, 1805.

Sipilä, Helvi. "Yhdistyneitten kansakuntien toiminta sukupuolten tasa-arvon edistämiseksi." In *Toisenlainen tasa-arvo*, edited by Sirkka Sinkkonen and Eila Ollikainen, 13–20. Kuopio: Kustannuskiila Oy, 1982.

Skinner, Quentin. "Meaning and Understanding in the History of Ideas." *History and Theory* 8, no. 1 (1969): 3–53.

—— *Visions of Politics: Regarding Method*. Vol. 1. Cambridge: Cambridge University Press, 2002. doi:10.1017/CBO9780511790812.

Skinner, Quentin et. al. "Language and Political Change." In *Political Innovation and Conceptual Change*, 6–23. Cambridge: Cambridge University Press, 1989.

Skousen, Mark. "The Perserverance of Paul Samuelson's Economics." *Journal of Economic Perspectives* 11, no. 2 (1997): 137–52.

Sneedort, Frederik. "Vigtigheden af de tre nordiske Rigers Forening: En Tale af afgangne Professor F. Sneedorf, holden i det nordiske Selskab i London i Foraaret 1792." *Skandinask Museum* 2 (1798): 122–34.

Söderman, Jacob. "On Transparency." Presentation, IIAS conference, Monterrey, Mexico, 16 July, 2006. http://www.chydenius.net/eng/articles/artikkeli.asp?id=924.

—— "Salailusta on tullut maan tapa." *Helsingin Sanomat*, 19 November, 2006. https://www.hs.fi/sunnuntai/art-2000004441307.html.

Solum, Ove. "What is it about Nordic Noir?" In *Perspectives on the Nordic*, edited by Jakob Lothe and Bente Larsen, 109–26. Oslo: Novus Press, 2016.

Somers, Margaret R. "Citizenship and the Place of the Public Sphere: Law, Community, and Political Culture in the Transition of Democracy." *American Sociological Review* 58, no. 5 (1993): 587–620.

—— "Let Them Eat Social Capital: Socializing the Market versus Marketizing the Social." *Thesis Eleven* 81, no. 1 (May 2005): 5–19. doi:10.1177/0725513605051611.

—— "What's Political or Cultural about Political Culture and the Public Sphere? Toward an Historical Sociology of Concept Formation." *Sociological Theory* 13, no. 2 (1995): 113–44.

Somers, Margaret R., and Fred Block. "From Poverty to Perversity: Ideas, Markets, and Institutions over 200 Years of Welfare Debate." *American Sociological Review* 70, no. 2 (2005): 260–87.

Sondrup, Steven P. et al., eds. *Nordic Literature: A Comparative History*. Vol. I, *Spatial Nodes*. Amsterdam: John Benjamins Publishing Company, 2017. doi:10.1075/chlel.xxxi.

Sonne, Lasse. *Nordek: A Plan for Increased Nordic Economic Co-operation and Integration 1968–1970*. Helsinki: Finnish Society of Sciences and Letters, 2007.

Sørensen, Øystein, and Bo Stråth, eds. *The Cultural Construction of Norden*. Oslo: Scandinavian University Press, 1997.

Sørensen, Vibeke. "Nordic Cooperation: A Social Democratic Alternative to Europe." In *Interdependence versus Integration: Denmark, Scandinavia and Western Europe, 1945–1960*, edited by Thorsten Borring Olesen. Odense University Studies in History and Social Sciences 193. Odense: Odense University Press, 1995.

Spence, R.E. "Italy." In *Comparative Public Administration*, edited by J. A. Chandler, 126–147. London: Routledge, 2000.

Spiro, Jonathan Peter. *Defending the Master Race: Conservation, Eugenics, and the Legacy of Madison Grant*. Burlington: University Press of New England, 2009.

Stadius, Peter. "Happy Countries: Appraisals of Interwar Nordic Societies." In *Communicating the North: Media Structures and Images in the Making of the Nordic Region*, edited by Jonas Harvard and Peter Stadius, 241–62. Farnham: Ashgate, 2013.

—— "Hundra år av nordism." In *Meningen med föreningen*, edited by Henrik Wilen, 73–83. København: Föreningarna Norden, 2019.

—— *Resan till norr: Spanska nordenbilder kring sekelskiftet 1900*. Helsingfors: Finska Vetenskaps-societeten, 2005.

—— "Trekungamötet i Malmö 1914: Mot en ny nordisk retorik i skuggan av världskriget." *Historisk tidskrift för Finland* 99, no. 4 (December 2014): 369–94.

Stein, Joshua David. "Sleep Noma Editor-at-Large Joshua David Stein Pays a First and Final Visit to Noma." *Tasting Table*, 26 July, 2016. https://www.tastingtable.com/dine/national/noma-restaurant-copenhagen-rene-redzepi-joshua-david-stein.

Stein, Ringen. "Welfare Studies in Scandinavia." *Scandinavian Political Studies* 9 (1974).

Steiner, Ann et al. "World Literature and the Book Market." In *The Routledge Companion to World Literature*, 316–24. Houndmills: Palgrave, 2009.

Steinmetz, Willibald, and Michael Freeden. "Conceptual History: Challenges, Conundrums, Complexities." In *Conceptual History in the European Space*, edited by Willibald Steinmetz, Michael Freeden, and Javier Fernández Sebastián. New York: Berghahn Books, 2017. doi:10.2307/j.ctvw04kcs.9.

Stenius, Henrik. "Nordic Associational Life in a European and an Inter-Nordic Perspective." In *Nordic Associations in a European Perspective*, edited by Risto Alapuro and Henrik Stenius, 29–86. Baden-Baden: Nomos, 2010. doi:10.5771/9783845225944–29.

—— "The Finnish Citizen: How a Translation Emasculated the Concept." *Redescriptions: Yearbook of Political Thought, Conceptual History and Feminist Theory* 8 (2004): 172–88.

Stie, Anna Elizabeth, and Jarle Trondal, eds. *Rediscovering Nordic Cooperation*. Special issue of Politics and Governance 8, no. 4 (2020). doi:10.17645/pag.v8i4.3726.

Stiglitz, Joseph. "Information and the Change in the Paradigm in Economics." *American Economic Review* 92, no. 3 (2002): 460–501.

—— "Is There a Post-Washington Consensus Consenus?" In *The Washington Consensus Reconsidered: Towards a New Global Governance*, edited by Joseph Stiglitz and Serra Stiglitz, 41–56. Oxford: Oxford University Press, 2008.

Stigsdottir, Ingrid. "Crime Scene Skåne: Guilty Landscapes and Cracks in the Functionalist Façade in *Sidetracked, Firewall* and *One Step Behind*." In *Regional Aesthetics: Locating Swedish Media*, edited by Erik Hedling, Olof Hedling, and Mats Jönsson, 243–62. Stockholm: Mediehistoriskt Arkiv, 2010.

Stoddard, Lothrop. *The Racial Realities in Europe*. New York: Scribner, 1924.

Stoddard, Lothrop. *The Revolt against Civilization: The Menace of the Under Man*. New York: Scribner, 1922.

—— *The Rising Tide of Color against White World Supremacy*. New York: Scribner, 1920.

Stoltenberg, Thorvald. *Nordic cooperation on foreign and security policy*. Proposals presented to the extraordinary meeting of Nordic foreign ministers in Oslo on 9 February 2009. https://www.regjeringen.no/globalassets/upload/ud/vedlegg/nordicreport.pdf.

Stougaard-Nielsen, Jakob. "Nordic Noir in the UK: The Allure of Accessible Difference." *Journal of Aesthetics & Culture* 8, no. 1 (January 2016): 32704. doi:10.3402/jac.v8.32704.

—— "Revisiting the Crime Scene: Intermedial Translation, Adaptation, and Novelization of *The Killing*." In *Nordic Noir, Adaptation, Appropriation*, edited by Linda Badley, Andrew Nestingen, and Jakko Seppälä, 89–111. London: Palgrave, 2020.

Strang, Johan. "Georg Henrik von Wright och Ingemar Hedenius: rollen som intellektuell och analytisk filosof i Finland och Sverige." In *Tankens utåtvändhet: Georg Henrik von Wright som intellektuell*, edited by Johan Strang and Thomas Wallgren, 192–215. Finland: Svenska Litteratursällskapet, 2016.

—— "Introduction: The Nordic Model of Transnational Cooperation?" In *Nordic Cooperation: A European Region in Transition*, edited by Johan Strang, 1–26. London: Routledge, 2016. doi:10.4324/9781315755366–1.

—— "Kommentar: Vår älskade dystopi." In *Sverigebilden i Norden: En studie i Danmark, Finland, Island och Norge*. Stockholm: Svenska institutet, 2021. https://si.se/app/up loads/2021/03/bilden-av-sverige-i-norden.pdf.

—— ed. *Nordic Cooperation: A European Region in Transition*. London: Routledge, 2016. doi:10.4324/9781315755366.

Strang, Johan, and Jussi Kurunmäki. "Introduction: 'Nordic Democracy' in a World of Tensions." In *Rhetorics of Nordic Democracy*, edited by Jussi Kurunmäki and Johan Strang. Helsinki: Finnish Literature Society, 2010. doi:10.21435/sfh.17.

Stråth, Bo. "Den nordiska modellen: Historisk bakgrund och hur talet om en nordisk modell uppstod." *Nordisk tidskrift för vetenskap, konst och industri* 1 (1993).

—— *Europe and the Other and Europe as the Other*. Wien: PIE Lang, 2000.

—— *Nordic Industry and Nordic Economic Cooperation*. Sweden: A & W International, 1978.

—— ed. "Poverty, Neutrality and Welfare: Three Key Concepts in the Modern Foundation of the Myth of Sweden." In *Myth and Memory in the Construction of Community: Historical Patterns in Europe and Beyond*. Wien: PIE Lang, 2000.

—— "The Swedish Image of Europe as the Other." In *Europe and the Other, Europe as the Other*, edited by Bo Stråth, Vol. 10. Wien: Peter Lang, 2010.

Sundelius, Bengt. *Managing Transnationalism in Northern Europe*. Boulder: Westview Press, 1978.

Sundelius, Bengt, and Claes Wiklund. "Quo Vadis? Tretton insikter om Norden." In *Norden sett inifrån: Det fjärde spårbytet*, edited by Bengt Sundelius and Claes Wiklund. Stockholm: Santérus, 2017.

Supplement to Nordic Co-operation Programme on Gender Equality 2019–2022. Equal Rights, Treatment and Opportunities for LGBTI People in the Nordic Region. Copenhagen: Nordic Council of Ministers, 2020.

Svedjedal, Johan. "Svensk skönlitteratur i världsperspektiv." In *Läsarnas marknad, marknadens läsare: En forskningsantologi utarbetad för literaturutredningen*, edited by Ulla Carlsson and Jenny Johannisson, 209–220. Göteborg: Nordicom, 2012.

Svensk Konversationslexikon. Stockholm, 1845.

Svenska Akademiens ordbok (SAOB). https://www.saob.se/.

Svenska Dagstidningar, Royal Library of Sweden. Accessed 4 June, 2021. https://tidningar.kb. se/.

Sverdrup, Bjørn Otto. "Europeisering som de-institusjonalisering – Nordisk politisk samarbeid i endring." In *Europa i Norden: Europeisering av nordisk samarbeid*, edited by Johan P. Olsen and Bjørn Otto Sverdrup. Oslo: Tano Aschehoug, 1998.

Swedish Institute. "Sweden beyond the Millennium and Stieg Larsson." Stockholm: Swedish Institute, 31 October 2012. https://issuu.com/swedish_institute/docs/sweden_beyond_ the_millennium.

Tant, A. P. *British Government: The Triumph of Elitism: A Study of the British Politcal Tradition and Its Major Challenges*. Aldershot: Darthmouth, 1993.

"The Gods of Food." Editorial. *Time*, 18 November 2013. http://content.time.com/time/sub scriber/article/0,33009,2156845,00.html.

Thomson, C. Claire, and Jakob Stougaard-Nielsen. "A Faithful, Attentive, Tireless Following: Cultural Mobility, Crime Fiction and Television Drama." In *Danish Literature as World Literature*, edited by Dan Ringgaard and Mads Rosendahl Thomson, 237–68. London: Bloomsbury, 2017.

Thurlow, Richard C. *The Secret State: British Internal Security in the Twentieth Century*. Oxford: Blackwell, 1994.

Tiihonen, Paula. "Good Governance and Corruption in Finland." In *The History of Corruption in Central Government*, edited by Seppo Tiihonen, 99–118. Amsterdam: IOS Press, 2003.

Tiihonen, Seppo. *Herrus: Ruotsi ja Venäjä*. Helsinki: Hallintohistoriakomitea, 1994.

Timonen, Virpi. *Restructuring the Welfare State: Globalization and Social Policy Reform in Finland and Sweden*. Cheltenham: Edward Elgar, 2003.

Todorova, Maria. "Spacing Europe: What Is a Historical Region?" *East Central Europe* 32, no. 1–2 (2005): 59–78. doi10.1163/18763308–90001032.

Todorova, Maria. *Imagining the Balkans*. New York: Oxford University Press, 1997.

Toft Hansen, Kim, and Anne Marit Waade. *Locating Nordic Noir: From Beck to The Bridge*. London: Palgrave, 2017.

Trägårdh, Lars. "Swedish Model or Swedish Culture?" *Critical Review* 4, no. 4 (September 1990): 569–90. doi:10.1080/08913819008459622.

—— "Statist Individualism: On the Culturality of the Nordic Welfare State." In *The Cultural Construction of Norden*, edited by Øystein Sørensen and Bo Stråth. Oslo: Scandinavian Univ. Press, 1997.

—— "Sweden and the EU: Welfare State Nationalism and the Spectre of 'Europe.'" In *European Integration and National Identity: The Challenge of Nordic States*, edited by Lene Hansen and Ole Wæver. London: Routledge, 2002.

—— "Mellem liberalism og socialisme: Om det særlige ved den nordiske model." *Kritik* 45, no. 206 (2012).

Trier Morgensen, Lars. "Fogh frelste den nordiske model." *Politiken*, 5 September 2009.

Troebst, Stefan. "Introduction: What's in a Historical Region? A Teutonic Perspective." *European Review of History: Revue Europeenne d'histoire* 10, no. 2 (June 2003): 173–88. doi:10.1080/1350748032000140741.

Trubek, Amy. *The Taste of Place: A Cultural Journesy into Terroir.* Berkeley: University of California Press, 2008.

Tsarouhas, Dimitris. *Social Democracy in Sweden: The Threat from a Globalized World.* London: Tauris Academic Studies, 2008.

Turner, Barry, and Gunilla Nordquist. *The Other European Community: Integration and Cooperation in Northern Europe.* Houndmills: Palgrave, 1982.

Tydén, Mattias. *Från politik till praktik: de svenska steriliseringslagarna 1935–1975.* Stockholm: Almqvist & Wiksell International, 2002.

"Urlaub in Schleswig-Holstein – Offizielle Tourismusseite," 25 August, 2016. https://www.sh-tourismus.de/.

Urry, John. *The Tourist Gaze: Leisure and Travel in Contemporary Societies.* London: Sage Publications, 1990.

Valtioneuvoston kanslia. *Euroopan rakenteelliset jäykkyydet.* Helsinki: Valtioneuvoston kanslia, 2002.

—— *Osaava, avautuva ja uudistuva Suomi: Suomi maailmantaloudessa -selvityksen loppuraportti.* Helsinki: Valtioneuvoston kanslia, 2004.

Valdimarsdóttir, Friða Rós. *Nordic Experiences with Parental Leave and Its Impact on Equality between Women and Men.* Copenhagen: Nordic Council of Ministers, 2006.

Varanka, Jouni, and Maria Forslund, eds. *Possibilities and Challenges? Men's Reconciliation of Work and Family Life – Conference Report.* Copenhagen: Nordic Council of Ministers, 2006.

Vibe, Johan. "Norden – et samarbeite nedenfra?" In *Hva skjedde med Norden? fra selvbevissthet til rådvillhet*, edited by Iver B. Neumann. Oslo: Cappelen, 1992.

Vik, Hanne Hagtvedt et al., eds. *Nordic Histories of Human Rights.* London: Routledge, 2021.

"VILD MAD – Frequently Asked Questions." Vild Mad. Accessed 30 May 2021. https://vild mad.dk/application/files/5815/0227/5901/FAQ_US.pdf.

Villaume, Poul, and Thorsten Borring Olesen. *Dansk udenrigspolitiks historie V: I blokopdelingens tegn.* Copenhagen: Gyldendal, 2005.

Virrankoski, Pentti. *Anders Chydenius: Demokraattinen poliitikko valistuksen vuosisadalta.* Juva: Werner Söderström, 1986.

Waade, Anne Marit. "Crime Scenes: Conceptualizing Ystad as Location in the Swedish and the British Wallander TV Crime Series." *Northern Lights: Film & Media Studies Yearbook* 9, no. 1 (2011): 9–25. doi:10.1386/nl.9.9_1.

—— *Wallanderland: Medieturisme og Skandinavisk TV-Krimi.* Aalborg: Aalborg Universitetsforlag, 2013.

Wæver, Catherine, and Christian Peratsakis. "Engineering Policy Norm Implementation: The World Bank's Transparency Transformation." In *Implementation and World Politics: How*

International Norms Change Practice, edited by Alexander Betts and Phil Orchard, 179–94. Oxford: Oxford University Press, 2014.

Wæver, Ole. "Nordic Nostalgia: Northern Europe after the Cold War." *International Affairs* 68, no. 1 (January 1992): 77–102. doi:10.2307/2620462.

Waldemarson, Ylva. "Gender Equality the Nordic Way: The Nordic Council's and Nordic Council of Ministers' Cooperation with the Baltic States and Northwest Russia in the Political Field of Gender Equality 1999–2010." In *Gender Equality on a Grand Tour: Politics and Institutions – the Nordic Council, Sweden, Lithuania and Russia*, edited by Eva Blomberg, et al., 20–86. Leiden: Brill, 2017.

Wallem, Frederik. *Det norske Studentersamfund gjennom hundrede aar: 1813–1913*. Kristiania: Aschehoug, 1913.

Ward, Elisabeth I. "Viking Pop Culture on Display: The Case of the Horned Helmets." *Material Culture Review*, 54, no. 1 (2001). https://journals.lib.unb.ca/index.php/MCR/article/view/17894.

Weber, Max. *Economy and Society*. Vol. 1 and 2. Berkeley: University of California Press, 1978.

Weibull, Lauritz. "Efter Roskilde fred: Ur Skånska kommissionens och Taubenfelts bref till Kungl. Maj:t 1658–1660." *Historisk tidskrift för Skåneland* 1, no. 4–6 (1901): 175–253.

Weindling, Paul. "Weimar Eugenics: The Kaiser Wilhelm Institute for Anthropology, Human Heredity and Eugenics in Social Context.". *Annals of Science* 42, no. 3 (1985): 303–318. doi:10.1080/00033798500200221.

Wells, Pete. "The New Noma: Frequently Asked Questions." *The New York Times*, 24 April, 2018, Food. https://www.nytimes.com/2018/04/24/dining/noma-restaurant-copenhagen.html.

Wendt, Franz. *Cooperation in the Nordic Countries: Achievements and Obstacles*. Stockholm: Almqvist & Wiksell International for the Nordic council, 1981.

Weßel, Merle. *An Unholy Union? Eugenic Feminism in the Nordic Countries, ca. 1890–1940*. Helsinki: Unigrafia, 2018.

—— "The Concept of the 'Nordic Race' in German and Nordic Racial-Theoretical Research in the 1920s." *NORDEUROPAforum – Zeitschrift Für Kulturstudien* 2016 (2016): 29–49. doi:10.18452/8186.

Wetterberg, Gunnar. *The United Nordic Federation*. Copenhagen: Nordic Council, 2010.

Whiteley, Nigel. "Intensity of Scrutiny and a Good Eyeful: Architecture and Transparency." *Journal of Architectural Education* 56, no. 4 (May 2003): 8–16. doi:10.1162/104648803321672915.

Whyte, William. "How Do Buildings Mean? Some Issues of Interpretation in the History of Architecture." *History and Theory* 45, no. 2 (May 2006): 153–77. doi:10.1111/j.1468–2303.2006.00355.x.

Wiking, Meik. *The Little Book of Hygge*. London: Penguin, 2016.

Wischenbart, Rüdiger. "The Business of Books 2016: Between the First and the Second Phase of Transformation; An Overview of Market Trends in North America, Europe, Asia and Latin America, and a Look beyond Books." Frankfurt Book Fair, June 2016. https://fill-liv relecture.org/wp-content/uploads/2016/07/white_paper_business_of_books_june_2016.pdf.

Witoszek, Nina, and Atle Midttun. "Sustainable Modernity and the Architecture of the 'Well-Being Society': Interdisciplinary Perspectives." In *Sustainable Modernity: The*

Nordic Model and Beyond, edited by Nina Witoszek and Atle Midttun. London: Routledge, 2018.

Wivel, Anders. "What Happened to the Nordic Model for International Peace and Security?" *Peace Review* 29, no. 4 (2017): 489–96. doi:10.1080/10402659.2017.1381521.

Wood, John. "New Synergy Supreme+Unleaded Launched." *Forecourt Trader Online*, 1 September, 2017. https://forecourttrader.co.uk/news/new-synergy-supreme-unleaded-launched/640519.article.

Wooldridge, Adrian. "The next Supermodel." *The Economist*, 2 February, 2013. https://www.economist.com/leaders/2013/02/02/the-next-supermodel.

World Economic Forum. *The Global Gender Gap Report 2014*. Geneva: World Economic Forum, 2014. http://www3.weforum.org/docs/GGGR14/GGGR_CompleteReport_2014.pdf.

———.*The Global Gender Gap Report 2017*. Geneva: World Economic Forum, 2017. http://www3.weforum.org/docs/WEF_GGGR_2017.pdf.

———.*The Global Gender Gap Report 2020*. Geneva: World Economic Forum, 2020. https://www.weforum.org/reports.

Worsaae, J.J.A. "Om vigtigheden af et centrum for Nordisk Oldforskning." *Annaler for Nordisk Oldkyndighed og Historie*, 1846, 3–20.

Wright, Georg Henrik von. "Sverige och Ryssland." *Finsk Tidskrift*, 1941.

Würgler, Andreas. "Conspiracy and Denunciaion: A Local Affair and Its European Publics (Bern, 1749)." In *Cultures of Communication from Reformation to Enlightenment: Constructing Publics in the Early Modern German Lands*, edited by James Van Horn Melton. Aldershot: Ashgate, 2002.

Zahidi, Saadia. "What Makes the Nordic Countries Gender Equality Winners?" *Huffington Post*, 24 October 2013. https://www.huffpost.com/entry/what-makes-the-nordic-cou_b_4159555#:~:text=All%20Nordic%20countries%20reached%2099,to%20primary%20and%20secondary%20education.

Zaret, David. "Religion, Science, and Printing in the Public Spheres in Seventeenth-Century England." In *Habermas and the Public Sphere*, edited by Craig Calhoun. Cambridge: The MIT Press, 1992.

Zwicker, Charles. "Review of Modern Welfare States." *Presidential Studies Quarterly* 21, no. 1 (1991): 197–98.

Contributors

Professor Tero Erkkilä, University of Helsinki

Associate Professor II Ruth Hemstad, University of Oslo/National Library of Norway

Professor Mary Hilson, Aarhus University

Senior Lecturer Tom Hoctor, University of Bedfordshire

Assistant Professor Lily Kelting, Flame University

Dr. Jani Marjanen, University of Helsinki

Professor Pirjo Markkola, Tampere University

Professor Jakob Stougaard-Nielsen, University College London

Associate Professor, Academy of Finland Research Fellow Johan Strang, University of Helsinki

Dr. Merle Weβel, Universität Oldenburg